A WORDSWORTH COMPANION

A WORDSWORTH COMPANION

Survey and Assessment

F. B. PINION

MACMILLAN PUBLISHING COMPANY
NEW YORK

Macmillan Publishing Company
866 Third Avenue
New York, N.Y. 10022

Library of Congress Catalog Card
Number 83–82621

ISBN 0–02–924990–2

Printed in Hong Kong

Contents

List of Maps and Plates	*page* vii
Reference Abbreviations	viii
Acknowledgments	ix

Part I: 1770–98

Early Years and Adolescent Poetry	3
Cambridge, the Picturesque, and London	20
France, Annette, and Descriptive Poetry	33
War, the Salisbury Plain Poems, and *The Borderers*	48
Coleridge, Alfoxden, and *Lyrical Ballads*	65
'Peter Bell' and Reformation by Nature	84

Part II: 1798–1814

Germany and the North of England	99
Home at Grasmere	109
From Marriage to 'Intimations'	127
The Prelude and the Imagination	142
Fortitude in Life and Verse	160
Heroism Abroad and Grief at Home	177
The Excursion	192

Part III: 1814–50

Activity and Alarm	211
New Enterprise and Sonnet Sequences	223
More Trachoma, Poetry, and Travel	234
To the Sunless Land	252

Contents

Part IV: Supplementary

Tradition and Innovation   271
Poetic Theory and Practice   282
Critical Reactions   301
Conclusion   316

Notes   329

Appendixes
  i   Wordsworth's *Guide to the Lakes*   333
 ii   Observations and Experiences Recorded by both
       Dorothy and William   335
iii   Two Topographical Questions   337
 iv   Select Bibliography   338

Index   341

List of Maps and Plates

MAPS

Map 1   The Lake District   *pages* 4–5
Map 2   Area around Grasmere and Rydal   111
Map 3   Wordsworth's Scottish Tours   133

PLATES

1   Wordsworth's birthplace; Ann Tyson's cottage
2   Windermere Ferry House; view to the north
3   Furness Abbey; Brougham Castle
4   Ullswater from Gowbarrow Park; Skelwith Bridge
5   Cambridge: St John's College; King's College Chapel
6   Racedown Lodge; Alfoxden House
7   Coleridge, 1796; Wordsworth, 1798
8   Tintern Abbey; Dove Cottage; view from the orchard
9   Grasmere; the Rock of Names; head of Windermere
10   The Borrowdale yews; the Swan Inn; Thirlmere
11   Blea Tarn and the Langdale Pikes; Rydal Mount
12   Rydal Water; Patterdale Bridge
13   The harbour at Whitehaven; Scott and Wordsworth
14   Dorothy Wordsworth; Dora Wordsworth
15   Mary Wordsworth; Wordsworth (by H. Inman)
16   Benjamin Robert Haydon's portrait of Wordsworth

Reference Abbreviations

POEMS

Ex   *The Excursion*
Pr   *The Prelude* (1850 text)
Pr.05   *The Prelude* (1805 version)

(The following abbreviations are used with *page* references to Oxford University Press editions, the PW notations indicating *The Poetical Works of William Wordsworth* in five volumes.)

PR   *The Prelude*, 1805 and 1850 texts, ed. Ernest de Selincourt, *second edition*, revised by Helen Darbishire, 1959
PW1   ed. Ernest de Selincourt, 1940
PW2   ed. Ernest de Selincourt, *second edition*, 1952
PW3   ed. Ernest de Selincourt and Helen Darbishire, 1946
PW4   ed. Ernest de Selincourt and Helen Darbishire, 1947
PW5   ed. Ernest de Selincourt and Helen Darbishire, 1949
I.F.   Miss Isabella Fenwick's record of observations made late in his life by Wordsworth on many of his poems

LETTERS

All references are given by dates, e.g. (to take examples before and after 1800) 17.vi.91, 8.iv.08. See Appendix iv.

Acknowledgments

My main indebtedness is to the scholarly editions of *The Poetical Works of William Wordsworth* by Ernest de Selincourt and Helen Darbishire. I am most grateful to Oxford University Press for generous permission to quote from passages first published in these editions, as well as from Wordsworth's letters and other prose writings. Cornell University Press has kindly allowed me to present the text of the Cornell Wordsworth at certain points. Archaic capitalization and the most obviously unintentional orthographical errors have been removed from Wordsworth quotations, which follow as far as is reasonably necessary the most chronologically appropriate texts. Where the sense does not depart from that of the 1805 version, the 1850 text of *The Prelude* is given, since it is the more widely accessible.

The two volumes of Dr Mary Moorman's *William Wordsworth* have been of inestimable value for a long period, but the latest edition of William and Dorothy's letters has supplied much biographical detail; some derives from Z. S. Fink (ed.), *The Early Wordsworthian Milieu*, Oxford, 1958, and T. W. Thompson (ed. R. Woof), *Wordsworth's Hawkshead*, London and New York, 1970.

Illustrations have been included by kind permission of Mrs Mary Henderson, née Wordsworth, Rydal Mount (14 left and right, 15 left and right) and Dr Mary Moorman (13 below). 7 left and right, and 16 are from the National Portrait Gallery. The origin of 8 above and 9 below is indicated in their captions. 13 above is from the second volume of W. Daniell's *A Voyage round Great Britain*, London, 1815; 3 above, from J. Robinson, *Guide to the Lakes*, London, 1819. 2 below, 3 below, 4 below, 10 below, 12 above and below are from T. Rose, *Westmorland, Cumberland, Durham, and Northumberland*, London and Paris, 1832, and 4 above and 11 above, from J. B. Pyne, *The English Lake District*, Manchester,

1853 (all by courtesy of the Sheffield City Libraries). 5 above and below are from Le Keux, *Memorials of Cambridge*, London, 1842; 8 below right, 9 above left and right, 10 above left and right, from Professor Knight's *Through the Wordsworth Country*, illustrated by Harry Goodwin, London, 1887; 1 above and 11 below, from the Houghton Mifflin *Wordsworth* of 1910 (photographs by Walmsley); 1 below, 2 above, 8 below left, from E. Robertson, *Wordsworthshire*, illustrated by Arthur Tucker, R.B.A., London, 1911; and 6 left and right, from Professor Knight's *Coleridge and Wordsworth in the West Country*, illustrated by E. H. New, London, 1913.

I am especially grateful to Mrs Mary Henderson for her great generosity; Dr Peter Laver, Resident Librarian of the Wordsworth Library, Grasmere, for practical assistance on a number of issues; Dr Terry McCormick of the Grasmere and Wordsworth Museum for advice on illustrations; Dr Carol Landon for an introduction to Windy Brow and information relative to some of Wordsworth's early poems; R. H. Fairclough of Cambridge University Library, particularly for calling attention to Jefferys' 1770 map of Westmorland; E. R. Wilkinson, local historian of the County Library, Carlisle, for unstinted research and help at all times, especially with Whitehaven illustrations; Mary Wedd for allowing me the privilege of reading her illustrated thesis on the topography of Wordsworth's poetry; John Atherton for organizing memorable visits to the Hall and Hall Farm, Coleorton; John Pentney for topographical research above Alfoxden; and Charles Pettit for advice on Racedown and Alfoxden illustrations.

My obligations to the Inter-Library Loan service, and to photographic departments, in the University of Sheffield have been continual. Much is due to the ready co-operation of Miss Julia Tame and Mrs Ann Marangos on behalf of Macmillan. Above all, I am grateful to my wife for her unfailing interest and the many benefits which have resulted from her critical reading of the text at successive stages in its preparation.

Part I: 1770–98

Early Years and Adolescent Poetry (1770–87)

One summer, on his way home from school at Hawkshead, William Wordsworth stayed the night at Patterdale, near the head of Ullswater.[1] In the evening, eager for adventure, he set out alone. Catching sight of a boat within a rocky recess, he could not resist the temptation to row out into the lake. Suddenly he noticed a cliff-like peak rise above the craggy steep near the shore; the further he rowed the higher it towered between him and the stars, until it seemed to be striding after him. Such was the joint effect of guilt and loneliness. 'With trembling oars' he turned, and made his way back 'in grave and serious mood'. If he had heard of his grandfather's flight to Patterdale, he was too preoccupied to think of him.

Richard Wordsworth had been Receiver-General for Cumberland, and his aim in 1745, when the beacon above Penrith flared for the last time, announcing the approach of the Young Pretender and his Scottish supporters, was to secure the county moneys and documents in his charge. While he was at Patterdale, his wife kept watch over home and possessions at Sockbridge (between Penrith and the foot of Ullswater), which he had bought after a period as attorney in London. Owing to unfortunate mining speculations his father had been compelled to sell the family property in West Yorkshire, where his ancestors had lived for centuries.

Years later the Receiver-General was probably offended by his elder son Richard, who became Collector of Customs at Whitehaven, for the Sockbridge estate passed to the younger son John, who had served his legal apprenticeship at Penrith. There he fell in love with Ann Cookson, daughter of a linen-draper whose wife Dorothy belonged to the more distinguished Crackanthorpe

3

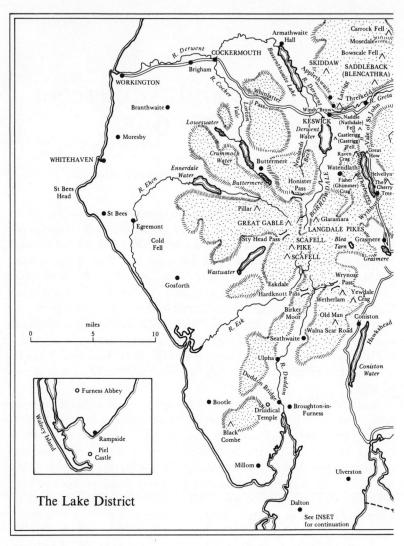

The Lake District

Map 1

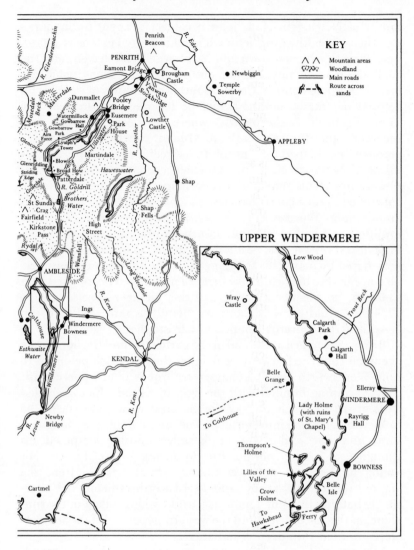

KEY

∧ ∧ Mountain areas
〜〜 Woodland
── Main roads
⊬–⊬ Route across sands

UPPER WINDERMERE

family of Newbiggin Hall. John became law agent to Sir James Lowther, a wealthy proprietor who had inherited extensive estates near Penrith, the new town and harbour of Whitehaven, and the coalfields in its vicinity. His numerous other possessions included a large handsome house in Cockermouth, the tenancy of which John secured not many months before he married Ann in February 1766. Both at Cockermouth, where he became bailiff and recorder, and further south at Millom, where he was made coroner, he helped to ensure that freeholders supported his master's cause at elections. Lowther exercised great political power through his 'ninepins', the parliamentary representatives he controlled in nine constituencies. So mean was he that, as far as is known, John Wordsworth received no payment for his Lowther loyalties, and had to continue in private practice as an attorney. His natural reserve, the position of trust he occupied as agent of a man hated by many, his frequent travel, and his private business, all conspired to make him few firm friends. When he married Ann Cookson, he was twenty-four, and she, eighteen. From 1768 to 1774 five children were born to them: Richard, William (on 7 April 1770), Dorothy, John, and Christopher.

Below the terrace at the end of the garden behind the house they occupied runs the Derwent. A field on the other side belonged to John Wordsworth, and it is characteristic of William's poetic spirit that, becoming familiar with the sight of a road which ascended through it, to reach the sky on the crest of a 'bare steep', he imagined it 'a guide into eternity'. The sound of the river delighted him, and day and night its 'ceaseless music' composed his thoughts, as nature continued to do during most of his life. His young mother was not over-anxious about her children; she wanted them to be happy, and Wordsworth remembered alternately bathing in a small mill-race, and basking naked in the sunshine, at the age of five, until the western slopes of distant Skiddaw were 'bronzed with deepest radiance'.

Sometimes the children were taken to stay with their grandparents at Penrith. One of the early experiences Wordsworth remembered somewhat confusedly was an outing on horseback with the servant 'honest James'; their course lay in the direction of Penrith Beacon. Suddenly young William found he was alone; afraid to ride down a rough stony slope, he dismounted and led his horse until he came to the remains of a gibbet on which a murderer had been hanged in 1767, not far from the scene of his crime. Whether he saw the letters in the turf commemorating this site, and imagined them near the gibbet, must remain conjectural. Not daring to linger, he reascended the bare common until he caught sight of a naked pool and, higher up, below the beacon tower at the top, a girl making her way with difficulty against the wind, as she carried a pitcher on her head. The sight was ordinary, but so perturbed was the boy by what he had seen in his loneliness that all the visual features of the ascent, and of the surrounding moorland, assumed a haunting 'visionary dreariness'.

Excursions to uncle Richard and his family had happier associations. It was on the road near Moresby that Wordsworth was first struck by the view of Whitehaven and its busy port, 'the white waves breaking against its quays and piers'; here too that Dorothy, when she first heard the sound of the sea 'and beheld the scene spread before her, burst into tears', a circumstance 'often mentioned among us', the poet noted late in life, 'as indicating the sensibility for which she was so remarkable'. He remembered it when they were living at Grasmere before his marriage: bright blue eggs in a sparrow's nest recalled her nervous approach for such a sight in the hedge of privet and roses which overtopped the wall of the garden terrace, their favourite playground, above the river at Cockermouth. A butterfly revived memories of the same period: in pursuit of one, he would rush like a hunter, but 'she, God love her! feared to brush The dust from off its wings'. The same kind of chase in conjunction with bolder feats was recalled by the sight of Cockermouth Castle in 1833; Wordsworth imagines the spirit of the place addressing him:

> Erewhile a sterner link
> United us; when thou, in boyish play,
> Entering my dungeon, didst become a prey
> To soul-appalling darkness. Not a blink
> Of light was there; − and thus did I, thy tutor,
> Make thy young thoughts acquainted with the grave;
> While thou wert chasing the wing'd butterfly
> Through my green courts; or climbing, a bold suitor,
> Up to the flowers whose golden progeny
> Still round my shattered brow in beauty wave.

Thoughts in the darkness of this dungeon initiated the taste for

Gothic horror which William exercised in some of his early poems and *The Borderers*.

In 1776 he began to attend the small grammar school which stood in Cockermouth churchyard. (In later years he probably remembered Fletcher Christian, a senior pupil who was destined to make his name as a leading mutineer on *The Bounty*.) One day, after being dared to enter the church, where a woman in a white sheet was doing penance, he was disappointed not to receive the penny he had been led to expect. Hearing this, his mother expressed the hope that he would remember the scene for life. Only he of her children gave her cause for worry, and she felt that he had capacities for good or for ill. She died in March 1778, probably from pneumonia, after a visit to a friend in London, where she slept in a cold, damp room. Wordsworth remembered how, after her death, his father never recovered his habitual cheerfulness; he recognised too how much time he and his sister and brothers had spent with her, and how much their affection and education had depended on her care. In one of his *Ecclesiastical Sonnets* he recalls a group of youngsters who stood nervously round the pastor at their catechizing, himself among them, each in new clothes and wearing a vernal posy, his mother anxiously watching; and how her 'happy hand' had bound 'with faithful tie' the flowers he wore:

> Sweet flowers! at whose inaudible command
> Her countenance, phantom-like, doth reappear:
> O lost too early for the frequent tear,
> And ill requited by this heartfelt sigh!

How long Wordsworth remained at Cockermouth Grammar School is uncertain, but his statement that he learned less Latin there in two years than in two weeks at Hawkshead suggests that he, Richard, and Dorothy were not transferred until after their mother's death to the dame school they attended at Penrith. Among the new friends they made there was Mary Hutchinson, whom Wordsworth married in 1802. They lived with their maternal grandparents, and William proved fractious. Discipline made him sullen or angry. Once, when he had retired to the attics in dudgeon, the sight of some foils made him think of suicide; another time, after daring Richard to do it, he slashed one of the family portraits. Undoubtedly he was thinking of this period and of later unpleasantnesses with the Cooksons when he referred to the miseries, vexations, and regrets which had played a part in the development of his eventual well-being; he admitted that his temper had been 'stiff, moody and violent'.

Although John Wordsworth's duties made it difficult to give his children much of his time, it was a relief to them, and to the Cooksons, when they spent their holidays at Cockermouth. From their mother's narration and reading they had learned to enjoy fairy tales, imaginative romances, adventure stories, and books of travel. Later, Wordsworth could not speak too highly of the value of such literature in satisfying the 'dumb yearnings' and 'hidden appetites' of children, and preparing them for life (Pr.v.426–533). After being at Hawkshead only a few days, when he was just over nine (not under, as he states), he joined a crowd by the shore of Esthwaite, expecting to see a drowned man brought to the surface:

> At last, the dead man, 'mid that beauteous scene
> Of trees and hills and water, bolt upright
> Rose, with his ghastly face, a spectre shape
> Of terror; yet no soul-debasing fear,
> Young as I was, a child not nine years old,
> Possessed me, for my inner eye had seen
> Such sights before, among the shining streams
> Of faëry land, the forest of romance.

At home, he borrowed from his father's 'golden store of books', and read voraciously; sometimes he was so enthralled that he gave them precedence over angling as he lay 'on the hot stones, and in the glaring sun' by the Derwent. One of the earliest books he treasured was a 'slender abstract' of *The Arabian Tales*; he remembered too the fascination of such books as *Gulliver's Travels*, *Don Quixote*, *Gil Blas*, and Fielding's novels. Interest in the poets was stimulated by his father, who encouraged him to learn 'large portions' of Shakespeare, Milton, and Spenser by heart.

By the end of 1778 Dorothy had settled happily with her mother's cousin at Halifax; she did not return to Penrith, or meet her brothers again, until 1787. Richard and William were sent to Hawkshead Grammar School in June 1779, just before the end of the first half-year term, presumably to help them settle quickly in their new surroundings when the second term began in August.

Whether they spent their holidays at Cockermouth or Penrith, they were usually escorted to and from Hawkshead on horseback, until they were old enough to travel independently. Roads were poor and narrow, and there were long steep climbs; the servant responsible for escorting them had a tiring day to endure, especially just before and after Christmas, when short days and inclement conditions demanded greater vigilance.

To the south of most of the Lake District mountains, in beautiful pastoral and sylvan country between Coniston Water and Windermere, Hawkshead provided a market centre for the neighbourhood. Pack-horses were used to bring homespun wool from distant farms and cottages, to be sold with other local products in the square. Among its frequenters Wordsworth remembered beggars and pedlars, and, at the centre of the scene, the old huckster who for sixty years had regularly displayed her wares on a grey outcrop of stone. Baskets and casks were a product of neighbouring woods, where the activity of charcoal-burners was commonly denoted by rising smoke. Below 'the snow-white church upon her hill' stood the school founded in 1585 by Edwin Sandys (a local boy who became Archbishop of York) to instruct the sons of neighbours in general knowledge, Latin and Greek, 'all such good authors which do contain precepts of virtue and good literature', and, once a week, in 'the principles of true religion'. Such was its reputation for scholarship that pupils came from further afield; it excelled in mathematical teaching, and sent students regularly to the two ancient universities, Cambridge especially. Most of its hundred or so boys were boarders, about sixty living in the headmaster's house, the others in or near Hawkshead.

The Wordsworth boys were fortunate to live with Ann Tyson; her husband was a joiner, and they lived in the village. Though childless and in her middle-sixties, she knew how to take charge of young people. In her youth she had been in service with the Knott family at Coniston; they owned an iron-foundry in Furness, and a more recent one at Bonawe on Loch Etive. Her success with children, and their regard for her, may be gauged from the fact that one of the Knotts whom she helped to bring up persuaded her to accompany his own family summer after summer for their holidays while he was there on business in Scotland. About this period she took her first school boarders; if not her first, Richard and William Wordsworth were two of her earliest, and she was a second mother to them. They were joined by their brother John in

January 1782. In the autumn of 1783 the Tysons moved to Colthouse, just outside Hawkshead; as her husband's health was declining, Ann had probably concluded that she would benefit if she
employed more assistance and supervised a larger boarding establishment. There were times before her retirement at the end of 1789
when she had eight school boarders at Colthouse. Christopher, the
youngest of the Wordsworths, arrived in August 1785, at the beginning of Richard's final term.

Wordsworth was not slow to explore the wealth of varied scenery
around Hawkshead. He was only 'a little boy' when he took a lad of
his own age, employed by an itinerant conjurer, to observe his
delight in 'the prospect of the islands below and the intermingling
water' from a high point above Windermere ferry-house peninsula. Few restrictions seem to have been imposed on the boys in
out-of-school hours, and Ann Tyson gave her charges considerable
trust and freedom. Kite-flying was a frequent pastime, and hazel-
nutting had its obvious attractions. For such raiding expeditions,
often in the woods south of Esthwaite, Wordsworth saved his old
clothes in accordance with the advice of his 'frugal dame'.
Whether she knew all his escapades is doubtful. In the autumn,
even in his first full term, he was out on open heights half the
night, visiting springes set by himself and other boys to catch
woodcocks for the table. He made numerous acquaintances; keen
on angling, he 'attached' himself one day to 'a person living in the
neighbourhood of Hawkshead, who was going to try his fortune as
an angler near the source of the Duddon'. After climbing over
Wrynose Pass, they fished most of the day with little success in
torrential rain, and Wordsworth was so exhausted on the way back
that he had to be carried. As he grew older, he became more
adventurous. To reduce the loss of lambs, the pillaging of ravens'
nests was encouraged, and youths took great risks in scaling mountain crags with such feats in view. Wordsworth remembered his
peril as he hung over his quarry, supported more by the wind's
force, it seemed, than by footholds in the slippery rock. He was
present when a school companion on the same ploy, after losing
nerve and being warned not to move, was rescued from a ledge on
Yewdale Crags.[2]

He remembered how, when he was very young, he emerged
above the 'silvery vapours' among the mountains, and caught sight
of a shepherd and his dog. 'Girt round with mists', they seemed to
be floating on an aerial island of grey pendent rocks. About the

same time he watched a shepherd in a valley directing his dog along the mazes of steep crags after a flock that fled upwards 'Through rocks and seams of turf with liquid gold Irradiate' (Pr.05.viii.81–119). So, from experience and stories told by Ann Tyson, he learned to admire the shepherd. 'Severest solitude' seemed more 'commanding' when he was there:

> Seeking the raven's nest, and suddenly
> Surpriz'd with vapours, or on rainy days
> When I have angled up the lonely brooks
> Mine eyes have glanced upon him, few steps off,
> In size a giant, stalking through the fog,
> His sheep like Greenland bears; at other times
> When round some shady promontory turning,
> His form hath flash'd upon me, glorified
> By the deep radiance of the setting sun:
> Or him have I descried in distant sky,
> A solitary object and sublime,
> Above all height! like an aerial cross
> As is stationed on some spiry rock
> In the Chartreuse, for worship. Thus was man
> Ennobled outwardly before mine eyes,
> And thus my heart at first was introduc'd
> To an unconscious love and reverence
> Of human nature . . .

Usually the Wordsworth boys spent their summer holiday at Penrith, and their winter recess with their father at Cockermouth. Just before Christmas 1783, after inquests at Millom, he lost his way in the gloom over Cold Fell, and was compelled to spend a shelterless wintry night there. He was ill when he reached home, and died on 30 December. Wordsworth remembered his funeral in wind and snow, and all the details of the scene on and around the craggy summit where he had waited at the end of term, hoping to catch sight, whenever the mist cleared, of the two roads along either of which the horses might be brought to take him and his brothers home. Subsequently the sorrow succeeding his joyful expectations had seemed like a chastisement or rebuke from God, in consequence of which the recollected scene of presumption —

> the wind and sleety rain,
> And all the business of the elements,

The single sheep, and the one blasted tree,
And the bleak music from that old stone wall,
The noise of wood and water, and the mist
That on the line of each of those two roads
Advanced in such indisputable shapes

— became imbued with an unknown imminence and the in-
clemency of fate.

Relief came to the three orphans when they joined their friends
at school. On winter evenings, when darkness or weather kept
them indoors, they read, listened to Ann Tyson's reminiscences,
played noughts and crosses on slates, or engaged in sessions of card
games such as loo and whist. Occasionally such pastimes were
interrupted by protracted yells from the movement of air under
'splitting fields of ice' on Esthwaite. Skating created excitement,
but rarely was it possible on Windermere, as it was in 1785.[3] In the
summer, senior pupils boated on Windermere, and explored its
islands. After the summer holiday, they soon spent most of their
terminal allowances on excursions: rowing across Windermere to
Bowness, where they played bowls, and enjoyed strawberries and
cream, at the White Lion; or riding to the Druid Temple near
Broughton or, much further, to Furness Abbey, whence they returned in haste, enjoying the sound of thundering hoofs as they
galloped over level sands in the Leven estuary.

The time came when the 'props' assisting Wordsworth's love of
the country were removed: he no longer depended on company
and exciting adventures, but was contented to commune with
nature in solitude. Before being consciously aware of it, he had
been spellbound by silver wreaths of curling mist or cloud reflections in stretches of water; he could gather pleasure like a bee
among flowers through 'every hair-breadth' of seascape at moon-
rise. At Furness Abbey he was entranced by the song of a wren;
when his party returned from Bowness, leaving Robert Greenwood
(who had come from Ingleton, Yorkshire, to board with Ann
Tyson in January 1786) to play his flute on an island as they rowed
off, the sky had never appeared more beautiful to Wordsworth,
and held him like a dream. One 'golden' day he wandered north
until suddenly, from the brow of a 'steep barrier', he saw Grasmere
Vale for the first time and, overpowered by the beauty of lake and
mountains, thought how fortunate it would be to live there. During the latter part of his schooldays, his favourite evening walk was

on an enclosed 'slip of common' by Esthwaite; at night he would walk alone 'under the quiet stars'; if a storm threatened, he would stand beneath a rock, 'listening to notes that are The ghostly language of the ancient earth'. Often, with his best friend, John Fleming of Rayrigg, Windermere, he would walk the five miles round Esthwaite before lessons began at 6 a.m. Sometimes, before 'one smoke-wreath had risen from human dwelling, or the vernal thrush was audible', he was out alone, on some 'jutting eminence' at daybreak.

> Oft in these moments such a holy calm
> Would overspread my soul, that bodily eyes
> Were utterly forgotten, and what I saw
> Appeared like something in myself, a dream,
> A prospect in the mind.

Already Wordsworth's 'religious love' of nature had awakened.

The second of the four headmasters during his attendance at Hawkshead Grammar School was Fletcher Christian's brother Edward. When he left in 1782 for Cambridge, where he became Professor of Common Law, he was succeeded by William Taylor, young (unlike the 'Matthew' of Wordsworth's poems), beloved by his pupils, and a lover of poetry. He encouraged Wordsworth to write poems, and lent him volumes of the English poets; through him William became familiar with the poetry of Thomson, Gray, Collins, Beattie, Chatterton, and others, including Elizabeth Carter and Helen Maria Williams. Just before his death in 1786, he called his senior pupils, including Wordsworth, to his bedside, and bade them farewell.

Late in life Wordsworth stated that he wrote his first 'voluntary verses' after attending a dance at Egremont. As he and his brothers spent their Christmas holidays not far away at Whitehaven after their father's death, it is probable that these verses were composed early in 1785, for the evidence at various points indicates that Wordsworth's poetry began when he was fourteen. The poem William Taylor invited him to write for the school bicentenary may have been begun soon afterwards; the result was a composition of more than a hundred lines in the style of Pope. These verses were so admired that Wordsworth was encouraged to write more. Personification is dominant, most of the poem comprising an address by the Power of Education which stresses the substitution of scientific philosophy for superstition from the time of Bacon and the school foundation, and indicates how its curriculum, influenced by Taylor and the Newtonian teaching from which he had benefited at Cambridge, provided a basis for philosophical development. Beneath 'Hawkshead's happy roof' the goddess has

> loved to show the tender age
> The golden precepts of the classic page;
> To lead the minds to those Elysian plains
> Where, throned in gold, immortal Science reigns;
> Fair to the view is sacred Truth display'd,
> In all the majesty of light array'd,
> To teach, on rapid wings, the curious soul
> To roam from heaven to heaven, from pole to pole,
> From thence to search the mystic cause of things,
> And follow Nature to her secret springs;
> Nor less to guide the fluctuating youth
> Firm in the sacred paths of moral truth.

Classical literary influences are strong in some of Wordsworth's early verse. One poem, on the death of a starling, imitates Catullus. 'Anacreon' is more ambitious; it expresses the beauty of the loved one in hints and directions to Reynolds for her picture. The technical influence of Elizabethan poetry and Milton's earlier verse is clear, and dramatic effect is increased by the preponderance of seven-syllabled lines in sprung rhythm over octosyllabics. Wordsworth's characteristic tendency to describe in terms of analogous natural images is already apparent, one being drawn from the curling white mist on Grasmere, which, 'like a veil of flowing light, Hides half the landskip from the sight'. The date of the poem, 'August 7th, 1786', suggests that the young poet's affection for Mary Hutchinson had grown during the summer holidays at Penrith, and this interpretation is confirmed by 'Beauty and Moonlight', the fragment of an ode in which, try as he will to forget Mary, he is reminded of her beauty by features in natural scenes. The closing thought conveys a luxury of adolescent feeling more typical of Keats than of Wordsworth: since it is impossible to forget his love, the writer invokes heavenly aid:

> Then might her bosom soft and white
> Heave upon my swimming sight,

As these two swans together ride
Upon the gently swelling tide.
Haste, haste, some god indulgent prove,
And bear me, bear me to my love.

Other early poems reveal the fictional taste for death and ghosts which was fashionable as a result of the Gothic influence of ballads and novels, and of Collins, Blair, and Beattie among the more contemporary poets. Its hold on Wordsworth's imagination lasted several years; only in retrospect (Pr.viii.377–91) did he realize the unreal and sentimental forms 'this new power' took:

the elder-tree that grew
Beside the well-known charnel-house had then
A dismal look: the yew-tree had its ghost,
That took his station there for ornament:
The dignities of plain occurrence then
Were tasteless, and truth's golden mean, a point
Where no sufficient pleasure could be found.
Then, if a widow, staggering with the blow
Of her distress, was known to have turned her steps
To the cold grave in which her husband slept,
One night, or haply more than one, through pain
Or half-insensate impotence of mind,
The fact was caught at greedily, and there
She must be visitant the whole year through,
Wetting the turf with never-ending tears.

The last lines seem to prefigure 'The Thorn'. The Gothicized story of 'A Ballad' (written in March 1787) originated from a story Wordsworth probably heard from Ann Tyson on the desertion and death of the daughter of one of her Colthouse neighbours. The first stanza of the laboured but inconclusive 'Dirge' contains an archaistic refrain from Chatterton: 'Mie love is dedde Gone to her deathbedde, Al under the wyllowe tree.'

Natural similes are generally sustained to create complete images; otherwise they would sometimes be more comparable to seventeenth-century conceits, as in 'Beauty and Moonlight':

I saw the white waves o'er and o'er
Break against a curved shore,

> Now disappearing from the sight
> Now twinkling regular and white;
> Her mouth, her smiling mouth can shew
> As white and regular a row.[4]

The trend is more tortuously obvious in the changing parallelism of a sonnet imagined to have been written by a husband after the death of his wife. The comparison in 'Dirge' of the eyebrow, 'Thrown o'er her soft dissolving eye' like 'a bridge all ivi'd o'er', is fancifully disproportionate.

Wordsworth's first published poem was a sonnet in which Helen Maria Williams is imagined weeping over a tale of distress. Printed in *The European Magazine* of March 1787 over a Greek form of his name ('Axiologus'), it expresses a taste for popular sentimental literature which is admitted elsewhere in fanciful and infelicitously completed metaphor:

> How sweet in life's tear-glistering morn
> While fancy's rays the hills adorn,
> To rove as through as Eden vale
> The sad maze of some tender tale,
> Pluck the wild flowers and fondly place
> The treasure in the bosom's face.

These lines occur in what remains of 'The Vale of Esthwaite', a compilation of octosyllabic passages with incomplete lines at many points of improvized recording. The manuscript suggests that Wordsworth may have used missing sections of this lengthy poem for later poetry; the picture of the dog and shepherd on the aerial island was developed from the descriptive opening of this interesting fragment, and the scene of Christmas holiday expectation before the death of Wordsworth's father was revived by some immature lines in this composite work. Here too will be found the first form of the descriptive couplet in *An Evening Walk*: 'And, fronting the bright west in stronger lines, The oak its dark'ning boughs and foliage twines.' This image marks an important preliminary step in the poet's history; he was not more than fourteen when it struck him, on the road from Hawkshead to Ambleside, making him aspire to illustrate 'the infinite variety of natural appearances' which, as far as he knew, had remained unnoticed by the poets.

Perhaps the best of the natural description in the complete script of 'The Vale of Esthwaite' contributed to the first unit of *The Prelude*; what remains gives occasional hints of Dyer and Cowper; some phrases echo Milton, Thomson, Gray, Collins, and Beattie. Dusky Twilight journeys from the cloudy cave where day-long she dreams of Philomela, and holy Melancholy casts 'o'er the soul a still repose'. In more sensational vein Superstition spreads 'cold and awful horror', conjuring up in the sable woods a vision of Druids; one, about to sacrifice the poet, proves to be a waterfall 'in robe of white', and this suggests a spectre in a castle dungeon. Yelling spirits and clanking chains are heard within roofless walls by a lost minstrel, and a grisly phantom causes his harp to shriek. Introduced likewise by a screaming owl, a further Gothic descriptive narrative makes imaginative play with the legendary associations of Calgarth Hall, near the eastern shore of upper Windermere. Castellated, ruinous, and traditionally spectre-haunted, it could not but attract boys like Wordsworth. He gives further indulgence to 'fond sickly fancy', giddy steeps by Windermere being scaled by murderers' ghosts which glare upon the blast as 'Heaven's terrific sire' angrily makes 'the mighty lyre of Nature' shriek, while Night laughs like a madman. On high pillars of rock which brood over a dark dreary vale, he sees forms 'of wild terrific mien': hell-born Murder with haggard eye, Suicide with savage glance, and moody Madness with 'wide-rent robe, and shaggy hair'.

The end of the poem is disjointed. Most, if not all of it, was written after Wordsworth's reunion with his sister at Penrith in the summer of 1787. The memory of his father's death had suggested that he would shortly be with them that rest, in a churchyard such as heard Gray's 'pensive sighs'. But he finds comfort in the thought of Fleming's friendship and of Dorothy. (After returning to Hawkshead, he was to leave for Cambridge, where he had been admitted to St John's College.) Towards the end of the poem he ventures to hope that he will reach old age. Then he remembers the thought he associated with a sunset which impressed him at the age of thirteen,[5] while resting with his friends in a boat under a row of magnificent sycamores on the edge of Coniston Water; already he was linking 'moral feelings' with the 'external forms' of nature. Afterwards he thought the lines he had written on the subject could be turned to advantage in a single poem. The result (cf. Pr.viii.458–75) was 'Extract, from the conclusion of a poem, composed in anticipation of leaving school':

Dear native regions, I foretell,
From what I feel at this farewell,
That, whereso'er my steps may tend,
And whensoe'er my course shall end,
If in that hour a single tie
Survive of local sympathy,
My soul will cast the backward view,
The longing look alone on you.

Thus, while the sun sinks down to rest
Far in the regions of the west,
Though to the vale no parting beam
Be given, not one memorial gleam,
A lingering light he fondly throws
On the dear hills where first he rose.

Cambridge, the Picturesque, and London (1787–91)

When Dorothy Wordsworth returned to Penrith after an absence of almost nine years, her friendship with Mary Hutchinson was renewed, and William enjoyed their company. Dorothy's letters to Jane Pollard of Halifax are very informative. She thought William and Christopher very clever; John, who was to be a sailor, had a 'most excellent heart'; and Richard[6] was diligent though 'far from being as clever as William'. Finding their grandparents and uncle Kit (Christopher) unfriendly, they frequently ended their discussions with the wish that they had a father and home of their own. If Lord Lonsdale (Sir James Lowther) failed to pay his debts, which were estimated at £4700, they would still have about £600 each, she believed. John, needing only £200 to fit him out for the merchant navy in January, wished to contribute the remainder of his share to the education of William, who fancied being a lawyer if his health would permit. Then, as often in his later years, he suffered from violent headaches and a pain in his side. Uncle Kit would not have him at Penrith after the holidays. . . . It must have been a relief for him to stay at Colthouse, with John and Christopher, during August and September.

Dorothy, who read much despite her grandmother's disapproval, was delighted to receive 'a very pretty collection of books' from her brothers. William had read an edition of Burns's poems, many of them with great admiration, and borrowed a copy from the Penrith book club for her to read. Ann Tyson's interest in his welfare did not diminish, and she bought velvet and silk for his university attire. During the first three weeks of October, Dorothy helped him with his preparations for Cambridge. Her favourite uncle William Cookson was staying with them at Penrith. He was engaged to the vicar's daughter and, when they were married a year later, took Dorothy with them to live at Forncett rectory near Norwich. It was he who introduced Wordsworth to St John's College, of which he was a fellow, after accompanying him and another nephew by chaise. On the way, about two hundred miles from Penrith (Pr.05.vii.415), Wordsworth for the first time heard a woman utter blasphemy, and was shocked at her abandonment and pride in public vice.

Academic Cambridge presented a strange new world to a northern 'stripling of the hills', but Wordsworth was not without friends. Eight other scholars from Hawkshead were there: Fleming was two years ahead of him at St John's; and two others, one at the same college, the other (Robert Greenwood) at neighbouring Trinity, had boarded with him at Colthouse. As Edwin Sandys had been a student at St John's, its link with Hawkshead was traditionally strong. The college had been founded by the Lady Margaret, mother of Henry VII, to replace the old Hospital of St John, and Wordsworth, partly as a result of his proficiency in mathematics, partly from William Cookson's acquaintance with his tutor, was awarded a Foundress scholarship soon after his admission. He had cheap upper rooms in the first court, so close to Trinity Chapel that he continually heard its 'loquacious clock', and sometimes its 'pealing organ'; from his bed he could see by the light of the moon the antechapel where Newton's statue stood.

Many years passed before Wordsworth set down his Cambridge recollections in *The Prelude*, and the question inevitably arises to what extent his impressions are coloured by later views. His disillusionment is hardly surprising. Cambridge fellowships were reserved for celibate clergymen, many of whom were absentees; and pride of place in the curriculum was given to mathematics, which Newton had established as the key to natural philosophy and wisdom. Wordsworth did not rebel in the manner of Blake ('May God us keep From single vision and Newton's sleep!'), but the gradual effect of such learning was the certainty that his 'under soul' was 'hush'd', 'lock'd up in such a calm, That not a leaf of the great nature stirr'd' (Pr.05.iii.539—41). The realization that he was 'not for that hour, nor for that place' probably came after his first year. His account of the period is shot through with ironic amusement and a maturer detachment than could be expected from a young student:

> And here was Labour, his own bond-slave; Hope,
> That never set the pains against the prize;

Idleness halting with his weary clog,
And poor misguided Shame, and witless Fear,
And simple Pleasure foraging for Death;
Honour misplaced, and Dignity astray;
Feuds, factions, flatteries, enmity, and guile
Murmuring submission, and bald government,
(The idol weak as the idolater,)
And Decency and Custom starving Truth,
And blind Authority beating with his staff
The child that might have led him; Emptiness
Followed as of good omen, and meek Worth
Left to herself unheard of and unknown.

All this variety is viewed philosophically as no more than 'a creek in the vast sea' of the 'live whole'. Similarly, a later judgment probably led to over-ascription in the poet's *conscious* religious response to the scenes around Cambridge, as he 'paced alone the level fields Far from those lovely sights and sounds sublime' with which he had been conversant. The autobiographical problem is frankly admitted: Wordsworth cannot tell 'what portion is in truth The naked recollection of that time, And what may rather have been called to life By after-meditation'.

A first-class award at the end of his first term suggests his initial keenness for academic success; the following June he was placed in the second class; by the end of 1788 he seems to have abandoned any plan he had of studying for a fellowship. The reason for this must be sought as much in Wordsworth as in 'the injurious sway of place or circumstance', for three of his school contemporaries finished high in the lists of Wranglers. He admits that, though he could 'cleave to solitude in lonely places', he could not resist the throng; his heart was 'social, and loved idleness and joy'. As time passed, the 'dazzling show' faded. Gangs of university Mohocks, some dissolute and violent, roamed the streets; wealthy students were given to pranks and ill-mannered comment; and Wordsworth was made to feel his social inferiority as a sizar. He was 'ill-tutored for captivity' by the freedom he had enjoyed at Hawkshead, and resumed his habit of taking long solitary walks. Much of the mathematical teaching he had to endure during his first year was already familiar, and there were no teachers to inspire the kind of respect and admiration he had for William Taylor; he missed too the affection and steadying influence of Ann Tyson;

Tutors showed little interest in their students beyond an ego-centred desire for examination successes; too many scholars were motivated by prizes and competitiveness, and Wordsworth's interest became cankered by the gnawing spirit of emulation which an examination-ridden system bred. Late in life (12.iii.46) he remembered it, telling a nephew that it was akin to envy. Knowledge, he believed, should be sought for its own sake, and he regretted that the syllabus prescribed from term to term was timid, and did not allow him to read as widely as he hoped. In retrospect he wished there had been more plain living and high thinking at Cambridge. Most of the numerous fellows at St John's were waiting for appointment to livings, and the common lack of respect for their teaching ability, even more for that of the 'grave elders' among them − 'men unscoured, grotesque in character, tricked out like aged trees' which 'Give ready place to any random seed That chooses to be reared upon their trunks' − must have weakened any resolve Wordsworth ever had to follow their example.

Interest stimulated in the Lake District by the poet Gray was given fresh impetus at Cambridge when William Gilpin's two volumes on its 'picturesque' scenery appeared in 1786. Perhaps Wordsworth bought his copy of the work during his first year at Cambridge; a contemporary noted his enthusiasm for 'the beauties of the North', and it is significant that, after staying the whole academic year (as most students did), Wordsworth turned aside on his way north to visit Dovedale in Derbyshire. His main route rook him to Kendal; the next morning he crossed Winder-mere, and hurried to greet Ann Tyson, the 'old dame, so kind and motherly' whom he and others had learned to honour 'with little less than filial love'. It was early June, near the end of the school term, and he stayed several weeks. The beauty of familiar scenes, and friendly meetings with many people he had known, renewed his spirit. He was invited to parties, and it was after dancing almost until cockcrow that he returned over the hills between Windermere and Colthouse, and saw day break over sea and mountains:

> Magnificent
> The morning rose, in memorable pomp,
> Glorious as e'er I had beheld − in front,
> The sea lay laughing at a distance; near,

> The solid mountains shone, bright as the clouds,
> Grain-tinctured, drenched in empyrean light;
> And in the meadows and the lower grounds
> Was all the sweetness of a common dawn —
> Dews, vapours, and the melody of birds,
> And labourers going forth to till the fields.

This animating scene made him realize his dedication to nature, to those enduring things in life which could easily be lost sight of (and often had been, in Cambridge) in 'trivial pleasures' and distracting aims. His 'deeper passions lay elsewhere', and led to poetry. Much that he wrote in the summer of 1788 contributed to *An Evening Walk*. He had already developed the lifelong habit of composing aloud as he walked, and he recalled the companionship of an adopted terrier at such times, and how he would express his gratification by patting him when, after great pains and little progress, 'some lovely image' came to his mind 'full-formed, like Venus rising from the sea'; he was grateful too when the dog, turning back to warn him of a pedestrian's approach, saved him from the suspicion of being 'crazed in brain'.

He visited his uncles at Penrith and Whitehaven. With Dorothy and his sweetheart Mary Hutchinson he climbed Penrith Beacon, his youthful feelings endowing the scene with a radiance the brighter for the dreariness with which he remembered it from childhood. He and Dorothy walked along the banks of the Eamont to Brougham Castle, a favourite spot from earlier visits; here they climbed among the ruins to view the landscape or, lying on 'some turret's head', to catch the whisper of harebells and tufts of grass in the breeze 'while mid-day heat oppressed the plains'. The last three weeks of the summer vacation were spent at Colthouse, and it was after a 'round of strenuous idleness', sailing on Windermere followed by late-night dancing (probably at the Ferry House), that, on the ascent between the Sawreys, he was jolted out of the peace induced by solitude and a murmuring stream. Suddenly, at a turning of the road, he saw the 'uncouth shape' of a tall, incredibly emaciated man propped against a milestone, his hands pallid, his mouth looking ghastly in the moonlight and emitting low sounds of pain. Wordsworth could see from his faded garb that he was a soldier. At length he summoned up courage to greet him; many questions followed, and Wordsworth learned that the sufferer had been discharged on returning from service in the

Tropic Islands. Knowing a cottager who lived beyond a neighbouring wood, he took the sick man along, and, late as it was, ensured that he would receive lodging and refreshment. He had been shocked into awareness of harsh realities by this strange encounter, but he was equally impressed by the soldier's endurance, his indifference to past hardships, his dignified calm and trust in Providence.

On her way to Forncett with her uncle and his wife, Dorothy spent a day with William at Cambridge in early November, and thought she was 'in a different country' as she walked in 'college courts and groves'; it looked odd, but becoming, 'to see smart powdered heads with black caps . . . and gowns, something like those that clergymen wear'. Wordsworth was already giving more time to his own reading, especially in poetry. His interest in classical literature continued, and he translated from Virgil, Horace, and Moschus (PW1.283–7). He read the poets with whom he was already familiar, and new poets past and present, among them Lady Winchilsea and John Langhorne, both of whom he esteemed highly; *The Country Life* by the latter was, he held, the first poem 'that fairly brought the Muse into the company of common life' (15.i.37). He may have read Crabbe; he certainly enjoyed reading Chaucer. Shakespeare was not neglected, but the poets he read most zealously were Spenser and Milton. With the former he felt a special affinity: 'Sweet Spenser, moving through his clouded heaven With the moon's beauty and the moon's soft pace, I called him brother, Englishman, and friend!' The thought that these and other great spirits had been students at Cambridge stirred his imagination. Milton's rooms at Christ's were occupied by one of his friends, and he saw them for the first time at a wine-party, where he was so elated that he drank again and again to the poet's memory, having to run as best he could ('ostrich-like') for chapel, which he reached 'after the importunate bell Had stopped, with wearisome Cassandra voice No longer haunting the dark winter night'.

With travel and the picturesque as well as literature in mind, Wordsworth began the study of French, Spanish, and Italian, the last particularly, since he had regular lessons from the great scholar Agostino Isola, editor of *Gerusalemme Liberata*. He was very old and charming, once a friend of Gray, who, as Professor of History, had given him responsibility for the teaching of modern languages in the University. Wordsworth translated Addison's

'The Vision of Mirzah' for Isola, and his proficiency in Italian may be judged by some of his later translations, notably of sonnets by Michelangelo.

Though no contender for academic distinction, Wordsworth was too occupied at Cambridge to write much verse; and creative composition was mainly confined to revision and tentative sketches or notes. The religious love of nature which had been awakened in the Lake District did not wholly sleep: to 'every natural form, rock, fruit or flower' he gave a 'moral life'; he 'saw them feel' or 'linked them to some feeling'. Thus, in response to the 'quickening soul' of the universe, his mind became activated; looking for 'universal things', he felt

> Incumbencies more awful, visitings
> Of the Upholder of the tranquil soul,
> That tolerates the indignities of time,
> And from the centre of eternity
> All finite motions overruling, lives
> In glory immutable.

Alone on winter evenings amid college groves, he indulged in lighter musings; 'scarcely Spenser's self' in his youth could have enjoyed visions more tranquil than were his when, looking up at the graceful ivy-wreathed branches of an ash beneath the frosty moon, he fancifully created bright appearances of 'human forms with superhuman powers'.

William's long vacation in 1789 was spent first with Dorothy and the Cooksons at Forncett, then in the Yorkshire dales; he may have spent some time on the farm of Tom Hutchinson, Mary's brother, at Sockburn-on-Tees. After staying at Whitehaven, and almost certainly with a cousin at Branthwaite and another at Broughton, he spent a month with Ann Tyson. (When she retired at the end of the year he lost the one place where he had felt most happily at home.) The terrier companion of his vocal outdoor composition had been drowned, and he began some verses imitative of 'Lycidas' on the subject; his main poetic endeavours were devoted to *An Evening Walk*. After the briefest of calls on his uncle Kit at Penrith, he returned to Cambridge. The French Revolution had broken out, and he had no idea of the extent to which it would affect his life and thought. Perhaps it was at the beginning of his last academic year that he saw the uncertainty of his future imaged in a scene on the Cam, and was reminded of Collins' 'Ode on the Death of Thomson'. Accordingly, in the verses which were written at the time, and which appeared in the 1798 volume of *Lyrical Ballads*, the scene was transferred to the Thames.

Although Wordsworth had neglected his mathematics, his interest in universal things kept him in touch with the natural philosophy which was taught and discussed at the University. The general view was that the mysterious universe was explicable in terms of mathematical principle or law; God governed, and pre-served the stars from wrong. Yet statements in Newton's *Principia* that 'He is omnipresent', 'In Him are all things contained and moved' may, like the following passage from Virgil's *Georgics* (which Wordsworth studied) have helped to sustain his intuitions: 'for God, they say, pervades all things, earth and the sea's expanse and heaven's depth; from Him the flocks and herds, men and beasts . . . draw, each at birth, the slender stream of life'.[7] The seventeenth-century Cambridge Platonists probably co-operated to counteract a mechanical interpretation of nature. Euclidean geometry retained its fascination (Pr.vi.115–41) but, though it 'held acquaintance with the stars, And wedded soul to soul in purest bond of reason', Wordsworth came to regard it as a stone beside the resplendent shell of poetry (Pr.v.50–140) which imparts 'authentic tidings of invisible things' (Ex.iv.1132–47). Fittingly therefore the Wanderer of *The Excursion*, while lingering 'in the elements of science', applied his geometrical knowledge to realize actuality among crags and stars, but turned in vain to science for the key to experience when 'Nature and her overflowing soul' had steeped his thoughts in feeling (PW5.384–5).

Wordsworth's first visit to London seems to have been in 1788 (Pr.vii.65). When he reached the heart of the city, he was momen-tarily overwhelmed with 'a weight of ages', an impression which remained with him 'as a thing divine' (Pr.viii.530–59). There can be little doubt that in 1789, probably at Christmas, he met his brother Richard, who had been transferred to the city; he cer-tainly met John, who, after two or three transatlantic voyages, was now waiting to serve on a new merchantman, the *Earl of Aber-gavenny* of the East India Company, under the captaincy of his cousin John, uncle Richard's second son. Years later, in conversa-tion with the poet Samuel Rogers, Wordsworth recalled how he bought William Bowles's *Fourteen Sonnets* soon after publication in 1789, and annoyed John by stopping to finish reading them in a niche of London Bridge. Heartfelt recollections of country scenes in these poems appealed to Wordsworth, as they did to Coleridge a few years later.

William was unclassed in the 1790 examinations, and placed among those who showed 'considerable merit in the subjects which they undertook'. Of greater moment to him were the preparations which he and his college friend Robert Jones were making for a visit to the Swiss Alps. They had studied the route described by William Coxe, a fellow of King's College, Cambridge, in his 'Swisserland' *Sketches* of 1779. This they proposed to do in reverse; their visit to the Grande Chartreuse en route probably arose from interest which had been excited by Gray's letters. Such a tour on foot would have daunted most people, but Wordsworth was lured by prospects of 'the sublime and beautiful' (which it is reasonable to assume he had studied in Burke's well-known essay) and of finding 'the picturesque' in scene after scene, as his first letter to Dorothy during the tour clearly proves. 'I am a perfect enthusiast in my admiration of Nature in all her various forms', he writes; repeatedly, after quitting a 'fortunate station', he returned avidly to it 'with the hope of bearing away a more lively picture'. He was to be stirred by more than spectacle: 'Among the more awful scenes of the Alps, I had not a thought of man, or a single created being; my whole soul was turned to him who produced the terrible majesty before me.'

The French Revolution lent added interest to the two pedestrians, for, on the first day of their journey through France, the anniversary of the storming of the Bastille was celebrated with festivities and dancing which continued throughout the country a week or two; France seemed to be 'standing on the top of golden hours', and human nature 'born again'. National rejoicing in the liberty which the Revolution had brought appeared wholly natural to the travellers, who sailed down long stretches of the Saône and Rhone with a festive group of delegates returning from mass celebrations in the Champ de Mars. Resuming their journey on foot, they reached the Grande Chartreuse, where they were the monks' guests for two days in early August. After making their way along the northern shore of Lake Geneva, and visiting Chamonix, to view Mont Blanc and the glaciers, they proceeded along the upper Rhone and climbed the Simplon Pass. Not realizing they had crossed the Alps, they had to return down a mountain track to the bed of a stream leading to the three-mile stretch of the Gondo gorge, which was narrow, and difficult to traverse at times. There had been heavy rains; the weather was still tempestuous; and Wordsworth and Jones were fatigued. A succession of awe-inspiring spectacles, with dizzying crossings and prospects, violent gusts of wind, and continual changes from gloom to dazzling brightness, coupled with the tumult of roaring waterfalls and of wind buffeting wind and crags, took their toll; the sublime turned at times into the terrific. Stunned and bewildered, they went on to a hostel where they spent 'an awful night', their sensations being prolonged by a tremendous torrent 'that came thundering down a chasm of the mountain on the opposite side of the glen'. So Wordsworth recalled his experience when he revisited the 'Spittal' with Dorothy thirty years later.[8] The description he wrote in 1799 of his impressions in the Gondo gorge conveys Wordsworth's feelings unforgettably, for externalization in 'bewildered', 'sick', and 'giddy' is psychological; but the Apocalyptic conclusion reflects the subsequent re-creation of a sequence of scenes (Pr.vi.624–40).

Nearly two months of their tour lay ahead. By Lake Como 'it was impossible not to contrast that repose, that complacency of spirit, produced by these lovely scenes, with the sensations . . . experienced two or three days before, in passing the Alps'. After losing touch in a wood during a violent thunderstorm, Wordsworth and Jones wandered all night, ending miles apart. They were lost again in woods outside Gravedona, after being roused by Italian clocks which made them think it was near dawn, when the lake would be at its loveliest; afraid of rustling noises around, they sat on a rock above the water, watching the dull red reflection of the moon change its form 'like an uneasy snake'. Moving north via the Splügen Pass, they came to the upper reaches of the Rhine and, after a devious route, descended the Reuss valley to Lake Uri, where they saw a wonderful sunset and listened, before 'the pictured fane' of William Tell, as their boatman narrated the hero's exploits with glowing pride. From Lucerne they proceeded to Lake Zürich, then to the Catholic shrine of Einsiedeln, to Glarus and, north again, to Lake Constance. From Schaffhausen and the Falls of the Rhine they made their way to Lucerne, Grindelwald, Lauterbrunnen, Berne, and Avenches (presumably to visit Rousseau's haunts by the Bieler See), on to Basle, whence they floated down the Rhine to Cologne, which they reached on 28 September. They were in no hurry. In Belgium they were reminded of revolutionary movements by the sight of armed forces, but looked on these things 'as from a distance'. Wordsworth was more occupied with 'the ever-living universe', and returned to Cambridge inspired by a sense of youthful independence. How much he studied is not known; perhaps he made notes on his tour for the poem which became *Descriptive Sketches*. Before taking his final examination in January 1791, he spent about six weeks with Dorothy at Forncett, and a few days, if his statement to a nephew can be accepted precisely, reading Richardson's *Clarissa*. Like Jones, he obtained his B.A. without honours.

Unlike Wordsworth, Jones entered the Church, and thereby qualified for a vacant fellowship at his college. Feeling that he must observe the way of the world as well as nature, Wordsworth decided to find lodgings in London. He had heard of Vauxhall and Ranelagh, their green groves and 'wilderness of lamps', their 'gorgeous ladies, fairy cataracts, and pageant fireworks'; if he had not already seen these and other public attractions, he soon did. His uncle Richard (who had given him considerable financial assistance at Cambridge) sent him £60, and this sum determined the length of his metropolitan term. He was 'Frugal as there was need, and, though self-willed, From dangerous passions free'. The record of his 1791 sojourn (Pr.vii) presents the motley and charivari of busy streets, menageries, picture displays, exhibitions, and a variety of stage-shows at Sadler's Wells. The theatre had attracted him from boyhood; he attended numerous plays but, outside Shakespeare, little passed beyond 'the suburbs' of his mind or stirred his imagination deeply. With the exception of Edmund Burke, whose respect for tradition Wordsworth admired even then, almost all the well-known speakers in the House of Commons tired him with their long-winded oratory. Oratory of another kind pleased his satirical palate in churches, where he observed 'the crook of eloquence' entwined with flowery phrases from Dr Young, Shakespeare, and even Ossian. His critical evocation of a pretentious narcissist preacher recalls Cowper and Anne Brontë: a comely bachelor, 'fresh from a toilette of two hours', begins his address with seraphic look, and leads his voice 'a minuet course' through many a maze, sometimes contracting his mouth to an almost imperceptible orifice, which then opens with an exquisite smile of 'rapt irradiation'. He was impressed by the quiet of London at night, when sky, moonshine, and sounds of desert infrequency caught his attention. Most people, he thought in retrospect, would find the city a 'blank confusion', epitomized in

Bartholomew Fair, the spectacle of which he presents in seething graphic detail; the discerning philosopher would see it differently, 'with a feeling of the whole'.

On this crowded canvas three scenes are particularly memorable: outside a theatre, among admiring dissolute men and shameless women (including his mother), a beautiful child 'like one of those who walked with hair unsinged amid the fiery furnace'; an artisan father heedless of passers-by, as he sat in the sunshine with his sickly babe, regarding it with unutterable love; and (as Wordsworth, 'amid the moving pageant' of unknown people, was lost in 'thoughts of what and whither, when and how' until the shapes before him became 'a second-sight procession') the sudden view of a blind man against a wall with a paper on his chest to tell his story. Struck by the thought that here was the human condition personified, 'the utmost we can know, both of ourselves and of the universe', the poet's mind turned round 'as with the might of waters', and he gazed on the 'steadfast face and sightless eyes' as if 'admonished from another world'.

'I quitted London about three weeks ago, where my time passed in a strange manner; sometimes whirled about by the vortex of its *strenua inertia*, and sometimes thrown by the eddy into a corner of the stream, where I lay in almost motionless indolence.' So Wordsworth wrote (17.vi.91) from the home of his friend Jones in northern Wales, where he stayed nearly four months, excluding the three-week tour on foot among the mountains which he recalled in his dedication of *Descriptive Sketches* to Jones, with reference to 'the sea-sunsets, which give such splendour to the vale of Clwyd, Snowdon, the chair of Idris, the quiet village of Bethgelert, Menai and her Druids, the Alpine steeps of the Conway, and the still more interesting windings of the wizard stream of the Dee'. His most vivid memory was the moonlight scene from the top of Snowdon (as described near the end of *The Prelude*).

On the advice of his uncle William, Wordsworth returned to Cambridge in September to study oriental languages (mainly Hebrew, Arabic, and Greek) as a preparation for the Church. His friend William Mathews, recently of Pembroke College and now unhappy as a teacher, had suggested they take to the roads for a living; he replied that, were he without relatives to whom he was accountable (many years passed before his debts to them were cleared), he would prefer Mathews' recommendation to his own position or to 'vegetating on a paltry curacy'. He was doomed to be an idler all his life, he wrote in November, having realized that, with little knowledge of Latin and 'scarce anything of Greek', he lacked the linguistic discipline for 'a course of Oriental literature'. He was at Brighton, on his way to Orléans, having obtained his guardians' permission to spend the winter there, primarily to improve his French, in the hope of securing his independence as a travelling tutor to some young aristocrat.

France, Annette, and Descriptive Poetry (1791–3)

Wordsworth was eager to see Paris, and stayed there for five days at the beginning of December. He sought places to which the Revolution had given éclat (including the site of the Bastille, the Faubourg St Antoine, and the Champ de Mars), heard 'hissing factionists' in public places, and attended stormy meetings at the National Assembly and the Jacobin Club. As in London, his interest was that of a sight-seer and student of humanity; nothing in the political scene impressed as much, he afterwards maintained, as Le Brun's popular 'Magdalene' picture.

Unaware of the significance of events, Wordsworth spent much time at parties and clubs in Orléans, with the object of learning French manners and speech. In such elegant society all the vexed questions of the day were scrupulously avoided; Wordsworth conversed and joined in card-play, but soon tired of the formalities. Mixing with people more freely, he became interested in public affairs and the Revolutionary cause. Three cavalry officers had rooms in the house where he lodged, and through them he became acquainted with other members of the nobility who had been stripped of their privileges. Most were prepared to join the émigrés assembling in the Rhineland in readiness for war. Wordsworth could not share their feelings, for he had grown up in a region, and attended educational institutions, where distinction lay open to all and, by and large, little respect was paid to wealth or blood. To one who had never questioned the principle of equal rights, the Revolution seemed 'nothing out of nature's certain course'.

Soon after his arrival in Orléans, Wordsworth spent evenings with a 'very agreeable' family; Annette Vallon and her brother, whom she was visiting, may have been among their guests. Her home was at Blois, where her mother had recently remarried. She

33

must have been fascinated by the young Englishman (nearly four years her junior). Perhaps he raised romantic hopes of life abroad, away from political turmoil and war; she had strong anti-revolutionary sentiments. Wordsworth could survey mankind and political passions disinterestedly, but he could not resist the winsome ways of this excitable young woman. They were soon passionately in love and, not long after Annette's return, he followed her to Blois. Her pregnancy, and the need for a steady income, made him conclude, after all, that he must enter the Church (19.v.92).

France had declared war on Austria, and he was certain that the country's future would be decided that summer. Once again his lodgings brought him into close contact with army officers, among them Michel Beaupuy, from whom he heard the story first included in *The Prelude* (05.ix.555–934), then rightly withdrawn because of its disproportionate length, and revised for publication in 1820 under the title of 'Vaudracour and Julia'. The tale must have been well known; it was reported by Helen Maria Williams in her *Letters Written in France* (1790),[9] and Wordsworth's I.F. note states that he heard it from a French lady 'who had been an eye-and-ear witness of all that was done and said'. Though written not much more than two years after his marriage, and imaginatively influenced by *Romeo and Juliet*, Wordsworth's poem communicates some of the romantic intoxication he experienced thirteen years earlier in France. Its tragic sequence of events is movingly and more effectively narrated than some critics allow. Too much autobiography has been read into the poem, and it seems quite improbable that Wordsworth, with no career or income in sight, deliberately chose, in the hope of overcoming objections which his guardians or Annette's family might raise, to 'entrust himself to nature', assuming that the birth of a child would lead to 'a happy end of all'.

His greatest friend was Beaupuy, and they walked frequently along the Loire, or through forest tracts, where Wordsworth sometimes forgot the present in imaginative re-creation of scenes in Ariosto or Tasso or Spenser. So strong was his love of tradition that, whatever his sympathies with the Revolution, the sight of a sacked convent grieved him, nor could Beaupuy's stories of past wrongs and vice destroy the 'chivalrous delight' with which he viewed local châteaux. The sight of hunger brought him back to reality, and he believed that the new 'benignant spirit' was unconquerable; he saw frequent evidence of it in young patriots as they bade farewell to loved ones before posting to the frontier. Beaupuy was honourable, scholarly, gentle, and courteous to all. He and Wordsworth talked

> Of civil government, and its wisest forms;
> Of ancient loyalty, and chartered rights,
> Custom and habit, novelty and change;
> Of self-respect, and virtue in the few
> For patrimonial honour set apart,
> And ignorance in the labouring multitude.

To discuss the principles of liberty, and its historical successes and failures, with a man of such idealism and faith, at a time when events gave abstract rights a living reality, made Wordsworth feel in after years that Beaupuy stood 'near the worthiest of antiquity'; 'such conversation, under Attic shades, did Dion hold with Plato'. His influence on Wordsworth never faded; he contributed to the composite character of 'The Happy Warrior'; and he strengthened the poet's belief in common man. 'Man he loved as man', however mean and obscure; he believed in the nobility of his nature, a God-given gift which made him capable of seeing 'clear truth' and of building liberty

> On firm foundations, making social life,
> Through knowledge spreading and imperishable,
> As just in regulation, and as pure
> As individual in the wise and good.

Beaupuy left Blois with his regiment at the end of July to defend his country against the Prussians, and Wordsworth continued working assiduously on *Descriptive Sketches*, which he completed in Orléans. In his 'Autobiographical Memoir' he stated that he was there at the time of the September Massacres, but the evidence suggests that he reached the city later, while alarm and debate over the surrender of Verdun and the blood-letting in Paris still continued. (About this time, ironically, his sister Dorothy was attending balls, and meeting members of the royal family at Windsor, where her uncle William, the newly appointed Canon, was in residence.) To avoid scandal as much as possible, Annette had been sent to Orléans for the final period of her pregnancy; she probably took shelter in the home where she may first have met Wordsworth. More favourably received here, no doubt, than by her mother at Blois, he stayed most of September and October in the city, the defeat of the Prussians at Valmy enabling him to close *Descriptive Sketches* optimistically in the name of Liberty.

'Bliss was it in that dawn to be alive, But to be young was very heaven', he had felt that summer. He was an ardent supporter of the Revolution when he returned to Paris at the end of October. One night, after viewing the prison where the king and his family were immured, and the Carrousel from which the attack on the Tuileries palace had been made with great bloodshed that August, he retired, thinking of the September massacres until he seemed to hear a voice that cried to the whole city, 'Sleep no more', and felt that it was as 'defenceless as a wood where tigers roam'. Had he not been financially compelled to return to England, after staying six weeks or more in Paris, he might have made common cause with the Girondins who perished ten months later. They were moderates, impressed by seventeenth-century English republican writers, including Milton, Harrington, and Algernon Sidney, the influence of whom on Wordsworth was soon to become apparent. He could have studied and discussed them in Paris, where their works were readily available in translation. He retained his faith in 'equity and reason', believing that 'the virtue of one paramount mind' would quell 'outrage and bloody power'. Yet his visionary night-fears had been traumatic; he realized that the fate of France depended on what faction got control of the capital, and dread of politically excited mob rage and violence troubled his imagination for life.

Just before Christmas 1792, and a few days after the birth of his daughter Caroline, Wordsworth joined his brother Richard at Staple Inn, where he was to stay for more than half a year. He was soon to discover that his guardians would not consent to his proposed marriage, and that uncle William's support for ordination would no longer be available if he remained loyal to Annette. He could not play the loiterer; he now had personal responsibilities and strong political convictions, the latter strengthened by the failure of all legal efforts to obtain financial restitution from Lord Lonsdale. Having every reason to support himself without delay, and wishing to prove he could do something after his undistinguished university career, he lost no time seeking a publisher for

An Evening Walk and *Descriptive Sketches*, and the two poems appeared separately towards the end of January 1793.

Not surprisingly, Wordsworth regretted with hindsight that he 'huddled up those two little works and sent them into the world in so imperfect a state' (23.v.94). Dorothy and Christopher Wordsworth at Forncett were dismayed to find obscurities in the text, and wished William could have benefited from the criticism of a sympathetic reader. Both works bear ample testimony of highly wrought composition, an excess of artful attention rather than spontaneity confirming Wordsworth's acknowledgment that his early verse was the product of 'extreme labour and tardiness' (28.xi.16); their faults sprang from the immaturity of apprenticehood. Samuel Taylor Coleridge, reading *Descriptive Sketches* in 1794, recognised 'the emergence of an original poetic genius', but found 'harshness and acerbity' combined with 'images all a-glow', the difficulty of the one and the 'novelty and struggling crowd' of the other demanding greater attention than descriptive poetry 'has a right to claim'.

Wordsworth revised *An Evening Walk* in France. Most of it had been composed during his summer vacations of 1788 and 1789, but how much of it was drawn from 'The Vale of Esthwaite' is conjectural. Especially interesting is the transformation of a passage in the latter (ll.200−05, on the sound of the owl as the moon changes the colours of cloud and sky) from clear uncluttered simplicity and vividness to elaboration in picturesque style:

> The bird, with fading light who ceas'd to thread
> Silent the hedge or steaming rivulet's bed,
> From his grey re-appearing tower shall soon
> Salute with boding note the rising moon,
> Frosting with hoary light the pearly ground,
> And pouring deeper blue to Aether's bound;
> Rejoic'd her solemn pomp of clouds to fold
> In robes of azure, fleecy white, and gold,
> While rose and poppy, as the glow-worm fades,
> Checquer with paler red the thicket shades.

With additional imagery in the last two lines from Lady Winchilsea's 'A Nocturnal Reverie', such details would impress more as a whole in a picture than in the successive viewpoints of the above, where Wordsworth, characteristically at this stage of his career, shows a Keatsian desire to 'load every rift with ore', especially from literary sources. The 'boding note' of the owl recalls Cowper (*The Task*, i.205), but the 'sob long and tremulous' of the original cannot be foregone; it appears in a draft version, and finally, with a closer approximation to Gray, in the 'tremulous sob of the complaining owl' at the end of the poem.

Literary allusiveness had become traditional in eighteenth-century poetry; in a neo-classical age, the adaptation of fine phrases from Greek and Latin authors was a commonplace. Gray's 'Elegy' abounds in them, and, as they are resonant with universal feelings, a scholarly reader will find enrichment in their overtones. Similarly, cultured readers welcomed literary echoes in Wordsworth's early poetry. The frequency of his allusions and borrowings indicates what can be achieved through zeal for effect by an immature writer endowed with perseverance and an unusual memory for apt imagery and epithet. He had yet to realize the danger of allowing the 'trade in classic niceties', the 'craft of culling term and phrase', to divert him from his own 'world of eye and ear'. In his later poetry he did not avoid literary echoes, his aim being (like Eliot's in *The Waste Land*, where the technique reaches an extreme form of concentration) to recall thought, events, themes, or imaginative scenes, of special significance to his subject.

In *An Evening Walk* he was indebted not only to poets but, less consciously perhaps in language, to writers on the Lake District, from Gray to the more recent Hutchinson, Clarke (mentioned in a footnote), and Gilpin. The poem shows wide reading, including Spenser, Shakespeare, and a number of forgotten poets. Milton is the dominant influence, from the 'wizard' course of the Derwent in the introduction to the 'aëreal music' at the close. Among the eighteenth-century poets who are heard are Thomson, Goldsmith ('Sweet are the sounds', 'village murmurs'), Gray ('breezy morn', 'drowsy tinklings'), Collins ('folding star' — from Milton's 'star that bids the shepherd fold'), and Beattie ('embattl'd clouds', the ponderous wagon, the 'slow clock tolling deep', the hare in the 'rustling corn'). Acknowledged borrowings include 'sweetly ferocious' from Tasso.

The heroic couplets are noticeably more end-stopped than the 1794 additions, often reflecting the cumulative style of composition. Inversions are sometimes so awkward that fluent reading is hampered. Personification is rife: 'Echo dallies with the various din' and the poet loves to view 'obsequious Grace the winding swan pursue'. An introductory passage illustrates this characteristic freely (and the fashionable affectation of melancholy) in conjunction with other tendencies and points of interest:

> Return Delights! with whom my road begun,
> When life rear'd laughing up her morning sun;
> When Transport kiss'd away my april tear,
> 'Rocking as in a dream the tedious year';
> When link'd with thoughtless Mirth I cours'd the plain,
> And hope itself was all I knew of pain.
> For then, ev'n then, the little heart would beat
> At times, while young Content forsook her seat,
> And wild Impatience, panting upward, show'd
> Where tipp'd with gold the mountain-summits glow'd.
> Alas! the idle tale of man is found
> Depicted in the dial's moral round;
> With Hope Reflexion blends her social rays
> To gild the total tablet of his days;
> Yet still, the sport of some malignant Pow'r,
> He knows but from its shade the present hour.

The second line, with 'laughing' an obstacle to sense ('reared up'), is indefensibly gauche; 'april tear' is quaint, whether it refers to youth or to the comparison between 'April-drops' and tears by Lady Winchilsea; the quotation which follows is excellent if one knows the sentence in Milton's *Areopagitica*, 'There be delights . . . that will fetch the day about from sun to sun, and rock the tedious year as in a delightful dream.' The 'little heart' echoes 'The Vale of Esthwaite' and the venial overuse of diminutives in a sorrowful passage recalling Wordsworth's youthful grief at his father's death; 'total tablet' (like 'mental tablet' at the end of the same poem) is a reminder of the rather mechanical *tabula rasa* theory of mind and memory originated by John Locke. Here it occurs in a somewhat baffling conceit, which Wordsworth recorded in an early notebook, 'Human life is like the plate of a dial: Hope brightens the future, Reflection the hour that is past, but the present is always marked by a shadow.'[10] Following the precedent of his age, he moralizes his song, less cryptically towards the end of the poem, where his reflections run parallel to the changing scene, the supervention of darkness suggesting Death and the extinction of 'those fair Shadows, human joys' (from the poet Young), the moonlight which follows raising Hope with particular significance for the poet.

As can be expected, most of the poem is pictorial. It is composite, being confined to no particular place or walk; and piecemeal expansion tended to diminish the unity of the whole. Even the sense of a particular evening is lost when human tragedy in winter interrupts description of summer sights and sounds. Nor does the changing landscape always emerge clearly, successions of scenic glimpses tending to leave a conglomeration in the mind, especially in the earlier stages of the poem. Not surprisingly one of the most successful passages in this section remained unchanged in the final edition of 1849, except for the substitution of 'or' for 'and' in the penultimate line, the elimination of old-fashioned elisions ('silver'd, wat'ry, scatter'd'), and slight punctuational improvements:

> While, near the midway cliff, the silvered kite
> In many a whistling circle wheels her flight;
> Slant watery lights, from parting clouds, apace
> Travel along the precipice's base;
> Cheering its naked waste of scattered stone,
> By lichens grey, and scanty moss, o'er-grown;
> Where scarce the foxglove peeps, or thistle's beard;
> And restless stone-chat, all day long, is heard.

An ambitious picture of a farmyard cock, largely copied from Rosset's *L'Agriculture, ou Les Géorgiques Françaises* (to which Wordsworth acknowledges only indebtedness of recollection) is less successful. Even if, in the couplet 'Bright sparks his black and haggard eye-ball hurls Afar his tail he closes and unfurls', the sense is understood without the comma after 'Afar', the hyperbolical metaphor of the verb (consonant perhaps with 'monarch' and 'regal brow') is slightly absurd. The simile of the unfurled tail 'like pine-trees, waving to and fro' suffers from disproportion to the point of the ridiculous, especially in a writer whose similes from nature were to be singularly appropriate. More felicitous is the ending, with the crow of the cock assonantly conveyed in contrast to the diminished repetition of distant replies: 'On tiptoe rear'd he blows his clarion throat, Threaten'd by faintly answering farms remote.'

It would be misleading to compare the landscape views by and large with pictures, for all is in process of change, from the approach of sunset to the re-illumination of scenes by moonlight. The poet, moreover, selects from various points, near and far. The setting sun broadens and spreads tides of gold which touch the purple steep and casts its shadow on the 'pictur'd' lake. (The 1849 version is more clear and accurate: 'Whose softened image penetrates the deep.' 'The gilded turf arrays in richer green Each speck of lawn the broken rocks between' is made intelligible in 'Each slip of lawn the broken rocks between Shines in the light with more than earthly green', where 'slip' adds a visual dimension which is absent in 'speck'.) In the distance, yellow beams light up branches at various points in a level wood. Then a shepherd appears, waving his hat as he directs his dog, which winds its way up glittering rocks to round up intercepted sheep. A Druid fane is illuminated (the note indicates the Druid 'Temple', a circle of stones near Broughton), and all the 'babbling brooks' turn to 'liquid gold'. An admirable image suggested by *Paradise Lost*, 'Such the dark spear that crossed the sunbroad shield Of Satan striding o'er the empyreal field', was added in 1794 to describe the long blue bar dividing the 'aegis orb' of the sun at the opening of this passage, but its dramatic splendour is distracting, and Wordsworth wisely withdrew it.

His admiring interest in swans is amply reflected in the description of a pair and their brood on Windermere, and in the closer observation of their home; any disproportion here is slight compared with the sequence. With 'Ye ne'er, like hapless human wanderers, throw Your young on winter's winding sheet of snow', the subject turns abruptly to man's inhumanity to man, and a contrived incursion of Langhorne's deliberately startling realism. Wordsworth imagines some unhappy mother, 'faint, and beat by summer's breathless ray', yearning for the return of her soldier husband, now 'asleep on Bunker's charnel hill afar'. This reference to the American War of Independence recalls the discharged soldier whom Wordsworth had met not far away, perhaps on the very road along which he imagines her dragging her young children. (The 1793 text, with 'Minden's charnel plain' − 'Bunker's charnel hill' appearing among the *errata* − presents unequivocal evidence of the influence of Langhorne's *The Country Justice*: 'Cold on Canadian hills or Minden's plain'.) Perhaps Wordsworth, with Pope's gibe in mind, felt that something more than 'pure description' was required in poetry worthy of serious regard, and introduced this section, and his moralizing reflections, for this reason. It is rather intrusive, and strikes an incongruous note when it concludes with the children's perishing in the cold of winter. Implicit in this is a challenge to the social conscience which anticipates 'The Ruined Cottage'.

The tendency to congestive description returns with twilight sounds, one producing an image of visual appeal, like a Bewick vignette: 'And heron, as resounds the trodden shore, Shoots upward, darting his long neck before.' More harmonious are the closing scenes, as moonlight endows the lake with 'restless magic', touching waves with 'fairy light' or 'tracking with silvering path the changeful gale'. Mountain steeps appear like a black wall, as cottage lights stream across the water. When the moon reaches its zenith, shadows among the mountains are reduced, plains extend 'rimy without speck', and the only visible movement is that of 'silver'd wreaths of quiet charcoal smoke' that move 'o'er the ruins of the fallen wood, Steal down the hills, and spread along the flood'. Fittingly for a writer who has recurrently shown a zeal for communicating aural sensations, *An Evening Walk* ends with late night sounds. As 'the song of mountain streams' beguiles his homeward way, the 'aëreal music' is broken at intervals by

> the slow clock tolling deep,
> Or shout that wakes the ferry-man from sleep,
> Soon followed by his hollow-parting oar,
> And echo'd hoof approaching the far shore;
> Sound of clos'd gate, across the water born,
> Hurrying the feeding hare thro' rustling corn;
> The tremulous sob of the complaining owl;
> And at long intervals the mill-dog's howl;
> The distant forge's swinging thump profound;
> Or yell in the deep woods of lonely hound.

The poem was concluded before Wordsworth left England or met Annette. It is dedicated to his sister Dorothy, and, 'although dark and broad the gulf of time between', the moon of hope gilds 'with her fondest ray' the distant cottage where they will share 'golden days'. It is the 'sole bourn, sole wish, sole object' of his life.

Nearly twice as long as *An Evening Walk*, *Descriptive Sketches* is based on some of Wordsworth's recollections of his tour with

Robert Jones, who is remembered in the dedication and concluding lines. The two were brimful of zest and confidence when they
made their journey, Wordsworth finding it sweet, 'with such
delight On every side, in prime of youthful strength, To feed a
poet's tender melancholy' (Pr.vi.364−6). The serious conclusion of
the poem recalls the gravity with which it opens, the lover of
nature plodding 'his road forlorn', her charities enabling him to
forget his sorrows and bestowing 'chast'ning thoughts of sweetest
use' to 'moralize his pensive' way. If anxiety about Annette Vallon
contributed to this strain, it is hardly confirmed by the supposition
that, like the poet in Gray's 'Elegy', he is afflicted with 'crazing
Care' or 'desperate Love'. The moralizing style which casts its
shadow over the work at the outset, making the lone traveller pass
'o'er Gallia's wastes of corn' in dejection, is reminiscent of Beattie's
The Minstrel, and more traditional and affected than personal.
This eighteenth-century role produces rather sombre realistic
impressions, with little of the enthusiasm for scenery that Wordsworth actually felt, and nothing akin to Byron's individual
response to nature's magnificence. Wordsworth's feelings are
tethered too much to philosophical generalities:'

> − The mind condemn'd, without reprieve, to go
> O'er life's long deserts with its charge of woe,
> With sad congratulation joins the train
> Where beasts and men together o'er the plain
> Move on, − a mighty caravan of pain;
> Hope, strength, and courage, social suffering brings,
> Freshening the waste of sand with shades and springs.
>
> *   *   *
>
> Soon flies the little joy to man allow'd,
> And tears before him travel like a cloud.
> For come Diseases on, and Penury's rage,
> Labour, and Pain, and Grief, and joyless Age, . . .
> Till Hope-deserted, long in vain his breath
> Implores the dreadful untried sleep of Death.

The poem is disappointing; rarely does it equal the vivid detail,
concentration, and subtle rendering which are to be found in *An
Evening Walk*. Wordsworth knew the Lake District far more
intimately than any region in the Alps or northern Italy. So much
was encompassed in his tour that much of it probably left little

more than a blurred or general impression by the time the poem was written.

Nevertheless, there are, as Wordsworth claimed, 'many new images, and vigorous lines' in both poems. In describing them as 'juvenile productions, inflated and obscure' (9.iv.01), he was embarrassingly aware of how, laboured, sometimes contorted, and frequently dressed in borrowed robes, they differed from the individual style he had achieved in poems such as 'The Brothers' and 'Michael'. *Descriptive Sketches* is written more freely than its predecessor, and occasionally varied with triplets in the manner of Dryden. Some of its obscurities may have been unintelligible to their author in later years; 'hollow ringing ears', 'lip-dewing song', 'bosom'd cabin' (ll.97−101), for example, were wisely omitted from the perspicuous text of 1849. Inversion, after spiking attention in rapid succession (ll.62−7), is not very noticeable; but personification, although not general, occurs here and there in massed profusion.

Much of the poem is relatively void of quotation and literary allusion, but it contains echoes from Addison's *Cato*, Dyer's 'Grongar Hill', a poem by Smollett, another by Langhorne, Rogers' recently published *The Pleasures of Memory* (1792), and the more familiar works of Milton, Thomson, Gray, Collins, Cowper, and Beattie. In addition, Wordsworth was indebted to French writers, and especially to the observations which Ramond de Carbonnières added to his translation of William Coxe's *Travels*. From this source came the description of the chamois-hunter's unusual way of securing a footing on the sun-baked heights, and all those impressive effects associated with him, of broken silence and extraordinary manifestations of star, moon, and sun, as experienced only in the higher Alps (ll.375−97). Ramond's enthusiasm for Rousseau may account for Wordsworth's evocation of natural man in his primeval freedom and nobility (ll.520−5). Repetitions of imagery and expression from *An Evening Walk* occur incidentally; and two phrases, 'Thy torrents shooting from the clear-blue sky' and 'Black drizzling crags' were transferred in 1799 to the description of the Gondo gorge.

As in *An Evening Walk*, human tragedy is not overlooked. The chamois-hunter and the Grison gipsy are representative figures, and the grim tragedy of each reaches a horrible climax which adds to the prevailing sombreness of the poem. Wordsworth's imagination is psychological, externalizing the woman's fear as she wearily walks with her baby. Her alarm and anxiety are communicated by forest moan and thunder, a startling torrent, crashing trees, and water-spirits when she shelters from a battering shower. A waning red moon confronts her in the darkness; a wolf howls below, and she is stricken with fright by a sudden burst of bird-chatter, the barking of a fox, the growl of a bear, the stir of leaves, and banditti's voices. The moon reappears 'all crimson', and the inevitable end is near:

> — Vex'd by the darkness, from the piny gulf
> Ascending, nearer howls the famish'd wolf,
> While thro' the stillness scatters wild dismay,
> Her babe's small cry, that leads him to his prey.

No such inevitability is suggested in the 1849 version, where the more lurid descriptive effects are absent. Similarly Wordsworth judged the macabre touch which he added to the death of the chamois-hunter excessive. After being lost in mists and engulfed in snow, he is 'craz'd by the strength of hope at morn' to think the raven a heaven-sent bird (as it was to Elijah):

> Then with despair's whole weight his spirits sink,
> No bread to feed him, and the snow his drink,
> While ere his eyes can close upon the day,
> The eagle of the Alps o'ershades his prey.
> — Meanwhile his wife and child with cruel hope
> All night the door at every moment ope;
> Haply that child in fearful doubt may gaze,
> Passing his father's bones in future days,
> Start at the reliques of that very thigh,
> On which so oft he prattled when a boy.

No doubt the main scene and the couplet on wife and child waiting vainly in hope were suggested by an episode in Thomson's 'Winter' (*The Seasons*), 276—321.

   In a long, more generalized, descriptive account of the pastoral Swiss and their seasonal migration to and from the heights, occurs a passage which Wordsworth was to develop significantly. It originated in James Clarke's *A Survey of the Lakes*, where a description of a similar view from Skiddaw ends, as Wordsworth's does, with sounds audible below a sea of mist, each account including bird song, human voices, and the distant roar of torrents, with other sounds appropriate to their respective settings. Clarke was influenced by a verse which he quotes from Beattie's *The Minstrel*, one of Wordsworth's favourite poems:

> And oft the craggy cliff he loved to climb,
> When all in mist the world below was lost.
> What dreadful pleasure! there to stand sublime,
> Like shipwreck'd mariner on desert coast,
> And view th' enormous waste of vapour, tost
> In billows, lengthening to th' horizon round,
> Now scoop'd in gulfs, with mountains now emboss'd!
> And hear the voice of mirth and song rebound,
> Flocks, herds, and waterfalls, along the hoar profound!

From Beattie to Clarke, and from Beattie and Clarke to Wordsworth, a view moves from Skiddaw to the Alps, thence (at the end of *The Prelude*) to Snowdon. Wordsworth's two seas of mist are distinguished by a central gulf or chasm through which the various sounds ascend, and this feature is crucial to the figuration of the imaginative process which the scene ultimately assumes.

Wordsworth did not choose to describe a large number of scenes from his tour; the most outstanding relate to the Grande Chartreuse, Lake Como, the Reuss ravine, Lake Uri, Einsiedeln, and Chamonix. He presents the first as he imagined it in 1792, when Revolutionary soldiers approached to occupy it; his regrets at this desecration are expressed in the horror which he ascribes to nature. The departure of the *genius loci* spreads a gloom which contrasts with the more human, sunlit scenes, softened by love and music, around Lake Como. At Einsiedeln, where pilgrims come to cure their ailments, Wordsworth is again sympathetic; he does not despise their hope, but his incredulity merges into conventional dejection: 'Without one hope her written griefs to blot, Save in the land where all things are forgot, My heart, alive to transports long unknown, Half wishes your delusion were its own.'

The Chamonix passage, with its reference to Mont Blanc and the two glaciers like enormous serpents, contains nothing more remarkable than 'The voice of Ruin, day and night, resounds.' The Reuss descent offers a Salvator Rosa impression 'embrown'd by Terror's breath' which contrasts with the vivid stormy picture of sunset over Lake Uri selected by Coleridge in *Biographia Literaria* to illustrate Wordsworth's early genius:

'Till the Sun walking on his western field
Shakes from behind the clouds his flashing shield.
Triumphant on the bosom of the storm,
Glances the fire-clad eagle's wheeling form;
Eastward, in long perspective glittering, shine
The wood-crown'd cliffs that o'er the lake recline;
Wide o'er the Alps a hundred streams unfold,
At once to pillars turn'd that flame with gold;
Behind his sail the peasant strives to shun
The west that burns like one dilated sun,
Where in a mighty crucible expire
The mountains, glowing hot, like coals of fire.

Wordsworth achieves the 'picturesque' magnificently, but the note in which he belittles (as Jane Austen did about the same time) the 'cold rules' prescribed for achieving it indicates that his enthusiasm for Gilpin was wearing thin. He had once given to sketches like the above 'the title of Picturesque', but 'the Alps are insulted' by the term. For this scene he prefers a manner more in accordance with Turner's: 'The ideas excited by the stormy sunset I am here describing owed their sublimity to that deluge of light, or rather of fire, in which nature had wrapped the immense forms around me; any intrusion of shade, by destroying the unity of the impression, had necessarily diminished its grandeur.'

Although he visited the mountains of Savoy early in his tour, Wordsworth placed his 'sketch' of Chamonix and its Savoyard scenes immediately before the ending of his poem, the better to turn to the subject which inspired him most with ardour at the time, his belief in the Revolution and its principles. The liberation of Savoy took place soon after the poem was completed, but the defeat of the Prussians by the French, near the border where Beaupuy served, renewed his faith. Following the traditional association of mountains and liberty (as in Milton's 'L'Allegro' and Gray's fragment 'The Alliance of Education and Government'), he had referred to the content bred by independence in mountain wastes (ll.317–24). After extolling the virtues which spring from freedom, he rejoices in the prospect that the millennium, the 'virgin reign' of nature, will be restored by force of arms, and concludes with the prayer that freedom will 'ride sublime' over all forms of oppression.

War, the Salisbury Plain Poems, and *The Borderers* (1793–7)

When France declared war on England on 1 February 1793 Words-worth suffered an unprecedented shock; there could be no recon-ciliation between his patriotism and his conviction that the French Revolution, by freeing the common man from injustice and tyranny, represented a righteous cause; he had too much integrity to betray his principles. How strongly he felt may be seen in his response to a protest against the execution of Louis XVI which came from Richard Watson, an absentee bishop who lived at Cal-garth Park near Windermere. Coupled with a panegyric on the British constitution, this had been hurriedly penned and added to a reprint of the bishop's sermon on 'The Wisdom and Goodness of God in having made both Rich and Poor'. Neither pleased Words-worth, for the sermon was based on the assumption that within the 'vast scale of Being' there was a natural, hierarchical order which justified the socio-economic inequalities of the class system. Wordsworth's reply, *A Letter to the Bishop of Llandaff*, was written during February and March, but not pursued to the point of publication. The text at various points lacks final revision, and the ending has been lost. Perhaps Johnson, his publisher and a friend of radical authors, warned him of the danger of government action; perhaps Wordsworth realized, when uprisings and civil war in loyalist parts of France were reported in April, that his main argument had been undermined.

Watson was a liberal who had defended both the American Revolution and the French Revolution. For this reason, and in order to enlist a favourable response to his views, Wordsworth adopted a reasoned, courteous style, not above irony at the bishop's complacency on the equity of the British constitution. His views derive from innate conviction, discussions with Beaupuy, conversance with French debates and authors, the writings of Milton, Harrington, and Algernon Sydney, the well-known arguments of Rousseau and Tom Paine, and some acquaintance with Godwin's *Political Justice*, which had just been published. Burke, after his attack on the Revolution, is criticized as an 'infatuated moralist' for asserting that chivalry, the extinction of which he philosophically lamented, deprived vice of 'half its evil'. Wordsworth argues that a revolutionary period is not a time of liberty; despotism, deplorable though it is, may be necessary at such a time to remove tyranny. He defends the execution of Louis XVI for this reason, and insists that 'a republic legitimately constructed contains less of an oppressive principle than any other form of government'. He has faith in the virtue and educability of ordinary people; they can make a good choice of representatives, whereas under a monarchical government the popular mind can be debauched. Since it is 'the natural tendency of power to corrupt the heart of man', a wise republic will allow a legislator only a limited length of office; with the knowledge that he will soon revert to citizen status, he will act with wise restraint. Wordsworth contends that monarchy creates instability, that no one is equal to its demands, and that court corruption is inevitable. He is opposed to any system which produces hereditary privilege, the 'unnatural monster of primogeniture', titles and honours, the division between rich and poor (God's estate, according to the bishop), and 'the class of wretches called mendicants' (a view interestingly inconsistent with 'The Old Cumberland Beggar'). Such a system will pass laws inimical to the will of the people, he maintains, pressing for electoral reform. The young Wordsworth of 1793 was bold compared with the Wordsworth of the post-Napoleonic era; if there is 'a single man . . . who has no suffrage in the election of a representative' he is 'a helot'. The poet of *Lyrical Ballads* is heard in the statement that, to be a suitable legislator, 'you should have felt like the bulk of mankind' and know their sorrows.

Of the letters from Annette Vallon to Wordsworth at Staple Inn during this period, two, sent from Blois on 20 March (one for 'Williams', the other for Dorothy), have survived, after interception by a French official. They reveal an unusually emotional mother, full of tendresse (as 'Williams' had been when he kissed all the baby clothes she made at Orléans); they prove that Dorothy had been taken into confidence and was full of sympathy (Annette is unhappy because she knows that Dorothy is unhappy for her); and they show unequivocal realization of the obstacles to marriage raised by uncle William at Forncett. She advised that he be kept uninformed of their communications, and held that war with England would not last long, but that, although she would be happier if they were married, it was dangerous for 'Williams' to return to France. She looked forward to the time when brother and sister, mother and daughter would be 'just one', their life centred in 'dear Williams'.

With five guineas from his brother Richard, Wordsworth was able to accompany his school friend William Calvert in June for a month's holiday on the Isle of Wight, where each evening the sound of the fleet at Spithead reminded him of imminent war with France (PW1.307−8; cf. Pr.x.315−30). How far they intended to travel afterwards is not clear, but the whisky conveying them over Salisbury Plain broke down, and Wordsworth proceeded alone on foot. Solitude promoted musings on war and man's inhumanity, but it was not until he reached Robert Jones's home that 'Salisbury Plain' was written. 'More like a man flying from something that he dreads', he made his way from Bristol up the Wye valley, recalling no doubt Gilpin's illustrated observations on its river scenes, and finding solace as his zest for natural beauty grew, until the eye held his mind in 'absolute dominion' (Pr.xii.127−51). At Goodrich Castle, beyond Monmouth, he met the heroine of 'We are Seven'. Much further on, still following the Wye, 'between Builth and Rhayader' (as he told George Venables: *Kilvert's Diary*, 28.ix.70), he walked 'many a mile' one evening with a wild rover, the original of Peter Bell, from whom he heard 'strange stories'; such was their mutual suspicion, each had a hundred eyes, Wordsworth wrote.

The statement in his I.F. commentary on 'Peter Bell' that they walked downwards from Builth to Hay conflicts with the note to 'We are Seven': 'I proceeded by Bristol up the Wye . . . to the Vale of Clwydd, where I spent my summer under the roof of the father of my friend, Robert Jones.' Dorothy expected to meet him at Halifax in the winter, three years after last seeing him. (The claim that Wordsworth returned to France in the autumn should be treated with caution. It began with a statement in Carlyle's *Reminiscences*, based on what Wordsworth told him late in life. Carlyle formed the impression that the poet had witnessed the execution of Gorsas early in October. Wordsworth probably told him that he knew Gorsas (cf. Pr.ix.176), the first of the Girondin deputies to be guillotined. How, with hardly any resources, he could have planned and effected a visit to the heart of enemy country, and what his motives could have been to risk capture and imprisonment, are baffling questions. It is unreasonable to suppose that he acted for political reasons, or to assume that he thought there was a chance of marrying Annette, who would not have encouraged such a desperate enterprise; it is strange, moreover, that, had he gone, Wordsworth left no reference to it in *The Prelude* or elsewhere.)

While he stayed with Jones in Montgomeryshire, his smile of incredulity incensed a bibulous Welsh parson, who threatened him with 'a huge sharp-pointed carving knife', to the consternation of their host (14.v.29). Towards the end of the year he spent several weeks with friends and relatives in the Lake District. At Christmas, and perhaps before, he was with his uncle at Whitehaven; he then stayed in the Keswick region, probably at Windy Brow, the home of William and Raisley Calvert near Latrigg, certainly with John Spedding, his old school friend, of Armathwaite Hall, Bassenthwaite, 'moving backwards and forwards' before joining Dorothy at Halifax. In the spring of 1794, after travelling by coach to Kendal, they walked to Windy Brow, sleeping at Grasmere. William took a familiar route by upper Windermere (where they picnicked, as he recalled in 'There is a little unpretending rill'), along the southern side of Rydal Water, and over White Moss, past Dove Cottage. The way was new to Dorothy, and the beauty of the scenery filled her with unforgettable delight. At Windy Brow they received 'great civilities from many very pleasant families', especially the Speddings, with whom they stayed several days. Dorothy read French again, began the study of Italian, and sent a spirited reply to Mrs Crackanthorpe of Newbiggin Hall (the wife of uncle Kit, who had taken her esteemed family name), after being censured for taking risks in rambling about the country and living in an unprotected situation. She made a fair copy of 'Salisbury Plain', and William began revising and extending *An Evening Walk*.

The new impressions which Wordsworth added to his published poem, though not retained in the 1849 text, are interesting. His recent view of the school in Grasmere churchyard recalled playtime at Cockermouth Grammar School, with happy children unaware of the link between their 'sensible warm motion' and 'the dull earth that crumbled at their side' (a subject clearly connected with 'We are Seven' and 'Intimations of Immortality'). Quiet pastoral scenes around Penrith Beacon reminded him of ancient warfare in the region and traditional superstitions relative to the Giant's Cave. Most significant of all are hints of Wordsworth's mature belief in his developing thoughts on nature, which he links with mankind and the illimitable in time and space. The love of nature creates love of virtue; particularly does it enable those to whom Science has 'unbarred celestial stores' to see in common forms 'the endless chain Of joy and grief, of pleasure and of pain'. In this way the 'social accents' of nature can breathe 'a melancholy calm' on morbid passions, roll 'the bright train of never ending dreams' through the mind rapt as by magic 'into worlds beyond the reign of sense', and create a heart which is sensitive to all forms of life, and 'sees not any line where being ends'. Wordsworth has retained the eighteenth-century rationalization of the 'vast chain of Being', but it is subsumed in the vaster concept of a universal spirit which exercises moral power through nature. 'Septimi Gades', a very free adaptation from one of Horace's odes (PW1. 296–8) probably belongs to this period; it confirms Wordsworth's longing to settle at Grasmere, and reveals a revival of his love for Mary Hutchinson.

William Mathews, now at the Middle Temple, proposed a monthly miscellany to be called 'The Philanthropist', and wished Wordsworth to collaborate. Wordsworth, who could not 'bow down' his mind to enter the Church, and had 'neither strength of mind, purse, or constitution' to take up law, replied that he was too impecunious to live in London and act as editor. Deeming it prudent to state his political views in advance, he declared his permanent allegiance to 'that odious class of men called democrats'. He disapproved of 'monarchical and aristocratical governments', but recoiled from every form of revolutionary violence, and deplored 'all inflammatory addresses to the passions of men'. With wise guidance England could be spared the scourge which afflicted France. 'No opportunity of explaining and enforcing those general principles of the social order' which are universally applicable should be allowed to slip. They include 'an entire preservative from despotism' and, 'if a revolution must afflict us, they alone can mitigate its horrors and establish freedom with tranquillity'. He vigorously objected to governmental repressive measures such as transportation and imprisonment. Wordsworth's principles were firmly rooted, and did not change radically. Perhaps the suspension of the Habeas Corpus Act dampened Mathews' enthusiasm, for nothing came of his project.

In the meantime William and Dorothy spent several weeks with their cousin John's wife at Whitehaven, while their uncle Richard was ill at Branthwaite, where he died in June. Dorothy then stayed with another cousin at Rampside on the Furness coast. After returning to Windy Brow, to befriend young Raisley Calvert, who was a victim of tuberculosis, William in his turn enjoyed a few weeks at Rampside. It was while crossing the sands of the Leven estuary, on his way back from the grave of his headmaster William Taylor at Cartmel, that he heard the joyful news of Robespierre's death, and felt his shaken faith in France restored (Pr.x.511–603).

He had been promised a legacy by Raisley, and tended him to the end. Preparations were made to accompany him to Lisbon for the winter, but his patient was too ill to travel beyond Penrith. After a period at Windy Brow, they returned to Penrith, where Raisley died in January. With great foresight and generosity, he had increased his bequest to £900, to be invested in the hope that it would help the poet to pursue his literary ambition. After staying with Dorothy in Newcastle, William proceeded to London, where he remained until the summer and frequently met Godwin, whose radical idealism he held in high esteem. Their friendship lasted until Godwin's death, long after Wordsworth had realized that some of the revolutionary theory set forth in *Political Justice* was too intellectually detached from life to satisfy human nature.

In the capital Wordsworth met other radicals, and a number of his Cambridge contemporaries, including Basil Montagu, sixth Wrangler in 1790, who persuaded him to share his rooms at Lincoln's Inn. Montagu needed friendship, for he was a widower with a very young son, and his inability to cope had led to intemperance; in retrospect, he was convinced that Wordsworth's steadying influence had been 'the most fortunate event' in his life. He introduced him to the two Pinneys, sons of a rich Bristol merchant, and to Francis Wrangham, winner of the Chancellor's Medal for Latin verse at Cambridge in 1790. John, the elder Pinney, offered Wordsworth the loan of Racedown Lodge in Dorset, provided he and his brother could come occasionally, as paying guests, for hunting and coursing. Though she regretted the loss of her Halifax friends, Dorothy Wordsworth accepted the opportunity with delight, calculating that with the interest from

Raisley Calvert's legacy, William's literary earnings, and guardianship of two or three young children, their income would be adequate. (Unfortunately Montagu's child was their only charge, and the legacy came in instalments, the last in August 1798, by which time Montagu, to whom Wordsworth had lent £300 of the first, was in such financial straits, that he was unable to pay much in return for about two years.)

At Bristol in August Wordsworth met the ex-Pantisocratic partners Southey and Coleridge, and hoped to become better acquainted with the latter; he may also have been introduced to Joseph Cottle, bookseller and publisher. Dorothy arrived on 22 September, and a few days later they travelled, probably with Basil Montagu (not yet three years old) to Racedown, high up on the Dorset-Devon border. The poverty of country people, for most of whom coal was prohibitively expensive, was soon apparent. The Wordsworths were comfortable, and so well was their house equipped they had to purchase little. After a month without a servant, Dorothy obtained 'one of the nicest girls' she had ever seen; Joseph Gill, general manager of the Pinney farm, was very helpful. There was a good library, including Euclid, to which Wordsworth returned, and Italian authors, some of which Dorothy studied with his assistance. She found time to read widely, and proceeded to bring up Basil on Rousseauistic principles, the evidence of the senses being given priority over literacy, and no punishment being meted beyond emphasis on the deprivations naturally consequent on offences.

The first poem William prepared at Racedown, with publication in mind, was 'Adventures on Salisbury Plain', a revision of that written in 1793; in less than eight weeks it was almost another work. Two fragments, more mature in style than seems possible in the earlier period to which they have been assigned, contain descriptive details which, found also in 'Adventures on Salisbury Plain' and *The Borderers*, probably derive from observations in the Racedown area. In the second of these fragments (PW1.292−5) the story of the female vagrant begins; she tells it to a sympathetic mother. Perhaps Wordsworth thought of recasting the poem in this way to give it greater probability, and abandoned it for 'The Ruined Cottage'. It was written in a variant of the Spenserian stanzas which are found in all the other versions of the tale. The woman's story was extracted from 'Adventures on Salisbury Plain' for inclusion as 'The Female Vagrant' in *Lyrical Ballads*, and the whole poem revised for its first publication in 1842. Less politically animated, it still roused Wordsworth's humanitarian sympathies; at heart he was as much opposed to the division between rich and poor as he had been when he wrote *A Letter to the Bishop of Llandaff*, in which he had referred to 'an infatuation which is now giving up to the sword so large a portion of the poor and consigning the rest to the more slow and more painful consumption of want'. This subject had preoccupied him intermittently ever since he met the discharged soldier; he could not exclude it from *An Evening Walk*; he could forget it in *Descriptive Sketches*, when exhilarated by thoughts of the liberty which war seemed to ensure the French, but it had returned almost obsessionally after England's declaration of war against France, and it was to reach a climax in 'The Ruined Cottage'.

'Salisbury Plain' (1793) impresses less by its narrative than by the concentration of political satire in the vision of traditional Stonehenge barbarities (cf. Pr.xiii.312−49, where the contrast between this revelation and that of the Druidic teachers versed in celestial lore repeats that of 'Salisbury Plain'). Recurring twice in vivid detail, the vision makes a lasting impact, finally embodying all those horrors of imperialistic war and social injustice which it parallels. One abusive form of superstition has replaced another. In a long homiletic conclusion the poet asks what 'reason's ray' can do more than 'reveal with still-born glimpse' the terrors that surround us, while 'tempests rise, With starless glooms and sounds of loud dismay'. Only the insensate can find wisdom in the 'iron scourge' of law, with its infliction of force, terror, bonds, and exile. 'Heroes of Truth' are urged to destroy 'the oppressor's dungeon', and rear 'the herculean mace of Reason' over the towers of Pride, 'till not a trace Be left on earth of Superstition's reign, Save that eternal pile which frowns on Sarum's plain'.

Recourse to bare personification tends to devitalize Wordsworth's denunciation; and poetic diction persists with 'finny flood' and 'fleecy store'. Gothic touches are borrowed from Spenser's *The Faerie Queene* ('his hair in horror rose', 'Cold stony horror all her senses bound'), in addition to the personified image which concludes the hope of one whose trust is in Reason: 'let foul Error's monster race Dragged from their dens start at the light with pain And die'. A few memorable lines occur ('The very ocean has its hours of rest', 'Roaming the illimitable waters round'), apart from the Miltonic 'Oh, what can war but endless war still breed?' Visual and aural details give reality to the landscape, and the unhappiness of the 'friendless hope-forsaken pair' who meet in the 'lone spital' (the traveller who takes shelter from the storm, and the woman whom he startles there and who tells him her tale) is contrastingly emphasized by the brightness of dawn, the whistling 'carman', and the crowing cock, as they continue their journey; by 'The very ocean has its hour of rest' as she resumes her story; by the sudden appearance of Salisbury's spires as she finishes ('The city's distant spires ascend Like flames which far and wide the west illume, Scattering from out the sky the rear of night's thin gloom'); then by the cheerful notes of the brook, 'the linnet's amorous lays', a merry milkmaid, and lowing herds. In this way reinforcement is lent to the hope with which the poem ends. The symbolism which pervades it in loneliness ('Where all the happiest find is but a shed And a green spot 'mid wastes interminably spread'), and in storm, gloom, and dawn, is its strongest feature. The woman's story anticipates Margaret's in 'The Ruined Cottage', but the contrast of her past and present introduces a certain incongruity, with Keswick associations and the imagery of 'sister breasts of snow' that swell and sink like two swans amid Derwent water-lilies (a modified resurrection from 'Beauty and Moonlight'). The traveller seems ultimately to be little more than a listener; he remains a mystery, and the narrative is manifestly contrived.

No 1795 manuscript of 'Adventures on Salisbury Plain' survives, but nothing indicates that it varied significantly from that of 1799. Unlike its precursor, this version does not use high-frequency personification for critical ends, but conveys its political animadversions through overcomplicated narrative. The philosophical introduction of 'Salisbury Plain', with its contrast between the suffering of those who have been deprived of refinement, love, and friendship, and that of the savage whose hardships are permanent, is discarded for new narrative. The woman's story is extended, and greater emphasis is placed on the traveller (a sailor, as might be guessed from his imagery in the previous poem) and his plight from first to last; Stonehenge receives scant attention. Wordsworth's object is to attack not just war and its causes and effects but also the penal code, and it is with this that the poem ends. Interest in humanity increases, but one must ask whether this elaborate recension is more effective than the original. It provides more fuel for radical agitation, concentrating on State-created ills to such an extent that the gloom which is reinforced by the 'waste' of the plain is almost unrelieved; but the abandonment of the recurring image of Stonehenge superstition and horror results in a loss of imaginative unity, vividness, and power.

The extensions to the woman's story are interesting from first to last. The loss of her father's Derwent property as a result of a rich man's cunning is based on the 'Naboth's vineyard' tradition from which originated the superstitions attached to Calgarth Hall.[11] In North America with her soldier husband, she sees mining, bombings, conflagration, murder, and rape. Her sufferings continue in England, where she finds most kindness among vagrants, whose nightly pilfering (graphically delineated in rapid strokes) so little suited her that she is forced to fend for herself, as Wordsworth movingly describes in a verse which already equals the best style of his dramatic humanitarian poems in *Lyrical Ballads*:

> I lived upon the mercy of the fields,
> And oft of cruelty the sky accused;
> On hazard, or what general bounty yields,
> Now coldly given, now utterly refused.
> The fields I for my bed have often used:
> But, what afflicts my peace with keenest ruth
> Is, that I have my inner self abused,
> Foregone the home delight of constant truth,
> And clear and open soul, so prized in fearless youth.

The roles of the two principals are changed. Wordsworth ensures that the listener is not forgotten while the vagrant tells her story. When she mentions the British ship on which she returned to England after losing her husband and children, he is anguished; when she ends her tale, he stands trembling with ashen cheeks. It is she who tries to console him. From first to last he can never be out of the reader's mind. The opening scene with the old soldier emphasizes his kindly disposition, which is confirmed when he saves a child from his brutal father. The latter's remark that he deserves the gallows for his interference makes perspiration start from the sailor's brow, and we are reminded of the dominant feature of plain and poem, the premonitory gibbet-corpse, the sight of which in the tempest had caused the sailor to fall senseless before seeking shelter in the spital.

Influenced by Godwin on Necessity, Wordsworth stresses the force of chance as well as State inhumanity. After two years' hard service, the sailor had been press-ganged for war immediately on his return. When he was released years later, officials, seeing him unfriended, refused to pay his dues. The thought of his beloved wife and children when he was returning home penniless had made him madly rob and murder a traveller. His comment, when remorse overcomes the brutal father, that the 'bond of nature' needs to be more closely drawn, since "Tis a bad world, and hard is the world's law; Each prowls to strip his brother of his fleece', serves to moralize the tale; but the assertion is mild compared with succeeding events. He is called to assist a dying woman who has been driven from her home with her children, after her husband, who had been seen fleeing, had been suspected of a murder near their home. 'Never on earth was milder creature seen,' she says before dying. 'Bred in solitude, unus'd to haunt the throngs of men', the good people of the inn to which she had been brought do not 'repine mortality's last claim to grant'; but their suspicions of the sailor are awakened, and they are intent on observing the law. He walks straight to the city, however, and confesses his crime with relief. His 'piteous claim' is granted, and the poem ends in savage irony, a fair's festivities being presented beneath his corpse as it hangs in iron case, left to swing when the tempest rises (like the one he himself had seen on the plain) for some kindred sufferer to view, 'and drop, as he once dropp'd, in miserable trance'.

Wordsworth wasted time in misguided efforts to give greater structural unification to his tale. Three stanzas of uncertain date (PW1.341) show the old soldier as the sailor's father-in-law, and (it seems, though the evidence is uncertain) the female vagrant (Rachel) as the unsuspecting widow of the murdered traveller. A letter from Germany (27.ii.99) indicates the poet's intention to discard Robert Walford (probably the old soldier) and 'invent a new story for the woman', making her the widow or sister or daughter of the man her companion had killed, 'by way of a pretty moving accident and to bind' the story 'in palpable knots'. The result would have been an improbable complication of coincidences.

In his maturer years Wordsworth never regarded the poem highly, and for that reason did not choose to publish it (or *The Borderers*) until late in life, when he had little to lose. It was too extreme; he pruned and clarified the narrative, and modified his denunciations, making the rich less explicitly unjust, and war (after his long opposition to the imperialistic tyranny of Napoleon) less reprehensible. Very significantly, he changed the title to 'Guilt and Sorrow'. There is no bitterness at the end of the poem; the sailor's wife dies peacefully after he has asked her forgiveness; there is no threat to expose him; he welcomes the sentence, and trusts in his Saviour's forgiveness. His fate is pitied; though hanged, he is not exposed like a criminal to public gaze.

Wordsworth had agreed to collaborate with Francis Wrangham in a verse satire, loosely based on Juvenal and directed against the government, the aristocracy, and the royal family. 'Must honour still to Lonsdale's tail be bound?' he asks in a sample transcribed in November 1795. A letter of 7 March 1796 affirms his resolution to bring the project to a 'speedy conclusion', and reports that Basil is 'quite well *quant au physique mais pour le moral il-y-a bien à craindre*. Among other things he lies like a little devil.' The *Imitation of Juvenal* was deferred. When Wordsworth sent Wrangham an instalment the following February, he had almost completed the first draft of *The Borderers*. It had been his pre-occupation during the autumn and winter, and was nearly finished by the end of May 1797.

Wordsworth's confidence in human nature was returning. With Beaupuy and 'a sounder judgment than later days allowed', he had believed in an innate ability which made people in general capable of seeing truth and of becoming sufficiently enlightened to create a just society (Pr.ix.331–3, 355–63). But his faith in the French Revolution had been shaken by its factional tyranny and carnage, and even more by the aggressive, dominating role which France had assumed towards neighbouring countries. For a while Godwin's *Political Justice* had shored up his idealism but, though still an opponent of the harsh repressive measures enforced by the British government (which seemed to be 'thirsting to make the guardian crook of law a tool of murder'), he had realized, partly through resuming acquaintance with country people, and seeing life (nature) more closely, partly through the insights and affection of Dorothy, that faith in Godwinian reason had misled him. Like French revolutionary extremists, he had worshipped reason. Now, with Rousseau and Burke, he recognised that it plays a smaller part in life than instinct, tradition, and feeling; that 'genuine knowledge' and motivation depend on the heart as well as the head. Godwin later admitted that he had overlooked 'the culture of the heart', but Wordsworth had accepted his basic necessitarianism, which rejected a belief in innate goodness, and insisted that knowledge and judgment come from experience only (an assumption based on the mechanical theory of sensation — sense-impressions — which originated with Locke and developed in Hartley). Godwin, believing that man's perfectibility depended on reason, had concluded that, in the light of it, the individual should be free to do as he pleases. Wordsworth now realized that such libertarianism could run counter not only to human feeling but also to Rousseau's 'general will' or the collective reason of time-honoured morality.

His reawakening or renovation did not come suddenly. He had summoned his 'best skill, and toiled, intent To anatomise the frame of social life', examining and discarding theories until, 'sick, wearied out with contrarieties', he had 'yielded up moral questions in despair'. His analysis of the dilemma is exact: he had welcomed a philosophy 'that promised to abstract the hopes of man out of his feelings', and fix them in 'a purer element', and assumed that the transition to liberty could be achieved by means which 'did not lie in nature' (Pr.05.x.844). He had reasoned that liberty for all would result from personal freedom,

> Which, to the blind restraints of general laws
> Superior, magisterially adopts
> One guide, the light of circumstances, flashed
> Upon an independent intellect.

Discussing this in retrospect (Pr.xi.223–305), he alludes to *The Borderers*, hoping that it would illustrate the errors into which he fell, betrayed

>   by reasonings false
> From their beginnings, inasmuch as drawn
> Out of a heart that had been turned aside
> From Nature's way by outward accidents,
> And which was thus confounded, more and more
> Misguided, and misguiding.

From this it can be seen why Wordsworth had a healthy scorn for 'toiling reason' and books which 'neglect the universal heart'; why, in the hope of promoting the regeneration of man, he hoped to look deep into the human mind, and make it the main region of his song; and why, in a fragment he probably wrote in 1798 occur passages for which ample support may be found in Sir Philip Sidney or in George Eliot:

> Can it be imagined . . . that an old habit will be foregone, or a new one formed, by a series of propositions, which, presenting no image . . . can convey no feeling which has any connection with the supposed archetype or fountain of the proposition existing in human life? . . . bald and naked reasonings are impotent over our habits, they cannot form them . . . they are equally powerless in regulating our judgments concerning the value of men and things. They contain no picture of human life; they *describe* nothing, [and therefore cannot move us, 'melt into our affections', much less change our habits].[12]

Whether Wordsworth's fragment of a 'Gothic' tale (PW1.287– 92) was written as late as the spring of 1796, after he had requested his copies of Gilpin's *Observations* in the Lake District and in Scotland to be forwarded from London, is uncertain. Much of it is laboured, but it is influenced by Gilpin in setting and even in style, as 'The unimaginable touch of time' indicates. (In the preliminary part of the former work, with reference to Kenilworth Castle, Gilpin writes, 'the touch of time, crumbling it imperceptibly away'.) It shares a vivid image with 'Adventures on Salisbury Plain', and it supplies the half-ruined castle scene (II.3) in *The Borderers*. In both scenes the man who wishes to murder is inhibited by a star seen through a crevice in the dungeon roof. In the play the association of love with the star and the face of the man whose murder is contemplated is presented without comment; the star appeals to the conscience, and it is evident that the would-be murderer is human, that his heart, 'awake to feeling for all forms that Life can take', sees no 'line where being ends' (PW1.10). The disarming effect of the old man's face recalls *Macbeth*, and with it there are other echoes of Shakespeare's play, especially in an early version; there is also a reminder of *King Lear*, which suggested the moor scenes; the effect of the villain's murderous intentions on the hero's credulity owes much to *Othello*.

True knowledge, Wordsworth had discovered, comes from the marriage of heart and head (Pr.xi.350–4). To illustrate the danger of reason divorced from feeling, he selects a special type of character, not a typical Godwinian who would exercise reason in the cause of benevolence, but a criminal whose self-justification needs reassurance in friendship. Godwin had looked forward to the dissolution of political government, 'that brute engine, which has been the only perennial cause of the vices of mankind'; but he recommended some form of local rule for the benefit of society, and Wordsworth provides this under Marmaduke, the tragic hero. Again, for his purpose, he chooses a period when law and government are suspended, and the individual leader can act independently. Oswald (Rivers) persuades Marmaduke (Mortimer) — the names in parenthesis belong to the early text — that the girl he loves and her blind father are false to him. Marmaduke finds that, on the brink of action in the dungeon, he cannot murder the father, as Oswald wishes, and leaves him exposed on a moor, his fate to be decided by the will of Heaven. Intervention, after the discovery of Oswald's treachery, comes too late, and Marmaduke gives up his command, to wander in expiation, 'the spectre of that innocent man' his guide.

Unlike Iago's, Oswald's malignity is not motiveless. His criminal character is analysed with rare psychological perspicacity in Wordsworth's prefatory essay. Motivated by pride and contempt for humanity, he is betrayed into crime; he recovers pride and power through the suppression of his remorse. Exercising reason relentlessly, he justifies his own enormities until his appetite for the 'unnatural' is whetted; 'like a worn out voluptuary', he 'finds his temptation in strangeness'. Benefits conferred on such a person ultimately breed hatred, and Oswald's greatest satisfaction therefore is in contriving a crime by Marmaduke to parallel his own. Thus he hopes to find the sympathy he needs, and a degraded companion who will assist him slavishly in the enlargement of 'man's intellectual empire'. Having thrown off the 'soft chain' of feeling, they will be bound in 'a chain of adamant'. He is a compound of contradiction. He has deceived himself into thinking that feelings are the wiles of women and old age, that the heart is 'the toy of fools', and that Marmaduke (whom he envies) is one of those 'fools of feeling'. His one aim is the extinction of his own remorse, and he affects strength in suffering. Yet he knows that, compared with the momentariness of physical action, consequent suffering is 'permanent, obscure, and dark, And shares the nature of infinity', and that guilt-ridden introspection, pursuing 'a dim and perilous way' through 'words and things', can create 'A slavery compared to which the dungeon And clanking chains are perfect liberty'.

In his demonstration that, judging by 'the immediate law' of circumstances and not by general principles, rationalization can lead a poisoned mind to crime after crime, Wordsworth expressed a conviction which had developed from various sources, including self-justification for the abandonment of Annette to which he was becoming reconciled; the bloody actions of power-loving French revolutionaries who had been decent citizens; the example of Falkland in Godwin's *Caleb Williams* (cf. *The Borderers*, III.4: 'Power is life to him And breath and being; where he cannot govern, He will destroy'); the trial of Fletcher Christian, leader of the much publicized mutiny on the *Bounty*, and Edward Christian's vindication of his brother. Wordsworth's interest in the case at the time he was writing *The Borderers* is shown in a letter (23.x.96); Fletcher's 'I am in hell' is repeated by the remorseful Mortimer of the early version, and Oswald's initial crime varies little essentially from Fletcher's. His self-justification provides Wordsworth's interpretation of an event which must have preyed on his mind:

> On a dead sea under a burning sky
> I brooded o'er my injuries, deserted
> By man and nature; − if a breeze had blown
> It might have found a way into my heart.

In 'Adventures on Salisbury Plain' he had depicted a murderer as a victim of Godwinian necessity. Through Marmaduke he rejects such a philosophy and vindicates the rightness of heart and conscience. Marmaduke refuses to become a slave to rationalizing self-vindication; instead of casting off the soft chain, he welcomes 'every sting of penitential anguish', and concludes, as Wordsworth in his disillusionment with France must have done, that the world is tainted:

> Lacy! we look
> But at the surfaces of things; we hear
> Of towns in flames, fields ravaged, young and old
> Driven out in troops to want and nakedness;
> Then grasp our swords and rush upon a cure
> That flatters us, because it asks not thought:
> The deeper malady is better hid;
> The world is poisoned at the heart.

Though set in the reign of Henry III, the overt crime of *The Borderers*, from the cruelty of the sensual Clifford to the unjust imprisonment of the peasant Elfred, had its parallels in stories of pre-Revolutionary France with which Wordsworth must have been familiar. Whatever his views on the fallibility of cold reason, he had not rejected *Political Justice* wholly, nor would he ever associate 'the wisdom and goodness of God' with the existence of wealth and poverty.

Wordsworth did not write the play initially for the stage; he adapted it with this in view, and it was seriously considered for production at Covent Garden Theatre. It is well constructed, and more dramatic than poetical, though it is by no means lacking in poetical touches. Oswald's choice of a plant 'strong to destroy' and 'strong to heal', which prefigures the action, is recalled just before his death; proud of his proven power and overconfident of moulding Marmaduke to his purpose, he still believes he is 'strong to o'erturn, strong also to build up'. Marmaduke's credulity is made more convincing than Othello's, and dramatic ironies are skilfully wrought. Villainy is Gothicized and over-contrived with melodramatic stage stuff, but the play has more merit than is often allowed. Its theme is too specialized and intellectual to have wide appeal, but it occupies a crucial place in Wordsworth's development, and is a logical precursor to *Lyrical Ballads*.

Coleridge, Alfoxden, and *Lyrical Ballads* (1797–8)

Mary Hutchinson stayed at Racedown from November 1796 until June 1797; she had travelled from Sockburn with her sailor brother Henry, who was on his way to Plymouth. Her presence during the severe winter was a pleasure to Dorothy and William, but it must have made him think seriously at times about his future vis-à-vis Annette. Basil's father arrived in March, and he and Wordsworth, after visiting Bath, called on Coleridge at Nether Stowey in the Quantocks. About this period Wordsworth wrote a short dramatic fragment, possibly for *The Borderers*, illustrating the suicidal reasoning of a perverted mind. 'The Convict' may be earlier; based on Godwin's arguments against prison iniquities (in *Caleb Williams*, for example) and published in *The Morning Chronicle* (14.xii.97), then in *Lyrical Ballads*, it is the first of a number of Wordsworth's poems in anapaestic verse, the movement of which hardly allows one to settle seriously to the seriousness of the subject. He also composed the first two cantos of 'The Three Graves', a supernatural story which was continued (but not completed) by Coleridge. Wordsworth's ballad moves easily and powerfully, giving passionate reality to the subject. The opening, with its sinister graveyard associations and arresting catechetic technique, was prompted by one of William Taylor's Bürger ballad translations, 'The Lass of Fair Wone', in *The Monthly Magazine*. Mary Hutchinson took back with her a copy of a passage intended as the ending of 'The Ruined Cottage' (PW5.398–9, ll.696–742). Wordsworth (whose memory, especially on dates, was often deceptive) said it was the first part of the poem he wrote; a precursor will be found, both in subject and narrative technique, in 'Incipient Madness' (PW1.314–16). All these subjects indicate that, though Wordsworth was 'the life of the whole house', as Dorothy wrote, cheerfulness had not yet animated his poetry.

Yet a new spirit was at work. The healing spirit of nature which is hinted at in *The Borderers* becomes the climactic theme of 'The Ruined Cottage'. It is evident in two poems which, though they turn to Wordsworth's pre-Revolutionary period, express his departure from Godwinian rationalism. 'Lines left upon a Seat in a Yew-tree' developed from a paragraph written in his last year at school. The poem is based on the Revd William Braithwaite of Satterhow, who died at Hawkshead in 1800. He built a summer-house to enjoy the view over Windermere from the station above the ferry-house peninsula, and lived a life of seclusion after graduating at Cambridge. In the statement that he would gaze until the lovely scene became far lovelier, Wordsworth's theory of the imagination is beginning to emerge; more significant are the reflections of benevolence in the world which this beauty inspires. The morbidity of the spectator's thoughts on his own life provokes the memorable sentence, 'The man whose eye Is ever on himself doth look on one, The least of Nature's works.' Pride, Wordsworth continues, is littleness, and 'he who feels contempt for any living thing' has never grown up. The conclusion that true knowledge leads to altruism shows how far Wordsworth had moved. Something deeper than political revolution was needed; the maladies of the world could not be removed without a change of heart. 'The Old Cumberland Beggar', based on boyhood memories, presents a new point of view on mendicity; the proposed poor-law measures were calculated to diminish the spirit of altruism in the public, the feeling that 'we have all of us one human heart'. The old beggar, focused with fine detail in three unelaborate, matter-of-fact, but wonderfully evocative sketches, is a 'silent monitor', who imparts to children (even more than books or 'solicitudes of love' can do) those first kindlings of sympathy and thought, in which they find 'a kindred with a world' of want and sorrow. The benevolence he diffuses is part of 'the benignant law of heaven', and Wordsworth's restored faith makes him declare that there is 'a spirit and pulse of good' in everyone, however degraded.

This belief explains why Wordsworth wrote 'A Somersetshire Tragedy'. He had met Thomas Poole, Coleridge's friend, when he visited Nether Stowey, and became interested in the story of John Walford, a murderer, after passing the gibbet where he was hanged. (The ordnance map shows Walford's Gibbet near the woods of Danesborough). Poole had prepared an account for Wordsworth, and Coleridge was so impressed by its poetic power that he wished to publish it years later in *The Friend*. Unfortunately the poem was destroyed in 1931 by Gordon Wordsworth, who said that it had little poetic merit. Some idea of the original can be obtained from the second volume of *Thomas Poole and his Friends* (1888), where Mrs Henry Sandford describes it as 'an account of the tragical fate of a wretched charcoal burner, a man well known to Poole in his boyish days, who, having met with a disappointment in love, drifted into evil courses, and was forced into a disastrous marriage with a poor degraded creature whom he almost loathed, and whom in the end he murdered'. It is characteristic of Poole 'that he compels the reader to realise that there is in this John Walford, this being of undisciplined impulses and brutal passions, a capacity for better things, and to feel sympathy for him to the very end. And there are certainly vivid, poetic touches. The execution, for instance, which took place on the spot where the crime was committed, "amidst the beautiful scenery of the Quantock Hills", is wonderfully described, and yet with what I should call the rudest simplicity.' As Walford was led to the gallows, the woman whom he had loved and had been prevented from marrying by her mother, suddenly appeared, climbed into the cart, and spoke to him for a few minutes. 'At the very last' he called for her, and she was eventually found 'back behind the brow of the hill', and dragged 'almost lifeless' to the cart. As she knelt on the straw, he bent over her, and talked for nearly ten minutes. The officer held him back as he was about to kiss her, but, as she was being drawn away, he snatched her hand and kissed it, shedding some tears for the first time. When she was removed, he recollected himself, wiped his tears, and said he was ready. After joining audibly in the Lord's Prayer and Creed, he mounted the board across the cart, and the rope was tied around his neck. He then addressed the crowd 'with a loud, firm, unbroken voice: "I am guilty of the crime I am going to die for; but I did it without fore-intending it, and I hope God and the world have forgiven me." All were amazed − afraid to breathe; the buzz of the multitude was so hushed that even the twittering of the birds in the neighbouring woods was heard. . . .' A great writer, humanitarian and poetic like Hardy in his prime, might have been equal to the subject; whether Wordsworth in 1797, with no hope whatever of publication, could have persisted with it and wrought it to his satisfaction is doubtful.

After visiting a Unitarian minister at Taunton, Coleridge walked to Racedown, finishing his journey, as Wordsworth remembered all his life, by leaping over a gate and bounding down a pathless field to 'cut off an angle'. Dorothy thought his conversation teemed with 'soul, mind, and spirit'; writing to Mary Hutchinson, perhaps a week or two after her departure, she reported that the first thing read was 'William's new poem *The Ruined Cottage*', and that the next morning he read *The Borderers*. Coleridge remained about three weeks, and his hosts were invited to Nether Stowey, where they stayed during the first half of July. With deep green valleys, heather slopes, and woods, the Quantock Hills afforded a variety of walks; and so much pleasure did the Wordsworths derive from Coleridge's company and literary stimulus in such delightful country that they did not hesitate to move to Alfoxden House, nearly four miles away from Nether Stowey, almost immediately after agreement for its lease had been negotiated by Thomas Poole. A commodious mansion in a large deer-park, with a clear view of the Bristol Channel beyond open country to the north, and facing an amphitheatre surmounted by woods to the south, it was set in complete seclusion. A deep glen with brook and waterfalls from the wooded heights near the entrance provided a favourite haunt. This was the 'roaring dell' to which Charles Lamb, on a visit to Coleridge, was taken while his host, incapacitated after his wife Sara had spilt a pan of boiling milk over his foot, sat in the arbour of Tom Poole's garden writing 'This Lime-tree Bower my Prison'. Shortly afterwards John Thelwall, who had been tried for treason with Horne Tooke in 1794, visited Coleridge and called on the Wordsworths. 'Citizen John,' Coleridge said to him, 'this is a fine place to talk treason in!' 'Nay! Citizen Samuel,' he replied, 'it is rather a place to make a man forget that there is any necessity for treason.' Coleridge whose anti-government complaints had been publicized in his short-lived periodical *The Watchman*, discouraged Thelwall from settling in the district (where he wished to write poetry), arguing that it would be unfair to his radical friend Poole, who was responsible for the arrival of two strangers at Alfoxden. When it was reported that they and Coleridge (who projected a poem, to be called 'The Brook') were French spies, making notes on the navigability of a local stream, the Home Office sent a detective, who (according to Coleridge) used to eavesdrop behind a bank on the shore and imagine that their discussion of Spinoza referred to him and his physiognomy ('Spy Nosy').

Susceptible to all that philosophy could offer in the formulation of his religious thought, Coleridge had moved from Hartleyanism to Berkeleyanism, and thence to Spinoza. However stimulating his metaphysical eloquence, his religious love of nature was never as deeply rooted as that of Wordsworth, whom he regarded as a semi-atheist. His monism is best expressed in 'the one Life within us and abroad' of 'The Eolian Harp' (1795). In 'This Lime-tree Bower' he hopes that Lamb, after being pent in the great city, will stand, as he had done, regarding the landscape until all seems 'less gross than bodily' and 'of such hues As veil the Almighty Spirit, when yet he makes Spirits perceive his presence'. Such experience recalls the 'holy calm' of Wordsworth at Hawkshead, when 'bodily eyes were utterly forgotten' as he communed with God and nature. Coleridge's relatively free expression of personal feelings in such poems as the above may have encouraged the more intimate style in Wordsworth which first made itself felt in 'Tintern Abbey',[13] where a more fully communicated awareness of the 'one Life' is found:

> Until, the breath of this corporeal frame
> And even the motion of our human blood
> Almost suspended, we are laid asleep
> In body, and become a living soul:
> While with an eye made quiet by the power
> Of harmony, and the deep power of joy,
> We see into the life of things.

The 'eye made quiet' suggests that Wordsworth had found something deeper or more transcendental in nature than those visual aspects which had once been an appetite to him.

Coleridge, who knew too well his lack of 'those inferior abilities' which 'the common duties of life' require, and found the companionship of his practical-minded wife increasingly irksome and tedious, delighted as much in the company of Dorothy and William as they did in his. After walking along the coast to Linton in November, they proceeded to the Valley of the Rocks, which suggested to the volatile Coleridge the absurdly impracticable scheme of writing a prose imitation of Gessner's *The Death of Abel* in three cantos, Wordsworth to write the first, he the second, and whoever finished first the third. Soon afterwards, on another excursion, 'The Ancient Mariner' was conceived, Wordsworth suggesting the

main action of the story, and some detail such as the image of the
ribbed sea-sand. There and then composition began but, their respective styles proving 'widely different', Wordsworth soon concluded it would be better to give Coleridge a free hand. Basil
Montagu, who was in financial difficulties, stayed at Alfoxden
with his son several weeks, during which the Wordsworths visited
London, in response to a recommendation that *The Borderers*
should be altered for performance at Covent Garden. Had this
effort succeeded, they would have been compensated for
Montagu's failure to pay his dues.

What remains of Dorothy's Alfoxden journal begins on 20 January 1798, and the delicacy of her recorded observations prompts
the question how much she contributed incidentally to the poetry
of both William and Coleridge during their *annus mirabilis*. It
shows that she was a poet in the finer perceptions of nature, but it
does not prove that Coleridge or Wordsworth was indebted to her
in the first place. Each sensitized the other; in the words of Coleridge, they were 'three people, but one soul'. There are descriptions
in the journal which precede similar images in 'Christabel', but
one cannot conclude that Dorothy or Coleridge or Wordsworth
was the first to observe them. One can only conjecture what, if
anything, she contributed to 'A Night-piece', which Wordsworth
composed on the road from Nether Stowey to Alfoxden; with it
should be compared her note for 25 January, which must have
been recorded after their return from Tom Poole's:

> The sky spread over with one continuous cloud, whitened by the
> light of the moon, which, though her dim shape was seen, did
> not throw forth so strong a light as to chequer the earth with
> shadows. At once the clouds seemed to cleave asunder, and left
> her in the centre of a black-blue vault. She sailed along, fol-
> lowed by multitudes of stars, small, and bright, and sharp.

Composition probably began as a result of their observations on the
scene as they walked home. If Dorothy gave William eyes and ears,
his was the more creative spirit, as may be seen by comparing 'A
whirl-blast from behind the hill' with her note of 18 March 1798:
'sheltered under the hollies, during a hail-shower. The withered
leaves danced with the hailstones. William wrote a description of
the storm.' Her journals were to restore to memory scenes which he
re-created in poems such as 'I wandered lonely as a cloud'. Her

sensitive responses also encouraged him to write on natural subjects which were condemned as trivial by fashionable reviewers,
following the lead of Jeffrey, redoubtable editor of *The Edinburgh
Review*.

Wordsworth did further work on 'The Old Cumberland Beggar', and completed an account, probably the first draft, of his
meeting with the discharged soldier nearly ten years earlier. His
main task, however, was the extension of 'The Ruined Cottage',
his attention being devoted to the development and philosophy of
a pedlar, designed to play a prominent part in *The Recluse*, a
poem vaguely conceived on a grandiose scale in areas which Coleridge had contemplated for 'The Brook'. Dorothy observed that
William's faculties seemed to expand every day: 'he composes with
much more facility than he did, as to the *mechanism* of poetry,
and his ideas flow faster than he can express them'. The quiet confidence of his new faith (already adumbrated in the yew-tree
'Lines') is best expressed in a passage incorporated in *The Excursion* (iv.1207–75; cf. PW5.400–3), where he speaks of release
from morbidity and hatred in the joy of the 'pure principle of love',
and of the philanthropic lessons communicated by nature. With
this in mind, but in a different spirit, 'Peter Bell' was begun on 20
April, and read to Hazlitt at Alfoxden about six weeks later.

All these poems, with the exception of the last, are in blank
verse, the natural unpretentiousness of which reflects Wordsworth's stylistic aims far more than some of the poems in *Lyrical
Ballads*. This volume does not include any of the more important
poetry he had written before March 1798, apart from one or two
excerpts. By this time Wordsworth knew that the Alfoxden lease
would not be renewed after midsummer, and Coleridge, who had
received a pension from Tom and Josiah Wedgwood which
enabled him to avoid entering the Unitarian ministry and devote
himself to literature and philosophy, persuaded him and Dorothy
to accompany him to Germany, where he wished to pursue such
aims. For this the Wordsworths needed further income. Cottle
made various proposals for publication, among them two volumes
of Wordsworth's poems, one comprising 'Salisbury Plain' and
'Peter Bell'. Wordsworth was opposed to this, and it was not until
the end of May that agreement was reached to publish anonymously a selection of his poems with some of Coleridge's. Most of
Wordsworth's contributions had been written during the previous
three months.

Three additions were made: 'Expostulation and Reply', 'The Tables Turned', and 'Tintern Abbey'. The first two were written after a discussion with 'a friend who was somewhat unreasonably attached to modern books of moral philosophy'; probably Hazlitt, who (as he tells us in 'My First Acquaintance with Poets') 'got into a metaphysical argument with Wordsworth' at Alfoxden. The last poem in the volume was a late addition. When the Wordsworths left Alfoxden, they stayed with Cottle and others in the Bristol area, and then proceeded to the Wye valley, walking to Tintern Abbey and on to Goodrich Castle. On the return journey, after revisiting Tintern, Wordsworth began composing the 'Lines' which were imagined 'written a few miles above' the abbey, concluding his poem just before entering Bristol, where it was written down and handed without alteration to Cottle.

It is doubtful whether a single first publication of English poetry has ever appeared with two greater and more dissimilar poems than 'Tintern Abbey' and 'The Ancient Mariner'; doubtful also whether they are the most remarkable items in this extraordinary volume. Yet its reception was surprisingly mild and favourable on the whole. The fact that Wordsworth had withdrawn from supernatural subjects ('The Three Graves', 'The Ancient Mariner') in favour of Coleridge, and had started a work with aims like those of Coleridge's abandoned poem 'The Brook', supports the claim made afterwards in *Biographia Literaria* that an agreement was reached whereby Coleridge chose supernatural or romantic subjects, and Wordsworth the natural and ordinary, and that both aimed at exciting the reader's sympathy ('that willing suspension of disbelief for the moment, which constitutes poetic faith') by fidelity to human nature whatever the circumstances, real or supernatural, and by presenting their subjects imaginatively. On this second aspect of Wordsworth's poetry Coleridge writes with lyrical understanding: 'to give the charm of novelty to things of every day, and to excite a feeling analogous to the supernatural, by awakening the mind's attention to the lethargy of custom, and directing it to the loveliness and the wonders of the world before us; an inexhaustible treasure, but for which, in consequence of the film of familiarity and selfish solicitude, we have eyes, yet see not, ears that hear not, and hearts that neither feel nor understand'.

Only a few of Wordsworth's poems, notably 'Goody Blake and Harry Gill', 'The Last of the Flock', 'The Thorn', and 'Simon Lee, the Old Huntsman', were experimental; and in these, trusting for humanitarian reasons that his poems would appeal widely among the lower classes of society, Wordsworth ventured a style similar to that of the halfpenny ballads he had seen hawked about (5.vi.08). Perhaps the title 'Lyrical Ballads' was chosen for this reason and also because Taylor's translations of Bürger had created new enthusiasm for the ballad, for there is hardly a ballad in the volume, and 'The Rime of the Ancyent Marinere', with its elaborate machinery directed to a moral end ('For the dear God, who loveth us, He made and loveth all'), takes us, despite its stanza and archaisms, outside the realms of traditional balladry.

Five of Wordsworth's inclusions were written before *Lyrical Ballads* was projected: the yew-tree 'Lines', 'The Female Vagrant', 'The Convict', 'Old Man Travelling', and 'Lines written near Richmond'. The last of these, consisting of five verses written at Cambridge, was divided on Coleridge's recommendation, into two poems for the 1800 edition: 'Lines written while sailing in a Boat at Evening' and 'Remembrance of Collins'. The sub-title 'Animal Tranquillity and Decay' was preferred to 'Old Man Travelling' in 1800, the original poem consisting of 'an overflowing' from 'The Old Cumberland Beggar' with the addition:

> — I asked him whither he was bound, and what
> The object of his journey; he replied
> 'Sir! I am going many miles to take
> A last leave of my son, a mariner,
> Who from a sea-fight has been brought to Falmouth,
> And there is dying in a hospital.'

These lines were eventually removed, perhaps because Wordsworth had become hypersensitive on the score of matter-of-factness; and most critics think that the poem gains by their absence. The sketch suggests that nature gives the man composure in his decay, but the first version is more striking in its implicit emphasis on the ability which comes from 'the calm oblivious tendencies of Nature' (PW5.403) to sustain heartfelt suffering.

The remaining fourteen contributions by Wordsworth (who provided nineteen of the twenty-three poems in the 1798 edition) fall clearly into two groups, the first of which may be described as humanitarian. Of these Wordsworth thought 'Goody Blake and Harry Gill' 'one of the rudest' in the collection. Its 'chatter, chatter, chatter still', its colloquial idiom ('Two poor old dames,

as I have known', 'Sad case it was, as you may think'), and its linking of narrative strokes with rapid 'and' successions, are all part of
a dramatic presentation, the poet hazarding the role of a simple
but not unlettered narrator who becomes excited in the telling of
his story. The feelings of the two protagonists are imparted
through skilful rhythmic changes, the climax of Goody's curse as
she kneels and prays being accentuated by the freezing intonations
of 'The cold, cold moon above her head'. Wordsworth could
imagine the situation from his observations near Racedown in
the winter of 1796–7, but the story (from Erasmus Darwin's
Zoonamia, or the Laws of Organic Life) arose, like 'The Three
Graves', from his interest in the psychosomatic effects of the curse.
The moving story of 'The Last of the Flock' is presented (as if by
the crofter himself) in very simple diction, with effective use of
repetition and a psychological insight that succeeds through the
realism of its language. Unable to find parish relief (the events
took place at Holford near Alfoxden), he sells his sheep to maintain his family: 'And they were healthy with their food; For me –
it never did me good.' Like 'Michael' the poem conveys an anti-
Godwinian vindication of the inherited love of possessions; even
more, through its love of family and flock, it illustrates (like the
poems which follow) Wordsworth's revolt from rationalism, and
the value he attaches to the affections. He appeals to the heart and
the imagination, presenting pictures of life, as if to say (with
Beaupuy), ''Tis against *that* that we are fighting.'
    The subject of 'Simon Lee, the Old Huntsman' is a worthy one,
but it is doubtful whether Wordsworth did it full justice except at
the end, despite the rearrangements, omissions, and improvements he made after 1798. It is not the contrast between youth and
age, important though that is; nor is it primarily the gratitude of
an old man for assistance in a task which would never have taxed
his strength in his prime. Gratitude is significant directly and
allusively, for it implies a critical comment on Godwin, who did
not regard it as a virtue. The climax of the poem (and Wordsworth
achieves this admirably) is the inadequacy of words to com-
municate one's feeling in response to a moving expression of
gratitude, and particularly one which intensifies one's sense of the
pathos of life's decay. Deep though this theme is, it has its humour;
old Simon's thanks and praises continue as if they will never end.
Wordsworth removed weaknesses in the main body of the poem,
including factuality, colloquialism ('not over stout', 'poor old

ancles'), and the blundering circumlocution 'Of years he has upon his back, No doubt, a burthen weighty.' Others remain: the detail about the legs and ankles is superfluous, and detracts from the dignity of the subject; the address to the reader begins with otiose facility and is wholly unnecessary. It is the 'picture' or action which should tell; the reader needs no more comment or appeal than is provided at the end.[14]

Two dramatic lyrics on maternal love in strange situations afford excellent illustrations of 'the fluxes and refluxes of the mind when agitated by the great and simple affections of our nature'. 'The Mad Mother' ('Her eyes are wild') owes much to 'Lady Anne Bothwell's Lament' in Percy's *Reliques*, and 'The Complaint of a Forsaken Indian Woman' was suggested by facts in Samuel Hearne's account of his journey from a fort in Hudson's Bay to the Northern Ocean. The deserted mother of the first lyric has crossed the ocean from North America, and thinks of building 'an Indian bower' for her babe. Her thoughts, which form the main substance of the poem, reflect her madness when her baby first sucked, and she saw fiendish faces pulling at her breasts; the soothing that she now feels as he feeds; and the wild impulses within her to cross howling torrents and haunt high cliffs above the sea. She longs for the boy to give her the love she has lost, then fearfully detects a wild look in his eye as he finishes feeding at her breast. If the child has inherited madness, it cannot be from her, she thinks; and she breaks off on a note of elation, 'Now laugh and be gay, to the woods away! And there, my babe, we'll live for aye.' The second poem is sadder, and most dramatically imaginative when the Indian woman who has been left behind in the snowbound wastes remembers the last look of her child:

> My child! they gave thee to another,
> A woman who was not thy mother.
> When from my arms my babe they took,
> On me how strangely did he look!
> Through his whole body something ran,
> A most strange something did I see;
> – As if he strove to be a man,
> That he might pull the sledge for me.
> And then he stretched his arms, how wild!
> O mercy! like a little child.

The passage gives lyrical expression to the natural perceptions of a

woman not highly articulate and yet movingly expressive despite
Wordsworth's daringly repetitive use of 'something' (later changed
to 'working').

'Came home the Crookham [Crowcombe] way, by the thorn,
and the little muddy pond', Dorothy wrote in her Alfoxden journal
(20.iv.98). The thorn may have reminded Wordsworth of the
Scottish ballad:

> And there's she lean'd her back to a thorn . . .
> And there she has her baby born . . .
> She has houked a grave ayont the sun . . .
> And there she has buried the sweet babe in.

If the pond recalled 'The Lass of Fair Wone', whose betrayed
heroine tore out a shallow grave, beside a pond, with her bloody
nails (and the influence of the translation on 'The Three Graves',
which has the same presentational technique as 'The Thorn', suggests it may have done so), 'The Thorn' embodies a criticism of
Bürger's romantic improbabilities, and brings the reader back to
life. Thoughts of Annette may have made Wordsworth more alive
to a mother's sufferings, but it was Beaupuy more than Annette
who awakened his mind to the sufferings of the poor, and helped to
make him the imaginative humanitarian he became. 'The Thorn'
presents a common tragedy to which most people were either
unsympathetic or indifferent. Wordsworth presents it as it was
commonly known, not as a clear, complete story (as in Bürger) but
as a subject of local gossip with its conjectures and varied interpre-
tations. He assumes (and wished he had written an introductory
poem to make this clear) a narrator who is credulous but slow to
make up his mind. Such an addition was unnecessary; all that
Wordsworth wrote on the subject, including his brief note in the
1798 preface, is superfluous. The poem is explicit; the rustic narrator, too tender-hearted to believe that a mother can murder her
child, is obvious at all stages, and adds considerably to the interest
of the subject. He presents the diversity of communal views, some of
them superstitious. The ridiculed 'I've measured it from side to
side; 'Tis three feet long and two feet wide' reflects, not Wordsworth's matter-of-factness but the simple confirmation of rustic
suspicion; the factuality (which is found elsewhere in the stanza,
and is not devoid of humour) is psychological, an index of character
which is more significant and relevant than the substitution made

in 1820 (after Coleridge's criticisms in *Biographia Literaria*), 'Though but of compass small, and bare To thirsty suns and parching air'.

Coleridge was sceptical of poetic talent in the less literate, but Wordsworth has no hesitation in attributing imaginative and lyrical gifts to his narrator. The poem combines naive repetition and expression with vision and feeling, in a manner so accordant with the variables of the subject (which cannot be divorced from the presentation) that it never shakes conviction. There is a parallel between the thorn and the woman; wretched and forlorn, weighed down with moss and lichens, it is exposed to storms on a mountain ridge. It has the appearance of a stone; so too has Martha Ray[15] when the narrator first sees her on the height through the driving rain. Some say the mossy mound which is 'like an infant's grave in size' is red with child's blood, but the narrator finds it beautiful; whatever people think, he concludes:

> I cannot tell how this may be:
> But plain it is the thorn is bound
> With heavy tufts of moss that strive
> To drag it to the ground;
> And this I know, full many a time,
> When she was on the mountain high,
> By day, and in the silent night,
> When all the stars shone clear and bright,
> That I have heard her cry,
> 'Oh misery! oh misery!
> Oh woe is me! oh misery!'

The verse illustrates the lyricism of a 'ballad' with a new kind of realism and a vision that extends from the individual to the whole universe. The storm scenes convey an imaginative reinforcement of the human plight or man's inhumanity to man; the stars are a reminder of universal nature, to whose laws man is indifferent. Later imaginative writers like Hardy and George Eliot (whose *Adam Bede* contains a legacy of Martha Ray and her red cloak) had a scientific vision of the universe which stressed the opposite conclusion, that nature is indifferent to man.

In subject and spirit 'The Idiot Boy' provides a bold contrast to 'The Thorn'; Wordsworth 'never wrote anything with so much glee'. Many readers have found its free-and-easy ambivalence disconcerting, if not inimical to its underlying seriousness; yet its author regarded it at least as highly as 'The Thorn', as is indicated at the end of *The Prelude*, where he recalls the Quantock days when Coleridge recited 'The Ancient Mariner' and 'Christabel', and he himself 'steeped in soft forgetfulness the livelong hours', 'Murmuring of him who, joyous hap, was found, After the perils of his moonlight ride, Near the loud waterfall; or her who sate In misery near the miserable thorn'. Though written entertainingly, the poem succeeds in conveying maternal love and anxiety. Writing to John Wilson (7.vi.02), Wordsworth stated that his aim was to delineate not merely feelings which 'all men *do* sympathise with' but those which 'all men *may* sympathise with'. He had often associated with idiots the 'sublime expression of scripture that, "their life is hidden with God"', and hoped that the false delicacy or prejudice which operated against them, and which was unusual among the lower classes of society, might be removed. It was part of a great poet's duty 'to rectify men's feelings, to give them new compositions of feeling, to render their feelings more sane pure and permanent, in short, more consonant to nature, that is, to eternal nature, and the great moving spirit of things'. He had often thought the conduct of lower-class parents towards idiot children 'the great triumph of the human heart. It is there that we see the strength, disinterestedness, and grandeur of love . . .'.

Coleridge took the view that Wordsworth's 'burr, burr, burr' is a reminder of 'ordinary morbid idiocy', and that 'the idiocy of the boy is so evenly balanced by the folly of the mother, as to present to the general reader rather a laughable burlesque on the blindness of anile dotage, than an analytic display of maternal affection in its ordinary workings'. He refers to 'The Idiot Boy' as 'that fine poem', and says nothing in its favour. If the mother's character is 'an impersonation of an instinct abandoned by judgment',[16] the reason is that Wordsworth has sought to be true to life rather than sentimental. Betty Foy is a recognisable type; her 'fiddle-faddle' has the comicality of detached observation, but the poem ensures that her maternal distress and affection ultimately transcend all the accidentals of the story, and make the most moving appeal. The author's dual role enriches his poem.

But for Betty's 'bustle' and 'mighty fret' the story was inconceivable. Her action in risking Johnny on a long nocturnal ride for medical help ('the like was never heard of yet') would put any mother 'in a fright'. Alarmed at his failure to return, she leaves her patient Susan Gale; and her anxiety reaches such a pitch that she can blame her for all that has happened. When she reaches the doctor's house, Susan and her illness are completely forgotten. This late-night visit produces a dramatic vignette which seems like a quintessence of the eighteenth-century novel at its best:

> And now she's at the doctor's door,
> She lifts the knocker, rap, rap, rap;
> The doctor at the casement shows
> His glimmering eyes that peep and doze!
> And one hand rubs his old night-cap.
>
> 'Oh Doctor! Doctor! where's my Johnny?'
> 'I'm here, what is't you want with me?'
> 'Oh sir! you know I'm Betty Foy,
> And I have lost my poor dear boy,
> You know him — him you often see;
>
> He's not as wise as some folks be.'
> 'The devil take his wisdom!' said
> The doctor, looking somewhat grim,
> 'What, woman! should I know of him?'
> And, grumbling, he went back to bed.

The daring ambivalence of the poem is compounded by animated literary satire. When Betty is most distressed, the reader is left in suspense, the poet-narrator suggesting, in an obvious leg-pull, a variety of adventures the hero of the story may have undertaken. The last of them runs:

> Perhaps, with head and heels on fire,
> And like the very soul of evil,
> He's galloping away, away,
> And so will gallop on for aye,
> The bane of all that dread the devil!

This romantic jocosity is a witty thrust at Bürger's popular ballad 'Lenore', recalling in particular Blake's frontispiece illustration of the rider's horse for J. T. Stanley's translation.[17] 'The Idiot Boy' opens with mock-solemn allusion to two recurring narrative details in William Taylor's translation: 'The moone is bryghte, and blue the nyghte' and 'Halloo! halloo! away they goe'. The triple effects ('happy, happy, happy John', his 'burr, burr, burr', and Betty's 'rap, rap, rap' at the doctor's door) are high-spirited flourishes which show that Wordsworth can go one better than Bürger in his excitatory repetitions.

The happy ending is artistically anticipated, and nowhere are the excitable mother's emotions conveyed more delightfully than at the point of reunion, where the comment of humour and contrast in no way diminishes the reader's empathy. Perhaps the alarm of this kind-hearted woman had exaggerated her patient's crisis, for whom should she and her son meet on their return journey but old Susan, whose anxiety for both of them had summoned up resolution and driven away pain as if by magic. The psychological realism of this feature of the story has been emphasized by critics, but it is characteristic of the whole. The hooting of the owls is a motif that leads to the ending. When Betty is high on the down, after her visit to the doctor's, she is at her wits' end; her strained attention is communicated in 'The grass you almost hear it growing, You hear it now, if e'er you can'. The hooting of the owls is heard again, and they lengthen out the 'tremulous sob' (from 'The Vale of Esthwaite') that 'echoes far from hill to hill'. Johnny hears the owls in tuneful concert all night long. The poem begins with them, and returns to them at the end, which brings us to the origin of the story, as it was told by Thomas Poole. When asked where he had been, what seen, what heard, the idiot boy replied (and Wordsworth gives his 'very words'): 'The cocks did crow to-whoo, to-whoo, And the sun did shine so cold.' 'And that was all his travel's story', the poet adds, the 'bold' traveller's 'all' being the final thrust at the Bürger ballad.

Indirectly nearly all the philosophical poems in *Lyrical Ballads* hint at the inadequacy of intellectualism. Two of them relate to childhood. How alien reasoning is to a child, who, as Wordsworth remembered from boyhood, has no conscious awareness of mortality, is the subject of 'We are Seven'; some lines in the early version of 'Intimations of Immortality' are relevant, the child's conception of the grave being 'a lonely bed without the sense or sight Of day or the warm light, A place of thought where we in waiting lie'. The persistent questioning of the poet in illustration of his belief is a development of an error he made at Goodrich Castle. 'Anecdote for Fathers', based on experience with Basil Montagu, also shows the meddling intellect of the adult at work; here, in its zeal to promote adult reasoning in the child, it provokes spurious answers.

Shorter poems on nature ('To my Sister', 'Lines written in early Spring', Expostulation and Reply', 'The Tables Turned') are off-shoots of the religion which had been more fully expounded in the pedlar section of 'The Ruined Cottage', its variant passages, and other blank verse fragments of 1798 (PW5.381–8, 401–3). Its central tenet is God's love, a 'universal birth' in spring. The one Life is a 'power that rolls about, below, above', and imparts benevolence to those who attend in 'wise passiveness'. Hence Wordsworth's reference to nature's 'holy plan', and his claim that the spirit of nature ('One impulse from a vernal wood') can impart 'spontaneous wisdom' more vital than 'the spirit breathed from dead men to their kind' through the medium of books. Darwinism and modern science have not nullified Wordsworth's creed; there are many thinkers besides D. H. Lawrence who believe that the re-formation of society depends on becoming in tune, or establishing 'living organic connections', with nature and the cosmos.

Wordsworth had received so much from nature's 'overflowing soul' that 'all his thoughts were steeped in feeling', and he was not contented until he felt 'the sentiment of being' throughout the universe; he saw 'one life, and felt that it was joy'. He finds an in-adequate response in science to the rainbow hues of a cloud of mist in sunlight, and asks if we were intended to pore, 'and dwindle as we pore', on minute things, seeing them 'in disconnection dead and spiritless' until by continual analysis we 'break down all grandeur'. We murder to dissect. 'Let us rise from this oblivious sleep', he urges, so that the senses and the intellect can enrich each other until the mind finds sustenance everywhere, from 'a stone, a tree, a withered leaf, To the broad ocean and the azure heavens Spangled with kindred multitudes of stars'. By 'drinking in the soul of things We shall be wise perforce', he concludes, confident that 'the joy of that pure principle of love' which it brings will prevail, and make us 'seek for objects of a kindred love In fellow-natures'. In this way he connects nature with God and man and the refor-mation of mankind.

After this, 'Tintern Abbey' contains little that is new. Elevated, but not grand, in style, it conceals its art in an apparently natural manner which contrasts with the more elaborate classical con-structions of *Paradise Lost*. The language is cultured but unpre-tentious; it follows a course varying from speech rhythms to those approximating periodic prose. Concentrations of thought are managed without disharmony, and rarely have musical variation and the smooth flow of movement in words achieved comparable effects. 'Tintern Abbey' is a blank verse triumph, the climax of experiment and practice in the medium for more than two years.[18] It presents the most personal and, at times, the most impassioned verse Wordsworth had ever written, its principal subject being the faith of 'Nature's priest'.

The poem contains little landscape. It glances at the 'glad animal movements' of Wordsworth's boyhood, when his interest in nature was incidental; gives more space to what it meant when he first visited the Wye valley in 1793, when the eye was despotic and sense-impressions were 'all in all'; deals with what the memory of it has done for him and, in the address to Dorothy with which it concludes, with what it will do for her; above all, it presents the significance that nature has for him now, when his eye has been 'made quiet' by awareness of its deeper realities.

In his self-presentation he describes (PW5.381) how the pedlar attained 'An *active* power to fasten images Upon his brain, and on their pictured lines Intensely brooded, even till they acquired The liveliness of dreams'. Such recollections had given Wordsworth a pleasure which restored him in body, mind, and spirit when he was weary with the din of city life. The happiness derived from them, he feels, may have had no 'trivial influence On that best portion of a good man's life, His little, nameless, unremembered acts Of kindness and of love'. He therefore trusts that the present visit holds 'life and food' for future years, and that, for Dorothy, when her wild ecstasies have matured into sober pleasure, and her mind is 'a mansion for all lovely forms', there will be 'healing thoughts' as she remembers him and this occasion. He believes that the moral and spiritual influences of nature are active in happy recollection.

The poem shows an advance in Wordsworth's theory of the imagination towards the development it was to take in *The Prelude*, where, in conjunction with nature, it is the key to the greater life of man. His awareness of the universal spirit makes him a lover

> of all the mighty world
> Of eye, and ear, − both what they half create,
> And what perceive; well pleased to recognise
> In nature and the language of the sense
> The anchor of my purest thoughts, the nurse,
> The guide, the guardian of my heart, and soul
> Of all my moral being.

The 'wise passiveness' proves to be creative; senses and intellect enrich each other. The mind does not allow the ear to be passive any more than it does the eye, as Milton recognised in 'L'Allegro': 'Lydian airs, Married to immortal verse, Such as the meeting soul may pierce, In notes . . .'. Wordsworth, who knew Milton's verse better than any other poet's, may have been influenced by 'the meeting soul' (which he quotes in his dedication to *Memorials of a Tour on the Continent*). He was certainly indebted to Young's *Night Thoughts* (vi.410ff.), where man's treasure is found in the senses, which are divine (like reason) and 'half create the wondrous worlds they see'.

Whether Wordsworth's actual experience of the 'one life' was mystical rather than visionary cannot be proved. Expression in 'Tintern Abbey', more than elsewhere, suggests that it could have been; 'we are laid asleep in body, and become a living soul'. Seeing 'into the life of things' may be commensurate with either the pedlar's 'high hour of visitation from the living God' or his vision of the 'perpetual logic' which linked him 'by an unrelenting agency' to all in the universe from the minute and immediate to the stars in their courses. The sentiment of universal being is 'a sense sublime Of something far more deeply interfused' through space 'and in the mind of man'. Nature for Wordsworth is not 'out there', as we might say; it includes man and his relationship to the living world. Undivorced from nature, the mind is so impressed 'with quietness and beauty', and so fed 'with lofty thoughts'

>   that neither evil tongues,
> Rash judgments, nor the snares of selfish men,
> Nor greetings where no kindness is, nor all
> The dreary intercourse of daily life,
> Shall e'er prevail against us, or disturb
> Our cheerful faith, that all which we behold
> Is full of blessings.

This is not a facile optimism; it does not evade the human problem. It reflects the faith of Wordsworth after involvement in human affairs and a crisis on a scale such as have befallen few English poets. His belief in nature did not make him deaf to 'the still, sad music of humanity'. For him the future of mankind depended on a deeper and more common realization of the responsibilities which our higher nature seeks.

'Peter Bell' and
Reformation by Nature

It may seem odd that Wordsworth could write 'Peter Bell' and 'Tintern Abbey' in the same year. Not only did he indulge his humorous whimsicalities with gusto; his nature-worship then, and in 1799 (when he completed the two-part poem of his boyhood reminiscences), was peculiarly subject to an almost primitive belief in the 'souls of lonely places', as well as in their ability to exert moral influences. He was apt also to interpret the psychological effects of guilt as the working of spiritual agencies in external nature. At this stage his ideas combine local manifestations peculiar to his belief, a spiritual philosophy which sees one Life in the whole universe, and in consequence (and more significantly today) a vision which is humanitarian. The inventiveness of 'Peter Bell' springs from these characteristics.

The serious faith behind the narrative which Wordsworth wrote with such inward glee is found in *The Prelude*. The blood-tie between the babe and its mother (ii.232ff.) forms 'the gravitation and the filial bond Of nature that connect him with the world'. Their mutual love creates the child's sense of beauty: frail and helpless as he is, he is emphatically alive, 'an inmate of this active universe'. Wordsworth believed that no one, not even Peter Bell, was irredeemable; that the original child of nature could be rescued from 'a universe of death', and enjoy a sense of grandeur as a result of the reawakening of the imagination in co-operation with spiritual love (Pr.xiv.150ff.).

He must have had doubts about his poem, for, after retrenching it in Germany and taking pains thereafter 'to make the production less unworthy of a favourable reception', he did not publish it until 1819. Its reception was unfortunate none the less. John Hamilton Reynolds, Keats's friend, must have glanced surreptitiously at the opening either in manuscript or proof copy, for his 'Peter Bell, A Lyrical Ballad' was published before Wordsworth's poem. Described by Shelley as 'the antenatal Peter, Wrapped in weeds of the same metre', it imitated Wordsworth's prologue, and developed a skittish narrative with reference to a number of his earlier poems. Other parodies on the subject were insignificant beside Shelley's lampoon 'Peter Bell the Third', which it was not thought prudent to publish until 1839. Starting from a verse which Shelley thought uproariously funny, and which Wordsworth omitted from later editions –

> Is it a party in a parlour?
> Cramm'd just as they on earth were cramm'd –
> Some sipping punch, some sipping tea,
> But, as you by their faces see,
> All silent and all damn'd!

– its theme was damnation. Shelley had been a great admirer of Wordsworth's poetry, but condemned him (as his 1815 sonnet 'To Wordsworth' shows) after reading *The Excursion*, even more after the General Thanksgiving 'Ode' of January 1816 (on the successful outcome of war against Napoleon), as a deserter of truth and liberty. So began the tradition, to which Browning affixed the seal, of Wordsworth 'the lost leader'. Shelley's poem was the occasion for a slashing attack on the repressive measures of the post-war government; it damned Wordsworth with the whole Establishment, and especially for the dullness which had overtaken his poetry.

Believing that the people (not the fashionable reading public) would enjoy 'Peter Bell', Wordsworth composed it originally in a plain, forthright style. Its high-spiritedness seems more laboured than that of 'The Idiot Boy'; occasionally it shows a bucolic tendency reminiscent of the 'convulsive inclination to laughter about the mouth' which Hazlitt noticed in Wordsworth's 'solemn, stately' features. Yet Edmund Gosse undoubtedly spoke for many when he asserted that the author shows no humour, and that 'the tale is not less improbable than uninteresting'. In recent years, however, the work has won much admiration. Lascelles Abercrombie wrote highly and at length in its praise; Ernest de Selincourt thought Wordsworth justified in regarding it as 'one of his greatest imaginative poems'; and Mary Moorman refers to it as his 'most brilliant narrative poem'.

Through 'God and Nature's single sovereignty' Wordsworth had grown to regard man and his potentialities with awe; he believed that reformation was possible, not in some imaginary Utopia but in 'the world of all of us', 'the place where, in the end, We find our happiness, or not at all' (Pr.xi.105—44). The failure of the Revolution ended his hope of renovation by political means, but it did not destroy the belief which he shared with Beaupuy in the inherent goodness of man. It was part of nature, as may be seen in 'The Old Cumberland Beggar':

> 'Tis Nature's law
> That none, the meanest of created things,
> Of forms created the most vile and brute,
> The dullest or most noxious, should exist
> Divorced from good — a spirit and pulse of good,
> A life and soul, to every mode of being
> Inseparably linked.

Something more basic than political change was necessary for social amelioration, and that was a change of heart in response to nature. ('The Dungeon', a passage from the play *Osorio* which was included in *Lyrical Ballads* shows that Coleridge shared Wordsworth's views.) Peter Bell had long withstood nature's benign influences, and needed shock treatment, like the hero of 'The Ancient Mariner'. The poem is a riposte to Coleridge's supernaturalism; it originated in the belief that 'the imagination not only does not require for its exercise the intervention of supernatural agency' but that it 'may be called forth as imperiously, and for kindred results of pleasure, by incidents within the compass of poetic probability, in the humblest departments of daily life'. The prologue is a jeu d'esprit which conveys this belief: the poet, tired of a voyage in space, yearns to return to reality, and feels a man again as he nears landing. As long as he can stray with 'sympathetic heart' and 'a soul of power' among 'the common growth of mother-earth', he has no craving for the dragon's wing or magic ring. To define his purpose further, he deliberately employs features and incidents which have their correspondences in Coleridge's poem. The narrator has just returned from a fantastic voyage; his tale requires an audience (only Bess, the squire's daughter, is remembered during the telling; and, unlike the wedding-guest, all the listeners are forgotten at the end). Parallels to the mariner's story may be seen in

Peter's brutality to the ass, his swoon when he catches sight of the dead man in the river, the spirits that work on his imagination, and the rumbling sound that comes from a mine.

The story originated in a newspaper account of how an ass was found 'hanging his head over a canal in a wretched posture' before his master's dead body was discovered in the water. Some of the details of Peter's past inhumanity may have been drawn from what the original rover told Wordsworth in Wales; the main narrative was invented. After creating suspense by taking the reader *in medias res* by a device made to look like an error of judgment, Wordsworth presents Peter's past and character. 'Nature ne'er could find the way' into his heart; he had never responded to 'the moral intimations of the sky'.[19] His keen, curst expression suggests that 'the man had fixed his face, In many a solitary place', against them. From the primrose by the river's brim to the soft blue sky with its witchery, no lovely natural form could 'melt into his heart'. Unlike Marmaduke in *The Borderers*, or the boy Wordsworth in 'Nutting', he was averse to 'skyey' influences; he was the sheer opposite of the ideal already portrayed in the pedlar (PW5.382):

> Oh! then what soul was his when on the tops
> Of the high mountains he beheld the sun
> Rise up and bathe the world in light. He looked,
> The ocean and the earth beneath him lay
> In gladness and deep joy. The clouds were touched
> And in their silent faces did he read
> Unutterable love. Sound needed none
> Nor any voice of joy: his spirit drank
> The spectacle. Sensation, soul and form
> All melted into him. . . .
> In such access of mind, in such high hour
> Of visitation from the living God,
> He did not feel the God; he felt his works . . .
> His mind was a thanksgiving to the power
> That made him. It was blessedness and love.

The story of Peter Bell depends on effects which sometimes appear ambivalent, the question being whether the dissonance between Peter and the other world is intended as an external factor or a psychological impression. He is in a rage at losing his way, after taking a short cut by moonlight in Swaledale, when he sees an ass which he regards as a prize. The animal refuses to carry him and, when beaten, sinks down by the edge of the river. Peter interprets his inability to move him as witchcraft at work, and his loneliness and guilty emotional excitement continue to make him highly impressionable. He is daunted by the echo of the ass's repeated bray (sounding 'Thief, thief!' from a quarry in the earliest version) and by strange appearances in the uneasy, dimming moon, the glimmering broad blue sky, and the staggering rocks. On the point of renewing his efforts to raise the beast, he catches sight of something strange in the river (his wonder at the sight evoked the picture which caught Shelley's creative fancy), is aghast on recognising a corpse, and falls in a swoon. When he attempts to lift the body, the ass rises and licks his hands; as soon as he has recovered it, the animal kneels for Peter to mount. A doleful sound is recognised by the ass as the crying of his master's son, and he stops as if to pursue it until it dies away. The love and loyalty of the creature make Peter feel that vengeance will befall him. In this unusual state of mind, he sees strange sights among the towering rocks and spires of the dell through which he rides; a rustling leaf disturbs him, and drops of blood in the white dust of the road rouse feelings of guilt, until he notices a bleeding wound in the ass's head. 'Ghastly pains' shoot through him as he thinks of the dead man and the animal's fidelity, but he soon recovers with the thought that, but for him, the poor man might never have a Christian burial; again, in the confidence that nobody would ever suppose that he could think such an emaciated creature worth stealing. Tapping his tobacco-box, he causes the ass to turn his head, and sees a toothful grin, which he is about to return when he is alarmed by a rumbling mine, and feels that the earth will swallow him. Then, after a chapel has reminded him of his sixth marriage, to a godly Highland girl who died of sorrow, a noisy drunken group recalls episodes from his past, and he is smitten with remorse; he thinks he sees her, and hears her calling for her mother, on her death-bed. A Methodist preacher, crying 'Repent, repent!' brings him back to reality, and he melts into tears. (The cross which he notices at this point — a reminder of Christ's entry into Jerusalem before his crucifixion — is a late addition to the text.) The ass returns home, and the grief of the family moves Peter until, like the ancient mariner, he is rescued from life-in-death:

> And now is Peter taught to feel
> That man's heart is a holy thing;

> And Nature, through a world of death,
> Breathes into him a second breath,
> More searching than the breath of spring.

A holy sense imbues him with a human sympathy such as he had never felt. The joy of the son who returns and heaps affection on the ass is more than he can bear. He forsakes a life of crime and, 'after ten months' melancholy', becomes 'a good and honest man'.

(A passage, originally part of 'Peter Bell', was used, with two new stanzas as introduction and conclusion, to form the poem 'Andrew Jones', which appeared in the second volume of *Lyrical Ballads*, 1800. The Highland girl whose marriage disillusionment with Peter caused her to pine and christen her babe 'Benoni, or the child of sorrow' was suggested by the story which Ann Tyson told Wordsworth of a neighbour's daughter: the subject of his early poem 'A Ballad', PW1.265–7. 'Peter Bell' may have influenced Hardy when he made Tess christen her child 'Sorrow', after she had remembered the marginal explanation of 'Benoni' in Genesis, xxxv.18).

English literature contains conversions (as in John Masefield's *The Everlasting Mercy*) less convincing than Peter Bell's, and the prototype of his emotional penitence can be found again and again in the annals of contemporary Methodism. Wordsworth's story may appear to be contrived at points, but one can quarrel little with the process and the outcome if the experience is interpreted purely in human terms, the 'spirits of the mind' being accepted as wholly psychological, and the awakening of Peter's conscience as the natural product of past and present events in his life. Such, however, is not Wordsworth's intention. The spirits of the mind are like those he has experienced 'in darkness and the stormy night', and the stanzas 'I love upon a stormy night' (PW2.464–5), in the same measure as 'Peter Bell' and probably written at the same time, afford an interesting essay on the subject. In the first version of his boyhood experiences which he was soon to write, Wordsworth assumes local spirits who reproved him with either 'gentle visitations' or 'severer interventions' (PR.22–3, *app. crit.*). His basic assumption is expressed in a fragment (PW5.340):

> Why is it we feel
> So little for each other, but for this,
> That we with nature have no sympathy,

> Or with such things as have no power to hold
> Articulate language?
> And never for each other shall we feel
> As we may feel, till we have sympathy
> With nature in her forms inanimate,
> With objects such as have no power to hold
> Articulate language. In all forms of things
> There is a mind.

With this should be connected the lines already quoted from 'The Old Cumberland Beggar' on the goodness inherent in all people, however base; they have 'a spirit and pulse of good' which is 'inseparably linked' to 'every mode of being'. The spirits which work on the mind of Peter Bell, and affect his visual sense, are spirits of nature, visitations from the mind that is in 'all forms of things'.

Wordsworth's views were rooted in Newtonian philosophy; they had been confirmed and enlarged by independent reading as well as in discussions with Coleridge. Addison, for example, in *The Spectator* (no. 571) had expounded views similar to those in the above passage:

> All the dead parts of nature are invigorated by the presence of their Creator . . . Man only, who does not co-operate with this holy Spirit, and is unattentive to his Presence, receives none of those advantages from it, which are perfective of his nature and necessary to his well-being. The divinity is with him, and in him, and every where about him . . . This single consideration one would think sufficient to make us open our hearts to all those infusions of joy and gladness which are so near at hand.

'Every particle of matter is actuated by this Almighty Being which passes through it', Addison claims, influenced by the concept of the 'active principle' which Newton had postulated, and which was in Wordsworth's mind when he wrote years later (Ex.ix.1–3): 'To every form of being is assigned . . . an *active* principle.' In the words of the 'argument', the Wanderer (originating from the pedlar of 'The Ruined Cottage') 'asserts that an active principle pervades the universe, its noblest seat the human soul'. This recalls 'Tintern Abbey': 'A motion and a spirit, that impels All thinking things, all objects of all thought, And rolls through all things'.

Circulating 'from link to link', it is 'the Soul of all the worlds', the Wanderer continues.

Wordsworth had found support for such a view at the end of 'Summer' in Thomson's *The Seasons*; 'angel-winged' Philosophy springs aloft, gaining 'the heights of science and of virtue', where 'all is calm and clear', and where reason can trace the 'chain of causes and effects' to Him, 'the world-producing Essence, who alone possesses being'. The idea received its stereotype in Pope's *Essay on Man* (i.233ff.), where the 'vast chain of Being' is seen from the infinite to the infinitesimal, from God to angels and man, from man to beast, bird, fish, and insect, all being 'parts of one stupendous whole, Whose body Nature is, and God the soul'. Its persistence in Wordsworth may be seen in a poem of 1831, 'The Primrose of the Rock', where the tuft of flowers is 'A lasting link in Nature's chain From highest heaven let down' to the earth in its constant course and the rock in which the plant is rooted. 'Blake, Coleridge, and Wordsworth, in rebelling against a mechanistic universe and upholding an animistic one, were much closer to Newton himself than they realized.'[20]

How closely the unity of all was linked with the reformation of mankind Wordsworth emphasized in his address to Coleridge towards the end of *The Prelude* (1805):

> Thy gentle spirit to my heart of hearts
> Did also find its way; and thus the life
> Of all things and the mighty unity
> In all which we behold, and feel, and are,
> Admitted more habitually a mild
> Interposition, closelier gathering thoughts
> Of man and his concerns . . .
> And God and man divided, as they ought,
> Between them the great system of the world
> Where man is sphered, and which God animates.

'Prophets of Nature', they would be 'bless'd with true happiness' as joint labourers in a work of redemption, he hopefully concluded.

Although the modern assumption of a neutral or Godless universe is ultimately a scientific admission of its ultimate incomprehensibility, it will have severed for most readers the link between human welfare and cosmic wisdom. George Eliot was a Wordsworthian, but her scientific outlook limited her hopes to the humanitarian level of promoting human sympathy as a force for altruism and justice. Fortunately much of Wordsworth's faith depends on such humanitarianism; his weakness is in his extra-human claims. There is no necessary correlation between the love of external nature (a primrose by the river's brim), moral integrity, and genuine human sympathy. A passage on which Wordsworth worked in 1798 (PR.613) suggests that he had experienced some *rational* uncertainty on this point. Returning almost to the thought of his yew-tree 'Lines', he argues that 'The mind must sink that hangs on its own works With an exclusive dotage', but that the spectacle of nature will be ennobling, and foster admiration. This in its turn will strengthen the affections, for, he asks (and the questioning implies an assumption), can he

> Who thus respects a mute insensate form,
> Whose feelings do not need the gross appeal
> Of tears and of articulate sounds, can he
> Be wanting in his duties to mankind
> Or slight the pleadings of a human heart?

Wordsworth adduced evidence at various times in support of his theory. In a letter to John Wilson (7.vi.02) he argues that characteristics of nature (colours, forms, scents, voices and movements of birds and animals, changing skies and weather) must be the 'nourishers' and even the 'fathers' of children's passions. 'Images of danger, melancholy, grandeur, or loveliness, softness, and ease' will affect inhabitants, even a nation if it is small, as it was in the Highlands of Scotland. Such influences on character are reduced by religion, law, industrial and commercial growth, and the consequent movement of people. In the poem 'Presentiments' (1830) he bases his claim that these intimations (when 'Truth shows a glorious face, While on that isthmus which commands The councils of both worlds') are '*heaven*-born' and 'star-guided' on the analogy that God, 'Whose wisdom fixed the scale of natures' (the chain of Being), 'instructs the brutes to scent All changes of the element'.

In his 'Reply to Mathetes' (Wilson), which was published in Coleridge's *The Friend* (1809–10), Wordsworth alludes to the 'high instincts' of 'Intimations of Immortality'. They indicate a beauty which has not been seen, a pathos which has not been felt, and a sublimity which has not been reached. The 'sacred light of childhood' can be no more than a remembrance for youth, but he can be 'remanded to Nature' with hopes 'founded less upon his sentiment than upon his intellectual being' (reason and will). Wordsworth has been discussing 'dispositions stealing into the spirit like music from unknown quarters', with 'Nature as a teacher of truth through joy and through gladness'. Nature develops 'precious feelings of disinterested, that is self-disregarding, joy and love', and unless this conscience is activated all precepts are nugatory. The best education of this kind is through nature, and through books which 'breathe the ancient spirit', the wisdom of the ages. In this way intellectual beauty unfolds. The virtue Wordsworth has in mind does not transcend human nature, but if it were sacrificed for worldly gain, our greatness would decline (here is the key to 'The world is too much with us. . . . Little we see in Nature that is ours'). There can be 'no confirmed and passionate love of truth for him who has not experienced the hollowness of error'; in other words, we learn by nature (experience). Lastly Wordsworth emphasizes the danger of too much instruction; it may create the 'lifeless decency' of the conventional.

The nature which inspires the great exists supremely in the works of mighty poets (Pr.v.594–5). Their creative energies are like those of the universe. In his sonnet on the departure of Sir Walter Scott for Naples, Wordsworth speaks of 'Spirits of Power' assembled over Eildon's 'triple height' and complaining at the loss of 'kindred Power'. The 'prospectus', as first appended to 'Home at Grasmere', shows that the powers inspiring the poet spring not only from nature or life but also from nature via the inherited wisdom of the ages:

> Come thou prophetic spirit, soul of man
> Thou human soul of the wide earth that hast
> Thy metropolitan temple in the hearts
> Of mighty poets, unto me vouchsafe
> Thy guidance, teach me to discern and part
> Inherent things from casual, what is fixed
> From fleeting, that my verse may live and be
> Even as a light hung up in heaven to cheer
> Mankind in times to come.

With this in mind he stated, late in life, his belief that his poetry 'must sooner or later work its way into the hearts and minds of the people', his familiarity with nature making it inevitable that nature would conquer for him.

When, in the 'prospectus', he stresses the importance of the imagination, the creative power that comes from the 'blended might' of the individual mind and the external world, his subject is the achievement of the ideal state. Since spiritual love is inseparable from this imagination (Pr.xiv.188–92), and 'minds Once wedded to this outward frame of things In love' see such achievement as 'the growth of common day', he asks why such a state should be thought merely a dream or fiction. This link between nature and humanity is manifest in the revision of a passage written in 1798 as part of a conclusion to 'The Ruined Cottage'. In this final version (Ex.iv.1230–49) Wordsworth states that by contemplating natural forms in relation to man we become aware of 'the spiritual presences of absent things'. There is nothing in the outward face of nature but will teach some acceptable lesson 'of human suffering, or of human joy'. So those whose eyes and hearts are open will learn,

> while all things speak of man,
> Their duties from all forms; and general laws,
> And local accidents, shall tend alike
> To rouse, to urge; and, with the will, confer
> The ability to spread the blessings wide
> Of true philanthropy. The light of love
> Not failing, perseverance from their steps
> Departing not, for them shall be confirmed
> The glorious habit by which sense is made
> Subservient to moral purposes,
> Auxiliar to divine.

'Home at Grasmere' supplies a local example of this:

> Look where we will, some human heart has been
> Before us with its offering; not a tree
> Sprinkles these little pastures but the same
> Hath furnished matter for a thought; perchance,
> For some one serves as a familiar friend.
> Joy spreads, and sorrow spreads; and this whole vale,
> Home of untutored shepherds as it is,
> Swarms with sensation, as with gleams of sunshine,
> Shadows or breezes, scents or sounds.

Even if these feelings spring from 'self-respecting interests', they are not unworthy or unhallowed. They 'lift the animal being' and refine; 'they breathe their own undying life Through this their mountain sanctuary',

> giving to the moments as they pass
> Their little boons of animating thought
> That sweeten labour, make it seen and felt
> To be no arbitrary weight imposed,
> But a glad function natural to man.

In the words of 'Yarrow Revisited', 'the visions of the past Sustain the heart in feeling Life as she is − our changeful life, With friends and kindred feeling'. Or, as Wordsworth writes in 'Not in the lucid intervals of life', 'O Nature, we are thine, Through good and evil thine, in just degree Of rational and manly sympathy.'

Objections to Wordsworth's theories of nature have been common. Mary Lamb, after reading *The Excursion*, concluded that, according to his creed, a town-dweller 'had not a soul to be saved'. George Eliot could not believe that country people enjoy moral privileges: 'To make men moral, something more is necessary than to turn them out to grass.' For many readers Darwinism will have sounded the death-knell to the beneficence of Wordsworth's nature, but Darwinism may not supply the whole answer, even if God or the one Life be in dispute. Wordsworth's nature, it should be remembered, often implies (in the traditional eighteenth-century manner) the whole creation, including humanity. In this sense, it still has validity; it is usually worthy of close attention, and often admirable for its perception and wisdom.

Part II: 1798–1814

Part II 1799 - 1814

Germany and the North of England (1798–9)

Before leaving for Germany, Wordsworth and Coleridge made an unpremeditated excursion into Wales, calling on Thelwall at Liswyn Farm[1] near Brecon. With Dorothy and Coleridge's acolyte John Chester, they then journeyed from Bristol to London 'per foot, per waggon, per coach, per post-chaise', and found time to view Blenheim and Oxford on the way. Wordsworth had borrowed money from the Wedgwoods, and asked Cottle to sell his expensive 'Gilpin's tours'. Victor Klopstock was very hospitable to the visitors at Hamburg, and introduced them to his aged brother the poet, with whom Wordsworth conversed in French. The notes he made on later interviews with him were included in *Satyrane's Letters*, Coleridge's high-spirited impressions of the Hamburg visit.

Wishing to study German philosophy, the latter soon made plans to settle at Ratzeburg, a more intellectual centre not far off. William and Dorothy, eager to find cheaper accommodation and more attractive country surroundings, travelled south in early October to the ancient walled city of Goslar near the Harz mountains. (By this time, after a restricted issue of *Lyrical Ballads*, Cottle had sold most of his copies, and the publication rights, to a London bookseller.) As the Wordsworths could not afford to live *en pension*, they took lodgings, in consequence of which they could not entertain, and made few acquaintances outside the tradespeople who occupied the old imperial city. William, who had not foreseen the social barrier Dorothy would create, the word 'sister' being regarded as a euphemism for 'mistress', made little progress with the German language. He had bought copies of Bürger and Percy's *Reliques* in Hamburg, but had found less to admire in the former than Coleridge had. He thought 'Susan's Dream' his best and most Shakespearian poem, but enjoyed 'Lenore' less in the

99

original than in English translations. He wished he could find more human character and less of the author in his works. Everywhere in Burns, by contrast, he found 'the presence of human life' which communicated itself with 'the charm of recognitions'. Apart from the incidents, which were seldom original, Bürger showed a lively narrative genius, but lacked the 'higher beauties' of a great poet. Wordsworth loved his *Tra ra la*, but preferred less of the horn, more of the flute, and far more of the pencil or living character.

During the 'perishingly cold' winter of 1798–9 at Goslar, he was very industrious; having few books to read, he wrote 'in self-defence'. Clad in a fur-lined pelisse and dog-skin bonnet, he would leave the living-room stove to walk each day on the ramparts or in a small park where a beautiful pond-haunting kingfisher was his sole companion. From Coleridge they received the hexameters which conclude, 'William, my head and my heart! dear William and dear Dorothea! You have all in each other; but I am lonely, and want you!' When milder weather arrived they left, walking through the Harz forests and mountains, sometimes more than ankle-deep in water. At Osterode, where well-dressed Sunday citizens stared her 'out of countenance', Dorothy was detained until William had presented their credentials to the burgomaster. At Nordhausen they found letters from Coleridge, now a student at Göttingen. Here they met him in April, on their way back to Hamburg. They were returning to the north of England, where they hoped to find a home, preferably in the Lake District and near a large library. They reached Sockburn early in May, and stayed with the Hutchinsons until December.

Wordsworth not only wished to be back in England; he longed to see Mary Hutchinson, as the poem 'I travelled among unknown men' makes clear, if it is remembered that it was sent to her, to be read after 'She dwelt among the untrodden ways' (29.iv.01). The Lucy poems are love poems which were inspired largely by thoughts of Mary, whom many a time, when his conscience made him feel committed to Annette, he must have imagined lost or dead to him. Absence from both told ultimately where his heart lay.

The poetry he wrote in Germany contains some of his choicest work, and he would have written more but for the physical pains he suffered from excitement during composition. He had experienced such effects since adolescence, and they were to continue, making dictation or the copying of his poems by an amauuensis a necessity rather than a convenience. When he did not read, he was consumed with thought and feeling, composition driving him with tempestuous force. No doubt he thought much about *The Recluse*, the philosophical poem Coleridge had encouraged him to write. The many short poems he wrote on varied subjects are indicative of a 'redundant' but frustrated poetic energy. He thought of changing the Salisbury Plain poem; he pruned 'Peter Bell' and probably prepared 'Andrew Jones'. Uncertainty of purpose, combined with thoughts of Annette, made him read Burns's 'Despondency' with 'the deepest agitation' (27.ii.99).

The most eminent of the more miscellaneous poems he wrote in Germany are 'A Poet's Epitaph' and 'Ruth'. The first, taking its thematic form from an epigram by Theocritus (whom Wordsworth contrasts with Bürger, 27.ii.99), and even more from Burns's 'A Bard's Epitaph', is unsparingly sharp in its satire of the intellectual who lives in a world of abstractions, divorced from form and feeling, or from the actual realization of nature and his fellow men. In contrast the poet enjoys 'the harvest of a quiet eye', penetrates the externals of nature, ponders the reality, and does not neglect common life. Fragments (PW5.343–4) throw light on those 'impulses of deeper birth' that 'come to him in solitude', linking them with lines in 'Tintern Abbey', and showing how the poet, 'by sensible impressions not enthralled', sees 'into the life of things'. The stirring, inquisitive mind is 'laid asleep', and the 'godlike senses' (creative as well as receptive) give 'short impulses of life' that seem 'to tell of our existence' and then pass away. At such times of quiet the ear hears not but holds 'manifest communion with the heart'. No sound is heard 'which the heart does not make'; 'all melts away', and 'things that are without Live in our minds as in their native home'. At another time, it seems as if 'the life of the vast world' is 'hushed into a breathless dream'.

'Ruth', the story of another woman driven to madness by desertion, grew from the account Wordsworth heard of a Somerset vagrant. Its exotic impressions, including the head-dress of the seducer and the imaginative magnificence of 'flowers that with one scarlet gleam Cover a hundred leagues, and seem To set the hills on fire', were suggested by Bartram's account of his travels in North America. The poem adds a new dimension to Wordsworth's conception of nature, and may help to explain the lines 'Whate'er exists hath properties that spread Beyond itself, communicating good, A simple blessing, or with evil mixed' (Ex.ix.10−12). The stripling with the dancing crest had roamed with Indians; his impetuous blood had derived a kindred impulse from tropical storms, and 'voluptuous thought' from nature's luxuriance. 'Pure hopes of high intent' must have come to him from the 'beauteous forms' of nature, Wordsworth adds, but his 'moral frame' had been impaired by 'wild men's vices', and he lacked self-control. The implication is that some natural forms lend themselves to immoral suggestion, but only when the mind is corrupted. 'The Danish Boy' was 'entirely a fancy', Wordsworth wrote, but it may have been suggested by a tradition in the Quantock region (which seems to supply the setting), though it has been ascribed to West Cumberland.[2] It was designed to introduce a ballad on a prince who had fled battle and, 'for the sake of the valuables about him', been murdered by the cottager in whose home he had taken refuge. As in 'Hart-leap Well', the place of the crime is smitten with nature's curse, but the boy is serene, though he sings of war, and his melody pleases hill flocks, herds, and mountain ponies.

Enforced leisure at Goslar had set Wordsworth thinking about Hawkshead. Hence the 'Matthew' poems, including the 'Address to the Scholars of the Village School of −'. The latter shows that the schoolmaster of these poems is a composite figure; his death recalls that of William Taylor, but he is aged, with white hair, and remembered for his wild ways and mother-wit. The elegies from which the dirge was drawn (PW4.452−5) show plainly (like the title of the poem) that the subject is the village schoolmaster, and T. W. Thompson has identified him with John Harrison, whose daughter died at the age of eight. The tablet with 'Its history of two hundred years' continues the disguise in 'Matthew', though Wordsworth's notes on the poem do not indicate that the school is Hawkshead Grammar School or that the master is Taylor. 'Like the Wanderer in "The Excursion", this schoolmaster was made up of several both of his class and men of other occupations', he states. Matthew's character remains consistent throughout, and comes to life in the two conversational poems, 'The Two April Mornings' and 'The Fountain'.

The first answers the question why Matthew sighs on a sunny April morning when he and the poet are walking merrily to spend a day among the hills. His reply evokes a scene brought back to memory by a cloud cleft with purple over a mountain to the east. On such a morning, when he was out angling, he visited his daughter's grave and, turning away, saw a beautiful girl tripping freely by the churchyard yew, and as happy as a dancing sea-wave. He could not suppress a sigh, but did not wish her his. Present and past combine to reinforce dramatically the emotional charge of a poem which moves with seemingly natural simplicity, and remains vividly fixed in the imagination. 'The Fountain' also has a deep undercurrent of regret. People, especially the 'man of mirth', accept old age reluctantly, unlike the birds and the streamlet which flows merrily from the fountain, as it will for a thousand years. The joy that Matthew describes belongs to the past, but the thought reverses that of Gray's 'Ode on the Pleasure arising from Vicissitude'; it is man only who, in Shelley's words, pines for what is not. Instead of presenting this in a familiar way, as in 'The Small Celandine' ('O man, that from thy fair and shining youth Age might but take the things youth needed not!'), Wordsworth presents the paradoxical obverse: 'the wiser mind', Matthew claims, 'Mourns less for what age takes away Than what it leaves behind'. The poet assures him that he will be a son to him in place of his dead children, but Matthew insists that this is impossible. Nevertheless, nature drives away his despondency, until he is in the mood to sing his witty song about the 'bewildered chimes' at Hawkshead, as the poet had requested earlier.

Thoughts of finding a home in the north of England mingled with boyhood recollections to produce some of Wordsworth's most successful description. The opening of one passage (retained for the inception proper of *The Prelude*) —

> Was it for this
> That one, the fairest of all rivers, loved
> To blend his murmurs with my nurse's song,
> And from his alder shades, and rocky falls,
> And from his fords and shallows, sent a voice
> That flowed along my dreams?

— suggests that he was already contemplating an autobiographical introduction to *The Recluse*. All the recollections except 'Nutting' were revised for inclusion in *The Prelude*: 'There was a boy' (not greatly modified, v.364—88), the 'stolen' boat and skating passages (i), and his impression of the Gondo gorge after crossing the Alps.

Dorothy's recollection of a child who was lost in a snowstorm near

Halifax led to the writing of 'Lucy Gray'. The actualizing detail of
the poem is soon evident, and the persistence of the parents' search
is effectively communicated in a succession of factually precise
images, boldly linked with repetitive conjunctions. This matter-of-
factness does not militate against the author's purpose, which was
to combine reality with imaginative effects. Above all, Wordsworth perpetuates the grace of the dead girl, and her vitality; it
abides in quickening imagery ('Not blither is the mountain roe
. . . smoke'). Together, they are communicated in the child's
happy self-confidence, the poet's music, and the song of life with
which, like 'The Solitary Reaper', the poem ends:

> — Yet some maintain that to this day
> She is a living child;
> That you may see sweet Lucy Gray
> Upon the lonesome wild.
>
> O'er rough and smooth she trips along,
> And never looks behind;
> And sings a solitary song
> That whistles in the wind.

It is unfortunate that 'Lucy Gray' has been associated with the
'Lucy' poems. Of the four which were written in Germany, 'Strange
fits of passion' and 'Three years she grew' are idiosyncratic.
Whether the first is based to any extent on actual experience, at
Racedown or elsewhere, whether the thought occurred first with
reference to Dorothy or to Mary Hutchinson when she was living
there, or whether the subject of the poem is wholly imaginary, are
all unanswerable questions. It presents a thought which surprises
the lover himself in a way which only a lover will understand. He
rides along, and the movement of his horse is deliberately evoked in
'hoof after hoof He raised, and never stopped'. Like the lover in 'A
slumber did my spirit seal', he is suddenly jolted out of his serenity,
when the bright moon (its emblem) on which he had fixed his gaze
suddenly drops behind the roof of her dwelling, and by a flash of
imaginative analogy he is smitten with the fear that Lucy may be
dead. Wordsworth is not interested in romance or passion, only in
the working of the mind at a point of heightened emotion. The
success of the poem could be measured by contrasting it with a
Bürger ballad.

'Three years she grew' was composed in the Harz Forest, and this might be regarded as presumptive evidence that its Lucy is Dorothy. But here, as in most of these poems, the heroine is an idealization. Personal and elegiac qualities are subordinated to a pattern of education which Wordsworth had deduced from his own early experiences, and which took its final form in the first book of *The Prelude*. Both Lucy and he are chosen or 'favored' beings; in girlhood and boyhood they learn from experience. Nature kindles or restrains; it is both law and impulse: it teaches by beauty and by fear; it impresses 'upon all forms the characters of danger or desire'. The love of nature which supervenes later affects not only the mind and spirit, as is stressed in 'Tintern Abbey', but features and physique, as Wordsworth re-asserts in *The Prelude* (xiii.279–87):

> Also, about this time did I receive
> Convictions still more strong than heretofore,
> Not only that the inner frame is good,
> And graciously composed, but that, no less,
> Nature for all conditions wants not power
> To consecrate, if we have eyes to see,
> The outside of her creatures, and to breathe
> Grandeur upon the very humblest face
> Of human life.

Death or the thought of death links the above two Lucy poems with 'She dwelt among the untrodden ways' and 'A slumber did my spirit seal'. The former takes its colour and tone from the middle stanza, where the imagery, like Wordsworth's skylark, is true to the kindred points of heaven and home; it emphasizes solitude and modesty, and suggests the co-ordinates of life on earth. The exclamatory emotional release with which the lyric concludes has been the frequent butt of parodists, but it expresses the inexpressible in a manner which compares favourably with, for example, Arnold's straining for grandeur at the end of 'Requiescat'. (Like the 'kisses four' in Keats's 'La Belle Dame', the 'springs of Dove' may have been dictated by the demand of rhyme, but it is possible that Wordsworth had north Yorkshire, not Derbyshire, in mind.)

'A slumber did my spirit seal' is philosophical and detached rather than personal; it excites reflection rather than emotion. Few poems of such brevity and apparent simplicity convey as much.

How well-chosen Wordsworth's metaphors are, and at the same time so general that they hardly call attention to themselves, may be seen in 'slumber' and 'seal'. The deftness of 'touch' illustrates the critical care with which simple words are chosen; 'diurnal' is exceptional in its uncommonness, but singularly appropriate, its sound imparting the grandeur which the sense demands (with double alliterative reinforcement from 'rolled round'), as in the 'diurnal round' of the skating passage. The force of the poem depends on the shock of contrasts: the lover's blithe assumption and the death of his love before he has discovered the fragility of life's thread; the vitality of the girl and her insensibility in death; the fleetingness and minute significance of individual life in the universe of space and time. The girl moulded by nature belongs to nature after her death; there is neither mourning nor consolation, only recognition.

Although Dorothy may have been in his mind when Wordsworth wrote 'Strange fits of passion' and 'Three years she grew', the elegiac theme of the Lucy poems associates them strongly with Mary Hutchinson for the reason already given, with confirmation in the circumstances connected with 'I travelled among unknown men'. In this respect, 'The Glow-worm', the last of the group to be written, is especially significant. Based on an incident at Racedown, it undoubtedly recalls Dorothy's transports; yet it was not written until seven years later, soon after Wordsworth parted from Mary Hutchinson on his way to Grasmere. Their marriage had been decided, and the poem is transfused with a lover's emotions; it was composed with Mary principally in mind.[3] Wordsworth had found the image which expressed her spirit (cf. Pr.xiv.270–5), and the image recalled his glow-worm offering to Dorothy. (Oversensitiveness to the kind of criticism spearheaded by Jeffrey in *The Edinburgh Review* induced him to withhold his most ardent love lyric from publication after 1807.)

William and Dorothy stayed on at Sockburn, simply because they had little income. Cottle paid the remainder of his debt and offered to add interest, which Wordsworth refused. He probably helped Tom Hutchinson on his largely pastoral farm, within a loop of the Tees east of Darlington. His poetical activities were concentrated on his boyhood and youth, and he completed the first (two-part) unit of his autobiographical poem, a far more satisfying whole than the first two books of *The Prelude* later assumed. It is devoted entirely to his early years, and contains four additional passages: on the recovery of the drowned man by the shore of Esthwaite; the two 'spots of time' (Pr.xii.208–61, 287–326); and the Coniston scene where 'that sense of dim similitude' which links moral feelings with external forms had been stirred, making him associate the love he would always retain for his native regions with the image of the lingering radiance cast by the setting sun on the hills where it rose.

The Prelude was under way. Coleridge had returned to England and, in his answer to Wordsworth on the subject, wrote:

> O let it be the tailpiece of 'The Recluse'! for of nothing but 'The Recluse' can I hear patiently. That it should be addressed to me makes me more desirous that it should not be a poem of itself. To be addressed as a beloved man, by a thinker, at the close of such a poem . . . is the only event, I believe, capable of exciting in me an hour's vanity.

He had already sent Wordsworth another idea for the poem: 'I wish you would write a poem, in blank verse, addressed to those, who, in consequence of the complete failure of the French Revolution, have thrown up all hopes of the amelioration of mankind, and are sinking into an almost epicurean selfishness, disguising the same under the soft titles of domestic attachment and contempt for visionary *philosophes*.' It might form part of *The Recluse*, he added, 'for in my present mood I am wholly against the publication of any small poems'.

At one point Wordsworth had thought of returning to Alfoxden should the opportunity arise, but now, to Coleridge's regret, he had decided to stay in the north. Cottle accepted an invitation to visit him, travelling with Coleridge by post-chaise. All three set out for a tour of the Lakes, but Cottle was soon deterred, and made his way home from Greta Bridge near Barnard Castle. Wordsworth and Coleridge travelled by mail-coach over Stainmore to Temple Sowerby, where John Wordsworth came to meet them at William's request. He was on leave, and had come north to attend the funeral of uncle Kit, who had died suddenly at Newbiggin Hall and left Dorothy £100. Wordsworth refused to visit his aunt, holding her responsible for the denial of dues to himself, his brothers, and Dorothy. The next day John joined the two poets. They walked to Haweswater, over to Long Sleddale, and on to Windermere and Hawkshead. Neither the new, whitewashed villages by

Windermere nor the Assembly Room which had been built where the old grey stone stood in Hawkshead market-place pleased them. They then proceeded to Rydal and Grasmere, which they made their centre for five days, staying at Robert Newton's inn opposite the church. After accompanying John as far as Grisedale Tarn on his return to Newbiggin, Wordsworth and Coleridge moved on to Keswick, where William wrote to Dorothy, informing her that he and John had discussed having a house built by the lake at Grasmere, and that there was a small one to let. The sightseers then went on to Bassenthwaite, Cockermouth, Crummock Water, and Buttermere, where they saw Mary Robinson of the Fish Inn (cf. Pr.vii.296ff.), then to Ennerdale (where they heard the story which led to the writing of 'The Brothers') and on to Wastdale Head, back to Keswick via Borrowdale, then via Threlkeld and Matterdale to Ullswater. So ended their tour of the Lakes. Coleridge returned to Sockburn, where he fell in love with Sara Hutchinson, before setting off for London and writing the poem finally entitled 'Love'. Meanwhile Wordsworth had returned to Grasmere and made arrangements to rent Dove Cottage.[4]

On 17 December he and Dorothy left Sockburn on their four-day journey to Grasmere. Starting by moonlight, they rode with George Hutchinson to a point eight miles beyond Richmond on their way into Wensleydale; before their walk began, they saw the setting, and heard the story, of 'Hart-leap Well'. The days were short, the weather bleak, the roads hard and frosty, and they encountered snow-showers; even so, they did not fail to visit spectacular waterfalls near their route. They stayed the third night at Kendal (after arranging to spend some of uncle Kit's legacy on the purchase of furniture) and the next day set off to Dove Cottage by post-chaise. There was much to do in a cold and almost empty house; soon they were 'overhead in confusion, painting the rooms, mending the doors, and heaven knows what!' Both were happy despite colds; they had kind neighbours, and William had realized the dream that had been his since, 'a roving school-boy', he had first seen the Vale of Grasmere from the brow of the hill across the lake. The hard weather continued, and soon Rydal Water was covered with ice as 'clear as polished steel'. William 'procured' a pair of skates, intending to 'give [his] body to the wind' on the morrow, which was Christmas Day. He had already made progress with 'The Brothers'.

Home at Grasmere (1800–2)

The small lattice-windowed house which William and Dorothy occupied at Town End, to the south-east of the main village of Grasmere, had once been 'The Dove and Olive Bough' inn, from which its name 'Dove Cottage' originated in more recent times. Dorothy made the wainscoted room downstairs (formerly the bar-room) her kitchen, and the adjacent room her bedroom; she had a scullery at the back, and Molly Fisher came in from one of the houses opposite to help her two or three hours a day at two shillings a week. The larger room upstairs, where Wordsworth kept his books and worked when severe weather kept him indoors, became the living-room, and the neighbouring one (which had smoked 'like a furnace') his bedroom. There were two other rooms upstairs, one overlooking the back garden, the other an 'out-jutting' one at the side (which Dorothy papered with local news-papers).

As the cottage was open to the Ambleside-Keswick road, a small space at the front was enclosed with upright stone flags to form a garden in which Dorothy grew wild and cultivated flowers; William found room for peas and other vegetables, including scarlet-runner beans which were strung to the house. Behind it, a small garden, called 'the orchard' because it contained a few fruit trees, rose sharply and provided, over the cottage roof, a view of the lake and, away to the right, of the church, Helm Crag, and 'two-thirds of the vale'. The lower slopes of Rydal Fell, thick with bracken and saplings, came down to the garden. The road to Ambleside rose steeply and branched, one route passing White Moss Tarn, the other rounding White Moss above Bainriggs wood and the lake, and turning east to join the other above Rydal Water. The road through Grasmere climbed the Vale to the north, passed over Dunmail Raise, and continued above Thirlmere and below the slopes of Helvellyn towards Keswick.

About two hundred people lived in and around Grasmere, and of these twenty-six were 'statesmen', small farmers whose freehold estates remained undivided on inheritance. Wordsworth tended to regard the place as a perfect republic of shepherds and agriculturists, but, whatever the traditional equality of respect, changes were already making inroads for the worse. The decline in home production of yarn and cloth caused by the growth of manufacturing towns forced poorer 'statesmen' to sell land to the rich, and inequality increased. Wordsworth, who had once accepted the Godwinian doctrine that private property was undesirable, soon realized at Grasmere how much depression was caused by its loss. Feeling assured of Charles James Fox's conviction that 'the most sacred of all property is the property of the poor', he wrote to this eminent politician, emphasizing the importance of land as a 'permanent rallying point' for the domestic affections (14.i.01). 'Repentance, A Pastoral Ballad' is based on the experience of the Ashburners, who lived opposite the Wordsworths and had exhausted themselves, by carding and spinning from five o'clock in the morning, in fruitless efforts to save their fields. The same question underlies 'Michael'; and the moral strengthening which comes from family ties with the landscape is, as has already been noted, one of the subjects of 'Home at Grasmere'.

John Wordsworth arrived in January 1800 and stayed until the end of September; he was waiting until the *Earl of Abergavenny*, to which he had just been appointed captain, returned from the East. Rather taciturn but devoted, he deeply appreciated William's poetry, and was ready to help him in every possible way. His ambition was to make enough money by private trading to build a house for William and Dorothy, and another for himself, at Grasmere. The two brothers went fishing together, often with Mr Sympson, an octogenarian who lived at High Broadrain near the head of the Vale, and had long been vicar of Wythburn, just beyond Dunmail Raise. Mary Hutchinson stayed at Dove Cottage from the end of February until early April. She was followed by Coleridge, who had been working in London for *The Morning Post*. At Keswick, he found that Greta Hall was to let; he admired its prospect above the river and, knowing that Poole had tried in vain to find him a house, became interested in the possibility of living near Wordsworth again. After his departure, William and John made their way across the Pennines to see the Hutchinsons. Dorothy walked with them as far as Low Wood, and returned to

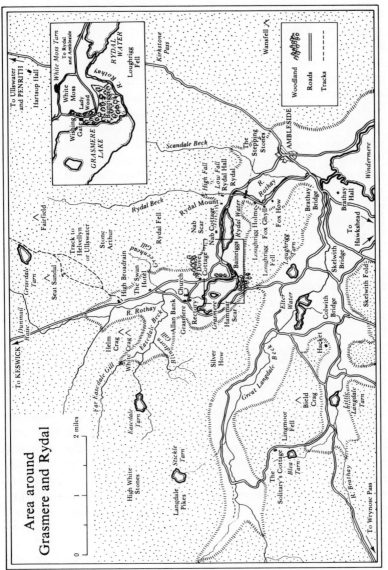

Area around
Grasmere and Rydal

Map 2

begin her Grasmere journal. 'My heart was so full that I could hardly speak to W. when I gave him a farewell kiss. I sate a long time upon a stone at the margin of [Windermere], and after a flood of tears my heart was easier', she wrote. Little is known of the brothers' itinerary; they did much sight-seeing undoubtedly, for the only evidence that exists indicates that they went out of their way to visit Yordas, a cave near Ingleton,[5] and Gordale Scar near Malham. Tom and George Hutchinson had each taken a farm, the former at Gallow Hill near Scarborough, his sisters Mary and Joanna keeping house for him, the latter at Bishop Middleham (near Bishop Auckland) with Sara. The Wordsworths, who were absent three weeks, stayed most of the time with Tom, and William was disappointed not to meet Francis Wrangham, his former co-adjutor in Juvenalian satire, at Hunmanby, where he held a rich living.

At the end of July, Coleridge reached Grasmere with his family, on their way to Keswick; they remained with the Wordsworths nearly four weeks, during two of which Coleridge was rheumatically ill. Domestically unhappy, and a prey to opium since 1797, he was more dependent on William and Dorothy than they realized. He had told Southey that William was the only man to whom he felt in every way inferior; more recently he had declared that Wordsworth's equal had not appeared since Milton. When he had recovered, they all picnicked on the island in the middle of Grasmere. A few days later the Coleridges left for Greta Hall. A second volume of *Lyrical Ballads*, for which he hoped to complete 'Christabel', was being planned. Visitors continued in September, among them Mr Marshall, husband of Dorothy's friend Jane, and Robert Jones, who returned to stay for a week. It was on their way home, after parting from the latter, that William and Dorothy met the leech-gatherer, 'an old man almost double', and learnt about his life. John left at the end of the month, and they accompanied him as far as Grisedale Tarn, where they remained, with Ullswater in view, till he was out of sight. It was the last time they saw him in the Lake District.

Wordsworth had just completed his lengthy preface for the forthcoming edition of *Lyrical Ballads*; he would never have thought of it but for Coleridge's persuasion. Some difficult decisions were eventually reached, Coleridge judging that Wordsworth was the true poet, and he himself no more than a metaphysician. The most crucial led to the omission of the incomplete 'Christabel', which meant that all the poems in the second volume were Wordsworth's. Modifications in the first volume included the transfer of 'The Ancient Mariner', in a less archaic form, from the beginning to the end. The emphasis was to be on poems of common life, and Coleridge would agree to no more than an anonymous acknowledgment to himself as 'a friend' who had furnished 'The Ancient Mariner', 'The Foster-Mother's Tale', 'The Nightingale' (new), 'The Dungeon', and 'Love' (substituted for 'The Convict'). The publication of *Lyrical Ballads* (1800) was delayed until January 1801, principally because Wordsworth was busy until December preparing 'Michael' to replace 'Christabel'. He had suffered from ill-health at various times during the year.

Nearly all the poetry in the second volume had been written in Germany or since. To the latter period belong all but the last of 'Poems on the Naming of Places'. A wild vernal nook in Easedale is associated with Dorothy; a calm recess (among the untrodden ways in the woods above Rydal Water), with Mary Hutchinson; Stone Arthur peak, with William's love of solitude. The scene in each reflects the character. The dedication of the second poem in this blank-verse group to Joanna Hutchinson arose from the memory of her laughter. She had not passed her youth 'amid the smoke of cities', and had she been at Grasmere in the summer of 1800 she would surely have been mentioned in Dorothy's journal. The question does not arise, for the poem states that she had been living afar for two long years. Dorothy's indication in *Recollections of a Tour in Scotland* (21 August) that the story is untrue applies to the whole poem, not merely to the part where the author admitted extravagance. The passage illustrates an admirable manipulation of mountain names:

> The rock, like something starting from a sleep,
> Took up the lady's voice, and laughed again;
> That ancient woman seated on Helm-crag
> Was ready with her cavern; Hammar-scar,
> And the tall steep of Silver-how, sent forth
> A noise of laughter; southern Loughrigg heard,
> And Fairfield answered with a mountain tone;
> Helvellyn far into the clear blue sky
> Carried the lady's voice, — old Skiddaw blew
> His speaking-trumpet; — back out of the clouds
> Of Glaramara southward came the voice;
> And Kirkstone tossed it from his misty head.

As narrator, Wordsworth had given free rein to his fancy, intending his echoic effects 'to divert or partly play upon the vicar', and preparing the reader for this in the lines which begin, 'Now, by those dear immunities of heart Engendered between malice and true love'. The fourth poem records an incident when Wordsworth was walking with Coleridge and Dorothy along the shore by Bainriggs wood. The rash judgment theme presents one of Wordsworth's solitaries memorably, but without the imaginative overtones of 'Resolution and Independence'; it ends with needless underscoring: 'Nor did we fail to see within ourselves What need there is to be reserved in speech, And temper all our thoughts with charity.' The heavy human implications of the climactic scene contrast with the light diversionary images that precede it, and with the alien grace delectably associated with the tall Queen Osmunda fern, lovelier in its retired abode than 'Naiad by the side Of Grecian brook, or Lady of the Mere, Sole-sitting by the shores of old Romance'. 'The Fir Grove' ('When to the attractions of the busy world') commemorates fraternal sympathies. When the poet came to Grasmere in the bleak winter, he used to visit Lady Wood on the western side of White Moss, hoping to find a sheltered space where he could walk to and fro as he composed. Not finding it, he worked elsewhere until the spring, when he returned to find a track worn among the trees by his brother as he paced up and down as if on deck. He remembers John's love of nature at Hawkshead, and regards him as a silent poet. In the final passage, written when John was at sea (perhaps as late as 1802) Wordsworth imagines that often while he treads the path, the fir grove murmuring with a sea-like sound, his brother may be pacing the deck far away, 'muttering the verses which I muttered first among the mountains'. The wish that they and others whom they love may meet again in 'Grasmere's happy vale' was never granted.

Among the miscellaneous poems of 1800 are 'The Waterfall and the Eglantine' and 'The Oak and the Broom', a late but idiosyncratic contribution to the variety of eighteenth-century fable. Two poems of ballad origin are of interest. The story of 'The Seven Sisters' (a version of which Coleridge was allowed for financial reasons to publish in *The Morning Post*) stems from a German poem, and compares very favourably with 'Ellen Irwin', which is moulded on the stanza of Bürger's 'Lenore'. Its story derives from a ballad which appeared later as 'Fair Helen of Kirconnell' in Scott's *Minstrelsy of the Scottish Border*. One need only compare the second part of this with 'Ellen Irwin' to see how Wordsworth's versification is afflicted with prosiness: 'From many knights and many squires The Bruce had been selected; And Gordon, fairest of them all, By Ellen was rejected.' The classical comparison introduced at the outset to prepare the reader for a new experimental style accentuates the artificiality of the poem.

Wordsworth's adoption of fashionable anapaests in 'The Reverie of Poor Susan' and 'The Childless Father' marks another misjudgment. His date for the former (first 1801–2, then 1797) is unreliable; it draws its title from the poem which he thought Bürger's 'most perfect', and its subject (as Legouis pointed out) from the Abbé Delille. Outward appearances are deceptive: a note of enchantment makes Susan pine for her home in the country, and the tragic past is not forgotten as old Timothy goes to the chase. The same metre befits the poet's unsqueamish attitude in 'The Farmer of Tilsbury Vale' (whose story he had heard from Thomas Poole); like Susan's, the sense of exile in an 'old Adam' is expressed in visions conjured up by natural appearances in London. Similarly the anapaestic beat in 'The Two Thieves' (a recollection of Hawkshead) accords with the poet's amused tolerance.

Although sketched with graphic detail, an arresting pastoral incident in 'The Idle Shepherd-Boys' lacks imaginative power, and is finally reduced to a cautionary tale. 'A Pet-Lamb' is a difficult subject, dependent on the excited thoughts and feelings of a child; Wordsworth is carried along too uncritically by a tripping metre, touching the sentimental at times, and concluding ingenuously with the reckoning that the 'ballad' he recalled line by line was more the singer's than his own. ''Tis said, that some have died for love' is more convincing and poetical; the disconsolate lover's feelings are movingly expressed in rhythms and responses to visible and audible images which catch his attention as he tries vainly to find peace of mind.

 'Hart-leap Well' is written in Wordsworth's more assured manner, the first part telling the story he had heard from a shepherd between Richmond and Wensleydale. Two similes describing Sir Walter's horse at the end of the chase are notable: 'weak as a lamb the hour that it is yeaned' and 'white with foam as if with cleaving sleet'. The anticipatory note of 'doleful' in the first part is confirmed in the 'more doleful place did never eye survey' of the second, and the impression is reinforced when the 'last deep groan' of the hart as he expires by the spring is recalled in the 'dolorous groan' of the water at subsequent intervals. The second part of the poem supplies the comment, the most imaginative being implicit in the shepherd's reflections on the 'thoughts' and feelings that may have urged the hart in the last stages of his desperate flight. In the opening lines Wordsworth repeats the gist of his aerial pro- logue in 'Peter Bell': rather than attempt to 'freeze the blood' or resort to moving accidents, he prefers 'a simple song for thinking hearts'. The shepherd's 'thinking heart' contrasts with the patron- izing tone of Sir Walter, who builds a pleasure-house to celebrate the feat of the 'gallant stag'. The poet-narrator shares the shepherd's feelings, but his final comment, 'Never to blend our pleasure or our pride With sorrow of the meanest thing that feels' seems superfluous. The bad taste of the jubilant Sir Walter is suf- ficient evidence of his lack of feeling, and the poem has its place in the Ancient Mariner-Peter Bell category. More important, but more questionable, is the contention that the Being which exists in all nature 'Maintains a deep and reverential care For the un- offending creatures whom he loves', that the hart's death was 'mourned by sympathy divine', and that Nature would express her sorrow and condemnation for an act of inhumanity until 'the coming of the milder day'. 'Hart-leap Well' was one of the first poems to be concluded at Dove Cottage, and a passage written not long afterwards in 'Home at Grasmere' not only clarifies this hope of man's amelioration (in response to nature) but indicates that Wordsworth's use of 'God' does not necessarily imply orthodox belief, even in *The Excursion*:

> And when the trance
> Came to us, as we stood by Hart-leap Well,
> The intimation of the milder day
> Which is to be, the fairer world than this,
> And rais'd us up, dejected as we were,
> Among the records of that doleful place,
> By sorrow for the hunted beast who there
> Had yielded up his breath, the awful trance,
> The vision of humanity, and of God
> The Mourner, God the Sufferer, when the heart
> Of his poor creatures suffers wrongfully —
> Both in the sadness and the joy we found
> A promise and an earnest that we twain . . .

Might, even thus early, for ourselves secure,
And in the midst of these unhappy times,
A portion of the blessedness which love
And knowledge will, we trust, hereafter give
To all the vales of earth and all mankind.

'Thrice hath the winter moon been filled with light' since the 'dear vale' of Grasmere 'received us' and 'heard the poet mutter his prelusive songs', runs one of the passages of 'Home at Grasmere' which were written in 1800. Another refers to their 'beautiful and quiet home'; to John, the 'never-resting pilgrim of the sea', a 'stranger of our father's house' who is with them; and to prospective visits from 'sisters of our hearts' (the Hutchinsons) and from Coleridge, 'a brother of our hearts, philosopher and poet'. Another concerns two swans which had been conspicuous at the centre of the lake, and been loved not just for their beauty, placidity, and constancy, but because they were a solitary pair and strangers, like themselves; now they have disappeared, perhaps been parted or killed by the 'deadly tube' of dalesmen. As, when low-hung mists rise, features of a new region are steadily revealed, so people, animals, and birds in the Vale are becoming familiar. Such passages were to be linked and extended; like 'The Ruined Cottage', they were 'prelusive' to *The Recluse*, which never reached even a final planning. The subject-matter of 'Home at Grasmere' illustrates the danger that lay ahead for Wordsworth in undertaking so comprehensive a work. An interesting fragment, never finally prepared for publication, it shows a tendency to write freely and at random, even on little things; and clearly underlines Wordsworth's need for the discipline of a limited design to elicit his best creative thought.

The year began with 'The Brothers' and ended with 'Michael', two of the most genuine poems in the English pastoral tradition. The merit of the former lies not only in its seemingly natural dialogue but also in the artistry with which it is directed towards achieving irony, suspense, and a climax of emotional effect, without ever transgressing the limits of a chance conversation. For Coleridge, it was a pastoral model, which he could never read with unclouded eye. Wordsworth's apology for its abrupt opening, with the explanation that the poem was intended as the last of a series, is redundant; it is arrestingly dramatic, and stresses the repeated irony of the vicar's rash judgment, his self-centred failure to recognise Leonard, and his bland assumption that he is an idle tourist. The tension created by the garrulity of the one and the restrained heartfelt curiosity of the other acts with increasing cogency. Leonard, the brother who has returned from sea, is drawn from John Wordsworth. The dark cleft caused by lightning in the huge crag (Pillar Rock, Ennerdale), with the consequent disappearance of one of its two companion springs, is a pre-monitory image cast up amid the informative chatter of a priest whose 'gay complacency' makes one wonder if he was any the sadder and wiser when he learned the truth. Leonard, hearing of his brother's death, returns to sea, relinquishing his cherished hope of living for the remainder of his days in his native vale. His role suggests that, had Hardy's John Lackland been given a com-parable tragic involvement in one of the tales he heard, he would have been more memorable, and the whole design of *A Few Crusted Characters* would have benefited in artistry and depth.

Two local stories supplied a basis for 'Michael': one, like Luke's, from a family who had lived at 'The Dove and Olive Bough'; the other, that of a shepherd who had spent seven years building a sheepfold in Greenhead Gill. Much that Wordsworth composed, after visiting its remains with Dorothy on 11 October, was rejected, including two passages (PW2.480–2) of special interest. One des-cribes how the boy Luke dislodged a tuft of snow which, gathering size and pace as it fell down the slope, divided, spreading a host of subdivisions, until the mountain side seemed to be 'Raced over by a thousand living things, Ten thousand snow-white rabbits of the cliffs'; and how he would whoop for joy at the sight, and point to the form of a gigantic tree, traced by those elfin runners in the snow and starting at his feet. The other emphasizes how emotions from such experiences of childhood onwards are 'sanctified' by such memorable scenes, which bind them together, preserving affinities 'between all stages of the life of man':

> Hence with more pleasure far than others feel,
> Led by his son, this shepherd now went back
> Into the years which he himself had lived;
> And natural feelings coming from within
> And from without, he to the present time
> Link'd the dear memory of old histories,
> Not with the loose and garrulous tongue of age,
> But even as with a young man's eloquence,

Adding thereto the tenderness of years.
Hence may you guess the joy of Michael's heart
When with his son he clomb on Fairfield side.

One incident in Luke's life found a place in *The Prelude*, 1805 (viii.222–311), and was later omitted because of its disproportionate length. Wordsworth heard the tale from Ann Tyson, and this suggests that she told him the Luke story, for the opening of 'Michael' refers to it as the first of those domestic tales which appealed to him as a boy, making him love shepherds not 'For their own sakes, but for the fields and hills Where was their occupation and abode'. The story of Robert (not Richard) Bateman was well known, and Wordsworth had often passed the church he founded at Ings on the Kendal road near Windermere.

Wordsworth told Fox (14.i.01) that 'The Brothers' and 'Michael' were faithful copies from nature, illustrating the 'domestic affections' of statesmen, whose 'little tract of land' was like 'a fountain fitted to the nature of social man from which supplies of affection, as pure as his heart was intended for, are daily drawn'. He often thought of Poole's character in delineating Michael, his aim being 'to give a picture of a man, of strong mind and lively sensibility, agitated by two of the most powerful affections of the human heart; the parental affection, and the love of property, *landed* property, including the feelings of inheritance, home, and personal and family independence' (9.iv.01). 'Michael' is a moving story, for which Wordsworth assumes imaginative readers or 'thinking hearts'. Its preliminary emphasis is on the bond which grows between father and son, the 'forward-looking thoughts' that the child brings to Michael in his old age, the 'feelings and emanations' that spring from companionship with the boy, and the association of him with acts in particular places, happy reminders which give new life to 'the old man's heart'. Humour lights up the realism of Luke's early efforts to assist, 'the urchin, as you will divine', being 'something between a hindrance and a help'. The emotion is implicit rather than overtly expressed, and the poet can ensure the effect he desires only through rhythmical control and rightly proportioned presentation. The story is carefully prepared, and moves more rapidly as it nears its conclusion. Little attention is given to the way in which the covenant is betrayed by Luke in 'the dissolute city', and this more than any other feature underlines the discipline Wordsworth imposed on his material. Its climactic subject is not the extrinsics of sensation, but the suffering of an old man whose lifelong hopes are broken. These hopes are conveyed musically in the simplest of words as Michael asks Luke to lay the stone:

> do thou thy part;
> I will do mine. – I will begin again
> With many tasks that were resigned to thee:
> Up to the heights, and in among the storms,
> Will I without thee go again, and do
> All works which I was wont to do alone,
> Before I knew thy face.

In memorable lines Wordsworth characteristically stresses the support in lasting sorrow of the love which he felt was the key to life's grandeur: 'There is a comfort in the strength of love; 'Twill make a thing endurable, which else Would overset the brain, or break the heart.' The sorrow is expressed less in the statements (which could have been plain prose) than in their unfaltering purity of tone:

> And to that hollow dell from time to time
> Did he repair, to build the fold of which
> His flock had need. 'Tis not forgotten yet
> The pity which was then in every heart
> For the old man – and 'tis believed by all
> That many and many a day he thither went,
> And never lifted up a single stone.

Such writing illustrates what Wordsworth had in mind when he asked in 'Home at Grasmere':

> Is there not
> An art, a music, and a stream of words
> That shall be life, the acknowledged voice of life?
> Shall speak of what is done among the fields
> Done truly there, or felt, of solid good
> And real evil, yet be sweet withal,
> More grateful, more harmonious than the breath
> The idle breath of sweetest pipe attuned
> To pastoral fancies?

'The Affliction of M —' (intended originally, it seems, for *Lyrical Ballads*) was written in the hope of helping the poor widow at Penrith whose sorrows are the subject of this dramatic soliloquy; having received no tidings of her son for years, she had formed the habit of leaving her shop to ask any passing stranger if he had news of him. Among the poems in which Wordsworth traces the thoughts of maternal grief, none contains finer verse than this; it illustrates the virtues of simplicity, but does not exclude a more elevated language; and it clearly demonstrates that, whenever it was finished, he was no longer bound by any theory of poetic diction. The question, he had realized, depends not so much on the kind of language appropriate to the 'speaker' in a dramatic lyric as on the language most likely to evoke the right response in the reader.

Sara Hutchinson arrived in November, and stayed several weeks, helping Dorothy in the final copying of poems for *Lyrical Ballads*. William, tired from exertions (including the writing of the Preface) and illnesses, made little strenuous effort to write. He was worried about Coleridge's domestic unhappiness and ill-health, and sometimes about his own prospects. John sent him his old clothes, and made Dorothy an allowance of £20 a year, before leaving for his next voyage, in which Wordsworth had invested part of his capital. Visits were paid to Greta Hall, and to Eusemere, home of Thomas Clarkson, an eminent campaigner for the abolition of slavery; his wife became a great admirer of William's poetry, and one of Dorothy's chief correspondents. In September Wordsworth made his first visit to Scotland, accompanying Basil Montagu (and his bride's family) to witness his marriage in Glasgow. In November Coleridge left Keswick, ostensibly to spend the worst of the winter in London and Somerset; Mary Hutchinson came to Grasmere, where she remained until the end of the year.

Poetically 1801 had been almost fallow for William. 'I travelled among unknown men' had been sent to Mary in April. 'Louisa' and 'To a Young Lady' may have been written early in the new year, for the latter was published in *The Morning Post* of 11 February 1802. These poems, first intended as one, are felicitously written in the stanza of 'Three years she grew'. In them the poet sees the vitality of a 'child of Nature' first in her youth; then beyond, from marriage to 'an old age serene and bright, And lovely as a Lapland night'. The lady of the two poems is thought to be an idealization, though the adjunct to the title of the second ('who had been reproached for taking long walks in the country') suggests Dorothy; their general tenor, and the probable time of their composition, however, point to Mary Hutchinson.

Wordsworth could not afford to buy books, and had read nothing new since he came to Grasmere. In the autumn he turned to Spenser and Chaucer, the latter in John's set of Dr Anderson's *Works of the British Poets*. But for this massive collection, he would not have become acquainted as soon as he did with Daniel, Drayton, and other Elizabethan poets. In December, probably as a diversion when he was unable to settle to *The Recluse*, he began modernizations of Chaucer in verse; first, 'The Manciple's Tale' (which suggests he was far from prudish), then 'The Prioress's Tale' and a passage from *Troilus and Cressida*. He also translated 'The Cuckoo and the Nightingale', unaware that Anderson's text was faulty, and that Chaucer was not the author of the latter. His admiration of Chaucer remained undimmed; as late as 1840 he regarded him as 'one of the greatest poets the world has ever seen'. He thought he was 'indecent' at times in his comic tales, but never 'insidiously or openly voluptuous'. 'He had towards the female sex as exquisite and pure feelings as ever the heart of man was blessed with, and has expressed them as beautifully in the language of his age, as ever man did.' At Christmas Wordsworth worked on the third book of *The Prelude*, after returning to the pedlar section of 'The Ruined Cottage', the publication of which he contemplated with 'Peter Bell'. His attempts to finish 'The Pedlar' to his satisfaction did not end until March 1802.

With the spring came revival: 'The Sailor's Mother', 'Alice Fell', and 'Beggars' were written within a few days; before the end of March he had completed 'To a Butterfly' (a companion poem to 'The Sparrow's Nest' of the previous year), 'The Emigrant Mother', 'To the Cuckoo', 'My heart leaps up', and the first four stanzas of his Intimations 'Ode'. After a week with the Coleridges, he and Dorothy stayed with the Clarksons, William leaving on his birthday (7 April) to see Mary at Middleham. They were already engaged to be married, and Annette Vallon had been informed. Riding back to Eusemere, he composed 'The Glow-worm'. As he and Dorothy returned to Grasmere, they saw daffodils dancing in the wind by the shore of Ullswater; between Brothers Water and Kirkstone Pass, he finished 'The cock is crowing' (misleadingly entitled 'Written in March'). Early in May, after completing 'The Leech-Gatherer' ('Resolution and Independence'), he inscribed in his copy of Thomson's *The Castle of Indolence* those stanzas which, imitating its Spenserian verse, describe himself with some self-denigratory exaggeration and Coleridge in his happier moods. Wordsworth's self-portrait conveys a sense of the demonic power which possessed him until he was exhausted by composition, as Dorothy's journal repeatedly testifies with anxiety and loving admiration. The more joyous mood of June is reflected in the impromptu 'The sun has long been set', probably also in the skylark poem 'Up with me! Up with me into the clouds!' (long attributed to 1805).

Some of the vernal poems are light and occasional. 'The cock is crowing' excited Keats to parodic imitation, satirical of Oxford, but inferior to Wordsworth's verse, the visual evocativeness and joyous spirit of which nothing can diminish. Five poems on daisies and celandines are admittedly *de trop*; and the celandines fare less distinctively in subject and verse-form than the former. Playful simile-fancies are less impressive than the style, especially in 'To the Daisy', where the stanza, moulded on Elizabethan forms, is gracefully turned throughout. That the 'unassuming common-place of nature' should fulfil a 'function apostolical' for man ('Bright flower! whose home is everywhere') in its meekness and endurance might have appealed to seventeenth-century readers, but was too much for the author of *The Simpliciad*: 'Of apostolic daisies learn to think, Draughts from their urns of true devotion drink.' Such poems, for all of which man has his moods if he is in touch with nature, were to bring ridicule and contempt on Wordsworth from worldly-brash *littérateurs* whose insensitivity was regarded as the hallmark of sense. 'The Redbreast and the Butterfly' reveals a playful acceptance of nature's Darwinism. 'The Green Linnet' (probably written in 1802) elicits a more certain response, one verse, admired by Coleridge, illustrating the perspicuous skill with which Wordsworth can flash natural imagery kinetically before the eye:

> Amid yon tuft of hazel trees,
> That twinkle to the gusty breeze,
> Behold him perched in ecstasies,
>   Yet seeming still to hover;
> There! where the flutter of his wings
> Upon his back and body flings
> Shadows and sunny glimmerings,
>   That cover him all over.

'Beggars' is based on Dorothy's experience of 27 May 1800, as she added it to her journal entry for 10 June (probably after being reminded of it, and discussing it, with William on their way to Ambleside). Beyond the contrast between the cant of the mother and the more natural behaviour of her boys, its main interest is in the aggrandizement which Wordsworth lent his subject both in the early version (the gipsy mendicant being fit in person for a queen 'To lead those ancient Amazonian files; Or ruling bandit's wife, among the Grecian isles') and in 1827, when the blitheness of the boys made him think that, with wings, 'they might flit Precursors to Aurora's car, Scattering fresh flowers'. 'The Sailor's Mother' (branded a failure by Matthew Arnold) introduces a more impressive woman, who is compelled to beg. She is majestic, like a Roman matron in mien and gait; and the opening verses are noble, as befits the subject, without being in the least pretentious. Wordsworth met her on the road to Ambleside; 'her appearance was exactly as here described, and such was her account, nearly to the letter'. Oversensitive to Coleridge's criticism, he would have done better to retain the exquisite poetic reality of 'And I have been as far as Hull, to see What clothes he might have left, or other property'. The conclusion of the mother's reply is cunningly contrived to suggest a woman of strength who can hardly suppress her tears. 'The Emigrant Mother', originating in recollections of 'more than one French fugitive during the time of the French Revolution', consists largely of a lyric which, following a perfunctory narrative introduction, portrays with vivid and dramatic psychology the distress of a young mother deprived of her child. The last two poems are plainly successors to imaginative lyrical dramatizations in the first *Lyrical Ballads*.

Wordsworth's most successful work of 1802 is 'Resolution and Independence'. Detail in the life of the leech-gatherer he and Dorothy met in 1800 had undoubtedly heightened his awareness of the old man's faith and fortitude, but it was not the material for poetry. He had imagined him wandering about the moors, and he presents him there, beside a pool which is significantly 'bare to the eye of heaven'. The work is built on a cycle of contrasts: first in the change of the weather, then in the bright morning scene and the poet's mood as he thinks of his uncertain prospects, then between his over-anxiety and the unaccountable faith of the leech-gatherer, finally between the poet before and after his encounter, a change which is prefigured in the opening. Chatterton was in

Wordsworth's mind to a considerable degree when he prepared the poem, for the 'Balade of Charitie' not only supplied his stanza (the Chaucerian improved with a finalizing alexandrine); it suggested those major contrasts in weather and background which have their counterpart in the changing human situation. Wordsworth's anxieties had been deepened by thoughts of other poets, including Burns. Coleridge's unhappiness had long been familiar, but his plight had never been more despairingly revealed than on 21 April, when he read the first draft of his 'Dejection' ode (the verses he had written to Sara Hutchinson). That evening Dorothy read a biography of the Scottish poet Robert Fergusson, and Wordsworth's reference to 'despondency and madness' suggests that she discussed it with him.[6] Unlike Coleridge, he was no longer immersed in his personal problems; his recovery had been a necessary prelude to artistic creation and control. Imaginatively presented, 'Resolution and Independence' is a personal affirmation, all the more acceptable because its moral import is not heavily underscored.

The imaginative power of the main poem is visionary. It seems as if the poet has been led by 'peculiar grace' to the lonely spot. The old man, 'bent double' as he stands by the pool, seems almost part of the landscape, 'not all alive nor dead, Nor all asleep'. So preponderant is the imagery in the similes intended to convey this state that it may leave a false visual impression or obstruct the conveyance of the idea:

> As a huge stone is sometimes seen to lie
> Couch'd on the bald top of an eminence;
> Wonder to all who do the same espy
> By what means it could hither come, and whence;
> So that it seems a thing endued with sense:
> Like a sea-beast crawl'd forth, that on a shelf
> Of rock or sand reposeth, there to sun itself.

As the leech-gatherer describes how he has managed 'with God's good help' to gain an honest living despite all his hardships, his voice becomes 'like a stream scarce heard',

> And the whole body of the man did seem
> Like one whom I had met with in a dream;
> Or like a man from some far region sent,
> To give me human strength, by apt admonishment.

Here, as the poet's mind turns inward in self-communion, losing touch with the phenomenal world, we have an approximation to those 'fallings from us, vanishings' which Wordsworth regarded as intimations from 'God, who is our home'.

The finest descriptive effects are to be found in the first two verses, which constitute a poem. Tennyson's artistry in matching sound to sense is admirably contrived, but a comparison will show how artificially wrought it usually is beside the natural imagery that seems to well from Wordsworth's inspiration. The brooding of the stock-dove contrasts with the magpie's chatter, but nothing equals the auditory recall of 'And all the air is fill'd with pleasant noise of waters'. Here indeed, but not in the way signified by Matthew Arnold, nature seems to take the pen out of the poet's hand and write for him. The picture of the hare that raises a glittering mist wherever she runs is fascinating, but it should not blind us to the animated splendour inherent in the one word 'rejoices' ('The sky rejoices in the morning's birth'). Instead of straining at the picturesque, Wordsworth assumes an imaginative reader sustained by experience.

From Marriage to 'Intimations' (1802–4)

The depression referred to in 'Resolution and Independence' befell Wordsworth while he was journeying from Eusemere to meet Mary Hutchinson. It could have been caused by financial worries; the question was not only how he could afford his marriage, but what could be done to support his daughter Caroline. Correspondence with Annette had continued from December, when peace negotiations with France began. Deeply involved in the Royalist cause, she was prepared to accept her situation, but was anxious about Caroline's future; William and Dorothy had already decided to meet her in France, to give her what assurances they could. Plans for this meeting and for his marriage must have been completed by May, for at the end of the month he wrote the poem 'A Farewell', in which he contemplates a two months' absence before returning with Mary. A few days previously the Earl of Lonsdale died, and this event raised hopes that the debts due to the Wordsworths would soon be settled. Richard counselled patience, and it was not until 1803 that agreement for the sum of £8500 was reached.

On 9 July William and Dorothy left for Gallow Hill via Keswick and Eusemere. From Eamont Bridge they travelled by coach. It was cold, but they liked the hills and rain for bringing them 'so close together'. Dorothy never rode so snugly, until (at Bowes) she was driven into the coach by adverse weather. That evening (probably at Piercebridge) they enjoyed their fire; next morning they took a post-chaise for Thirsk, whence they walked past Rievaulx Abbey to Helmsley, where they slept at the Old Manor House, 'a very nice inn'. The next day, after meeting Mary and Sara seven miles out, they reached Gallow Hill. Ten days later William and Dorothy began their journey to London, where, after unspecified 'troubles and disasters', they mounted the Dover coach and crossed Westminster Bridge early on 31 July. Soon after breakfast in Calais the next morning they were with Annette and Caroline. Although the rooms they hired were ill-furnished, they stayed four weeks. It was hot, and their main walks were in the evening, by the shore, usually with Annette and Caroline. Relations must have been agreeable, but what was discussed and what pledges were made remain conjectural.

The whole Wordsworth family met in London. William and Dorothy were able to occupy the Montagus' rooms in the Temple; Christopher came up to Richard's from Cambridge, and John arrived from China. It was their first reunion for many years, and it was destined to be their last. Wordsworth and Dorothy visited Windsor to see uncle William while he was in canonical residence. They also saw Charles and Mary Lamb, who had just returned from a visit to Coleridge and the Lakes, and had spent a day or two with the Clarksons, who were staying at Dove Cottage. Gallow Hill was reached on 24 September, and on 4 October William and Mary were married at Brompton (where Francis Wrangham had been married in 1801). Dorothy was ill with nervous excitement, and the only witnesses of the ceremony were three of the Hutchinsons. Breakfast over, the married couple set off with Dorothy for Grasmere, travelling via Thirsk and Leyburn, then by the route William and Dorothy had taken when they made their first journey to their Lakeland home. Molly Fisher was overjoyed when they arrived on the third evening; they walked into the garden by candlelight, and were astonished at the growth that had taken place.

They had been absent three months, and during that period Wordsworth had written several sonnets. Dorothy had read Milton's aloud in May, and he had been so impressed by their 'dignified simplicity and majestic harmony' that he 'took fire' and produced three the same afternoon, one being 'I grieved for Buonaparté'. The question of national independence and freedom, vis-à-vis Napoleon, was to preoccupy him for years. He must have felt that peace with France (which ended in May 1803) was an uneasy lull, for he continued his sonnets on the subject of liberty while he was at Calais. Of the more personal written during his absence from Grasmere, the first was 'Composed upon Westminster Bridge'. 'The sun shone so brightly, with such a fierce light, that there was even something like the purity of one of nature's own grand spectacles', Dorothy wrote, almost certainly after discussing the scene with Wordsworth, or reading his poem, which was written while they were riding on the roof of the Dover coach. The thought expressed by Dorothy explains the utter bareness of 'Ships, towers, domes, theatres, and temples'; they were not beautiful in themselves, but invested with 'the beauty of the morning', so astonishingly that Wordsworth declares he had never seen 'sun more beautifully steep In his first splendour, valley, rock, or hill'. The sonnet ends with deep wonderment at the stillness which can overtake the heart of a great trading nation. Another peaceful scene, at Calais, is the subject of 'It is a beauteous evening'. Sunset suggests that 'the gentleness of heaven broods o'er the sea'. The eternal motion of the water reminds Wordsworth of the 'mighty Being' (the spirit that 'rolls through all things') as it sounds like muted thunder ('everlastingly', he adds with daring tautology which may be forgiven for its wonderful evocation of sound). The child (Caroline), living in her own world, evokes the thought of his Intimations 'Ode'; heaven lies about her in her infancy.

Of the political sonnets composed or thought to have been composed at Calais, two contrast the exhilaration of the people when he was there with Jones in 1790 and their lack of gaiety now, especially on 'young Buonaparté's natal day', set aside for rejoicing over his being made Consul for life. The poet's scorn for 'feeble heads, to slavery prone' (including foreign visitors, English largely, the Whig statesman Fox among them), eager to pay homage to Napoleon, is expressed in 'Calais, August, 1802'. 'On the Extinction of the Venetian Republic' and 'To Toussaint l'Ouverture' are greatly inspired by Wordsworth's passionate love of freedom. The first is more subdued, but perfectly designed and turned, its 'espouse the everlasting sea' recalling the imagery of 'It is a beauteous evening'; the second expresses in matchless verse the powers working through nature (human especially) for freedom and justice.

In 'September 1, 1802' Wordsworth invites sympathy for negroes expelled from France. 'Composed in the Valley near Dover, on the Day of Landing' conveys his pleasure and pride in the English scene and English freedom, but the patriotic feeling is complacent and ordinary compared with the deep resonances of 'September, 1802. Near Dover', where he recalls how he stood in the same valley, contemplating the Straits and how alarmingly near was the coast of France. Here his faith in the final conquest of right receives twofold expression: the thought that the 'span of waters' is a mighty influence for evil and good leads to the reflection that 'Even so doth God protect us if we be Virtuous and wise'; natural defence, however, is nothing in itself: 'by the soul Only, the nations shall be great and free'. He does not find this greatness in London. Algernon Sidney, Marvell, Harrington, Vane, 'and others who called Milton friend' taught 'how rightfully a nation shone in splendour'; but now he finds, instead of 'plain living and high thinking', ostentation, getting and spending ('rapine, avarice, expense') – the worship of materialism. In one of his best sonnets, he implies that the river of greatness no longer flows in England; 'she is a fen of stagnant waters', and he wishes the spirit of Milton would return and bestow 'virtue, freedom, power'. National strength depends less on material wealth than on moral and spiritual. This theme continued to produce some of Wordsworth's finest poems; it was based on a wisdom which was born of rare political experience and insight, and remarkable because it was to be justified by the course of events in Europe. (The invasion of Switzerland in October 1802 not only hardened Wordsworth's antipathy to imperialistic France but turned him against the Whigs, whose principles were not above commercialism and private enrichment.)

The post-nuptial journey to Grasmere produced two sonnets, the first on the skyscape from the Hambleton Hills. Opposite Bolton Castle, where Mary Queen of Scots had been imprisoned, the Wordsworths were compelled to stay in their post-chaise during a severe storm, while another horse was being fetched to replace one that had become too fractious; 'to beguile the time' Wordsworth composed a sonnet, contrasting their confinement with hers. It was not thought worthy of preservation, and the same may be said of the first, the real substance of which is better conveyed in Dorothy's journal. Wordsworth was dissatisfied with the conclusion, and returned to it with unconvincing results in 'Those words were uttered as in pensive mood'. Late in the year, in 'Nuns fret not', he expressed the artistic pleasure he had derived from working within the restricted form of the sonnet. About the same time he began a translation of Ariosto's *Orlando Furioso*, only ten stanzas of which survive (PW4.367–9).

Sara Hutchinson spent Christmas at Grasmere, and was there again during April 1803. On 18 June, some weeks before he was expected, a boy was born to Mary and William; he was named

John after his uncle and grandfather. When Mary had recovered, her sister Joanna came to stay with her while William and Dorothy were on tour in Scotland with Coleridge. For this Wordsworth bought a horse and jaunting-car, an open Irish vehicle, the occupants of which sat with their feet over each side and so near the ground that they could easily alight. They were away six weeks from the middle of August. Dorothy's recollections of the tour were written at length and at leisure; she had made no notes, and the last part was completed nearly two years later.

The party reached Carlisle on the day Hatfield, forger and bigamist deceiver of 'the maid of Buttermere', was condemned to death; Wordsworth and Coleridge entered the gaoler's house, where Coleridge saw the prisoner. Across the Border, they proceeded to the grave of Burns and his house at Dumfries; the next day they passed his farmhouse at Ellisland. Following the route taken previously by William, they reached the suburbs of Glasgow, where their vehicle became an object of interest, and children hooted after them; they had 'the pleasure of spreading smiles' from one end of the city to the other. The upper part of Loch Lomond recalled Ullswater; beyond the lower lake, Dumbarton Castle on its high rock looked ghostly in the mist, reminding Dorothy of Glastonbury Tor from the Dorset hills. From Tarbet they were rowed across to Rob Roy's Caves and thence to Inversnaid. They followed a rough horse-track towards Loch Katrine, and were debating whether to return when a Highlander rode up in Highland dress, a sight more thrilling than their first view of the lake. A boatman offered to row them down to the Trossachs, but Coleridge, who had been ill, was afraid of the cold and walked. He was there to greet them on landing, and they were not disappointed in the scenery, despite the rain. They returned the way they came, hoping to cross the mountains from Glengyle to the head of Loch Lomond. Heavy rain compelled them to walk back to Inversnaid, where they met the Highland lass who reminded Dorothy of Peter Bell's Highland girl, and whose beauty Wordsworth recalled in verse.

From Tarbet they resumed their journey by jaunting-car, but Coleridge, dreading the rain and being out of spirits, decided to turn back. They passed the Cobbler, and proceeded to Inverary, then north to Loch Awe, with an impressive view first of Ben Cruachan, finally of ruined Kilchurn Castle on its island. The sight of Mr Knott's iron-foundry at Bonawe delighted Wordsworth 'for poor Ann Tyson's sake'. Further west, after being ferried across Loch Etive, they saw their frightened horse whipped ashore 'in brutal triumph'. The next ferry caused the horse to run away but, as there was no way round the head of Loch Creran, he was brought back and made to swim by the side of the boat. The soft green islands of Loch Linnhe from Portnacroish reminded the Wordsworths of the isles of the blessed in 'The Vision of Mirzah'. At Ballachulish the bridge was broken, and Highlanders pulled their car across the stream after the horse had taken fright again. Next morning, terrified at the sight of roller shafts above a wall, on the way to Glencoe, it backed and was dragged by the car down the bank into Loch Leven. Dorothy and William had leaped down in time; with the assistance of a man who was providentially at hand, the horse was extricated, and no serious damage was done. Though impressed by the grandeur of the mountains, the tourists were disappointed by the glen itself, having expected 'images of terror' from overhanging rocks.

After a long but easier route via Tyndrum and Killin to Loch Tay and Aberfeldy, they travelled in darkness through the historic Pass of Killiecrankie. They planned to see it the following day after a tour on foot, but were compelled to postpone their visit until the next morning, when (a French invasion of England being hourly expected) they wished that forty or fifty thousand Highlanders could pour down for the defence of the country, under leaders such as Montrose. Their return took them to Dunkeld, then via Strath Bran and the Narrow Glen to Crieff, Loch Earn, Callander, and the Trossachs. Having seen this beauty spot again, they set off to Inversnaid, then to the head of Loch Lomond, from which they descended to Glengyle and visited (they supposed) Rob Roy's grave. The weather being fine, they took a circuitous route back to Callander (where their horse and conveyance had been left), first over mountains to the head of Loch Voil, where they discovered the burial-place of the MacGregors. At the foot of the lake, they joined the road they had travelled from Loch Earn, but were so tired they stopped for the night at 'the most respectable-looking house' in Strathyre. Dorothy talked to the mistress while she was baking, and was asked, among other questions, 'the old one over again', whether she was married. When she heard she was not, the mistress of the house looked surprised, and said with 'pious seriousness and perfect simplicity, "To be sure, there is a great promise for virgins in heaven."'

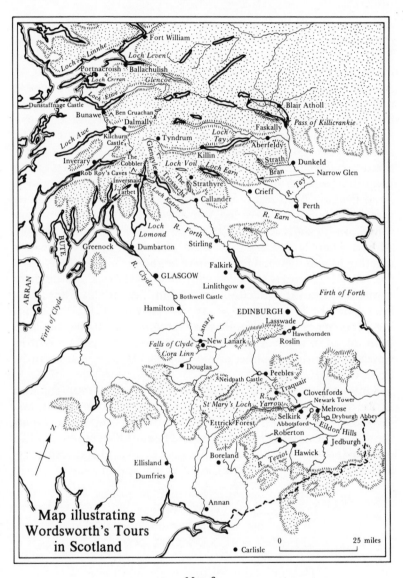

Map illustrating
Wordsworth's Tours
in Scotland

Map 3

From Callender they went to Stirling, where, after walking up to the castle, they bought a copy of Burns's poems. Their route to Edinburgh lay through Falkirk and Linlithgow. After sight-seeing in the capital, mainly from the castle and a point near St Anthony's Chapel on Arthur's Seat, they slept at Roslin. The next morning they walked through the glen, past Hawthornden (once the home of the poet William Drummond) to Lasswade, where they called on Walter Scott before he and his wife were up. In the afternoon Scott drove them back to Roslin, and promised to meet them two days later at Melrose. Before dinner they surveyed the beautiful architecture of Roslin Chapel; in the evening they went on to Peebles. Next morning they walked up to Neidpath Castle, where the felling of trees led Wordsworth that day to write his sonnet on 'degenerate Douglas'. Scott took them round Melrose Abbey; when he left for the assizes at Jedburgh, they followed, meeting him in their lodgings, where he recited part of *The Lay of the Last Minstrel*. He travelled with them to Hawick, telling them stories about all the places of interest in Teviotdale. Three days later, not long after Coleridge's return, they reached home, finding 'Mary in perfect health, Joanna Hutchinson with her, and little John asleep in the clothes-basket by the fire', not before Wordsworth had written a sonnet on the subject ('Fly, some kind spirit, fly to Grasmere-dale').

Some of the most important poems relating to this tour, those on Burns and Rob Roy, for example, were composed in later years. Of those written soon after Wordsworth's return, two are outstanding. Perhaps the more lyrical and beautifully expressed is 'To a Highland Girl'. It illustrates the poet's habit of imparting the almost inexpressible through the aid of natural imagery:

> With no restraint, but such as springs
> From quick and eager visitings
> Of thoughts, that lie beyond the reach
> Of thy few words of English speech:
> A bondage sweetly brook'd, a strife
> That gives thy gestures grace and life!
> So have I, not unmov'd in mind,
> Seen birds of tempest-loving kind,
> Thus beating up against the wind.

The girl and Inversnaid remain a dream and vision, emphasizing the importance of memory, 'To give new pleasure like the past,

Continued long as life shall last'. 'Yarrow Unvisited' was an inven-
tion (since the actual reason for not turning aside at Clovenfords to
see the stream was shortage of time), destined to be followed by
two Yarrow poems in the same verse, based on that of 'Leader
Haughs', a Yarrow ballad. Wordsworth's poem echoes another
Yarrow ballad and, like its prototype, makes effective use of place-
names. As a lyrical conversation poem, it is a remarkable achievement, light and engaging throughout. 'Glen Almain' refers to the
legend of Ossian's burial-place in the Narrow Glen, and is of less
interest than 'The Matron of Jedborough and her Husband',
where the animation of the old lady with whom the Wordsworths
lodged when Scott visited them is the subject of praise 'to Him who
is our lord and friend'. This poem was composed between 1803
and 1805, and illustrates, in view of the husband's plight as well as
the matron's afflictions, how Wordsworth's 'cheerful faith that all
that we behold is full of blessings' moved towards orthodox expression long before his poetic vigour declined.

October 1803 was a time for action. Wordsworth joined the
Volunteer movement which was being organized throughout the
country against invasion; and soon the Grasmere redcoats
marched past his cottage twice a week for drill at Ambleside.
Never was there 'a more determined hater of the French nor one
more willing to do his utmost to destroy them if they really do
come', Dorothy wrote. He attended drill sessions, and expressed
his thoughts and feelings in several sonnets. Not one rises to the
level of 'It is not to be thought of' and 'When I have borne in
memory', both of which had appeared in *The Morning Post*. He
thinks of the spirit of England and of France, and finds greatness
in neither, though he considers France more abject. England's
dearth of magnanimity makes him begin to question Providence,
and the fear of 'monied worldlings' convinces him that riches are
'akin to fear, to change, to cowardice, and death'; yet the attitude
of most people in the face of war strengthens his belief that 'every
gift of noble origin' is inspired by hope. He strikes bravura notes
'To the Men of Kent' and 'Anticipation', and, without being
trumpet-tongued, declares in 'What if our numbers' (thought to
belong to this period) his faith in the people at a time of crisis.

The painter Sir George Beaumont and his wife, both admirers of
Wordsworth's poetry, had stayed at Keswick in the summer and met
Coleridge. Concluding that it would help both poets, especially
Coleridge in his failing health, if they lived nearer each other,

Sir George bought land at Applethwaite below Skiddaw as a present for Wordsworth. It was an embarrassing gift, for Coleridge was already planning to live abroad, and Wordsworth could not afford to build a house. Hazlitt had painted their portraits, and returned in the autumn to paint another of Coleridge for Beaumont. He and Wordsworth became involved in a philosophical argument with Coleridge, who objected to the irreverence he detected in his friend's remarks on Ray, Derham, and Paley, though there could have been nothing objectionable in Wordsworth's critical reaction to the idea of a Creator outside the universe. Hazlitt was forced to flee from Keswick by the anger his sexual proclivities provoked; on his way back to London, he called in the middle of the night on Wordsworth, who provided the clothes and money he needed for his journey.

After persuading Southey to leave Bristol with his family and occupy half of Greta Hall, Coleridge was happier to think that in his absence his wife could share her sister's company. Rheumatic illnesses having aggravated his addiction to drugs, he hoped a warmer climate would restore him. Wordsworth had generously borrowed, and lent him, £100 to that end. Encouraged by the enthusiasm with which Coleridge had heard the second part of his autobiographical poem on 4 January 1804, he continued the work with vigour, the result being that 'the poem on his life' (in five books) was the major item among the copies of Wordsworth's unpublished work which Coleridge took with him, when he left England in April to assist his friend John Stoddart, King's Advocate in Malta. They had been transcribed by Dorothy and Mary, and included 'Ode to Duty' and the complete 'Intimations' ode.

Both odes have been grossly misunderstood. They are often assumed to mark the weakening of Wordsworth's independent judgment, his meek acceptance of orthodoxy and convention, and the onset of his poetic decline. In fact, they show his advance to maturity. They are both influenced by Henry Vaughan, and both are responses to Coleridge.

Coleridge's notebooks disclose that he spent some time at Wordsworth's in January 1804 analysing the dislike of doing one's duty. The subject preyed on his mind; he had long realized his failure as husband and father, his failure in self-control, and his failure to settle intellectually to any self-imposed task. He thought Wordsworth fortunate in all respects, and probably discussed his problems with him. Wordsworth, on the other hand, knew his own readiness to shrink from a major task, 'in smoother walks to stray'; and this realization, reinforced by his growing awareness of his family responsibilities, is amply demonstrated by the energy with which he set to work on *The Prelude* until its completion in 1805. A letter from Coleridge in February 1804, after stating that happiness comes from 'the exact performance of duty', stresses the blessing Wordsworth enjoyed because his path of duty lay 'through vine-trellised elm-groves, through love and joy and grandeur'. He associates grandeur with Wordsworth's poetic achievement and promise; and his linking of love and joy with duty is a key to 'Ode to Duty'.

Wordsworth remembered his waywardness at Cambridge, and his lack of conscience towards those who supported him, condemning it severely later in the year (Pr.05.vi.29−48); it was not Nature (the universal Spirit) but the 'mighty forms' of nature or the love of the picturesque which gave 'a character to irregular hopes' when he prolonged his tour in the Alps (ibid. 342−8). Now, at a time of national crisis, he may have found support for his new spirit of resolve in such poems by Henry Vaughan as 'The Constellation' and 'Misery'. Vaughan finds enviable order, light, and calm in stars obedient to God's law; in His service he wishes to be bound 'a prisoner' to his liberty. Wordsworth finds virtue in universal law from flowers to stars, and wishes to become a bondman to duty 'in the light of truth'. As a passage on duty in *The Excursion* shows (iv.73−99), he believes that man, as a link in the 'chain of Being' ('scale of being'), is subject to 'transcendent truths' through conscience. He recognises those inescapable human laws (with consequences) which parallel natural or scientific law in the thinking and imaginative creation of George Eliot. One stanza in the first version of Wordsworth's ode indicates expressly that he was no conformist; acting according to conscience gives a freedom which can result in heterodoxy and progress. Unfortunately the poem sets up a resistance akin to rejection by such lines as 'Stern daughter of the voice of God!' and 'I long for a repose that ever is the same', in addition to the final emphasis on 'bondman'. All this suggests overreaction by a poet, eager not to defer the task, but 'plagued' by the knowledge that the major task which lay ahead, imposed by Coleridge rather than by himself, was being deferred indefinitely for *The Prelude*. The key to his poem, to the sense of duty well fulfilled, is to be found in 'Character of the Happy Warrior',

> the generous spirit, who, when brought
> Among the tasks of real life, hath wrought
> Upon the plan that pleased his boyish thought:
> Whose high endeavours are an inward light
> That makes the path before him always bright.

The lawgiver is benignant; the genial spirit of youth is not frozen. Conscience and reason (which implies 'self-sacrifice' or self-discipline and concern for others) remand us to nature (as Wordsworth argues in his 'Reply to Mathetes'), and we accept moral principles, not as precepts but by voluntary choice, so moving 'along the orbit of perfect liberty'. 'Ode to Duty' expresses the wisdom of experience summed up in the familiar expression 'Whose service is perfect freedom'. Wordsworth goes further, believing that the growth of responsibility is a prelude to 'the milder day', 'the fairer world than this', of which he received an intimation by Hart-leap Well: 'Serene will be our days and bright, And happy will our nature be, When love is an unerring light, And joy its own security.'

Two years had passed before Wordsworth was able to complete 'Intimations', and the two parts relate primarily to past and present, with a sense of loss and of recompense. The complementary section which was added in 1804 (v–xi) opens with an explanation of the loss in terms of Platonic theory. Though this was not an article of faith with Wordsworth (Pr.v.507–12), he thought it had 'sufficient foundation in humanity' to justify its use as a means of giving coherence to his subject. He saw himself in the position of Archimedes, who said that 'he could move the world if he had a point whereon to rest his machine'. The 'shadowy . . . notion' which he borrowed is given definition and splendour, and the point of leverage becomes almost an intercalary poem, of such length that its centrality may make it appear the main part of the ode. The function of this section is subordinate nevertheless to the personal experience of the poem. To quote at length from the *Phaedo* or *Phaedrus* in support of the view that the child is the best philosopher is therefore superfluous. Wordsworth had discussed the subject no doubt with Coleridge, whose sonnet on the birth of his son Hartley in 1796 is based on Plato's 'strange fancy'; he was familiar with it in seventeenth-century writers,[7] particularly in the poetry of Vaughan. 'Corruption' may have supplied the angelic metaphor which he was to use for intimations of immortality in

'Composed upon an Evening of Extraordinary Splendour'; the association of angels and heaven with Abraham in 'Religion' may have enriched the significance of 'Abraham's bosom' (from St Luke) in 'It is a beauteous evening'. 'The Retreat' is even more closely related to Wordsworth's ode:

> Happy those early days, when I
> Shin'd in my angel-infancy!
> Before I understood this place
> Appointed for my second race . . .
> When yet I had not walk'd above
> A mile or two from my first love,
> And looking back — at that short space —
> Could see a glimpse of His bright face;
> When on some gilded cloud, or flow'r,
> My gazing soul would dwell an hour,
> And in those weaker glories spy
> Some shadows of eternity.

Although Vaughan's Christian idea of childhood innocence is not adopted, his Platonism relates to the 'celestial light' associated with Wordsworth's 'shadowy recollections', and more specifically to the passage where the latter speaks of the babe, 'no outcast' but 'an inmate of this active universe', the love in which he lives awakening his imagination and beautifying the flower to which he points (Pr.ii.232–65). Boyhood hours that had 'the charm of visionary things' are recalled in 'To the Cuckoo'; at such times he felt 'gleams like the flashing of a shield' (Pr.i.585–8, 631–5).

For Wordsworth the 'glory' is in the dreamlike vision of the child; and intimations of 'God, who is our home' confirm his adult faith that 'looks through death'. The extra-dimensional element of the poem, however, resides not so much in immortality (or pre-existence, which is only an accepted possibility) as in oneness with the universal spirit (in which Wordsworth did believe). Not long after completing 'Intimations', he affirmed that 'Our destiny, our nature, and our home Is with infinitude, and only there', and that our greatness is achieved through its revelation, when 'the light of sense Goes out in flashes that have shewn to us The invisible world' (Pr.05.vi.532–9). He would have agreed with the D. H. Lawrence who wrote that 'to be oneself' is 'a supreme, gleaming triumph of infinity'.

The 'obstinate questionings Of sense and outward things, Fallings from us, vanishings; Blank misgivings of a Creature Moving about in worlds not realised' refer to experiences similar to, or identical with, those when 'bodily eyes' were forgotten, and what was contemplated seemed like something in Wordsworth himself, 'a dream, a prospect in the mind' (Pr.ii.348—52). His psychological interest in the subject is clear from the I.F. note to 'Intimations', particularly when he asks, with reference to his Archimedean analogy, 'Who has not felt the same aspirations as regards the world of his own mind?' If the mind of man was 'the main region' of his song, the intimations theme is crucial to it, higher minds enjoying release from 'sensible impressions' to 'hold fit converse with the spiritual world' (Pr.xiv.86—129).

Coleridge's 'Ode: to Dejection' was written on 4 April 1802,[8] and its allusive 'I too will crown me with a coronal' shows that he had heard or read the first part of Wordsworth's ode (i—iv). He sees the beauty of nature but no longer feels it; he cannot hope 'from outward forms to win The Passion and the life whose fountains are within'. Afflictions suspend his 'shaping spirit of imagination', the key to the 'beauty-making power' of which is joy. The conclusion of 'Intimations' answers Coleridge's cheerlessness. Wordsworth finds joy in his shadowy recollections; they are his fountain-light, and he is grateful; the thought of his past years breeds 'perpetual benedictions'. Though nothing can restore 'the hour of splendour in the grass, of glory in the flower', his love of nature is not lessened. More mature and philosophical, he now finds strength in what remains; his imagination associates nature with humanity; 'The clouds that gather round the setting sun' take 'a sober colouring from an eye That hath kept watch o'er man's mortality', and 'the meanest flower that blows can give Thoughts that do often lie too deep for tears'. Imagination does not always reflect joy, as Coleridge implies in his ode. Nor, though experience brought intimations of the invisible world more rarely, was Wordsworth's more normal imagination suspended, as the conclusion of *The Prelude* was to demonstrate and proclaim.

Some features of Wordsworth's ode have special interest. The opening lines are from a poem he had allowed Coleridge to modify and publish as 'The Mad Monk' in *The Morning Post*. The 'timely utterance' which gave relief to the thought of the vanished radiance is probably the affirmation of 'My heart leaps up', which anticipates 'Intimations' in its assumption (rather than hope) that his 'natural piety', the love of nature he inherited in childhood, will be preserved. Echoes of 'The Idle Shepherd-Boys' are heard in 'jubilee' and 'coronal'. The 'imperial palace' metaphor, contrasting in splendour with the 'prison-house', conveys a sense of artificiality and of definition less imaginative than the natural imagery of 'trailing clouds of glory do we come From God, who is our home'. The omitted lines, 'To whom the grave Is but a lonely bed without the sense or sight Of day or the warm light, A place of thought where we in waiting lie', give a child's impressions, not Wordsworth's; the passage often associated with them from Dorothy's journal (29.iv.02) records an 'if only' thought, a supposition, not a belief. 'High instincts, before which our mortal nature Did tremble' refers not only to the workings of conscience but also to a vague sense of ideal beauty in many ways of life.[9]

Whatever shortcomings may be found in 'Intimations' in thought, expression, or proportion, they are slight compared with the general grandeur and masterly management of its difficult subject. Variety and ease of movement, grace and appropriateness of diction and imagery, are admirably evident from start to finish. Ambitions as the poem is, it has little of the cumbrous artificiality that characterizes too many of our great odes.

The Prelude and the Imagination (1804–5)

The Wordsworths had regretted the Clarksons' departure from Eusemere; they were equally disappointed when the Beaumonts' hopes of acquiring land for a summer residence by Loughrigg Tarn were frustrated. Lady Beaumont and Catherine Clarkson, two enthusiastic Wordsworthians, were to become Dorothy's chief correspondents. Devotion to Johnny, her little nephew, involved her in increased domesticity. A daughter was born to Mary in August, and christened Dorothy in accordance with a wish William had long entertained, though he thought 'Mary' the most musical and English of names. Dove Cottage was already crowded, but uncertainty about where Coleridge would live when he returned made it inexpedient to move in the meantime. A hut lined with moss was built in the orchard to eke out accommodation. In September William and Dorothy, after taking the Southeys and Mrs Coleridge to Buttermere in their jaunting-car, walked from Keswick by Whinlatter and Lorton Vale (where they visited 'the patriarch of yew trees') to Ennerdale, Wastdale, and the Duddon valley. Soon after this excursion, Wordsworth returned to his autobiographical poem, aiming to complete it before the summer of 1805.

Such purposefulness did not preclude the writing of shorter poems, among them a few of his best. 'The world is too much with us' is notable for its animated outburst against the spiritual poverty of Mammon-worshippers. 'Great God!' Wordsworth protests, 'I'd rather be a pagan suckled in a creed outworn.' The lines which follow echo Spenser's 'Colin Clouts Come Home Againe' with its 'pleasant lea', Proteus, and 'Triton blowing loud his wreathed horne'. 'The Small Celandine' shows how, 'thanks to the human heart by which we live', a small flower can 'take a sober colouring

from an eye That hath kept watch o'er man's mortality'; its closing
lines undoubtedly derive from Burns's 'Man was made to Mourn'. 'I
wandered lonely as a cloud', based on recollections of the Ullswater
scene described by Dorothy in April 1802, illustrates the manner in
which the imagination selects and concentrates: the daffodils, the
waves, and the heart of the poet as he remembers, all dance with
pleasure. The verse added for the 1815 edition indicates how the
imagination enhances by aggregation: 'Continuous as the stars that
shine And twinkle on the milky way, They stretched . . . Ten
thousand saw I . . .'. Wordsworth thought the best lines in the
poem were the two contributed by Mary: 'They flash upon that
inward eye Which is the bliss of solitude.'

The lyric on Mary, 'She was a phantom of delight', epitomized
in *The Prelude* (xiv.268–70: 'She came, no more a phantom to
adorn A moment, but an inmate of the heart, And yet a spirit'),
indicates how much thought could be given to the substance and
design of a short poem without sacrifice of melody. Rarely has so
much experience been concentrated in so little space, from the
haunting imagery of boyhood captivation to courtship vicissitudes,
and thence to the full realization of a partner's being in marriage.
There is no false sentiment; the woman is humanly perfect in her
imperfections. There is a sense of spirituality in love throughout,
from the romantically remote to the familiar countenance in
which can be read 'Sweet records, promises as sweet', and from the
variations of 'Praise, blame, love, kisses, tears, and smiles' to a less
emotional, more serene and philosophical appreciation ('Endurance, foresight, strength, and skill', 'A traveller between life and
death'). The word 'machine' for 'body' is antiquated; it occurs in
Hamlet, but Wordsworth remembered a passage in Bartram's
Travels which suggests Coleridge's 'one Life within us and abroad':
'the pulse of nature becomes more active, and the universal vibra-
tion of life insensibly and irresistibly moves the wondrous
machine'. It would be hard to find a short poem which presents the
stages of love with as much fidelity and in as many aspects. Wordsworth's admission that the idea of his poem sprang from the opening four lines when they were part of 'To a Highland Girl' adds to
its interest.

'Yew-trees', assigned to 1803 by Wordsworth but almost certainly written after his recent visit to the 'pride of Lorton Vale', is a
remarkably compact poem, evocative historically and Gothically,
with suggestive personification reminiscent of Gray, and a masterly

choice of descriptive words, notably in 'each particular trunk a growth Of intertwisted fibres serpentine Up-coiling, and inveterately convolved'. The language and its order are Miltonic, remote from everyday speech, and unimpeachable in sense and sound. The poem ends felicitously, on a note which dispels battle and 'ghostly shapes', as the sound of the 'mountain flood' is imagined in the stillness, 'Murmuring from Glaramara's inmost caves'.

1805 had hardly dawned when Grasmere was frozen over, and the Wordsworths were on the ice, Mary and Dorothy, each with a child, being pushed about on chairs by the skaters, William and Mary's youngest brother. Sunshine tempted them the next day to travel over Kirkstone Pass to Park House (between Eusemere and Penrith), a farm now occupied by Tom and Sara Hutchinson. On his return, William was alarmed to discover that the building of Allan Bank had begun, on a conspicuous site, threatening to ruin the seclusion and simplicity of the Vale. A few days later, Dove Cottage was stunned by the news that John Wordsworth had been drowned off Portland Bill; during a calm, the tide had swept his ship on to the Shambles, where it had foundered. Assisted by Sara, who brought the news, William did his utmost to sustain Dorothy and Mary. Sir George Beaumont, knowing that they had invested a considerable sum of money in the abortive voyage, asked if he could give financial help. They were covered by insurance, it appears, and Wordsworth's main concern was to discover that John had done his duty to the last; Charles Lamb helped him in this investigation. Robert Southey's deep and immediate sympathy endeared him to the Wordsworths as never before; and Coleridge wished much later that he could have died in John's stead, leaving him to marry Sara Hutchinson and protect his 'poor little ones'. Coleridge knew John's greatness and nobility of character; all respected him. For Wordsworth he was the ideal man, showing prudence, meekness, self-denial, fortitude, refinement in pleasure, and simplicity in manners and living.

Wordsworth's faith was shaken and restored. He was driven to ask the question which later obsessed Thomas Hardy: have we more love in our nature than the Cause and Ruler of things? The idea was monstrous, but he could dismiss it only on the supposition of another and better world (12.iii.05). His sorrow did not allow him to sacrifice his faith in the greatness of man's soul 'by nature and gift of God'; whatever destruction and waste took place in a warring world, he could think of virtue, courage, heroism, and 'triumphs of disinterested love' everywhere (12.ii.05). He had never written poetry without a thought of pleasing John, refused to be cast down, and was at length able, after trying in vain to write a poem on him, to continue *The Prelude*, which he finished near the end of May.

It was composed in three stages. First, there was the two-part section on his boyhood which had been structured from accounts of isolated experiences in 1798–9, beginning open-endedly to accommodate whatever introduction proved most suitable. It was then conceived as a work in five books, ending with the ascent of Snowdon and its significance relative to the imagination. When Wordsworth was working towards this conclusion, however, he realized that, in order to complete the account of his poetic evolution, he must show how his disillusionment with revolutionary France and with rationalistic political theory arose. Hence the 1805 version in thirteen books, posthumously presented in fourteen, after much revision, including the division of the unusually long tenth book on France.

The chronology of composition with respect to the main work presents no problems; considerable evidence is found in the letters of Wordsworth and Dorothy, and there are two internal pointers of interest. The third paragraph of Book Sixth tells us that he was writing just after his thirty-fourth birthday (in April 1804; also, it is worth noting apropos of 'Intimations', at a time when the 'morning gladness' or 'radiance', as he subsequently wrote, had not faded). Book Seventh was resumed after a break which extended through the summer of 1804, and which Wordsworth attributed to 'voluntary holiday' and 'outward hindrance'. His need for recuperation was undoubtedly complicated by concern for Mary before his daughter's birth; his strenuous walking holiday with Dorothy in September may have been followed by a brief reflective period before he resumed composition in the grove associated with his brother John.

It is with the opening lines that chronological problems arise. The preamble (ll. 1–54 in 1805, 1–45 in 1850) was once thought to have been written at Racedown; it now seems improbable that it existed in any form as a whole before the late autumn of 1799, and it could have been composed in November of that year, while Wordsworth was on his return journey from Ullswater, after parting from Coleridge, whose enthusiasm that the poem addressed to him was to form a 'tailpiece' to *The Recluse* may have prompted Wordsworth's zeal to begin.[10] This supposition is confirmed by the opening of Book Seventh in 1805, 'Five years are vanish'd since I first pour'd out . . . A glad preamble to this verse.' 'Five' remained in all the manuscripts until 1839 at least, when it was erroneously changed to 'Six' by Wordsworth's daughter Dora. The 'city's walls' (once assumed to refer to Goslar) became the 'vast city', a change which gives complete congruency with the ending of the work (xiv.348–87). With its immediate sequel, it will be seen that the preamble compresses a period of at least three years, glancing at the recovery which came ultimately to Wordsworth at Racedown, after a period, the first part of which was spent in London, when the 'reasonings false' of moral and political theory had turned his heart 'aside from Nature's way', making him forget men as men, and drying up the fount of poetry within him. How that burden of his 'unnatural self' was shaken off is the subject of the closing books of *The Prelude*, and this particular passage (ll.20–3) could not have been introduced in the 'glad preamble' before the final extension was planned in 1804.

At this time Wordsworth expected one part of *The Recluse* to be narrative, and he still had such an epic poem in mind when he completed *The Prelude* (3.vi.05). The post-preamble of this work (i.46–269), after a continuation of the poet's imaginary journey from the city to the 'sweet vale' of his choice (Grasmere), refers to the subjects he had considered. They included romantic tales contemplated by Milton or similar to Spenser's; principally, actions in defence of liberty by a number of heroes; lastly (his favourite aspiration), 'some philosophic song Of truth that cherishes our daily life'. Not feeling mature enough to cope with any of these, he is 'Baffled and plagued by a mind that every hour Turns recreant to her task', and feels like 'a false steward who hath much received And renders nothing back'. Was it for this, he begins his autobiographical poem on the growth of a poet's mind, that the Derwent made ceaseless music during his infancy, giving him a foretaste of 'the calm that Nature breathes among the hills and groves'? 'Home at Grasmere', to which Wordsworth returned after completing *The Prelude*, announces his resolve to persevere with his 'favourite aspiration' (*The Recluse*) and abandon the narrative or epic schemes he had contemplated: 'Then farewell . . . All hope, which once and long was mine, to fill The heroic trumpet with the muse's breath!'

How far the two-part unit of 1798—9 differs in subject from the first two books of *The Prelude* has already been discussed. Like 'Three years she grew', the first of these books gives greater definition to the moral education that comes from nature 'by beauty and by fear', linking it less with souls of lonely places, and more with the universal spirit:

> Wisdom and Spirit of the universe!
> Thou Soul that art the eternity of thought!
> That giv'st to forms and images a breath
> And everlasting motion! not in vain,
> By day or star-light thus from my first dawn
> Of childhood didst Thou intertwine for me
> The passions that build up our human soul,
> Not with the mean and vulgar works of man,
> But with high objects, with enduring things,
> With life and nature . . .

The psychological truth of solitary boyhood experiences in which Wordsworth is afflicted with guilt and fear is impressive. The 'low breathings' that he hears coming after him at night on the hills stir an echo in readers' minds. The rebuke of the sky in 'Nutting' (excluded from *The Prelude*) befits the boy who would not strike a flower and could not damage a foxglove accidentally with 'unreproved indifference' (PR.641), after being 'early tutored' to regard with fraternal love 'the unassuming things that hold A silent station in this beauteous world' (xiii.44—7). More haunting is the strangeness of sky and wind as he hangs alone on some perilous crag, seeking the raven's nest. Most striking of all is the image of the peak which pursues him by starlight and frightens him into rectitude on Ullswater; the subsequent working of guilt and fear is memorably true to childhood experience:

> No familiar shapes
> Remained, no pleasant images of trees,
> Of sea or sky, no colours of green fields;
> But huge and mighty forms, that do not live
> Like living men, moved slowly through the mind
> By day, and were a trouble to my dreams.

The belief that Nature was his guide and guardian came much later; and the question arises, how far Wordsworth's religious love of nature was awakened in his youth. Did he, when a schoolboy at Hawkshead, really know 'the sentiment of Being', the 'one life' in all things, however much he felt the beauty of nature? Wordsworth the writer, recalling how he felt, rather than what he felt, tends to interpret in the light of later beliefs. There were times when the 'vacancy' between past and present was such that he seemed 'two consciousnesses' (ii.27–33); others, one suspects, when the two selves almost merged. The experiences which illustrate how Nature moulded her favoured being are more faithful in their psychological and visual recall than in the religious interpretation of retrospect. 'It is difficult, impossible I am told,' writes W. H. Hudson, 'for any one to recall his boyhood exactly as it was. It could not have been what it seems to the adult mind, since we cannot escape from what we are, however great our detachment may be; and in going back we must take our present selves with us: the mind has taken a different colour, and this is thrown back upon our past.'[11]

The three stages of development (cf. i.562, ii.198–203) in Wordsworth's love of natural beauty are basic rather than exceptional; it is the emergence of his visionary imagination that is significantly idiosyncratic. If he is 'nature's priest', it is because nature is 'the breath of God' and he had been subject from the first 'to God and Nature's single sovereignty', 'the life of nature, by the God of love inspired' enriching his life, elevating him above 'little enmities and low desires', and giving him a confidence which sustained him in a world of self-seeking and apathy to great causes. In the confusion and trivial pursuits of London he had come to feel that through nature God inspires men in general with 'one sense for moral judgments'. As with Beaupuy, such belief in men's innate righteousness and nobility was the rockbed on which his faith in the ultimate triumph of liberty was grounded.

Man being one with the world of nature, and the highest of its creatures (viii.487), it was fortunate for Wordsworth that he became acquainted first with men whom he could admire. They were not Arcadian figures, but men whose highest qualities he could love and emulate. When intent on angling or stealing ravens' eggs, he had seen the shepherd at his task, magnified by the fog from which he emerged, or glorified in the radiance of the setting sun. Thus 'ennobled outwardly' in actions redounding worthiness and honour, man had earned Wordsworth's reverence. In retrospect he blessed 'the God of Nature and of man' that this was so, knowing that admiration of human virtues had safeguarded him against meanness, selfishness, and vulgar passions (viii.215–339). Though subordinate to nature's beauty and 'viewless agencies' at first, man came to be indissolubly linked with nature. Without such 'endearing union' the earth is 'valueless, even in its Maker's eye', Wordsworth asserts, exemplifying it (PR.577–8) in

> a path,
> A taper burning through the gloom of night,
> Smoke breathing up by day from cottage trees,
> A beauteous sunbeam in a sunny shed,
> A garden with its walks and banks of flowers,
> A churchyard, and the bell that tolls to church,
> The roaring ocean and waste wilderness,
> Familiar things and awful, the minute
> And grand . . .

In London therefore he had high hopes of God and man. In France he felt that there was 'one nature' which transcended 'all local patrimony', insisting that nothing has the right to last but equity and reason (x.146–208). Believing that God through nature endows all men with goodness, making them potentially divine, and that she has power 'to breathe grandeur upon the very humblest face of human life', whatever the conditions, Wordsworth subsequently hoped that as a poet he would become 'a power like one of Nature's' to stir people's hearts, and create imaginative sympathies which would lead to a 'fairer world than this'.

He is ironical at the expense of the model child, a moral paragon and learned prodigy, in Thomas Day's *Sandford and Merton*; like Dickens in *Hard Times*, he objects strongly to education which loads children's minds with facts and concepts beyond their realization or natural capacity. Far more important is it to fit knowledge to active interests, to prepare for life through imaginative stories, and to learn right and wrong through experience. Education should be enjoyable, not satiating, for true knowledge is acquired with increase of 'power' (v). Sought genuinely, for its own sake, it provides a fulfilment which may be described as 'holy'. From geometric science Wordsworth derived pleasure, a sense also of nature's laws, and hence an apperception of the 'one surpassing Life' beyond space and time which 'is and hath the name of God'

(05.vi.135—59). Enlightenment depends on nature or experience; it depends also on the diffusion of those 'imperishable thoughts' expressed by the 'one great Society' of 'the noble living and the noble dead'. 'Theirs is the language of the heavens', and when they are most God-inspired their words are mere 'under-agents' (xiii. 265—78), though capable of communicating Nature's power. Like the prophets, the poets are 'connected in a mighty scheme of truth' (xiii.302). Knowing how books 'debase the many' for the sake of 'the wealthy few, who see by artificial lights', and how they set forth 'extrinsic differences' and 'neglect the universal heart', Wordsworth resolves (xiii.207—49) to make his subject men as they are 'within themselves', his theme

> No other than the very heart of man,
> As found among the best of those that live,
> Not unexalted by religious faith,
> Nor uninformed by books, good books, though few,
> In Nature's presence: thence may I select
> Sorrow, that is not sorrow, but delight;
> And miserable love, that is not pain
> To hear of, for the glory that redounds
> Therefrom to human kind, and what we are.

In one important respect at least Wordsworth and Blake shared a great kinship: each attached great importance to the role of the imagination in the emancipation and elevation of man; each believed in man's divine potential. The imagination was 'the moving soul' of Wordsworth's 'long labour' in *The Prelude*, and the attention he gives it in the closing books implies more than the efflorescence of a poet's mind. He is a poet with a purpose, but the concluding note of optimism *in excelsis* suggests the overconfidence of one who still viewed his major problem too remotely; when he considered it more closely in *The Excursion*, he made no claim quite so hyperbolical. Wordsworth looks forward to the day when he and Coleridge will be a 'lasting inspiration' as 'prophets of Nature', and show how the mind of man may become 'a thousand times more beautiful than the earth on which he dwells', since it is 'of substance and of fabric more divine'.

This climactic pointer to the ultimate theme of *The Recluse* is reinforced with 'Paradise Regained' overtones. The contrast at the opening of Book Eighth (1805) between the 'wretchedness and vice'

of London and 'the paradise' where Wordsworth was reared is continued with reference to delusive revolutionary hopes at the beginning of the Eleventh: 'Long time hath man's unhappiness and
guilt Detain'd us', but 'not with these our song must end', rather
with 'breezes and soft airs that breathe The breath of Paradise'
and find a way to 'the recesses of the soul'. Miltonic echoes confirming this theme are found elsewhere in *The Prelude*, significantly at the opening, where the statement 'The earth is all before
me' recalls the ending of *Paradise Lost*. Wordsworth's main
subject is to be his own renovation. With its emphasis on the
imagination (moral and spiritual as well as creative), this is
intended as a preliminary to his major task, on the redemption of
man. His 'prospectus' indicates with every justification that this is a
more difficult subject than Milton's:

> Jehovah − with his thunder, and the choir
> Of shouting angels, and the empyreal thrones −
> I pass them unalarmed. Not Chaos, not
> The darkest pit of lowest Erebus,
> Nor aught of blinder vacancy, scooped out
> By help of dreams − can breed such fear and awe
> As fall upon us often when we look
> Into our minds, into the mind of man −
> My haunt, and the main region of my song.

The lines which follow this passage indicate the 'high argument' of
The Recluse, to 'arouse the sensual from their sleep of death', and
help, through the awakening of the imagination, to create a
paradise on earth.

More than any other known creature, man is 'instinct with god-
head' (viii.492−3); it is his birthright. Through the 'filial bond of
nature' the infant enjoys a love which 'irradiates and exalts All
objects through all intercourse of sense', making him 'an inmate of
this *active* universe'. No outcast (and Wordsworth here alludes to
his 'Intimations' theory), he is endowed with imaginative power
that makes him 'creator and receiver both'; like the poet, he is
potentially 'an agent of the one great mind'. In most people this
'first poetic spirit' is weakened or suppressed (05.ii.237−80). In
Wordsworth's youth it was roused until it generated a religious love
of nature; during much of his time at Cambridge it slept, his
'under soul' being locked in 'such a calm, That not a leaf of the

great nature stirr'd' (05.iii.260, 524–41). Then came a period when he mistook 'fancy and conceit' for imagination (viii.365ff.); later a passion for the picturesque made him glad 'to lay the inner faculties asleep' (xii.93ff.); then, after the Godwinian period, came the final renovation, when he seemed 'to have sight of a new world', a world he thought fit to be transmitted, since it is the source of both our spiritual and imaginative strength.

In the scene from the summit of Snowdon (the literary ancestry of which has already been traced from Beattie's *The Minstrel* to James Clarke's description of a scene from Skiddaw, thence to *Descriptive Sketches*) Wordsworth found an emblem of the higher, imaginative mind. The moon illuminates a vast sea of mist, above which rise hills like islands, while in the distance clouds form 'headlands, tongues, and promontory shapes'. This sea-change shows how the imagination modifies appearances, enduing, abstracting, and combining, to give unity of impression. More important is the deep, blue, gloomy chasm in the expanse of mist; through it mounts 'the roar of waters, torrents, streams innumerable' as with one voice. The scene is a 'perfect image of a mighty mind', but the key to it is this 'thoroughfare' for 'the homeless voice of waters' (1805). Wordsworth accordingly finds in it 'the soul, the imagination of the whole'. The mighty mind 'feeds upon infinity' and is 'exalted by an under-presence, The sense of God, or whatso'er is dim Or vast in its own being'. (The voice of many waters is associated with heaven in Revelation. Wordsworth's is homeless because it seeks 'God, who is our home'.) Such minds are 'Powers'. By the God of love inspired through nature (05.xi.99–100), their imagination implies 'clearest insight, amplitude of mind, And Reason in her most exalted mood'. Hence 'sovereignty within', 'cheerfulness in every act of life', 'truth in moral judgments and delight That fails not in the external universe' (05.xiii.106–19). From this imaginative love come all grandeur, truth, and beauty. Without it 'we are as dust'; it makes us aware of 'life endless, the great thought By which we live, infinity and God'. It gives man 'genuine liberty', and raises his awareness to the full; it springs from a vitalizing union between the individual and the universal.

Wordsworth felt, through the 'soul divine' of nature which we participate (05.v.16), that 'our home is with infinitude, and only there', with hope, effort, expectation, desire, 'and something evermore about to be'. The thought arose when he recalled his sensations on hearing, to his astonishment, that he had crossed the Alps.

Looking back, he interpreted the clouding of his mind as the supervention of the imagination:

> I was lost as in a cloud,
> Halted, without a struggle to break through.
> And now recovering, to my soul I say
> I recognise thy glory; in such strength
> Of usurpation, in such visitings
> Of awful promise, when the light of sense
> Goes out in flashes that have shewn to us
> The invisible world, doth greatness make abode.

'Higher minds', working in alliance with the soul of nature ('an ennobling interchange Of action from without and from within', xiii.375−6) cultivate 'the vision and the faculty divine'. In *The Excursion* these words (i.79) have a necessary connection with 'the mind's *excursive* power (iv.1263); in *The Prelude* the communion between earth and heaven, human and divine, which is given by the 'glorious faculty' is either 'discursive' or 'intuitive' (xiv.86−129). Such minds are not enthralled by 'sensible impressions', but 'by their quickening impulse made more prompt To hold fit converse with the spiritual world'.

Wordsworth's thoughts on the 'deathless spirit' of man, his inspiration from a divine source, and the perishability of all his wisdom and truth, led to the dream of the Arab (v) who crosses the desert on a dromedary, desperate to save the stone of geometric truth and the shell of poetry from the oncoming deluge. The stone that 'held acquaintance with the stars' is of high worth, but the shell of 'surpassing brightness' is worthier still, 'a god, yea many gods', with 'voices more than all the winds' and 'power to exhilarate the spirit' and 'soothe . . . the heart of human kind'.[12] Here, in this later version, Wordsworth proclaims his two principal aims as a poet, the first being further defined at the end of the book, God through nature inspiring the poets, giving them 'visionary power' to circumfuse forms and substances 'with light divine', and present them 'as objects recognised, In flashes, and with glory not their own'. He returns to the subject in *The Excursion* (iv.1141−7):

> Even such a shell the universe itself
> Is to the ear of Faith; and there are times,

> I doubt not, when to you it doth impart
> Authentic tidings of invisible things;
> Of ebb and flow, and ever-during power;
> And central peace, subsisting at the heart
> Of endless agitation.

Such a religion is closely connected with Wordsworth's 'intimations' theory, and there are allusions to it in *The Prelude*: with reference to the babe and the imagination (ii.241), to the 'yoke of earth' which threatened his creative mind at Cambridge (iii.182), and to those imaginative tales which satisfy the hidden appetites of young people before they become 'yoke-fellows to custom' (v.520). Here, and much later in 'Presentiments', he mentions the 'isthmus' we cross in the journey through life from our 'native continent' ('from God, who is our home'). It is a time when the 'eternal spirit', 'the soul of our first sympathies', enters like a breeze, creating those affinities that 'fit our new existence to existing things' and, 'in our dawn of being, constitute The bond of union between life and joy' (PR.636–7 and i.544–58).

The 'spots of time' passages which Wordsworth transferred to a late section of *The Prelude* have no such implications. They are recollections which he found efficacious in restoring his imaginative power. Creative feeling comes in aid of creative feeling. We receive but what we give, Coleridge wrote, and Wordsworth repeats the thought in this context (xii.208–335). 'Diversity of strength attends us, if but once we have been strong', but the feeling is a prerequisite for creative power: 'from thyself it comes, that thou must give, Else never canst receive.' The 'hiding-places' of his power which seem open but close as he approaches relate solely to vivid early experiences which are now receding from memory. The same expression, signifying recollections which are stored in the subconscious, and brought to life by a shy spirit that sometimes leaps from 'hiding-places ten years deep', occurs near the end of 'The Waggoner', which was written in 1805, almost certainly the year in which the commentary was added to the 'spots of time' passages.

Wordsworth's generalization on his increasing inability to recall his past should be qualified; all his most vivid recollections had already been recorded, and few were left, if any, of comparable appeal. It is no wonder that, when he tried to explore the past extensively, the hiding-places which seemed open tended to close as he approached them. The strenuousness of his efforts to write the greater part of *The Prelude* in 1804—5 did not give time for impressions to emerge always to advantage. He was in fact working against his usual practice, after finding it beneficial to let poetry originate from 'emotion recollected in tranquillity'. As far as inspiration was concerned, his belief in nature was based on experience, and it taught him to reject the view that 'nothing of itself will come, But we must still be seeking'. There were many parts of his life, chiefly the time of his residence in Cambridge, London, and France, which did not lend themselves to poetic treatment; and the wonder is, not that there are wide variations of quality in *The Prelude*, but that so much of the more prosaic parts is written in a commendable style, often with graphic detail and vigour. On the other hand, Wordsworth had become so habituated to the composition of blank verse that it came too readily at times; he can be self-indulgent to the point of garrulity. He had difficulty not only with proportion but with co-ordination, associative thinking leading him to embark on subjects to which he returned. This repetitiveness is noticeable in the later books, as a result mainly of combining thematic concentrations on developments relative to poetic growth with the relevant accounts of outward circumstances in his life.

In the 1805 version Wordsworth acknowledges the formal problem. At the opening of 'Residence in France' he compares the retrospect of his previous book to a river which turns back almost to its source, feels an impulse to 'precipitate' his verse, and adds (not very explicitly), 'Fair greetings to this shapeless eagerness, Whene'er it comes, needful in work so long, Thrice needful to the argument that now awaits us.' Asides to Coleridge, to whom *The Prelude* is addressed, lead sometimes to disproportion and irrelevance, notably on 'the maid of Buttermere' (vii) and on Sicily at the end of 'France' (xi). Thanks to Wordsworth's lack of restraint, we are given clues to the compositional chronology of the poem. At the opening of Book Seventh he addresses Coleridge at length, particularly on vernal signs which were conducive to composition. There is a charming immediacy about this private prattle; in it the correspondence of the preamble, between the outer breeze and the creative, is renewed, Wordsworth's favourite grove 'tossing its dark boughs in sun and wind' and spreading 'a commotion like its own' through the poet until he feels fit to resume his task. The river image appears: 'the interrupted stream broke forth once more, And flow'd awhile in strength, then stopp'd for years'. It recurs several times; sometimes, as in the examples above, with reference to the course of the poem, sometimes to Wordsworth's life; in 'Conclusion', to the development of his imagination (194–205).

Writing to Sir George Beaumont just before and after completing his work, Wordsworth indicated an awareness of its deficiencies. He had not written at such length about himself from self-conceit, being unprepared for anything more arduous; he was certain that it could be written in 'narrower compass', and was prepared to prune it wherever possible. When he completed it he was depressed; his performance seemed to have 'a dead weight about it'. It was not intended as a tailpiece to *The Recluse* (as Coleridge had supposed) but as a portico. Coleridge had taken the first five books to Malta; when the whole poem was read to him on his return, he was struck with admiration and a sense of his own failure; for him *The Prelude* was 'An Orphic song indeed, A song divine of high and passionate thoughts To their own music chaunted!' Whatever Wordsworth felt about its merits, he was anxious to improve the poem for posterity, and revised it assiduously, particularly in 1828, 1832, and finally before the spring of 1839.

If Wordsworth nodded during revisions of a poem of epic length, it is not surprising; few writers can look at their work with complete detachment, and re-reading tends to stimulate the same responses. Faulty syntax in one complicated sentence (viii.328–39) eluded him, and the prosaic qualities of large portions could not be altered radically, however much more effective they were made by trimming and bracing. The awkwardness of 'My drift hath scarcely, I fear, been obvious' may be smoothed into 'My drift I fear is scarcely obvious (v.293–4) without affecting its banality. The intimate tone Wordsworth adopted towards the reader (Coleridge initially) is rather disarming, but has obvious dangers, in contradistinction to marks of more restricted cordiality in the final text which reflect their later estrangement. Very occasionally Wordsworth's later manner introduced a poetic elegance reminiscent of the poet Thomson. Professor de Selincourt calls attention to this and, more significantly, to the loss incurred by the substitution of a more elaborate general introduction to the account of the meeting with the discharged soldier. Though misleading on the examples illustrating the imaginative potency which solitude held for Wordsworth when it had 'an appropriate human centre', he shows a convincing preference for the direct continuity of personal experience in the original, where the outer scene is followed by an unusually rich evocation of the poet's mind (PR.lxi, 128–30).

Changes for the better will be seen if the following passages are compared with those indicated in the 1850 references: 'with the din, Meanwhile, the precipices rang aloud' (i.439–40); 'Of Newton, with his prism and silent face' (to which was added 'The marble index of a mind for ever Voyaging through strange seas of thought, alone', iii.61–3);[13] the awkward repetition of 'Yet I could shape the image . . .' (05.iii.375–85; cf.iii.371–9); 'A pleasant sight it was when, having clomb The heights of Kendal, and that dreary moor Was cross'd, at length, as from a rampart's edge, I overlook'd the bed of Windermere. I bounded down the hill' (iv.1–12); 'Magnificent The morning was, a memorable pomp. . . . The sea was laughing. . . . The solid mountains were as bright as clouds' (iv.323–7); 'I turn'd my face Without repining from the mountain pomp Of autumn, and its beauty enter'd in With calmer lakes, and louder streams' (vi.9–13, where the vague grandeur of 'mountain pomp' is visually defined in 'coves and heights Clothed in the sunshine of the withering fern'); 'My heart leap'd up when first I did look down . . . aboriginal vale' (vi.517–19). Wordsworth could be ruthless in excising the otiose (cf.05.vi.19–29 and vi.20–5); the prosy superfluity of 'There comes (if need be now to speak of this After such long detail of our mistakes)' was eliminated, with much before and after (05.xi.121–2). Because of their disproportionate length, the story of the shepherd and his son, first intended for 'Michael' (05.viii.222–311) was removed, and that of Vaudracour and Julia (05.ix.555–934), reduced to minimal length.

Though changes in style are usually for the better, changes in substance lead to some loss. Sensitive on the score of egotism, Wordsworth changed constructions to avoid frequent pronominal references to himself. He also removed some interesting biographical details, notably in the account of boating by stealth, which was associated with Esthwaite before the publication of the 1805 text. Coleridge's criticism of his matter-of-factness had its effect; the 1805 version tells us that Wordsworth was 'not six years old' when he rode with 'honest James' on the moors near Penrith Beacon. More important than these details is the influence of his changing views on his revisions. It is easy to exaggerate them; he was never false to his former self. He is more self-critical about his Cambridge career, but his views of the University did not change.

His condemnation of the British government in its opposition to liberty during the early years of the French Revolution remains, though his criticism becomes more judicious, and the intemperate passage 'in their weapons and their warfare base As vermin working out of reach, they leagu'd Their strength perfidiously' (05.x. 654−6) is withdrawn. The most important change is the admission of Wordsworth's tribute to Burke, adamant opponent of the French Revolution and defender of 'institutes and laws, hallowed by time' (vii.512−43); equally significant is the omission of the reference to 'illustrious Fox', the Whig statesman, from this passage. Wordsworth never became a genuine Tory; he was still radical at heart, but his respect for the wisdom inherent in tradition grew, and his later obsessional fear of revolution made him lose confidence in the common man without education to guide him. This, the most important change in Wordsworth perhaps, is not reflected in *The Prelude*.

Nor did he ever become an orthodox Christian. He told Crabb Robinson that he had no sympathy for the orthodox believer who needed a Redeemer, and he does not appear to have changed his view that man's redemption depends upon the individual self; human happiness would be found 'in the very world, which is the world of all of us', or 'not at all' (xiv.209−18, xi.140−4). Realizing again how much our civilization owed to its tradition (as is manifest in *Ecclesiastical Sonnets*), he became more sympathetic to the Church of England. The result is an occasional preference in the later text of *The Prelude* for the metaphorical use of Church ritual. It does not affect his meaning; it glances obliquely and incidentally at a personal interest: for example, he substitutes 'Matins and vespers of harmonious verse' (i.45) for 'The holy life of music and of verse'; referring to noble deeds done during the worst of the French Revolution, he replaces 'As were a joy to hear of' with 'To which the silver wands of saints in heaven Might point with rapturous joy'. More important is the subduing of the more explicit forms of heterodoxy, as the vision spendid faded into the more common light of day. In the glad confidence of his youthful prime, he had felt (PR.525) that conscious thought was 'littleness of life' compared with

> the one interior life
> Which is in all things, from that unity
> In which all beings live with God, are lost

> In God and nature, in one mighty whole
> As indistinguishable as the cloudless east
> At noon is from the cloudless west when all
> The hemisphere is one cerulean blue.

As living experience of this world diminished, his faith in it seems to have become less positive, without ever being lost, and he tended to think more in terms of Christian theology, so that in 'Composed upon an Evening of Extraordinary Splendour' the 'light full early lost, and fruitlessly deplored' is suggested by vespers sung by choirs of angels in the grove. In *The Prelude* the magnificent clarity of 'Great God! Who send'st thyself into this breathing world Through Nature and through every kind of life, And mak'st man what he is, creature divine' is given a weakening ambivalence by the infusion of Christian grace (x.420—4); the precision of 'God and Nature's single sovereignty' is blurred in 'presences of God's mysterious power Made manifest in Nature's sovereignty' (ix.234—5); and the universal 'soul divine which we participate' is less clearly defined in a passage which does not change its central meaning (v.11—18). This kind of modification indicates the trend, a tempering, not a radical change of belief.

Fortitude in Life and Verse (1805–8)

The last books of *The Prelude* were written rapidly but, far from being exhausted by its completion, Wordsworth, after a brief respite, welcomed the freedom he at last enjoyed to write on a number of subjects he would willingly have undertaken earlier, particularly in memory of his brother. John's death had made him set aside *The Prelude*, only to return to it for relief from feelings which had precipitated such a torrent of composition that he could neither recollect it coherently nor write down the fragments he did remember (1.v.05).

By the summer the spirits of the Wordsworths had revived, and they had guests for several weeks. Catherine Clarkson, though still an invalid, came to see them, and took lodgings at Robert Newton's. Walter Scott and his wife made a brief excursion to the Lake District, and Wordsworth met him and Humphry Davy at Keswick. After walking with Southey to Watendlath, they left for Patterdale. The next day they climbed Helvellyn via Striding Edge, along which Scott, slowed down by his lameness, beguiled the time with anecdotes. From Wordsworth he heard the story of Charles Gough, whose skeleton had recently been discovered, unforsaken by his dog more than three months after he had fallen from the edge of the precipitous summit.

The poems which Scott and Wordsworth wrote independently on the loyalty of Gough's dog should be read, if only to accentuate the superiority of Wordsworth's 'Fidelity'. Nothing in 'Helvellyn' compares with the imaginative grandeur of

> There sometimes doth a leaping fish
> Send through the tarn a lonely cheer;
> The crags repeat the raven's croak,

In symphony austere;
Thither the rainbow comes — the cloud —
And mists that spread the flying shroud;
And sunbeams; and the sounding blast,
That, if it could, would hurry past;
But that enormous barrier holds it fast.

Typically but less appropriately Scott contrasts the setting in which his 'pilgrim of nature' has lain with that of a prince lying in funeral splendour. Wordsworth's description is remarkable for the range of its evocative effects, from the detailed to the more general, appealing to eye and ear. The conclusion on the dog's fidelity has a moving greatness of tone, a touch of the sublime, the pause before 'great' giving it an emphasis which ensures that the desired effect is achieved to the full. Far superior in metrical and narrative technique, Wordsworth's presentation varies artfully from the dramatic present to the narrative past, and shows a mastery of style which combines apparent ease with concision and clear-cut definition of sound and sense. Yet the general discipline came from afterthought, and from the omission of several stanzas replete with interesting detail (from reports of the inquest), such as that on the birth of puppies during the period of vigil.

Early in November William and Dorothy, who rode on her pony, enjoyed a week's tour in the Ullswater district. First they stayed with their friends the Luffs, near Goldrill Bridge, Patterdale; news of Nelson's death and the victory of Trafalgar came during their visit. Hearing that Broad How, a small farm near the head of the lake, was for sale, William decided they would move on to the Hutchinsons' and consult Thomas Wilkinson of Yanwath about its purchase.[14] With Sara Hutchinson, they found him working in one of his fields. He was a poet and Quaker who believed in the simple life, and Wordsworth's 'To the Spade of a Friend' was composed in his honour, probably the next year, while they worked in his 'pleasure-ground' by the river.

Two sentences in Wilkinson's unpublished account of a tour in Scotland had recently inspired Wordsworth to write 'The Solitary Reaper', perhaps the greatest of his lyrics. It originated from the melody of 'she sung in Erse as she bended over her sickle, the sweetest human voice I ever heard. Her strains were tenderly melancholy, and felt delicious long after they were heard no more.' The music and substance of the final words appealed, like the daffodils, to the poet's vivid sense of the pleasures of memory. He accentuates the solitude, the sweetness of the singer's voice, and the melancholy of her song by excursions into space and time. They have a superb comprehensiveness: the tragic themes from past and present, with a glance at the future, give universal overtones to the melancholy; the range over land and sea suggests that a sweeter single voice could not be imagined anywhere in a quiet natural setting. Such is the force of contrast, from a wide parching desert to a remote northern island amid ocean waters; the heat of the one making a withdrawal from the sun to rest in a shady haunt most welcome to weary travellers, and the nightingale's song in such surroundings an added pleasure; the prevailing cold of the other increasing delight in spring and in the voice of the cuckoo that proclaims it. Dramatic features at the opening, the quiet close, and success in communicating sounds, particularly at the end of the first and second stanzas, are further indications of the artist at work in the whole.

Perhaps a reading of Dorothy's *Recollections* of their Scottish tour renewed Wordsworth's poetic interest in certain subjects, for soon after finishing *The Prelude* he wrote 'Stepping Westward'. Its appeal lay not just in memory but more in its spiritual connotations. As the western sky was 'glowing with the departed sun', the question which greeted him had a heavenly significance. 'The echo of the voice enwrought A human sweetness with the thought' of travelling further from the east along an isthmus beginning and ending in eternity. Meeting Scott could also have revived memories of the Highland tour. 'Rob Roy's Grave' is largely mock-serious. The hero assumes that nature's law in opposition to man-made laws is the rule of right or God's appointment. 'The eagle, he was lord above, And Rob was lord below.' After this joke, Wordsworth adds that Rob might have been, if he had lived an age earlier; or rather, if he had been living now, for then he could have been another Napoleon. But this does Rob Roy wrong, for he loved liberty, and stood for principles which were always to enlist the poet's sympathy, being the poor man's heart and hand, and the supporter of all the oppressed. The two-edged irony at the expense of Rob and Napoleon is finally surpassed by the quality of the verse in unequivocal honour of the hero.

About this period Wordsworth worked on poems suggested by his visit in 1803 to places connected with Burns. Including one written much later, all three follow a stanzaic pattern to which

Burns was partial, and all convey Wordsworth's sympathy and humanity, a toleration of human frailty that makes Matthew Arnold seem frigidly squeamish. 'At the Grave of Burns, 1803' contains a striking image, 'As vapours breathed from dungeons cold Strike pleasure dead, So sadness comes from out the mould Where Burns is laid'; it acknowledges Wordsworth's indebtedness to the example of Burns in showing that verse may build her throne on simple truth; and its feelings issue from a deeper source than 'To the Sons of Burns', an adjuration which seems superfluous; half was added in 1827, the other half being tactlessly published in 1807. 'Thoughts' was written years later; in the spirit of his essays on epitaphs, Wordsworth prefers to dismiss 'sorrow, wreck, and blight', and remember the finer qualities of the dead.

His most important duty after completing *The Prelude* was to pay tribute to his brother John. He went up to Grisedale Tarn in June to fish with a friend, but the memory of his farewell to John near the outlet made him quit his companion and compose 'Elegiac Verses', a poem unremarkable by Wordsworthian standards, except in the comfort afforded the poet by a rare and modest flower, 'affecting type of him I mourn'. Recollection of a comparison between daisies and white stars in a letter written by John soon after taking command of the *Earl of Abergavenny* explains the opening of 'To the Daisy'; it refers to later voyages, evokes the final scene in graphic strokes, and concludes with gratitude that his brother had found his resting-place (at Wyke Regis, Weymouth) near what he had loved:

> The birds shall sing and ocean make
> A mournful murmur for *his* sake;
> And thou, sweet flower, shalt sleep and wake
> Upon his senseless grave.

The subject of 'Distressful Gift', an unpublished poem (PW4. 372–3), is the booklet John made for the inscription of poems by William which he hoped to read at sea. How genuine these elegiac tributes are may be felt most in 'Elegiac Stanzas, Suggested by a Picture of Peele Castle'; all is real, with no traditional embroidery such as Shelley was to employ in his elegy on Keats. (Wordsworth's sympathies would surely have been with Samuel Johnson in his condemnation of the pastoral convention in 'Lycidas'.) This poem, like many others by Wordsworth, is the expression of one who had thought and felt long and deeply on his subject. It was written in the summer of 1806, soon after Wordsworth had noticed the picture in the London home of its painter, Sir George Beaumont, to whom the poem is addressed. Wordsworth thinks of the calm 'glassy' sea he remembered by the castle when he stayed at Rampside, and of the illusion of youth — his readiness, if he had been a painter, to express what he imagined then, and 'add the gleam, The light that never was, on sea or land, The consecration, and the poet's dream'. He commends Beaumont's work, and finds an image of moral strength in his depiction of Peele Castle, braving the fierce storm at sea. Distress has humanized his soul; he does not believe in being 'housed in a dream', at distance from mankind, but welcomes the 'fortitude, and patient cheer' which enable him to face extreme adversity. He has recovered his faith: 'Not without hope we suffer and we mourn.'

'Character of the Happy Warrior' is a composite work, suggested first by Lord Nelson and written soon after news of his death had been received. Nelson was not a model of domestic virtue, and most of the qualities of the happy warrior were those which Wordsworth admired in his brother John; some, also in Beaupuy. In a letter to Beaumont (12.iii.05), after quoting a passage from Aristotle which exemplifies ways in which fortitude is shown, Wordsworth ascribes them to John. The qualities of heroism displayed by Nelson in battle are clear from two passages in the poem; the Wordsworthian virtues most emphasized are fortitude ('more able to endure, As more exposed to suffering and distress'), generosity inspired by 'filial piety' or 'the genial sense of youth' ('who, when brought Among the tasks of real life, hath wrought Upon the plan that pleased his boyish thought'), moral growth (based on reason and the good derived from painful experience), honourable conduct, unworldliness, homeliness, hope, and 'the faith that looks through death'.

In compliance with Mr Duppa's request to supply translations of Michelangelo's poetry for inclusion in his life of the Italian artist, Wordsworth succeeded with only three of the fifteen or more sonnets he attempted, 'so much meaning' did he find put 'into so little room'. He began 1806 with a diversion, 'The Waggoner'; lacking Matthew Arnold's high seriousness no doubt, it shows the spirit Wordsworth extolled in 'The Kitten and the Falling Leaves': 'Spite of care, and spite of grief, To gambol with life's falling leaf'. The poem was revised several times and not published until 1819, when it was dedicated to Charles Lamb, who recognised its 'spirit of beautiful tolerance' and 'a kind of shadowing affinity between the subject of the narrative and the subject of the dedication'. Knowing Benjamin the waggoner, who had passed his home regularly (once 'The Dove and Olive Bough', now occupied by 'a simple water-drinking bard'), Wordsworth could not resist the subject of his dismissal for intemperance, though he had long done so from timid scruples. The story, narrated in the metre of 'Christabel', is enriched with humour and topographical associations of the old route to Keswick. It was written, Wordsworth told Lord Lonsdale just before its publication, 'con amore, and in the opinion of my friends with spirit'.

Like much of the verse he wrote in 1806 and 1807, 'The Waggoner' reveals Wordsworth in his poetic prime. Though rapidly composed, the verse is smooth-flowing, and often beautifully finished. It varies excellently to suit the needs of the occasion, from the descriptive, narrative, and dramatic to the pleasant conversational ease of the epilogue:

> — Yes, I, and all about me here,
> Through all the changes of the year,
> Had seen him through the mountains go,
> In pomp of mist or pomp of snow,
> Majestically huge and slow:
> Or, with a milder grace adorning
> The landscape of a summer's morning . . .

It excels in atmospheric evocation, especially at the outset, in the presentiment of the storm that will bode ill for Benjamin. His thoughts and feelings on the way, and the manner in which he and his horses adapt themselves to conditions of road and weather, are vividly realized. Wordsworth's full sympathy with his subject takes a humorous turn which differs in its unequivocality from that of 'The Idiot Boy' or 'Peter Bell'. It presents the festive Cherry-Tree with an alluring degree of heightened fancy; equally, the effect of spirituous indulgence on optical impressions, and on the conversation of Benjamin and his sailor companion, whose model of Nelson's *Vanguard* gives the poem a topical interest. The effect of the screeching owl on the superstitious sailor, and Benjamin's explanation of his tricks, lead to the final impression of this fuddled pair, when the sailor, his forebodings allayed by the waggoner,

>   wheels − and, making many stops,
> Brandished his crutch against the mountain tops;
> And, while he talked of blows and scars,
> Benjamin, among the stars,
> Beheld a dancing − and a glancing;
> Such retreating and advancing
> As, I ween, was never seen
> In bloodiest battle since the days of Mars!

Wordsworth is happiest perhaps near the end of the narrative, where the steam from the horses mingles with the morning mist, and the whole is illuminated by the sun; Apollo never threw 'veil of such celestial hue' around the object of his care as he did then; whatever his power in classical epic, he could do nothing to save Benjamin from dismissal.

The need for change and relaxation drew Wordsworth to London, where he stayed eight weeks in the spring. Had Montagu not responded to his urgent request to pay some of his debts, this visit would have been impossible: Wordsworth owed his landlord two years' rent. He spent most of his time, first with his brother Christopher (now Rector of Lambeth, and married to Priscilla, sister of the poet Charles Lloyd),[15] then with the Beaumonts in Grosvenor Square. He probably called on Montagu, whose wife was ill, and he saw the Lambs, to whom he read 'The Waggoner'. William Godwin and he met several times, and they visited the artists David Wilkie and Henry Edridge; it was almost certainly on this occasion, perhaps on Beaumont's recommendation, that the latter made his well-known sketch of the poet. Samuel Rogers introduced him to Charles James Fox, whose greatness Wordsworth could still acknowledge, though he disapproved of his Bonapartist sympathies. Three weeks after his return home, his second son was born. The name chosen for him, until Southey pointed out what confusion it would cause, was William; he was christened Thomas after Mary's brother.

Five poems resulted from the London visit. As already indicated, one was suggested by Beaumont's picture of Peele Castle; another, by the hourly anticipation of Fox's death in September; 'Stray Pleasures', by a scene on the Thames to which Wordsworth felt compelled to draw Lamb's attention; 'Power of Music' and 'Star-Gazers', by street scenes. The last two present interesting human spectacles, but are wrecked as poetry by their jigging metres. Both have a serious undercurrent of meaning: the poor have little opportunity to enjoy the spiritual expansion they yearn for. In 'Stray Pleasures' the more varied metre more successfully conveys the participation of the poet in the glee of the dancers on the floating mill at the end of their day's work; the ending (a reminder of his 'faith that every flower enjoys the air it breathes') happily acknowledges the pleasure which Wordsworth continually finds in the movement of nature, a pleasure clearly dependent on the 'interchange of action from without and from within' which is characteristic of the imagination stirred by natural impressions. 'Lines', on the expected 'dissolution' of Fox, is brief but almost perfect in expression; the natural scene and the thought are one, the thought turning on the belief that greatness of human spirit, constituting 'Power', comes from God and returns to God through nature. Wordsworth's memory for quotation, not always accurate, was amost invariably felicitous; 'Importunate and heavy load' comes from Michelangelo. Earlier in 1806, a cuckoo's echo from Nab Scar above Rydal Water produced a poem ('Yes, it was the mountain echo') which testifies to Wordsworth's beliefs in those intimations which come like echoes to the 'inward ear' from God; the influence of this affirmation on Charlotte Brontë is revealed in *Jane Eyre* with reference to Rochester's call.

Wordsworth may have hoped that his London holiday would renew his zeal for *The Recluse*. After adding 700 lines during July, he was confident that discussion of the subject with Coleridge would enable him to 'go on swimmingly'. He had been extending 'Home at Grasmere', a piece which never reached finished form, though he worked at it years later; the reference to John as an in-mate of their Grasmere home was never removed. Two of the added stories were later revised for transfer to *The Excursion* (vi.1079–1191). The conclusion recalls 'Ode to Duty' and 'Character of the Happy Warrior'. Wordsworth feels that we are not born solely for enjoyment; that he, 'divinely taught', has unique possessions which he must impart. Once he loved to front danger, and he is still unable to read a tale of 'two brave vessels matched in deadly fight' without being pleased 'more than a wise man ought to be'. 'But me', he goes on, 'hath Nature tamed', and reason has sanctioned what she has performed by stealth. He therefore bids farewell to warrior subjects (such as those given at the opening of *The Prelude*), the kind of epic theme he had in mind when he wrote to Beaumont in June 1805.

Wordsworth's preference, as he stated in *The Prelude*, is 'some philosophic song Of truth that cherishes our daily life'. He intends, in short, to continue with *The Recluse*, and he gives its 'prospectus'. The date of this cannot be fixed; most of it in some form or other may belong to a period not later than 1800; the 'spousal verse' section on the imagination is a late addition, probably influenced in metaphorical expression by Coleridge's 'Dejection' ode. The whole unit was most probably revised when Wordsworth was working on 'Home at Grasmere' in 1806, and intended especially for Coleridge, as an earnest of things to come and a basis for discussion. After further revision it was included in the preface to *The Excursion*, where the omission, with reference to 'the individual mind', of 'and consists With being limitless, the one great Life' is notable.

The prospectus contains no new ideas; most of it will be found in *The Prelude* of 1805 (e.g. iii.168–94, xii.220–48, 278–312, xiii.84–119, 428–52). Central to it is the importance of the imagination in making man what he potentially is, 'creature divine'; by 'an ennobling interchange of action from without and from within' (in the words of *The Prelude*), it is capable of making 'the mind of man . . . a thousand times more beautiful than the earth on which he dwells'. The spousal passage does not give all the implications of Wordsworth's imagination; they are to be found in *The Prelude*, which shows why the mind of man is the keystone to the prospectus, and the 'haunt' and 'main region' of the poet's song. Instead of the 'thousand times more beautiful' claim, we have the protest: why should 'Paradise and groves Elysian' be dream or fiction ('history') 'when minds Once wedded to this outward frame of things In love find these the growth of common day'? The Miltonics upset Blake at a point ('Jehovah . . . angels . . . empyreal thrones I pass them unalarmed'), which serves to remind us that Wordsworth was not overawed by Christian conventionalism. In general they are rhapsodically grandiose, but the truthfulness of the claim that the proposed subject was more difficult than epic argument cannot dispel the suspicion that the invocation to Urania admits too much dependence on hope (including advice from Coleridge). Before the close, Wordsworth hints at the inclusion of *The Prelude* in *The Recluse*.

After being hampered for months as a result of the war with France, Coleridge reached England in August, and the news of his arrival made Wordsworth cancel the tour he had planned with

Scott in the Border country. As the cottage at Grasmere was too small for winter requirements, he arranged to take his family to Hall Farm on Sir George Beaumont's Leicestershire estate at Coleorton. It was not until they were on their way, at Kendal, that they met Coleridge. They were shocked by his manner and appearance. He was almost a complete stranger; only occasionally was there a hint of his former self. A slave to opium and drink, and faced with the crisis of leaving his wife and children, he was dejected, 'dismally irresolute', and loth to discuss matters of common interest. Wordsworth invited him to Coleorton, where he arrived with Hartley just before Christmas and stayed four months. He listened to *The Prelude*, and was moved by passages addressed to himself; but nothing, it seemed, could revive his interest in *The Recluse*. Sara Hutchinson, who had accompanied the Wordsworths, had a much greater appeal, but his envy, jealousy, and suspicions, fomented by opium-stimulated dreams and fancies, made him a difficult companion. 'A Complaint' registers the change Wordsworth felt; the fountain of friendship was now 'a comfortless and hidden well', which had not dried up for ever, he hoped.

The verse which he composed at Coleorton, among the groves by the hall which was being built, or along the path between it and Hall Farm, includes three narrative poems of varying quality. 'The Blind Highland Boy', based on a story told by the Grasmere parish-clerk, was intended for Wordsworth's children. No impartial or imaginative critic could have missed his intention, but the washing-tub in which the blind boy made his way towards the sea provoked derision, and the author, accepting Coleridge's suggestion from Dampier's *Voyage*, substituted the turtle-shell fiction. It would have been better, as Charles Lamb insisted, had he kept to the truth. 'The Horn of Egremont Castle' is an interesting tale, told in rather a business-like manner, and not always metrically satisfying. Its appeal for Wordsworth lay, as in a later story ('Artegal and Elidure'), in the brother's forgiveness. Interest in the subject of 'Song at the Feast of Brougham Castle', the restoration of Lord Clifford to his ancestral estates after the Wars of the Roses, is hinted at in 'The Waggoner' (iv). The young heir had been secured from danger in various retreats (one in Yorkshire, as a note to *The White Doe of Rylstone* indicates); at Threlkeld, disguised as a shepherd, he had been protected by Sir Lancelot Threlkeld. The superstitions of the region, below Saddleback or Blencathra, are given; but the subject once again hinges on the supersession of 'the savage virtue of the race, Revenge, and all ferocious thoughts'. The song, in the style of *The Lay of the Last Minstrel* (two copies of which Scott had sent Wordsworth), ends with the expectation that the shepherd will soon be mailed and horsed, making the field of death groan with victory. The minstrel did not know how adversity had bred wisdom, how 'Heaven's grace', through nature, had humanized Clifford's heart:

> Love had he found in huts where poor men lie;
> His daily teachers had been woods and rills,
> The silence that is in the starry sky,
> The sleep that is among the lonely hills.

Among the miscellaneous sonnets which belong, or are attributed, to the 1806 period are two very personal groups, 'To Sleep' (on sleeplessness) and 'Personal Talk'. The latter (with its introductory I.F. note) suggests an earlier period at Town End; the 'sweetest melodies . . . by distance made more sweet' seem to have been remembered by Keats in his 'Ode on a Grecian Urn', for Wordsworth's theme is the pleasure afforded by the imagination, especially in the poets he emulates. Too often his sonnet subjects fail to inspire lofty thoughts, tending to fanciful exercises in consequence, yet the Napoleonic war and the question of liberty could still inspire. Gustavus IV's appeals, in October 1805 and later, for resistance against Napoleon, 'the common nuisance', called forth admiration in 'The King of Sweden'. Another setback for the Coalition elicited, in 'November, 1806', the view that Britain would resist all the more spiritedly without an ally, if only its Ministry remained firmly patriotic; those who remember 1940 will find no hollowness in this. Wordsworth knew the national temper, and had the insight of a statesman and strategist of war. 'Thought of a Briton on the Subjugation of Switzerland' is implicitly a continuation of the subject: the title accentuates the link between countries whose natural defences help to secure Liberty; she has lost her mountain stronghold, and he hopes that she will be preserved through the sea-power of Britain. The thought and movement of this clean-cut, finely shaped poem are disciplined, yet it has the power of a deep invocation; in 1808 Wordsworth referred to it as his best sonnet. Another of merit, 'To Thomas Clarkson', was written when the Bill for the abolition of the slave trade was finally passed in March 1807.

Wordsworth spent much time at Coleorton selecting and arranging for the publication of *Poems in Two Volumes* in 1807. One of the latest lyrics to be ready for inclusion was 'O nightingale! thou surely art', in which his preference for the quieter and more steadfast virtues of the stockdove is characteristic. Although the selection contained many of his finest poems, it included too many on minor subjects to represent Wordsworth's merits fairly. The rough handling this publication received is the reflex of callous cultural smugness, but one could wish he had been more selective or had made room for more of his best work. In his letter to Lady Beaumont (21.v.07) he affected indifference to critical malevolence, though it ultimately contributed to his decline. He condemns the worldly insensitivity of his critics, insists that an original writer has to 'create the taste by which he is to be relished', asserts that his poems on civil liberty and national independence have a 'simplicity of style' and 'grandeur of moral sentiment' likely to have few parallels in contemporary poetry, and is confident that his writings will 'co-operate with the benign tendencies in human nature and society'. Their destiny, he trusts, will be 'to console the afflicted, to add sunshine to daylight by making the happy happier, to teach the young and gracious of every age, to see, to think and feel, and therefore to become more actively and securely virtuous'. Here, it is worth noting, he does not consider preaching or moral exhortation the duty of a poet; it is his business to make readers 'see', think, and feel.

A more welcome task at Coleorton had been the designing of a winter garden for Lady Beaumont; her idea for this came from paper 477 of *The Spectator*, by Addison, but Wordsworth planned and supervised the work. In February he travelled with the gardener to buy plants at Nottingham, which he found all the more interesting after having just read the memoirs of Colonel Hutchinson, its governor during the Civil War. He regretted the classical restoration of the castle, but thought the meadows below the rock and town 'a magnificent savanna with the Trent one of the grandest, if not the grandest, of our English rivers winding through it'. Near Castle Donington, perhaps on this journey, though he states on his way 'to and from Derby' (where he had probably met the poet John Edwards),[16] he saw the group which provoked him to write in 'Gipsies', 'better wrong and strife, Better vain deeds or evil than such life!' He assumes that the vagrants, like Peter Bell, are indifferent to nature's beauty. Their mode of life is unnatural: 'The silent heavens have goings-on; The stars have tasks — but these have none.' The 1807 version is better than its later form, but Wordsworth's defence of his irrational reaction is the product of hasty reflection (betrayed by the conventional facility of 'Then issued Vesper from the fulgent west').

In April the Hall Farm residents went to stay in London, where they met Scott, who returned with them to Coleorton. They accompanied him on his homeward journey as far as Lichfield, and had hardly time to look inside the cathedral. After staying at Halifax in June, Mary, Sara, and the children left for Kendal, while William and Dorothy were taken to Bolton Abbey, Wharfedale, by the Marshalls of Kirkstall, Leeds, before walking over the moors to Gordale and Malham. Wordsworth probably wrote 'Composed by the Side of Grasmere' soon after their return. The sonnet opens with a description of clouds and reflected stars which is typical of his best in distinct imagery. The reflection of ruddy-crested Mars reminds him of continuing war in Europe, but the voice of great Pan 'low-whispering through the reeds' tells him to be grateful for the tranquillity he enjoys. After further outings with Mary, including twelve days at Eusemere with the Beaumonts, and a tour to Wastdale, Ennerdale, Whitehaven, and Cockermouth, Wordsworth settled to work on *The White Doe of Rylstone*.

He had already written 'The Force of Prayer' in consequence of his visit to Wharfedale, and had made some progress with his major poem when, on 4 November, Hartley Coleridge burst in, the harbinger of his mother and Derwent and Sara, whom De Quincey had escorted from Bristol, where they had been staying. They remained a week before proceeding to Greta Hall, and it is to De Quincey that we are indebted for some vivid impressions of the Wordsworths: Mary, tallish, rather plain and taciturn, but redolent of sweetness and purity of heart; Dorothy, Egyptian brown, with wild eyes, ardent manner, sensibility, and an impassioned intellect that struggled for words; William, inelegant and ageing in appearance, with greying hair and a sanguine, weathered complexion in place of the bronze tint that once made him resemble a Venetian senator or Spanish monk. There is probably much truth in these impressions, though De Quincey's *Reminiscences* were written long afterwards, when he was not on good terms with Wordsworth; they are often untrustworthy, and even malicious.

The Marshalls had sent Wordsworth a copy of *The History and Antiquities of Craven* by Thomas Whitaker, and it was in this that he found not just the seed for his poem but a challenge to write it:

> After Rilston came into possession of the Cliffords, the same ground, with part of the fell above, was inclosed for a park . . . At this time a white doe, say the aged people of the neighbour-hood, long continued to make a weekly pilgrimage from hence over the fells to Bolton, and was constantly found in the abbey churchyard during divine service, after the close of which she returned home as regularly as the rest of the congregation. This incident awakens the fancy . . . Had the milk-white doe per-formed her mysterious pilgrimage from Ettrick Forest to the precincts of Dryburgh or Melrose, the elegant and ingenious editor of the 'Border Minstrelsy' would have wrought it into a beautiful story.

For the historical part of the narrative, which he regarded as of minor importance, Wordsworth relied on 'The Rising of the North' in Percy's *Reliques*. The idea of the white doe as a spiritual presence as well as companion may have come from a memory of November 1805, as recorded by Dorothy: 'Mrs. Luff's large white dog lay in the moonshine upon the round knoll under the old yew-tree, a beautiful and romantic image – the dark tree with its dark shadow, and the elegant creature as fair as a spirit.' The poem was completed in January 1808.

A mystery surrounds its revision. If the criticisms made by Cole-ridge (PW3.545) in a long rambling letter are to be taken at their face value, it must have been substantial, but there is no external evidence to this effect, though improvements and additions were made in 1809, and publication was delayed until 1815. For this Wordsworth wrote a dedication to his wife in gracefully modified Spenserian stanzas, which suggest the imaginative influence of the first book of *The Faerie Queene* on his story, and allude to the moral value of his poem for Mary after the death of two of their children. 'Personal Talk' (iii) shows that 'heavenly Una with her milk-white lamb' was a favourite story with Wordsworth.

The White Doe does not reveal the 'disproportion of the accidents to the spiritual incidents' which Coleridge found. Its proportions are satisfying, and the narration of the rebellion is both adequate and essential. Unlike Scott in his narrative poems,

Wordsworth is interested less in the externals of action than in a deeper subject, less amenable to success, but nearer to life. It focuses attention on Emily and Francis, and the latter's role is of great significance. The lines from *The Borderers*, 'Action is transitory . . . Suffering is permanent . . .', which Wordsworth prefixed to the poem relate not only to Emily's sorrow but also, as he states (18.i.16), to the effects of objects like the banner on the minds of those connected with them. Norton, assuming when he joins the rebels that he is one of heaven's delegates, chosen to fight for the old faith, looks up at the banner of the Cross, and is struck with dismay as he remembers the 'love divine' of Emily when she wrought it, the influence of Francis on her, and above all, the influence of their departed Protestant mother on both. Francis knows that the cause his father and brothers have rashly undertaken is doomed, but cannot desert them, and hovers 'like a tutelary power', ready to secure their safety; though spurned, he remains when all hope is lost. His life is spared as they are condemned to death, but he wins his father's forgiveness by swearing to recover the banner and lay it on St Mary's shrine at Bolton Priory. After seizing it and riding recklessly, blind to the outside world, he suddenly becomes aware of it, and realizes his folly. What end can such a vain oblation serve, and what right has he to carry such a symbol of disloyalty? In such irresolution, it is the thought of his danger that spurs him on foolhardily to the heroism of inevitable death.

The religious rift in the family is one of the accidentals of the story. The Cross which Emily embroidered for her father is an 'unblest work', done with religious love but for a cause which could not win her approval. Here begin the sufferings which continue until she is, as Francis predicted, 'the last leaf on a blasted tree'. The tragic flaw is denoted at the opening of the main narrative, which occupies five cantos between the introductory first and the last. Its first paragraph seems to imply Wordsworth's acceptance of Coleridge's criticism; looking back at the first canto and forward to the last, he writes:

> Beginning, where the song must end,
> With her, and with her sylvan friend;
> The friend, who stood before her sight,
> Her only unextinguished light;
> Her last companion in a dearth
> Of love, upon a hopeless earth.

Further evidence of change arising from the criticism that Emily had not been given enough prominence may be surmised in the fourth and fifth cantos. After introducing a friend of Emily's father, whose mission it is to bring her news of what befalls him and her brothers, the fourth changes its moonlight scene from one which brings her 'kindly sympathies' to one which swiftly presents the disastrous end of the revolt. In the fifth the old man completes his report with an account of the trial and of Francis' mission.

Wordsworth's artistic discrimination is seen to better effect when the white doe's appearances are considered in chronological order. Emily is seated ominously under a yew tree as Francis makes his gloomy forecast, and counsels her to seek 'fortitude without reprieve'. Eveything will be lost in desolation, he predicts, and the white doe feeding near will return to the woods it knew 'ere she had learned to love us all'. He urges her to be worthy of God's grace and fulfil her destiny, 'A soul, by force of sorrows high, Uplifted to the purest sky Of undisturbed humanity' (ii). The doe appears next when the moon shines on a beleaguered town and castle and on Rylstone Hall. Emily is soothed by the fragrance of 'breathing flowers' and of times recalled with her mother. She prays that her mother's spirit will descend in 'radiant ministry' on Francis, making him think better of 'the self-reliance of despair'. She has a mind to go to her father, but remembers her brother's interdiction, 'In resignation to abide, The shock, *and finally secure O'er pain and grief a triumph pure*'. The doe has come to seek her, but tries in vain to win a look of love (iv). Years after the disaster to her family, after much travel, she returns in spring to prove her fortitude. On a primrose bank, amid the desolation of Rylstone, she is 'serene':

> The mighty sorrow hath been borne,
> And she is thoroughly forlorn:
> Her soul doth in itself stand fast,
> Sustained by memory of the past
> And strength of reason; held above
> The infirmities of mortal love;
> Undaunted, lofty, calm, and stable,
> And awfully impenetrable.

Suddenly a deer leaves the troop which comes sweeping by, and approaches her as she sits beneath the 'self-surviving leafless oak' which typifies her state. 'A radiant creature, silver-bright', it lays its head on her knee, and looks up at her with 'pure benignity'. She remembers it, and her tears fall on the happy creature's face. It is a heaven-sent moment, the first of many meetings, the doe intuitively responding to her wishes. So its presence became dearer to her, giving gladness 'at morning to the dewy field' and a deeper peace to 'the hour of moonlight solitude'. At such times her favourite haunt was 'Bolton's sacred pile', and there she would sit on Francis' grave, her mute companion by her.

Adopting a more orthodox terminology without changing his religion radically, Wordsworth states his belief that he is inspired by the 'celestial power' which gave Emily fortitude and serenity. In her degree, too, the white doe partakes of 'Heaven's grace' (vii). The ending turns full circle into the beginning, where the splendour of the doe's presentation (its final appearance in the story) and conjectural explanations, among the outcoming worshippers, of its regular visits create a tone and mystery admirably suited to a narrative introduction. As he informed Wrangham (18.i.16), Wordsworth intended 'nothing less than the apotheosis of the animal', and he achieves this in a spiritualizing chiaroscuro manner reminiscent of Spenser. Gliding with a lovely gleam, the white doe emerges from the dusky trees and moves about the priory ruins before sinking gently by a grassy grave. She is 'a pledge of grace from purest heaven', filling gloomy nooks with 'glory' or the 'lustre of a saintly show', and shedding a 'more than sunny liveliness' on the flowers. She epitomizes the spiritual solace that comes to Emily; and the redolence of the imagery makes the reinforcing lines which were prefixed in 1837 to the final canto from 'Address to Kilchurn Castle' rather superfluous.

In the metre of 'Christabel', the style befits its more austere subject, and equals the best of Coleridge in technical accomplishment, especially at the opening and in the final canto. It affords a reminder that, given the right subject, Wordsworth in 1808 could equal its demands.

Heroism Abroad and Grief at Home (1808–14)

Expecting Coleridge and his two boys to share his home, Wordsworth had agreed to rent Allan Bank, the 'temple of abomination' which he had regarded as an offence to Grasmere Vale. In February, disturbed by news of Coleridge's continued illness, he travelled to London, taking the manuscript of *The White Doe* for publication, and intending to check the proofs while he was there. Dorothy, who wished to purchase furniture for their new home, was aghast to hear that he had decided to defer publication and leave the poem with Coleridge. She had been actively engaged in finding homes and organizing a welfare fund for the orphaned brothers and sisters of her young domestic help, Sally Green. Blinded by a heavy snowstorm, their parents had fallen over a steep edge on their way late at night over the mountain range between Langdale and their home in Easedale. Dorothy wrote an account of their tragedy and of the plight of their six children, left for three days in the care of the eldest, who was only eleven years old; the story made a deep impression on De Quincey, who recorded it more graphically than accurately in his Lake District *Reminiscences*.

Before returning to Grasmere, Wordsworth had an imaginative experience which struck him like an epiphany. Early one morning, after leaving Coleridge, he was immersed in gloomy thoughts; looking up, he was surprised to find Fleet Street empty, silent, and white with new-fallen snow; there was no traffic, only the soundless movement of a few dusky pedestrians here and there. Turning up Ludgate Hill, he saw the 'huge and majestic form' of St Paul's Cathedral towering beyond, 'solemnised by a thin veil of falling snow'. The lines in which he recalled the 'visionary scene' (PW4.374–5) are no more telling than his report of it to Sir George Beaumont (8.iv.08), but each flashes numinously Wordsworth's sense of communion with the 'invisible world'. His despondency was checked, and he knew the 'blessing' of 'exalted Imagination' as he had done in the experience which informed 'Resolution and Independence'. The ballad-elegy on the Greens ('Who weeps for strangers?') which he wrote soon afterwards in Grasmere churchyard is taut with feeling, but one cannot help reflecting what might have been made of both of these subjects had Wordsworth found more time to dwell on them.

In London he had met Henry Crabb Robinson, an admirer of his poetry and a friend of the Clarksons. Robinson noted Wordsworth's inelegant appearance and manners, his self-assurance and contempt for popular authors; but the more he saw of him, the more he respected the purity, dignity, and elevation of his mind and poetry. Coleridge became far from cordial; his annoyance when Wordsworth decided independently not to publish *The White Doe* was inflamed by jealous suspicion that he and Mary had supervised Sara Hutchinson's letters to him, and had convinced her that his attachment had destroyed her happiness. Such morbid accusations moved Wordsworth to write a lengthy rebuttal, telling Coleridge he had become habituated to venting the 'most lawless thoughts' and 'wildest fancies' of his 'lamentably insane state of mind'. It seems most likely that better counsel prevailed, and that this unfinished letter was not sent.

To the spring of 1808 belong two blank verse poems, which (like so much of Wordsworth's later blank verse) could be more aptly described as 'effusions'. 'To the Clouds' imparts with some exhilarating fluency and attractive fancifulness the eagerness which the poet shared with the clouds hurrying over Nab Scar as he followed the path from Rydal Mount to Grasmere; his thoughts 'admit no bondage', and his words 'have wings'. Inevitably it recalls Shelley's 'The Cloud', a superior poem by virtue of its disciplined design, its inwrought artistry, the inspired intensity of its varied imagery, and its sustained lyricism. By comparison, Wordsworth's poem remains largely an improvization, breath-takingly egotistical when he sees in the clouds and 'the bosom of the firmament, o'er which they move' a type of his soul's 'capacious self' with 'all her restless progeny'. The ending of the poem shows a lofty aspiration, but its thoughts of eternity hardly transcend prose.

'The Tuft of Primroses', a much longer, less unified, incomplete work, seems to have been written with *The Recluse* in mind, two passages from it being adapted for *The Excursion* (iii.367–405, vii.242–91). The early part suggests another 'Home at Grasmere'; it is highly personal with family allusions and reference, and records losses which Wordsworth had to face after a long absence at Coleorton. Its compositeness is twofold. The primrose survives to give gladness despite the tree-felling and rapid extinction of the Sympson family, finalized with the death of old Mr Sympson, the angling friend of Wordsworth and his brother John. The consequent loss of beauty, natural and cultivated, gives rise to the wish that warden spirits could prevent the spoliation of 'all growth of nature and all frame of art' that please the eye. The author of 'Ode to Duty' yearns for 'confirm'd tranquillity', 'the human soul consistent in self-rule', and 'heaven revealed to meditation'; he then proceeds to the story and scene of St Basil's retreat, with excellent descriptive effects in verse of sustained fluency, all derived from the original Latin. After recalling the ruins of religious shrines in France and Britain, Wordsworth turns for the third time to the expulsion of the monks from the Grande Chartreuse during the French Revolution. (Much of this version contributed to the final account in *The Prelude*, vi.441–71 especially.) The 'unwearied song' breaks off with reference to a convent of 'female votaries' in the contrasting mildness of a lonely vale, and leaves the second associative subject-cycle mysteriously incomplete.

Wordsworth had obviously realized the danger into which he was slipping with blank verse that came too readily, sustaining prose thoughts in easy conjunction with poetic feelings and imagery. 'In small proportions we just beauties see'; he would have done better to write unified and artistically finished poems on his several subjects instead of linking them loosely and disproportionately. Incidental splendours remain in the memory: the primrose which 'lives to proclaim her charter' in the Miltonic 'blaze of noon' and pierce 'the gloom of twilight with the vigor of a star' or 'with lustre somewhat dimm'd lovely and bright' like the moon; the trees lost to Grasmere, including the 'lofty band of firs' that appeared over the church, 'an aerial grove . . . suspended like a stationary cloud', and the avenue along which the priest, 'glistening in best attire', made his way from the parsonage towards the churchyard, where his 'ready flock' awaited him, 'While trees and mountains echoed to the voice Of the glad bells, and all the murmuring streams United their soft chorus with the song'.

The removal to Allan Bank took place at the end of May. Fortunately Henry Hutchinson, who had left the navy, was at hand; everything depended on him and Dorothy. William was 'not expected to do anything'; Mary had sprained her right arm; and Sara (whose serious illness Wordsworth could not exclude from 'The Tuft of Primroses') was far from strong. Sad though they were to leave their cottage, they were quick to appreciate the luxury of private rooms and the variety of beautiful prospects their elevated position afforded: sylvan and pastoral, lake and mountain slopes, sunrise and sunset. The children were happy to play freely 'without fear of carriages or horses'. These compensations were offset by the work which proved necessary, especially as the house filled. In September Coleridge made Allan Bank his home; and Hartley and Derwent, for whom a school had been found at Ambleside, joined them on Sundays. A few days after Coleridge's arrival, Catherine, the Wordsworths' fourth child, was born. De Quincey arrived in November, and was such a favourite with the children that he was soon persuaded to stay. Additional problems, often extremely trying, came from Coleridge, whose self-indulgence and aversion to plain living made him very demanding, as well as from smoky chimneys which made the kitchen and every other room except Wordsworth's study untenable at one time or another before improvements were made.

Some of Coleridge's eager, enthusiastic self returned as he wrote to numerous friends, hoping to enlist support for *The Friend*, which he planned to issue as a weekly paper. Wordsworth probably worked on *The Excursion*, but was soon plunged into deep concern for the cause of freedom in Europe. A Spanish revolt had encouraged the Portuguese to resist Napoleon, and a British expeditionary force had defeated the French at Vimiero, only for the government to accept the Convention of Cintra, which allowed the French troops in Portugal to be conveyed to France on British ships. From November 1808 to the end of March 1809 Wordsworth was busy writing his protest, and keeping as fully informed as possible about the war in Spain, in order to rouse public opinion. Often he walked to the top of Dunmail Raise to meet the carrier at two in the morning for his newspaper. Instalments appeared in *The Courier* on 27 December and 13 January, but postal problems and the loss of several sheets of script made Wordsworth discontinue this form of publication and prepare a lengthy pamphlet *Concerning . . . the Convention of Cintra.*

Coleridge collaborated at times, and De Quincey (to whom he had sublet Dove Cottage, after renewing its lease for six years) readily acted, in the final stages, as his representative with the printers in London, sometimes drafting amendments on Wordsworth's instructions. Revisions, additions, and De Quincey's punctiliousness finally upset the printer, and several weeks passed before the sheets were 'struck off' without a final check to ensure they contained nothing libellous, after Wordsworth had taken fright lest his criticism of Lord Wellesley, one of the signatories to the Convention, should lead to incarceration at Newgate or Dorchester – a prospect so unlikely that Dorothy and Sara found it highly amusing.

Wordsworth's tract would have been more effective had he written more directly, less abstractly, and less grandiloquently. His periodical, parenthetic sentences tend to lose point and vigour through accretion; his poetic idealization and repetition of sentiments breed impatience. Yet the magnanimity of his principles is unquestionable, and the sureness of his strategic sense (proved by subsequent history) is remarkable. It is based on a burning faith in the invincibility and instinctive wisdom of a people struggling for justice and freedom. Their ultimate salvation depends on 'moral virtues and qualities of passion' for great ends which transcend 'the principles and practice of governments'. The latter had been responsible for the Convention of Cintra and two wars against liberty, 'the American war, and the war against the French people in the early stages of their Revolution', momentous decisions affecting the people being made by men who live 'exclusive and artificial' lives, without imagination or true awareness of human nature. With this and self-vindication in mind, Wordsworth wrote:

This just and necessary war, as we have been accustomed to hear it styled from the beginning of the contest in the year 1793, had, some time before the Treaty of Amiens, viz. after the subjugation of Switzerland, and not till then, begun to be regarded by the body of the people, as indeed both just and necessary; and this justice and necessity were by none more clearly perceived, or more feelingly bewailed, than by those who most eagerly opposed the war in its commencement, and who continued most bitterly to regret that this nation had ever borne a part in it. Their conduct was herein consistent; they proved that they kept their eyes steadily fixed upon principles; for, though there was a shifting or transfer of hostility in their minds as far as regarded persons, they only combated the same enemy opposed to them under a different shape; and that enemy was the spirit of selfish tyranny and lawless ambition.

English people, to whom the rising in 'the Pyrenean peninsula' had given hope of further resistance to tyranny and oppression, had felt that the Convention was a betrayal. An 'inward liberty' which gratified their moral yearnings had been awakened, and Wordsworth's endeavour was to raise and steady this spirit, and help his countrymen to judge rightly 'in the present or any future struggle which justice will have to maintain against might'.

He believed that, by 'unnaturally clustering the people together', industry and commerce tended to promote Jacobinism, expediency, and materialism rather than imaginative or humanitarian vision and virtue. Such a danger, he held, did not exist in Spain, which had shown, notably at Saragossa, that the true army, in a contest for liberty, is the whole people. Even if Spain were overrun, the invading torrent would weaken as the water spread. Other nations in fetters would awaken. The time was auspicious, and Britain should use it to make 'a great and decisive effort', and redeem her failures, for 'upon liberty, and upon liberty alone, can there be permanent dependence'.

The pamphlet is inspired by principles which matured in Wordsworth during the French Revolution; they have a high and rare statesmanlike quality, and a nobility worthy of Milton, whom he quotes in conclusion. Though spoilt by diffuseness and persistence, his soul-animating strains in prose need to be savoured to appreciate the full force of the collateral sonnets he wrote while composing his Cintra pamphlet and later in 1809. They are neither numerous nor well known. Two relate to heroes of the resistance: Hofer in the Tyrol, Palafox at Saragossa; another returns to the heroic spirit of Gustavus IV of Sweden; one of the best ('Brave Schill! by death delivered') celebrates a German whose example would remain 'fixed as a star' in 'the spacious firmament of time', were earthly fame not the frail dependant of Fortune. In 'Alas! what boots the long laborious quest Of moral prudence . . .?' Wordsworth contrasts the 'haughty Schools' of philosophy, 'the pride of intellect and thought' in Germany, with the 'few strong instincts' and 'few plain rules' of Alpine peasants who had done far

Above Wordsworth's birthplace, Cockermouth

Below Ann Tyson's cottage, Hawkshead
(both about 1910)

1

Above the Ferry House, on the west side of Windermere, much as it was in Wordsworth's time

Below Windermere from the Ferry House, about 1830

Above Furness Abbey, about 1818

Below Brougham Castle, about 1830

Above Ullswater from Gowbarrow Park, with Keldas near the head of the lake and St Sunday Crag beyond

Below Skelwith Bridge and the Brathay river, with the Langdale Pikes in the distance

Cambridge (about 1840):

Above   St John's College

Below   a front view of King's College, showing the Chapel

Alfoxden House

Racedown Lodge

6

William Wordsworth, 1798

Samuel Taylor Coleridge, 1796

(both portraits by Robert Hancock)

Above Tintern Abbey, from William Gilpin's *Observations on the River Wye*, 1782

Below Dove Cottage about 1910, and view from the orchard above Dove Cottage, about 1886

Above left Grasmere *right* the Rock of Names (above Thirlmere, less than a mile north of Wythburn, and just beyond the Cherry-Tree of 'The Waggoner'). On this the initials of William, John, and Dorothy Wordsworth, Mary and Sara Hutchinson, and Coleridge were cut in the summer of 1800.
Below the head of Windermere, from Low Wood (by William Green, 1814)

Above left the four yews of Borrowdale *right* Helm Crag and the Swan Inn (Grasmere)

Below a view of Thirlmere and its bridge (about 1830), looking north

Above an artist's impression (about 1850) of Langdale Pikes with Blea Tarn in the foreground. (Beyond this, to the right of the scene, stands the house Wordsworth imagined as the Solitary's cottage.)
Below Rydal Mount, about 1910

Above a view of Rydal Water, showing the Rothay river and Ivy Cottage

Below Patterdale Bridge, with Keldas beyond, to the left. Broad How is on the opposite side of the head of Ullswater, to the right of the wood.

Above the harbour at Whitehaven, from a painting by William Daniell. Moresby lies beyond the hill in the background.
Below George Cattermole's impression of Sir Walter Scott and Wordsworth below Newark Tower in 1831

Dora Wordsworth as bridesmaid to
Sara Coleridge, 1829 (painting by Miss Rainbeck)

Dorothy Wordsworth, 1833
(from a painting by S. Crosthwaite)

14

William Wordsworth, 1844,
from a portrait by H. Inman

Mary Wordsworth, from a water-colour
on ivory by Margaret Gillies, 1839

15

William Wordsworth, 1842,

from a portrait by Benjamin Robert Haydon

more for the cause of freedom. The sonnet on Napoleon, 'Look now on that adventurer', is one of the most successful in this series, but the most stirring is the first, 'Composed while the Author was engaged in writing a Tract occasioned by the Convention of Cintra'. The affirmations remain unchanged, whatever the circumstances which occasioned them. Wordsworth's trust is in Heaven, and with those in whom nature lives, not with the worldly who are led astray by selfishness and factional interests. The 'mountain nymph, sweet Liberty' is writ large in 'Advance – come forth from thy Tyrolean ground'; but natural defences may fail, and the essential bulwark, the 'inward liberty' of his tract, is 'in the soul' ('And is it among rude untutored dales').

After much difficulty and delay, the first two numbers of *The Friend* were published at Penrith, where Coleridge had spent several weeks, engaged, it seems, less in its production than in spirituous indulgence. He recovered, after staying with Thomas Wilkinson. Sara Hutchinson transcribed for him, sometimes as he dictated; Wordsworth contributed seven of his recent political sonnets, and translations of six epitaphs by the Italian poet Chiabrera. His 'Reply to Mathetes', on the moral problems of adolescence, appeared on 14 December 1809 and 4 January 1810. In February, when Coleridge was 'utterly unprovided', he supplied the first of his essays on epitaphs. Not long afterwards *The Friend* made its last appearance. Wordsworth must have realized that Coleridge could give him no help with *The Recluse*, and nothing suggests that he himself found time to give it sustained attention. In the summer, almost certainly for financial reasons, he had agreed to write descriptive accounts of the Lake District for publication with Joseph Wilkinson's engravings, after ensuring that the enterprise did not conflict with the interests of his friend William Green, a superior artist.

The three essays on epitaphs were completed in February 1810. Wordsworth had discussed the subject occasionally with Coleridge, but his main thoughts arose from his admiration of Chiabrera's epitaphs. He argues, unconvincingly, that the desire to live posthumously in human memory would never have been awakened but for 'the consciousness of a principle of immortality in the human soul', and that there can be no repose, joy, or development of the social affections without such an implicit faith. In response to Dr Johnson's opinion that 'the greater part of mankind have no character at all', he argues that 'The light of love in our hearts is a satisfactory evidence that there is a body of worth in the minds of our friends or kindred, whence that light has proceeded. We shrink from the thought of placing their merits or defects to be weighed against each other in the nice balance of pure intellect. . . .' From this, as could be expected of the author of 'A Poet's Epitaph', he concludes that the epigraph-writer is not an anatomist; nor is he a painter: the character of a deceased friend or beloved kinsman should be seen not otherwise than 'as a tree through a tender haze or a luminous mist, that spiritualises and beautifies it'. In this way truth of the highest order, 'hallowed by love', is presented. The epitaph should make acknowledgments to our common nature; its thoughts and feelings should have a permanent and univeral significance; they should be controlled and tranquillizing. Great actions worthy of remembrance should not be omitted.

Nobody reading Wordsworth's second essay could accuse him of averting his ken from half of human fate, or wish to question his observation on churchyards that it is 'a happiness to have, in an unkind world, one enclosure where the voice of detraction is not heard'. He emphasizes that virtues are generally 'retired', particularly in humble life, and that 'many of the highest must be sought for or they will be overlooked'. He comments on epitaphs, 'not to lower the witling and the worldling in their self-esteem', but in the hope that he can 'bring the ingenuous into still closer communion with those primary sensations of the human heart, which are the vital springs of sublime and pathetic composition'. Further epitaphs are studied with the aim of distinguishing truth and sincerity from falsehood and affectation. Some of his statements in the third essay are epigrammatic, from 'no epigraph ought to be written on a bad man, except for a warning' to the self-revelatory idealism of 'In the mind of the truly great and good every thing that is of importance is at peace with itself; all is stillness, sweetness, and stable grandeur.' The aim of Wordsworth's ideal epitaph has a wider application: 'namely, to give to universally received truths a pathos and spirit which shall re-admit them into the soul like revelations of the moment.' His criticism of bad taste and artificiality leads to pronouncements which display fine independent judgment (he has already stated that expression should not be 'what the garb is to the body, but what the body is to the soul'):

Words are too awful an instrument for good or evil to be trifled with: they hold above all other external powers a dominion over thoughts. If words be not . . . an incarnation of the thought but only a clothing of it, then surely will they prove an ill gift; such a one as those poisoned vestments, read of in the stories of superstitious times, which had power to consume and to alienate from his right mind the victim who put them on. Language, if it do not uphold, and feed, and leave in quiet, like the power of gravitation or the air we breathe, is a counter-spirit, unremittingly and remorselessly at work to derange, to subvert, to lay waste, to vitiate, and to dissolve.

He dwells on the argument from deep conviction that the excellence of writing, in prose or verse, 'consists in a conjunction of reason and passion' which 'must be of necessity benign', and that intellectual power is inseparably linked with a country's morals.

In April, after being allowed to eat raw carrot by Sally Green, little Catherine was afflicted with vomiting and convulsed for hours; she was temporarily paralysed and subsequently lamed. On 12 May, soon after Coleridge's departure for Keswick, the Wordsworth's fifth child, William, was born. His father and Dorothy proceeded to Coleorton for a summer holiday with the Beaumonts. Wordsworth then travelled to Hindwell, Radnorshire, where Sara Hutchinson, despairing of Coleridge, had been staying with her brother Tom from the end of March. Dorothy was the guest of the Clarksons at Bury St Edmunds, Mr Clarkson meeting her at Cambridge, where her enthusiastic sight-seeing had been punctuated by a nervous crisis when she found herself alone with her guide on the roof of King's College Chapel. While staying at Allan Bank, Basil Montagu and his third wife (his former housekeeper and hostess) had arranged to place one of his sons at the Ambleside school which Coleridge's boys attended, and persuaded Coleridge, who had threatened to leave Greta Hall for Edinburgh, to accompany them to London, where they were confident that, with the help of their doctor, they would effect his cure. Meanwhile Dorothy had spent some time in London, staying with the Lambs and being escorted round the city by Charles in the evening and Henry Crabb Robinson during the day. She was with her uncle Dr Cookson, her aunt, and her cousins at Binfield near Windsor when she heard that Catherine was very ill again. On her return she was shocked to find her reduced almost to a skeleton. The children had not recovered from whooping-cough, and the

Wordsworths took them to Hacket, to stay with John and Betty Youdell, parents of their maid, hoping that 'change of air' would be beneficial.

One morning, as they sat in the warm sunshine on a crag near the cottage, white mists rising over the Brathay valley prompted William to recite the morning hymn from *Paradise Lost*: 'Ye mists and exhalations, that now rise From hill or steaming lake, dusky or grey, Till the sun paint your fleecy skirts with gold . . .'. Mary and Dorothy had never felt the power of Milton so deeply. The same evening, after walking some distance with William on his way home, Dorothy lost her way in the darkness, stumbling more than knee-deep in mud through a peat-bog until she reached a cottage, where she wept and sobbed with relief before being taken to Hacket. So cold was Allan Bank during a wintry spell on their return, and so great the fear lest the children caught scarlet fever from their neighbours, that they packed and went to live in a cottage belonging to John Wilson at Elleray, where they were very comfortable. They returned to Grasmere for Christmas, looking forward to residence in the summer at the old vicarage, a smaller, more manageable, less expensive house than Allan Bank.

They had been appalled to discover what a rift existed between them and Coleridge. On the road to London in October, Montagu had seen justification for the warnings he had received from Wordsworth; soon afterwards, having occasion to complain, and acting with more regard to Godwin's tenets on sincerity than to Wordsworth's interests, he told Coleridge what Wordsworth had said, trying to improve his case by saying that he was commissioned to speak as he did. Coleridge left the Montagus' in dudgeon. Full of maudlin self-pity, he entered his feelings in his notebook; nobody had ever loved him, and Wordsworth's friendship had been a sham. Writing to Dorothy ten days later, Lamb reported that Coleridge with his powdered head looked 'sleek and young' like Bacchus. 'He is going to turn sober, but his clock has not struck yet, meantime he pours down goblet after goblet. . . .' Wordsworth was responsible for his 'derangement' of brain, Coleridge apprised his wife; but for the kindness of the Morgans, with whom he was staying, he would have been out of his senses.

After dwelling on this misfortune, Dorothy informed her friend Mrs Clarkson that William had 'begun to work at his great poem' (12.v.11). This was *The Excursion*; he had added to it in 1810, but it is doubtful whether he achieved much then or in the summer of

1811. His other verse had been restricted to translations of Chiabrera's epitaphs, and to sonnets on the struggle for freedom in Spain. In them he pays further tribute to Palafox, and sees the Eternal smiling on the sword of Spain as it gleams like His lightning in the cause of justice. One of the guerrilla leaders reminds him of Sertorius, the Roman general whose struggle against tyranny in Spain he had once considered an epic subject (Pr.i.190ff.). These additions to his sonnet sequence are not greatly inspired, the most outstanding being his last ('Here pause . . .'). In the darkest hour of 'these evil days', Wordsworth had never abandoned hope, 'the paramount *duty* that Heaven lays, For its own honour, on man's suffering heart'. It was 'an accursed thing', he insisted, 'to gaze on prosperous tyrants with a dazzled eye'; nor should it be forgotten that 'the throne of tyranny' is built on man's weakness.

The attractiveness of 'Characteristics of a Child three years old', a delightfully touching poem on Catherine, results not least from the visual imagery related to the child's sportiveness:

> Unthought-of, unexpected, as the stir
> Of the soft breeze ruffling the meadow-flowers,
> Or from before it chasing wantonly
> The many-coloured images imprest
> Upon the bosom of a placid lake.

It was written before the Wordsworths left Allan Bank in May. Despite its advantages (including a dairy), the old vicarage had serious drawbacks; it stood in an undrained field, and the children had to play in an ugly white-walled court at the front, opposite the churchyard. One day, after the hay-making, the Coleorton landscape of a picture presented by Sir George Beaumont suggested to Wordsworth the sonnet 'Praised be the art', which he composed by the river near Grasmere Church; less well known than Keats's 'Ode on a Grecian Urn', it conveys more subtly the artist's skill in giving 'To one brief moment caught from fleeting time The appropriate calm of blest eternity'. A few days later, after seeing Dora (Dorothy) off to school at Appleby, he and Mary took their ailing children Catherine and Thomas for a seaside holiday near Bootle. They were driven by their cheerful maid Fanny, and soon caught sight of the old dog left to wander after the death of his master, curate of Grasmere forty years, noted for his avarice and drunkenness, and remembered for turning his hay in November moonlight during his senility. As Loughrigg Tarn came into view, Wordsworth thought of what might have been if Beaumont, who had bought it, had built a summer house there, as he had hoped to do. Further on, they acknowledged greetings signalled by Betty Youdell from an eminent point in front of Hacket. They breakfasted with friends at the head of Yewdale, which recalled Wordsworth's schoolboy exploits when he plundered ravens' nests on neighbouring crags. (Here ends the 'Epistle' to Beaumont, a poem which illustrates Wordsworth's ability to write with entertaining skill in measured couplets on anything of interest to him.) They stayed first at Duddon Bridge, then for three or four weeks by the sea. The weather was not very clement, but all thought Catherine greatly improved when she returned. She and Thomas had been driven home by Fanny, while their parents, parting from them at Duddon Bridge, had wandered up the Duddon valley, staying overnight at Seathwaite, before climbing Walna Scar Pass to Coniston and Yewdale. When they reached home thay were delighted to find a writing-desk and silver teapot, presents from Sara Hutchinson in Radnorshire. She returned to Grasmere in October. Though a minor beneficiary, like Mary, she had benefited financially from her rich uncle Henry's death.

In November William wrote some inscriptions for the grounds and garden at Coleorton, one to be placed in a grove of lime trees leading to the urn in memory of Sir Joshua Reynolds, two commemorating Sir George's distinguished Elizabethan ancestors, Sir John Beaumont the poet and his brother Francis the dramatist. Christmas Day was the finest Dorothy could remember, with 'a cloudless sky and glittering lake'; William bore Coleridge's misrepresentations with apparent calm, and the whole family was happy. Two days later she finished a long letter to Catherine Clarkson with the announcement that the fiddlers were playing in the kitchen, Dora was dancing, and she must join them.

It must be assumed that Wordsworth worked industriously on *The Excursion* during the first quarter of 1812, but he had two worries. After the successful conclusion of his London lectures, Coleridge had travelled to Keswick, collecting his boys at Ambleside and passing the Wordsworths' without calling, as Hartley and Derwent, who stayed there regularly, had expected him to do. Despite Dorothy's pleas that he should not leave without seeing them, he returned to London via Penrith. It was mainly to bring this estrangement to an end that Wordsworth went to London in April, hoping to confront Montagu and Coleridge. Coleridge refused such a meeting, and a long process of mediation took place with Crabb Robinson as the chief go-between. Robinson was impressed by Wordsworth's integrity, self-control, and refusal to break off relations with the Montagus, however much they were to blame. When an *éclaircissement* was reached, Coleridge was overcome. Wordsworth's second anxiety had led him to write to Lord Lonsdale in February, requesting consideration for any office at his disposal, as he could not honourably secure by his pen an adequate income for his family needs. He had received less than £140 from all his publications, he told his friend Wrangham about this time.

Mary had taken Tom for a long stay at Hindwell in Wales, and Wordsworth was with his brother Christopher, at Bocking in Essex, on his way to the Clarksons, when he received the shattering news that Catherine, who had been in good health, had been suddenly seized with fatal convulsions. Mary was too ill to return home immediately, as she wished. Almost six months later, she was beginning to recover when Thomas, 'the darling of the house', died of pneumonia after measles. Shortly afterwards, about the middle of December, Willy was very ill with measles. Anxious to have medical attention with the least delay, his parents took him to Ambleside and stayed there with him until there was no cause for alarm. Not until then was Wordsworth able to consider the gratuity of £100 per annum which Lord Lonsdale had offered until a post or pension was secured for him; it was no easy choice, but he decided to accept. Another important decision was made: they must move. The continual prospect of the churchyard where Thomas had played, and was now buried with Catherine, was too much for them. They had applied for Rydal Mount, the tenancy of which they hoped to obtain without much difficulty or delay. The arrival of Lord Lonsdale's annuity in January was welcomed because it would defray removal expenses and enable Wordsworth to proceed with *The Excursion* rather than with some 'task undertaken for profit'.

Rydal Mount had been bought by Lady Fleming, who lived with her mother at Rydal Hall. Both were well disposed towards Wordsworth ever since, after a visit by Dr Bell (a friend of Southey) in 1811, he had become actively interested in the adoption of his teaching system at Grasmere school. Previously Mr North of Liverpool had owned Rydal Mount, but his wife, 'a busy meddling woman', had resented the lead taken by the Wordsworths, especially by Dorothy in the neighbourhood, on behalf of the orphaned Greens; whatever the reason, Rydal Mount remained locked and empty for several weeks, until the wine (nine cartloads) was removed from the cellars. It was not until May Day 1813 therefore that the Wordsworths were able to leave Grasmere. In the meantime, on the retirement of the Distributor of Stamps for Westmorland (plus Whitehaven and Penrith), Lord Lonsdale had offered the post to Wordsworth. Its function was to grant licences and collect duties of many kinds; its main office was at Ambleside, but there were sub-distributors in market towns, and the Distributor's responsibility was to collect the money each quarter and forward it with accounts to the Board of Stamps in London. Wordsworth needed an accountant-secretary, and found an able one in John Carter, who, during slack periods, assisted in the garden at Rydal Mount, and succeeded in teaching Willy to read; he made a copy of *The Prelude* before 1820, and saw the final manuscript through the press in 1850. Wordsworth was not paid a regular salary; he had estimated that the Distributorship was worth at least £400 a year, but he soon found that he had to provide a pension of £100 a year for his predecessor in addition to John Carter's salary. Its income seemed unlikely to exceed half his expectations. The post was no sinecure, but it gave Wordsworth the security he needed.

The quip that he had exchanged the company of leech-gatherers for that of tax-gatherers came from Jeffrey in his review of *The Excursion*. Just when and how that work was completed is not clear; the poet must have devoted considerable time in 1813 to structuring and completing the sections he had prepared over a long period before the whole was planned. His new surroundings were probably a source of invigorating delight. House and garden commanded a richly variegated view down the wooded Rothay valley to Windermere, and there were numerous walks in other directions, back to Grasmere, and round Rydal Water and Loughrigg Fell. Many local visitors, including old friends from Grasmere, came to Rydal Mount in September, when much furniture was bought at sales; the carpets were expected to be laid by the end of the month. Such grandeur, it seemed to Dorothy, compared with the simplicity of the dear cottage at Town End: a Turkey carpet for the dining-room, and a Brussels for William's study! A strange visitor at the end of the year was young Basil Montagu, once the child *protégé* who lied like a devil at Racedown. After a period as a midshipman with his uncle, he had been ill and formed the habit of abusing people he knew, including his father, his uncle, and the Wordsworths. He stayed first at Ambleside, and then with Miss Barker at Keswick, where he suffered a haemorrhage, was nursed, and tended scot-free during the first four months of 1814, at a time when his father was persuaded to pay the last £200 of the £300 Wordsworth had lent him in 1796 from his Raisley Calvert legacy. Dorothy went to her friend Miss Barker's assistance; she stayed more than three months, and was sorry she could not help William, who was now preparing *The Excursion* for the press; he had made 'great alterations', and she had not yet seen any of the proofs. Clearly Wordsworth had high hopes, for he also planned to publish a new edition of his poems in two volumes, followed by 'Peter Bell', 'The White Doe of Rylstone', and 'The Waggoner' (24.iv.14). *The Excursion* appeared in July.

The Excursion

'My object is to give pictures of Nature, Man, and Society. Indeed I do not know any thing which will not come within the scope of my plan.' That is how (6.iii.98), when 'Life went a-maying with Nature, Hope, and Poesy', Wordsworth euphorically envisaged the philosophical work which the ebullient-minded Coleridge persuaded him to believe that he was supremely qualified to accomplish. He worked at it piecemeal, and procrastinated, finding relief for long periods in *The Prelude*, an introduction which absorbed most of the creative ideas for the mammoth tripartite sequel he contemplated. These had been set out with some grand succinctness as an appendix to 'Home at Grasmere', and then revised to appear as a prospectus in the preface to *The Excursion*. Unfortunately a sense of unfulfilled obligations dimmed Wordsworth's judgment, and made him persist in a task which never had a unified design to direct and discipline it. Piecemeal work and procrastination continued until a narrative framework was devised to give a semblance of a whole, in 'something of a dramatic form', to a collection of passages written or extended or revised on innumerable occasions from 1795 to 1814. The result was *The Excursion*, intended as the second part of *The Recluse*, the first and third of which were to 'consist chiefly of meditations in the author's own person'. The inherent initial weakness obviously remained, despite the poet's grandiose conception of the whole, in which *The Prelude* appeared like the ante-chapel to the main structure of a Gothic church.

Coleridge's recollection of what was planned[17] is probably sound, though he was not certain: 'Something of this sort was, I think, agreed on.' Its 'redemptive process' is based on a rejection of the rather mechanical psychology of Locke and Hartley ('compounding a mind out of the senses'):

Then the plan laid out, and, I believe, partly suggested by me,

192

was, that Wordsworth should assume the station of a man in mental repose, one whose principles were made up, and so prepared to deliver upon authority a system of philosophy. He was to treat man as man − a subject of eye, ear, touch, and taste, in contact with external nature, and informing the senses from the mind, and not compounding a mind out of the senses; then he was to describe the pastoral and other states of society, assuming something of the Juvenalian spirit as he approached the high civilization of cities and towns, and opening a melancholy picture of the present state of degeneracy and vice; thence he was to infer and reveal the proof of, and necessity for, the whole state of man and society being subject to, and illustrative of, a redemptive process in operation, showing how this idea reconciled all the anomalies, and promised future glory and restoration.

Coleridge had expected Wordsworth to adopt the pontifical stance of *spectator ab extra*, but it is to the latter's credit that he assumed a more humble role, and rejected dogma for persuasion through discussion, knowing that conviction on the subject he proposed could not be engendered intellectually but only through experience and reflection. His theme may be summed up in the conclusion of 'Elegiac Stanzas': 'Not without hope we suffer and we mourn.' The faith on which it is based combines stoicism with belief in a God of love, a spirit immanent in all life or nature, 'a Being Of infinite benevolence and power; Whose everlasting purposes embrace All accidents, converting them to good'.

Wordsworth's survey of life in *The Excursion* follows changes in his own outlook from the Racedown anti-war period through subsequent disillusionment with the French Revolution to renovation (the end of 'Despondency Corrected', which belongs to 1798) and religious faith in nature informed by God, the universal Being. The later books, comprising more than half the work, belong to the Grasmere period, as is suggested by their focus of interest in the Pastor and his churchyard. In the long I.F. commentary which he made late in his life, Wordsworth said that most of this section was written at Allan Bank, but Dorothy's letter of 12 May 1811 suggests very strongly that much of it was written later.

The narrator meets the Wanderer (whose development was the subject of Wordsworth's extension of 'The Ruined Cottage' in 1798, and again in the winter of 1801−2) and the tragic story of

Margaret (its setting in south-west England unchanged) is told. They then move on and meet the Solitary among the mountains. His political disillusionment and loss of faith from family bereavements are countered by the Wanderer, but the Solitary remains unconvinced. All three descend into another vale, and enter the church and churchyard. The Pastor arrives; the Wanderer tells him that they have been discussing whether hope and belief in progress are justified, and agrees that reason needs to be strengthened by feeling to create conviction. The narrator suggests that the humble labourer may err less on the graver questions of life than those who submit to reason, and the Solitary, in full sympathy, invites the Pastor to continue the subject, not with abstract argument but with 'solid facts' from the varied lives of those buried around them. (Here Wordsworth brings us in touch with the crux of the main artistic problem inherent in Coleridge's proposals for a philosophical poem.) After their tales have been told, the Solitary is still sceptical, and the Wanderer 'asserts the hollowness of all national grandeur if unsupported by moral worth'. The Pastor invites his interlocutors to his home, and the happiness of the children seen there illuminates the Wanderer's discourse on education and its importance to the State. After a picnic on the island, they all proceed to the other side of the lake, and climb a hill where the beauty of the evening scene inspires the Pastor to praise God, and glance at the debt of civilization to Christianity. Wordsworth ends with the hope that the effect on the Solitary of these discussions and experiences will not remain untold.

Hazlitt was right in contending that Wordsworth was 'the reverse of dramatic' in *The Excursion*, but erred in asserting that 'the recluse, the pastor, and the pedlar are three persons in one poet'. Had his trinity been the pedlar, the pastor, and the narrator, he would have been near the mark, for all three represent Wordsworth with varying degrees of emphasis, the Pastor, for example, using the language of the Church more freely than Wordsworth would have done, without ever infringing the essentials of the poet's belief. The one with whom Wordsworth is most identifiable is the Wanderer (cf. the I.F. note, PW5.373). He had not abandoned the contemplative position to the extent that Coleridge thought; he preferred a less egotistic form of expression, confident (like George Eliot) that ideas had to be incarnated in 'pictures' to have imaginative or aesthetic appeal. *The Excursion* needs to be judged by the extent to which it succeeds in this respect.

It pleased Jeffrey to ridicule the pedlar's role as 'chief prolocutor in this poetical dialogue'. Wordsworth did not intend any of his characters to be types, yet it may seem extraordinary that a pedlar should have the wisdom attributed to the Wanderer. Wordsworth believed that such a person, travelling long distances in the country and meeting all sorts of people, would probably be more aware of nature (the universe and humanity) than a typical city-dweller or intellectual or professional. In his boyhood at Hawks-head he had been singled out for his grave, over-thoughtful looks by an old pedlar whose experiences he loved to hear, and whose thought and knowledge he admired; he had been tempted to become a wayfarer himself rather than enter the Church; and he had heard much from Sara Hutchinson about 'the intellectual pedlar' James Patrick of Kendal, a kinsman with whom she lived in her childhood. Apart from Wordsworth's own development, he was the main influence in the creation of the Wanderer and his background.

The Wordsworthian character of the Wanderer *ab initio* may be seen in notable transfers from the 1798 text of 'The Ruined Cottage' (PW5.379—99) to *The Prelude* (1805): ii.416—34, with its reference to the 'one life' or universal Spirit, and such related passages as iii.124—9, 142—4, and 156—67. He can be identified with the author of 'Tintern Abbey', the first two books of *The Prelude*, and the preface to *Lyrical Ballads*:

> Far and wide the clouds were touched,
> And in their silent faces could he read
> Unutterable love. Sound needed none,
> Nor any voice of joy; his spirit drank
> The spectacle: sensation, soul, and form,
> All melted into him; they swallowed up
> His animal being; in them did he live,
> And by them did he live; they were his life.
> In such access of mind, in such high hour
> Of visitation from the living God,
> Thought was not; in enjoyment it expired.

> much did he see of men,
> Their manners, their enjoyments, and pursuits,
> Their passions and their feelings; chiefly those
> Essential and eternal to the heart,

> That, 'mid the simpler forms of rural life,
> Exist more simple in their elements,
> And speak a plainer language.

His heart 'lay open' to other people's enjoyment or suffering. Such
was his quiet cheerfulness that he was not turned aside from
wretchedness by 'coward fears'. 'He could *afford* to suffer with
those whom he saw suffer', and he was therefore rich in 'best
experience' and in 'the wisdom of our daily life'. Believing, at the
risk of shocking 'the prejudices of artificial society', that 'vigorous
human-heartedness' (Hardy's 'loving-kindness') is the key to true
taste, Wordsworth regarded the Wanderer as one of 'the aristocracy of nature'.

The story which he tells is deeply moving, but its ultimate subject (the one towards which Wordsworth struggled early in 1802) is
our attitude towards affliction (technically, with the role of the
pedlar as *spectator ab extra*). Wordsworth's views are sane and
realistic; he believed in moderation and self-control. He had suffered distressing family losses, and recovered. His optimism, far
from being facile, was based on reason and nature; it was rooted in
instinct, a principle of life recognised by Hardy:

> Thought of the determination to enjoy. We see it in all nature,
> from the leaf on the tree to the titled lady at the ball. . . . It is
> achieved, of a sort, under superhuman difficulties. . . . Even
> the most oppressed of men and animals find it, so that out of a
> thousand there is hardly one who has not a sun of some sort for
> his soul.

Only after repeated setbacks is Tess's 'appetite for joy' exhausted.
Margaret makes no supreme effort for herself or, less warrantably,
for her children. Such is her 'excess' of love towards her absent husband that her devotion is nothing less than a monomania. Whether
she could help herself is a critical question which Wordsworth
hardly admits, but his sympathy is undiminished. His psychological insight is displayed in the 'unnatural' behaviour of the
husband, especially to his children, when unemployment makes
him a prey to his gnawing sense of inadequacy. The subject began
as 'Incipient Madness' (PW1.314−16), and there can be no doubt
that indulged and uncontrolled grief does craze Margaret mildly.
She admits that her lack of resolution has 'done much wrong' to

her 'helpless infant'. Her steady decline (outwardly seen in the increasing neglect of her garden) produces 'The careless stillness of a thinking mind Self-occupied; to which all outward things Are like an idle matter'. The baby dies; the will to live (like the cottage) is sapped. Margaret remains devoted to her ruined home, and many years pass before her death, during which her mind is remote, her hope fixed upon the lengthy road of no return. We should not dally with misery; it is 'barren of all future good', and it has neither reason nor 'natural wisdom' to recommend it, the Wanderer argues.

Allied to a story which rouses sympathy in ever-deepening measure, such philosophic detachment opens *The Excursion* challengingly. Wordsworth's positive beliefs are adumbrated in the addendum he wrote for the 1798 version (PW5.400−3), a revised form of which provided the Wanderer's reply in 'Despondency Corrected'. If we rise from 'sleep', 'All things shall live in us and we shall live In all things that surround us'. The consequence will be that we shall 'seek for objects of a kindred love In fellow-natures and a kindred joy'; 'No naked hearts, No naked minds shall then be left to mourn The burthen of existence', as Margaret was left. To be roused, we need education that enlarges and enlightens the mind, senses and intellect invigorating each other and the feelings until, 'deeply drinking in the soul of things', we are wise, and the '*excursive* power' of the mind is developed. Believing in the 'soul which makes all one', Wordsworth felt that sympathies with all forms of nature are indivisible (PW5.340−1). In Margaret they die. Grief-ridden, she loses interest in her immediate surroundings, even in her children; she becomes 'reckless' or indifferent. The 'sleep' which overcomes her is reflected in externalities: the house that 'bespake a sleepy hand of negligence', the garden, and more particularly the waters of a spring, which, in conjunction with the broken bowl (cf. Ecclesiastes, xii.6) must symbolize life. The 'brotherhood' of sympathies that had existed between Margaret and these waters, before affliction began the slow destruction of her reason and will, had been broken. Once they had 'ministered to human comfort' daily, and 'the touch of human hand' had 'dislodged the natural sleep' that now 'binds them up in mortal stillness'. The later version of his addendum (Ex.iv.1207−75) shows that Wordsworth qualified the 'strict necessity' according to which wise behaviour follows the awakening he sketched, admitting free-will, and consciousness of free-will, without which the pedlar's critical commentary on Margaret would be invalid.

'We reap what we sow, but Nature has love over and above that justice, and gives us shadow and blossom and fruit that spring from no planting of ours', wrote George Eliot, still influenced by Wordsworthian belief, in 'Janet's Repentance' (v). The sympathies 'that steal upon the meditative mind', as if outbreathed by nature (as in 'Hart-leap Well') are referred to again when the narrator of *The Excursion*, after hearing the story of Margaret, and feeling the impotence of grief, returns to the cottage, and traces 'that secret spirit of humanity' which still survived amid 'the calm oblivious tendencies of nature'. The Wanderer's succeeding adjuration was quoted by John Wilson to illustrate the non-Christianity of Wordsworth's 'very high religion', and it may have been in response to this charge that Wordsworth in 1845 included (without committing the Wanderer or himself to orthodoxy) Margaret's consolation through faith in Christ Crucified, and strengthened his expression, on the power of tranquillity to transcend grief in the minds of the wise, by attributing its source to Faith. This tranquillity is reflected in the outer scene, in a manner characteristic of *The Excursion* as a whole and of the first book in particular.

Margaret's tragedy of self-centredness remains a unit, though linked to the sequel by the Wanderer and its theme; its discreteness is emphasized by the intensity of its texture compared with the leisurely treatment which is bestowed on the gloom and scepticism of the Solitary in the next three books. This episode is marked by some memorable natural imagery and a brilliant scene (ii.829–69). The discourse, at its best, is moving, but it descends to some dreary philosophical prosing, and is generally over-prolonged. The blank verse often shows unrivalled command and fluency (though it hardly became Wordsworth to boast that 'for *variety* of musical effect no poem in the language furnishes a parallel', as he 'whispered' to Catherine Clarkson in his letter of January 1815).

The home of the Solitary among the mountains (near Blea Tarn) is a three days' journey from the ruined cottage. His cynicism is reflected in his devotion to Voltaire and his comments on the poverty of the old man whose burial excited the Wanderer's enthusiastic evaluation of the family and community love which rustic funerals reveal. Wordsworth's account of the pauper is authentic but composite; the details of his rescue from the heights where he had been caught in a storm while seeking turf for winter fuel were told by Luff and recorded by Dorothy in her journal for

9 November 1805. The glorious scene of clouds and mountains (originating from that seen by Luff on 'that melancholy occasion' and from another witnessed by Wordsworth in the neighbourhood) evokes feelings in the Solitary which show that he is not spiritually dead, and that the revival of his *excursive* power is possible.

Although Wordsworth at times drew from his own past in sketching him, the Solitary remains a fictional character. Quantock memories appear in his recollections of married happiness; and, for the loss of his two children, Wordsworth, recalling his own, originally included 'Characteristics of a Child three years old' and much from 'Maternal Grief'. Two lines ('The intellectual power, through words and things, Went sounding on, a dim and perilous way') are adapted from *The Borderers* to express the Solitary's mental turmoil in affliction. The French Revolution gave him new hopes, and its reign of licence roused his sympathy:

> Here nature was my guide,
> The nature of the dissolute; but thee,
> O fostering Nature! I rejected — smiled
> At others' tears in pity; and in scorn
> At those, which thy soft influence sometimes drew
> From my unguarded heart.

When the Revolution turned into a power struggle, he sailed to America; here Wordsworth recalls having to leave France and Annette in 1792:

> For, like a plague, will memory break out;
> And, in the blank and solitude of things,
> Upon his spirit, with a fever's strength,
> Will conscience prey . . . *Beautiful* regards
> Were turned on me — the face of her I loved;
> The wife and mother pitifully fixing
> Tender reproaches, insupportable!

In the New World the Solitary discovered that 'primeval Nature's child' (the mythic ideal of one school of Revolutionary thought) was 'squalid, vengeful, and impure'. Now completely disillusioned, he looks languidly upon the 'visible fabric of the world' and is in love, he thinks, with easeful death.

The persuasion brought to bear on the Solitary owes something to the conclusion of 'Summer' in *The Seasons*, where Thomson asks what enlightened man would have been without philosophy (which traces 'the chain of causes and effects' to the Creator who 'alone possesses being'), and answers, 'A savage, roaming through the woods and wilds In quest of prey'. Like Wordsworth in 'The Tables Turned', the Wanderer urges the Solitary to come forth into the sun, and realize, by 'measuring through all degrees, until . . . time and conscious nature disappear . . . in unsearchable eternity', how much wisdom can be learned from nature. The Solitary, however, finds that the immediate scene reflects the element of chance, and thinks that the scientist has a greater assurance of truth than the philosopher. He is not interested in the question of pre-existence or life-after-death, and recalls, before telling his story, how his enjoyment of life was such that he did not need to entertain hopes of a world beyond or a golden age. Now he can sympathize with those who seek consolation in retirement from the world, and Wordsworth strengthens his case with the transfer of a passage (iii.367−405) from 'The Tuft of Primroses'.

The Wanderer's reply to the Solitary's 'mournful narrative' is too protracted and uneven. It contains fine passages, but it sinks almost to banality in advocating interests and activities to alleviate sorrow and renew one's spirits. Setbacks in society occur when weak and vacillating people allow leaders with wrong principles to have too much sway; even so, rapid improvements cannot be expected, nature's processes being gradual. The cogency of the moral and spiritual argument depends on faith in a Being of 'infinite benevolence and power', the 'Prime, self-existing cause and end of all That in the scale of being fill their place'. Like Wordsworth, the Wanderer worships in nature's temple, and is afraid that the vision splendid will fade as age draws on, but is convinced that if we possess our souls in quiet we are susceptible to intimations which are not mediated through the senses. Like the shell which traditionally expresses 'mysterious union with its native sea', the universe can impart 'Authentic tidings of invisible things; Of ebb and flow, and ever-during power; And central peace, subsisting at the heart Of endless agitation'. If science were worthy of the name it would excite a sense of wonder in life and the universe. The Wanderer prefers the liveliness of pagan superstition to the deadliness engendered by so much scientific analysis and research, but his homily nowhere has the force of Wordsworth's outburst in 'The world is too much with us'. A passage bringing Greek myth to life appealed strongly to Keats; another (iv.754−62) left its mark on his 'Ode to a Nightingale'; and another (956–68) suggested the idea for *Lamia* (ii.229–38). Wordsworth's real subject is the quality of life, and when the Wanderer proclaims 'We live by admiration, hope, and love' the element of wonder is implied. There are appeals to duty and to the 'imaginative will' by which faith is upheld, and the Wanderer is confident that through actions of loving-kindness the Solitary's recovery has already begun. The conclusion (iv.1207–75) insists that such humanity proceeds from a love of nature, but the reasoning (which, apart from its final insistence on free-will, belongs to 1798) is not always clear, and is based on peculiar conviction. Darwinism may conflict with Wordsworth's religion of nature but, far from invalidating what he says on the need for imaginative awakening and sympathy, it gives it added force. The weakness of the Wanderer's therapeutic argument is in its dependence on the will, and clearly Wordsworth does not pretend that it can be easily activated by reason; he can only state what is desirable for a full life with compensations for grievous loss. The Solitary's inability to respond immediately has to be accepted; he is like Hardy in 'The Impercipient' ('O doth a bird deprived of wings Go earth-bound wilfully?'): 'Alas! such wisdom bids a creature fly Whose very sorrow is, that time hath shorn His natural wings!'

The third phase of *The Excursion* takes us to the church and churchyard of a neighbouring valley, where the memorials of the dead prompt the Solitary to ask how far philosophy and religion helped them in life. Since his arguments so far have failed, the Wanderer asks the Pastor, a man of rank and refinement (fictional, though the setting is Grasmere), what can be learned from the lives of some who lie buried there. Before doing so, he speaks of the couple up at Hacket (the Youdells), living humbly in deprivation, but happier through the virtues of Christian charity than 'thankless thousands . . . clogged by ease and leisure' or those who falter through lack of faith. This example is countered by the Solitary, who recalls the loneliness of the unhappy pauper who was buried the previous day in the same churchyard. The Pastor, after reflecting Wordsworth's views on epitaphs, concludes that they express not only human feelings but also 'the pure soul' that communes with Heaven. His belief squares with Wordsworth's, that life truly lived is an expression of love, both human and divine; it is 'love and immortality'.

The opening of the sixth book reads like an interposition from

Wordsworth rather than an address by the narrator. Inspired by his brother Christopher's *Ecclesiastical Biography*,[18] it extols the Church of England and expresses the hope that its priests, like the Pastor, will maintain the high standards of the past in proclaiming the Faith. The stories which the Pastor tells seem to be selected on no consistent principle. Initially they are *exempla*. The first (based on the life of one of Wordsworth's school friends) shows how love for a lost one can be retained yet controlled; another, of a Patterdale miner, exemplifies hope and perseverance; the next affords a contrast in the life of a many-talented prodigal son with no firm principles, 'of contradictions infinite the slave'. The life of Molly Fisher's sister-in-law, a woman of high natural endowment whose thrift became avarice and whose love of a dissolute son her thraldom, illustrates the shrinking of a self-centred mind. One of the most interesting sketches, that of Wordsworth's friend Joseph Sympson, reflects 'a man of hope and forward-looking mind'; the life of Robert Walker which follows (vii.315−90) evokes the perennial question why much is made of war and love but little is heard in praise of 'the good man's purposes and deeds'. These stories, like those on the natural compensations which developed in a deaf man at Haweswater (a sketch used to complete the final essay on epitaphs) and in a blind man (based on John Gough of Kendal, who was still alive) could have been intended to have their effect on the Solitary after an interval for reflection. Two memorials which seem to rouse no more than his curiosity lead to moralizing on the vanity of worldly wishes; they concern the disappointed Jacobite and Hanoverian, who both sought seclusion at Hawkshead and became friendly despite their political differences (one of Ann Tyson's stories), and, finally, Sir Alfred Irthing, whose family history illustrates how 'the stars of human glory are cast down' and mutability reigns over earthly affairs.

Many of the buried have no tombstones; their memorials exist in the hearts and minds of the dalesmen, 'depositaries faithful and more kind than fondest epitaph'. Wordsworth (as narrator) repeats the thought in his second essay on epitaphs, that it is a happiness to have *one* enclosure where the voice of envy or detraction is not heard; and it is in this spirit, and not by way of evasion, that lives of criminal and vicious people are omitted, though the Pastor has no doubt that their examples may strengthen virtuous resolve. Through his Solitary, Wordsworth anticipates Hardy in

claiming that the tragic muse can find subjects as apt in humble
peasant life as among the mighty:

> Amid the groves, under the shadowy hills,
> The generations are prepared; the pangs,
> The internal pangs, are ready; the dead strife
> Of poor humanity's afflicted will
> Struggling in vain with ruthless destiny.

Obviously the Pastor cannot accept the philosophy implicit in such
terms, but he does not claim that Christian faith supplies all the
answers to human calamity. Some of the lives he tells may, by rousing sympathy in others' misfortunes, help the Solitary to realize
that life offers something more worthy than selfish withdrawal.
The most moving story is that of Ellen; it stirs the narrator of *The
Excursion* almost as much as that of Margaret (vi.1053–61), and
the Wanderer finds proof in it that Heaven deals gently with those
who suffer wrong. The tale of Wilfred Armathwaite which follows
shows how a wrong-doer was pitied when he could never forgive
himself ('absolved by God', a late change, was probably written for
dramatic reasons). A widower finds recompense in the happiness
brought to his family by the enthusiasm and industry of his eldest
daughter. Only time can soften regret for the death of a little girl
who had brought joy to her parents and seven elder brothers.
George Dawson, scholar, sportsman, and Volunteer, whose life
was cut short and who was buried with military honours, elicits
Wordsworth's admiration, with comments on the curse of Napoleonic oppression.

Wordsworth was tempted to add other stories, including that of
the shepherd who lost his life on Bield Crag (PW5.461–2), an
event recalling that of 'Fidelity' and omitted probably for that
reason. The Pastor is apprehensive that, in selecting from the
representative or universal 'forms of human nature', he has proved
wearisome; and Wordsworth sensibly provides relief to a long succession of tales, notably when attention turns to the noisy passing
of a horse-drawn waggon carrying a massive oak trunk; the Pastor
knows that the tree-feller's occupation is a threat to local beauty,
but sees in his cheerfulness of soul greater homage to Heaven than
that paid by many scrupulous worshippers.

Some of the outstanding qualities of the characters in these
stories shine memorably through images usually drawn from

nature but sometimes of classical origin. Ellen's movements 'might have quickened and inspired' a Titian 'to picture forth Oread or Dryad glancing through the shade What time the hunter's earliest horn is heard Startling the golden hills'. Mrs Sympson, though younger, is more spiritually prepared for death than her husband:

> Him might we liken to the setting sun
> As seen not seldom on some gusty day,
> Struggling and bold, and shining from the west
> With an inconstant and unmellowed light;
> She was a soft attendant cloud, that hung
> As if with wish to veil the restless orb;
> From which it did itself imbibe a ray
> Of pleasing lustre.

The deaf man who became attuned to nature is remembered by the tall pine that 'murmurs, not idly, o'er his peaceful grave'. In George Dawson the scholar's genius is revealed, just as the wandering gods, Pan or Apollo, though veiled in human form, were 'discovered in their own despite to sense of mortals'; the impression he made on all is like that of a mountain ash in berried glory reflected in the pool at its feet and brightening all the rocks around.

In the concluding stages of *The Excursion*, Wordsworth addresses himself to urgent needs in society, education in particular. If the recommended means seem inadequate, it is largely because (in England at least) the aims of education have been obscured by utilitarianism or, more recently, by political factions, stirred more by an engineered sense of class-division than by an enlightened urge for the common good.

The subject of mutability in society (arising from thoughts on Sir Alfred Irthing) suggests a parallel between the knight-errant of old and the pedlar whose time-honoured profession is threatened by industry. The Wanderer rejoices that the elements are being scientifically harnessed for human welfare, but insists that national greatness depends more on moral principles than on material prosperity. The sacrifice of the young in industry, and the unenlightenment of country children are both condemned. At this point the discussion breaks off with an invitation to the parsonage, where the happiness of the children (one a cottage boy) is clearly intended as a norm by which to measure national deficiencies and neglect. An ardent believer in the imagination (like Blake, whom he thought the greatest of contemporary poets), Wordsworth sees (like Blake) the 'human form divine' and the 'immortal soul' of children degraded and wasted in slavish labour, in fields as well as in Satanic mills.

Since there is an active principle in all that is natural, and the key to life is hope and 'meditated action', the Wanderer holds that human life is turned from its natural course

> wherever man is made
> An offering, or a sacrifice, a tool
> Or implement, a passive thing employed
> As a brute mean, without acknowledgment
> Of common right or interest in the end;
> Used or abused, as selfishness may prompt.

Oppression of 'active powers', the development of which would 'subvert our noxious qualities', can lead only to a perversion of rational beings, making them weak in goodness and strong in evil. Noble gifts such as reason, imagination, conscience, and free-will are bestowed on all, to whom 'The primal duties shine aloft − like stars.' As a result of what man has made of man, the ancient virtues have been overthrown, and injustice has created wide differences. Enthusiasm for 'that glorious time' when State education is provided for all gets the better of reason: we can ignore Malthusian fears of over-population, for the Empire invites Britain to 'cast off her swarms' and 'establish new communities on every shore whose aspect favours hope or bold adventure'. That Wordsworth is not quite as euphoric as the Wanderer is suggested in the immediate sequel. A perfect reflection is seen within a pool of a snow-white ram and its glowing mountainous background; a breath can destroy it, and nothing of highest worth can be lasting or certain in this world. The beauty of the vale at sunset inspires the Pastor to praise of God and to prayer that his Word will prevail. The thought is consistent, whatever its form. He discusses the progress of civilization since the age of superstition, and attributes it to Christianity and faith in the Cross. Undoubtedly Wordsworth's natural theology had moved much closer to Christian orthodoxy before he completed *The Excursion*; but, whether we believe the provenance of goodness is divine or wholly human, his general conclusions on life and the requisites for the development of man and society have lost none of their significance. He does not set out to justify the ways of God to men but, in the words of his revised prospectus, 'to weigh the good and evil of our mortal state', and to 'give utterance in numerous verse' to 'melancholy fear subdued by faith', 'blessèd consolations in distress', 'moral strength, and intellectual power', and the possibilities of 'joy in widest commonalty spread' through growth of the mind's excursive power. Much of this programme is achieved in *The Excursion*.

Its main weakness therefore is not so much in its substance as its form. To this extent one can always subscribe to Jeffrey's dismissive dictum 'This will never do.' Nothing can disguise its compositeness and disproportion; passages written early tend to be over-compressed, while late additions and linkages are often extended unduly. It is an assemblage rather than an artistic whole. It could be argued that certain parts ('The Ruined Cottage' and the story of Ellen pre-eminently) would have been better had they been prepared as independent units, and that Wordsworth (if at any time he was capable of writing a philosophical poem) could have achieved it, on the subject in hand, in a far shorter work than *The Excursion*. Only in connection with experience, real or imaginary, did his ideas seem to flow, however, and only when he had given experience time to mature did he seem able to keep its expression within due bounds. The faith which inspired him when he began *The Prelude* had been tempered by further reflection and experience, and the main tendency of the resultant change is revealed by certain modifications in the prospectus: his stress on the power of faith to subdue fear (how precisely Christian the faith is, is uncertain), and the change, with reference to the individual mind that keeps its 'own inviolate retirement', from '[that] consists with being limitless, the one great Life' to 'subject there To conscience only, and the law supreme Of that Intelligence which governs all'.

Sun imagery imparts a degree of thematic integration to the poem, though it detracts little from the unitary effect of the first book, where it is used more persistently. The narrator seeks shelter from the burning sun, and finds it in the brotherhood of elms by the ruined cottage. Here the Wanderer had quenched his thirst at a spring beside which he had seen a fragment of a wooden bowl green with moss (a symbol of death, as in the 1793 versions of *An Evening Walk*, 256, and *Descriptive Sketches*, 741–2). He remembers how Margaret had supplied cool refreshment from the same spring, and sees in its desolation a breaking of the brotherhood between humanity and nature. It is when he pauses in his story, and speaks of turning our hearts away through weakness from 'natural wisdom', that his listener (the narrator) leaves the breezy shade and stands 'drinking comfort from the warmer sun'. The calm oblivious tendencies of nature, seen and felt, are re-inforced at the end by the 'slant and mellow radiance' of the setting sun, and by the song of birds in 'the milder air' as the two men leave 'the shade'. They know, in short, 'the soothing thoughts that spring Out of human suffering'. When the narrator first entered the shade, he had been plagued by insects; at noon, when the Wanderer asks why 'the calm of nature' should be disturbed by restless thoughts, they fill the air with tuneful hum. As a philosopher, he must consider life as a whole, at a distance, as if he were on a mountain-top, 'above the host of ever-humming insects', hearing 'the mighty stream of tendency' down in the valley, but communicating also with the invisible world of eternity. The insect-hum reflects the 'giddy round of vain delight' and 'the fret and labour' of humanity on the plain below (ix.44–92).

The sun mounts slowly behind a dark hill as the Wanderer and the narrator make their way towards the Solitary's home. For a resumption of their discussion the Wanderer invites him 'forth into the sun', and he complies reluctantly. The sun represents the light of the truth that shines for all mankind (iv.630, 809–10), and the Wanderer knows the Solitary well enough to be convinced that, despite his readiness to seek comfort in the 'oblivious shades of death and night', he has 'caught at every turn the colours of the sun'. At the end of 'Despondency Corrected' the invisible sun had left behind on the mountain slopes a pomp of radiance contrasting boldly with the ample shadows. *The Excursion* ends with a glorious sunset, a foretaste of which the Solitary had experienced, after helping to rescue the pauper, when, emerging from dense mist, he had witnessed glory upon glory, and felt that the spectacle revealed the abode of spirits in beatitude. With that he had realized he had been spiritually dead and was alive again. An oblique comment on his pessimism comes when the Pastor remarks how cheerless the graves look when covered by April snowfall, if they are approached from the sullen north before the sun has attained 'his noontide height'; seen, however, from the quarter 'whence the lord of light, Of life, of love, and gladness doth dis-pense His beams', they look vernal, green and bright, hopeful and cheerful (v.515–57). Cynicism has given the Solitary the illusion that the sun shines equally on the just and the unjust (vi.573–99).

His happy self returns in cheerful company at the parsonage as he gazes on 'the landscape of the sun-bright vale'; at the end he looks forward to further meetings and discussions. 'Another sun, and peradventure more', will shine on us, he says. His judgment may still be warped, but the spirit of nature is revealed in his humanity.

Despite expression of his intention to continue *The Recluse*, Wordsworth made no significant progress with it; he had no defined plan to follow. If he had had some determined aim he would have pursued it, however harsh the criticism of *The Excursion*. It appeared in a magnificent quarto edition, the hope being that, winning favour among the rich and influential, it would create a wider demand which would make a cheaper edition possible. This did not happen until 1820.

Part III: 1814–50

Activity and Alarm (1814–18)

Wordsworth had suffered from trachoma,[1] an affliction of the eyelids which recurred periodically during the greater part of his remaining life, creating a disincentive to prolonged reading and an aversion to strong light. Inflammation caused by the first onset made him think it was due to exposure on Kirkstone Pass in January 1805; it was very troublesome in 1810 and 1811, when he began to fear he might lose his sight. Such fears are expressed in *The Excursion* (iv.109) and notably in '*A little onward lend thy guiding hand*' (1816), a poem prompted by the recollection of Milton and lines from *Samson Agonistes*.

In July 1814, shortly before *The Excursion* was published, he set off with Mary and Sara on a lengthy Scottish tour. They visited New Lanark, Robert Owen's model industrial village, and the neighbouring Cora Linn waterfall, Glasgow, Loch Lomond, the Trossachs, Glencoe, and Inverness, returning via Edinburgh, where they met R. P. Gillies, a young writer and Wordsworth admirer. At Traquair, they met Dr Anderson, editor of 'the British Poets', a selection which had been of inestimable value to Wordsworth. With James Hogg, 'the Ettrick Shepherd', they accomplished what William and 'his winsome marrow' Dorothy had reluctantly abandoned in 1803, exploring the beautiful valley of the Yarrow, renowned in balladry.

The tour was commemorated in four poems. 'The Brownie's Cell', entitled after the local name of a Loch Lomond island ruin once occupied by a solitary, was a favourite with Wordsworth. 'Composed at Cora Linn in Sight of Wallace's Tower' was highly esteemed by Landor for its Pindaric quality. 'Effusion', verses on Ossian's Hall, an eighteenth-century folly near Dunkeld (described in Dorothy's *Recollections of a Tour made in Scotland*, 8.ix.03), gives Wordsworth's thoughts on this 'intrusive pile, ill-graced with baubles of theatric taste', wherein a picture of Ossian divides and vanishes for admission to a hall 'almost dizzy and alive with waterfalls', reflected from the great cascade outside. Exquisitely expressed throughout, 'Yarrow Visited' is one of several poems which show that Wordsworth in his later years was capable of writing in strains rarely surpassed by other English poets. Some of the most felicitous lines in these Scottish 'memorials' testify the revival of his interest in classical literature, which he hoped to read with Johnny. The 'Brownie's Den' is as beauteous 'as the chosen spot In Nysa's isle . . . Whither, by care of Libyan Jove, (High servant of paternal love) Young Bacchus was conveyed – to lie Safe from his step-dame Rhea's eye'; and the spirit of the freedom-fighter Wallace recalls the association (first made in *Descriptive Sketches*) of the Marathonian tale and 'the votive shrine' of Tell by 'Uri's lake'.

A week after the travellers' return Dorothy Wordsworth accompanied Sara Hutchinson on a long visit to Hindwell. In that interval James Hogg and others visited Rydal Mount; they gathered to watch a meteor from the terrace, Hogg describing its path as a triumphal arch in honour of the meeting of poets. Hearing De Quincey say that Wordsworth had asked who were the poets, he made this an excuse for parodying his host in 'a further portion' of *The Recluse*, an act of petty revenge which he subsequently regretted.

When the sonnet 'Surprised by joy' was written is not known; Wordsworth said it was long after his daughter Catherine's death, but it was published early in 1815. It is one of the most moving personal poems in English literature. Its language is impeccable, but its most remarkable feature is the perfect accord of its varying movements with the poet's feelings, from sudden transport, through the shock of realizing he could ever forget his 'heart's best treasure', to heavy recollection of his sad loss. Such poetry never grows old, and exemplifies the highest strain of Wordsworth's music, evolved from ordinary language but subtly distinctive in tone. Too fine for complete oral transmission, like some of his later sonnets, it appeals hauntingly to the inner ear.

Wordsworth busied himself with the arrangement of his poems in accordance with a plan which began to unfold in the spring of 1809. He was preparing a two-volume edition, and this appeared in March 1815, with a dedication to Sir George Beaumont. The whole design, which has operated seriously against the appreciation of his poetry as a whole ever since, was based on a number of criteria: 'powers of mind' predominant in the creation of poems (e.g. fancy, imagination), form (e.g. descriptive, narrative, lyrical), subject (e.g. national independence and liberty). Yoked uneasily with these was a comprehensive time-scheme, ranging from childhood to old age, death, and immortality. Needless to say, the application of all principles was often impossible, and consequent decisions led to the separation of poems which are closely associated by personal links and developmental interest. The frequent collocation of dull inferior verse and first-rate poetry, often separated by wide chronological distances, is a deterrent to continuous or prolonged reading; and the difficulty of finding poems (except in a single-volume edition) cannot be exaggerated.

Needing new subjects for poetry, Wordsworth was glad to find them in books, especially after his success with 'Laodamia', which was quickly composed, and included in the 1815 edition of his poems, much to the delight of Lamb, who would not have recognised the authorship had he met the poem 'in a strange place'. Landor thought the subject could not have inspired more tenderness and passion in Euripides. Wordsworth was indebted to a number of classical sources (and Latin epithets are noticeable in 'redundant [locks]', 'conscious Parcae', and 'purpureal gleams'); he was particularly fascinated by the 'constant interchange of growth and blight' in the trees over the hero's tomb. The story turns on Laodamia's inability to control her feelings when the spirit of her husband Protesilaus is allowed to visit her briefly as a reward for his heroism. He wishes her to rise to a nobler spiritual level in preparation for life after death. The virtues he emphasizes may disclose a further appeal the subject held for Wordsworth:

> 'Be taught, O faithful consort, to control
> Rebellious passion: for the Gods approve
> The depth, and not the tumult, of the soul;
> A fervent, not ungovernable love . . .
>
> And thou, though strong in love, art all too weak
> In reason, in self-government too slow;
> I counsel thee by fortitude to seek
> Our blest re-union in the shades below.
> The invisible world with thee hath sympathised;
> Be thy affections raised and solemnised. . . .'

Yet Wordsworth kept closely to the spirit of the classical story; he wished it to be less severe, as the original ending showed, Laodamia being pitied and allowed 'to gather flowers Of blissful quiet 'mid unfading bowers' after her deliverance in 'a trance of passion' from 'the galling yoke of time'. The closing lines cost the poet much anxiety, but he restored the Virgilian doom in 1827, and preserved it with slight emendations.

The fall of Napoleon had led to a resumption of correspondence with Annette Vallon, chiefly on the forthcoming marriage of Caroline and Jean Baptiste Baudouin; a visit to France, to arrange a settlement with this in view, had been postponed but was considered again in February 1815. By March a Postmastership of £50 per annum had been obtained for Hartley Coleridge (through his uncle's influence) at Merton College, Oxford; and with further financial assistance, particularly from Lady Beaumont, it was thought he would have sufficient. Wordsworth, thinking of his own inadequacies at Cambridge, exhorted Hartley to apply himself zealously to prescribed studies, and not trust 'vaguely to his talents'. The visit to Paris, with Sara Hutchinson, which was planned for May, was again postponed when it was learned that Napoleon had escaped from Elba and landed in France.

During April, in preparation for the publication of *The White Doe of Rylstone*, Wordsworth wrote the dedicatory stanzas to Mary. Lord Lonsdale offered him the Collectorship of Customs at Whitehaven, a position once held by Wordsworth's uncle Richard. It was much more lucrative than the Distributorship of Stamps, but William could not leave Rydal Mount and its beautiful surroundings to live in a town, and he felt it incumbent upon him to explain in person why he declined the offer. He and Mary therefore left hurriedly for London, taking Hartley Coleridge to Oxford on their way. They met John Keble, who thought Wordsworth delightful; 'there was no affectation of poetical or metaphysical talk in him', rather the opposite. In the capital they visited the Beaumonts, and met many friends and people of distinction. The painter Benjamin Haydon made Wordsworth's life-mask, and took him to meet Leigh Hunt, editor of *The Examiner*, the current issue of which contained a review of *Comus* in which Hazlitt deviously sneered at Wordsworth's 'November, 1813', a heartfelt sonnet on George III's malady which exacerbated Hazlitt by its association of Napoleon's defeat at Leipzig with the will of Heaven. Haydon thought that, if Wordsworth had condescended to visit Hazlitt when he wrote favourably of *The Excursion*, 'his vanity would have been soothed and his virulence softened'. He

was charmed by Wordsworth's 'eager feelings' on all that interested him, but not blind to his egotism; Wilberforce found him
'independent almost to rudeness'. *The White Doe* appeared in
quarto, with an engraving of a graceful picture by Beaumont.
Though Dorothy realized the mistake of publishing *The Excursion*
expensively (only the wealthy could afford it, but they bought for
fashion's sake, 'and alas we are not yet in the fashion'), Wordsworth thought its successor deserved to be magnificently produced. Jeffrey maintained his jeering juridical stance by declaring
it 'the very worst poem we ever saw imprinted in a quarto volume'.
Yet admiration for Wordsworth was increasing, and *The White
Doe* received high praise in *The Gentleman's Magazine* (1815) and
Blackwood's (1818).

To 1815 belongs 'Artegal and Elidure', written 'as a token of
affectionate respect for the memory of Milton', from whose
History of England the story derives. The thought of Geoffrey of
Monmouth's chronicle, with its tale of Lear and legends beloved
by Spenser and youthful Milton, elicits a style of lively strength and
grace in the introduction, and the whole is transmitted in verse
well suited to historical narrative, each stanza being a shortened
modification of Spenser's, felicitously varied with a short sixth line
preparatory to its alexandrine close. The story is a striking
example of fraternal self-sacrifice and loyalty; Wordsworth placed
it after 'The Brothers' in the group labelled 'Poems Founded on
the Affections', but any resemblance the poems have is far out-
weighed by differences of setting and presentation.

The sonnet 'Weak is the will of man, his judgment blind', with
its emphasis on imagination, that 'glorious faculty assigned To
elevate the more-than-reasoning mind' and 'pluck the amaran-
thine flower of faith' to form an enduring wreath around the
sufferer's brow, could be regarded as the quintessence of *The
Excursion*. Copies of three other sonnets were sent to Haydon:
'September, 1815' welcomes the approach of winter, a season
'potent to renew . . . the instinctive joys of song, And nobler cares'
than those that come with 'listless summer'. 'November 1' presents
a distant view of Langdale Pikes strewn with the smoothest snow,
unstained by 'flight of sad mortality's earth-sullying wing' and
'destined to endure White, radiant, spotless, exquisitely pure,
Through all vicissitudes, till genial Spring Has filled the laughing
vales with welcome flowers'. 'To B. R. Haydon' was written in
response to the painter's news that weak eyesight impeded work on

his *Christ's Entry into Jerusalem*, a huge picture which was to include the faces of Wordsworth and Keats.

The final defeat of the French at Waterloo did not lead to a peace settlement until November. On 18 January 1816, the day appointed for national thanksgiving, Wordsworth began, 'almost extempore, in front of Rydal Mount, before church-time', the composition of his Thanksgiving 'Ode'. It appeared in May, with some shorter poems, as a finale to the series of anti-Napoleonic poems in the cause of freedom which he had already published. In an accompanying note, Wordsworth deplored the losses suffered for the cause, but praised the example and wisdom of Britain, and maintained that, despite the abuse of military power elsewhere, no people can be 'independent, free, or secure, much less great, in any sane application of the word, without a cultivation of military virtues'. He insisted at the same time on the need for 'civil, moral, and religious' enlightenment to ensure justice and equality throughout all social levels, so that 'courage may everywhere continue to rest immovably upon its ancient English foundation, personal self-respect'. Ultimately, to give a greater appearance of completion to his 'National Independence and Liberty' sequence, part of the ode relating to victory at Waterloo was detached and divided to form two independent poems, 'Ode, 1814' and 'Ode, 1815'.

Showing ample evidence of technical skill in their changes of movement, these odes are declamatory and grandiloquent rather than poetic; unlike the 'Intimations' ode, they are works of elaborate inflation, being based on a few simple ideas. 'Ode, 1814' is memorable for the composite English landscape above which the glorious form of St George is heard exhorting in outmoded style virgins and matrons to prepare garlands for the returning brave; the poem concludes with the hope that art and poetry will produce something more lasting as a reminder of heroic achievement and example for posterity. 'Ode, 1815', in celebration of Waterloo, is notable for the stanza which reveals in no uncertain measure Wordsworth's acceptance of the common belief that the 'just God of christianised humanity' uses natural disasters such as earthquakes and tornadoes, as well as man, for the prosecution of his designs. The statement that Carnage is the daughter of God was wrested out of context by Shelley; Wordsworth did not believe in war except for justice and freedom, was no lover of carnage (as his sonnet 'After visiting the Field of Waterloo' indicates), but accepted war with its horrors for justifiable ends: 'Thou cloth'st the wicked in their dazzling mail, And for Thy righteous purpose they prevail.' In the curtailed Thanksgiving 'Ode' he greets the rising sun as the 'orient conqueror of gloomy night', and hopes that its promise will not fail. The ascription of success to national 'magnanimity' rather than to strength of arms recalls the poet's conviction in 1802 that 'by the soul only' are nations great and free. He is proud of his country's example, but declares that any chauvinist who imputes victory to an indomitable Britain misses 'the sole true glory', which transcends earthly power: 'Say not that we have vanquished — but that we survive' by God's favour. In this spirit the ode continues to its prayerful conclusion. In general it is the product of easy-flowing thought, but deeper feeling survives, especially in the passage (ll.101–12) which emphasizes war's widespread waste. Among the minor accompaniments of these odes are two poems in praise of the role played by winter at Heaven's command in the destruction of the French army in Russia. Of the sonnets written early in 1816, that on the raising of the siege of Vienna by John Sobieski, king of Poland, is superior to the two on Waterloo; its last line He conquering through God, and God by Him, taken from the Italian poet Filicaia's ode on the same subject, encapsulates the leading thought in all Wordsworth's 1816 poems on the fight for freedom.

'A Letter to a Friend of Robert Burns' was finished in January and published by 1 May 1816. It was written to James Gray of Edinburgh, on hearing that Gilbert Burns was about to undertake a vindication of his brother. Wordsworth's pamphlet expresses his tolerance, humanity, and enjoyment of Burns's poetry. It has a special interest in its remarks on what is appropriate in the biographies of authors. He does not object to the truth, provided it is the whole truth. Lovers of freedom are lovers of the truth, but they will show discrimination and delicacy only when their love is intelligent. Facts produced by remorseless researchers which are inconsistent with the evidence of highly personal poetry are an irrelevance, and it is regrettable that 'inconsiderate intrusion has not left us at liberty to enjoy [Burns's] mirth, or his love; his wisdom or his wit; without an admixture of useless, irksome, and painful details, that take from his poems so much of . . . the right of imparting solid instruction through the medium of unalloyed pleasure'. Wordsworth makes Jeffrey's indictment of Burns an opportunity for an open attack on 'the happy self-complacency, the unsuspecting vain-glory, and the cordial *bonhommie*' of 'this persevering Aristarch'. He concludes by finding the same love of despotism in 'the anonymous conductor of a perishable publication' as in the fallen Napoleon, and the same vanity as in Robespierre, all three ostentatiously professing reverence for truth and concern for duty, while practising falsehood in the hope that it will prevail. Wordsworth's 'letter' was attacked, surprisingly by John Wilson, now living in Edinburgh, and characteristically by Hazlitt, whose aspersions during his lecture on Burns were hissed by Crabb Robinson.

'A Fact, and an Imagination' combines two sonnets, in the first of which (based on Milton's *History of England*) Canute concludes: 'He only is a king, and he alone Deserves the name (this truth the billows preach) Whose everlasting laws, sea, earth, and heaven obey.' The second gives what the more patient King Alfred might have said when the sea was calm after reaching its bounds, an image of the repose found by the wise, the brave, and the good, 'whose souls do, like the flood Of ocean, press right on; or gently wind, Neither to be diverted nor withstood, Until they reach the bounds by Heaven assigned'. '*A little onward lend thy guiding hand*' was written in the spring, it seems, when Wordsworth, after a recurrence of trachoma, wondered whether he would lose his sight. It is addressed to Dora, and he thinks of the walks they can take on the heights or in the woods, particularly 'in the still summer noon' when beams of light, either in repose or gliding through dusky aisles, recall 'the living presences of nuns', 'Whose saintly radiance mitigates the gloom Of those terrestrial fabrics, where they serve, To Christ, the Sun of righteousness, espoused'. Now, his eyes 'from bondage freed', he can turn with her to more glorious heights and shades in the Bible or the classics. The urge to take flight from the summit links the poem with 'To —, on her First Ascent to the Summit of Helvellyn', where the fancy is given free rein, and with 'Composed upon an Evening of Extraordinary Splendour and Beauty', where the vision splendid suggests wings playing in readiness to lift the poet heavenward.

Some of the 1817 poems to which the last belongs suggest that Wordsworth wrote without giving his subjects deep imaginative thought, and that he versified readily when little more than his fancy was stirred. 'Vernal Ode' repeats the device of 'Ode, 1814', a celestial stranger descending, to strike his golden harp and sing on 'the immortality of succession' (as it is described in the I.F. note) in the heavens (with the decaying stars) and on earth (with the seasonal changes in nature). The poem falls into two parts, each spoilt at one stage by over-complicated syntax. From the second emerges a strikingly defined passage on the immeasurable ancestry of the humming-bee,

> Mysteriously remote and high;
> High as the imperial front of man;
> The roseate bloom on woman's cheek;
> The soaring eagle's curvèd beak;
> The white plumes of the floating swan;
> Old as the tiger's paw, the lion's mane
> Ere shaken by that mood of stern disdain
> At which the desert trembles.

The wonders of natural revival through the ages suggest the presence of angels on earth; the bee's ancestry takes us back to the golden age, when 'Bright seraphs mixed familiarly with men; And earth and stars composed a universal heaven!' With this closing thought Wordsworth tries to give unity to the whole.

Two poems were designed to show that real sentiments are not incompatible with classical allusion; for this reason they are addressed to Lycoris, a character in Virgil's *Eclogues*. 'Ode to Lycoris' is one of Wordsworth's most finished compositions; it originated significantly from the reflected image at the end of the first stanza: 'These swan-like specks of mountain snow, White as the pair that slid along the plains Of heaven, when Venus held the reins!' The sequel, making use of an image, first intended for 'Nutting' in 1798, 'There let me see thee sink into a mood Of gentler thought, protracted till thine eye Be calm as water when the winds are gone', associates this with a cave like the grot where Numa the regal philosopher took counsel with the sage nymph Egeria. These are reflective poems. In youth we prefer twilight and autumn to dawn and spring, but with our declining years there comes a balancing inspiration which makes 'hopeful spring the favourite of the soul'. The second poem is expressed largely in descriptive metaphor. Climbing high in the heat is toilsome and perilous, making us apt to despise the familiar world below. But the heart, which has 'a truth and beauty of her own', is most itself in close contact with life, among 'moss-grown alleys, circumscribing shades, and gurgling rills'. At higher philosophical levels, how welcome the shade of some wild cave where we can reflect deeply on life as a whole. The thought implicit in this elaborate imagery is closely akin to that expressed by Wordsworth with simple lyrical directness in 1798, on 'toiling reason' and the heartfelt wisdom that comes from 'wise passiveness' rather than from books or the 'barren leaves' of science and art. Hence the concluding recollection of happy hours with his dearest friend in that inspiring period (a concealed reference to Dorothy rather than to the Coleridge of the past). Hence also Wordsworth's delightful I.F. note on the servant who told a visitor at Rydal Mount that her master's study was 'out of doors'. In the words of Robert Bloomfield, 'Nature was his book.'

'The Pass of Kirkstone', purporting to convey Wordsworth's thoughts and impressions from climbing the pass in all conditions, peters out, leading to nothing strikingly new. Worthier and well sustained is 'The Longest Day', a philosophical poem composed with Dora in mind, and much admired by Charles Lamb. Other reminders of Wordsworth's poetic revival may be found in 'Sequel to "Beggars"', which is gracefully penned and charitably inspired, and in the beautiful sonnet 'The Wild Duck's Nest'. Recollections of scenes of youth in 'Composed upon an Evening of Extraordinary Splendour and Beauty' show how habituated he had become to Church imagery. The poem provides an interesting interpretation rather than an evocation of the scene, and illustrates by dissimilarities how much of the glory and the dream which invested his childhood experiences had come from the transmutations of time and re-creative 'memory'. 'Dion', based on Plutarch and much revised, contains some of Wordsworth's noblest verse. It dwells on the tragedy of one who, 'Intent to trace the ideal path of right (More fair than heaven's broad causeway paved with stars)', commits an error and is afflicted by guilt, which Wordsworth communicates with an immediacy drawn from classical association, the Spectre being detected at the 'dusky bound' of a long gallery, and heard sweeping the marble floor

> Like Auster whirling to and fro
> His force on Caspian foam to try;
> Or Boreas when he scours the snow
> That skins the plains of Thessaly,
> Or when aloft on Maenalus he stops
> His flight, 'mid eddying pine-tree tops!

The poem pursues its way admirably to the end, where it sinks redundantly into a moral: 'Him only pleasure leads, and peace attends, Him, only him, the shield of Jove defends, Whose means are fair and spotless as his ends.' Had a minor poet written 'Lament of Mary Queen of Scots', it would probably be better known. It is an imaginative evocation of the prisoner's thoughts and feelings one New Year's eve, and is especially interesting from its creative origin, 'a flash of moonlight that struck the ground' when Wordsworth approached the steps leading from the garden to the front of Rydal Mount. Probably without realizing it, he recalled Helen Maria Williams' 'Queen Mary's Lament', a poem he had known years earlier.[2]

Coleridge's *Biographia Literaria* was published in the summer, and Wordsworth's disappointment at its treatment of his poetry suggests that he had not realized how incapable his former friend had become of responding wholeheartedly to his work. When they met in December, at the home of Thomas Monkhouse, Mary Wordsworth's cousin, Coleridge was cold and distant, Crabb Robinson reports. Wordsworth had travelled with Mary and Sara to London in November, primarily to discuss with Christopher at Lambeth the affairs of their brother Richard, who had died in 1816 leaving a widow and young son. They stayed in the capital two months. At Haydon's 'immortal dinner' Wordsworth sat with Keats under the huge picture which contained their portraits; after hearing Keats read his 'Hymn to Pan' from *Endymion*, he described it (not condescendingly) as 'a very pretty piece of paganism'. When they retired for tea, a Mr Kingston, Comptroller of Stamps, insisted on being introduced to his Westmorland agent; his subsequent attempts to engage in cultured conversation so convulsed Charles Lamb that he tipsily took a candle to examine the gentleman's phrenological development. At the time Keats was convinced that the period had 'three things to rejoice at': *The Excursion*, Haydon's pictures, and Hazlitt's criticism. He was astonished on seeing the poet he venerated splendidly attired to visit his overseer, and, after being Wordsworth's guest and finding that all present expected him to listen to his host as if to an oracle, readily responded to the strictures on his egotism which Hazlitt unleashed during his lectures.

Keats's views of Wordsworth must have sunk lower by the time he and his friend reached Rydal Mount in the summer, on their way to Scotland, and found none of the family at home. They had discovered at Bowness that Wordsworth had been there only three days earlier campaigning for the Lowthers, two sons of Lord Lonsdale. For years this family had held the two constituencies of Westmorland unopposed. At this election, Lord Lowther had a formidable opponent in Henry Brougham. Wordsworth had, in fact, left home to hear the announcement of the result at Appleby. While in London, he had been in correspondence with Lord Lonsdale on this campaign. Post-war disturbances had made him confessedly and obsessionally an 'alarmist'; he feared that a revolution by the uneducated masses would lead to 'Jacobinism', and was convinced that the steady powers of the landowners needed to be retained if orderly development towards justice and enlightenment for all were to be secured. His principles had not changed; his sympathies were still with the people, but he feared that progress and traditional values would be imperilled by revolutionary excesses.

So formidable a demagogue was Brougham that Wordsworth thought he would 'sweep all before him', if voting 'went by counting heads' instead of being restricted to freeholders; the same 'power of incitement' through England would endanger the government. As Distributor of Stamps, Wordsworth could not openly participate in canvassing; yet he contrived to be a leading adviser and influence. He prepared two published addresses to the freeholders of Westmorland; and Brougham, answering their charges, quoted 'Rob Roy's Grave' against its author, much to the delight of his audience. De Quincey then collaborated with Wordsworth, regaining favour after having lost it through opium-addiction and association with Margaret Sympson of Nab Cottage (who had since become an excellent wife to him). In return he was recommended for the editorship of the Lowther newspaper, *The Westmorland Gazette*, a post he managed to retain only fourteen months. Wordsworth had the satisfaction of seeing Brougham defeated in 1818, and again in 1820 and 1826, but it is regrettable that exaggerated fears drove him to devote so much time and energy to a cause which did him great harm, associating him with privilege, damning him in the eyes of Shelley and many liberal-minded contemporaries, and identifying him permanently with 'The Lost Leader' of Browning.

New Enterprise and Sonnet Sequences (1818–21)

Unfortunately Wordsworth's political agitation continued, as Brougham renewed his campaign for the emancipation of Westmorland and Whigs bought land to create partisan freeholders. John's educational future was another long-standing problem. In September 1818 Dorothy had to find accommodation for the numerous servants who heralded the coming of the Wilberforce family to Rydal Mount, where they stayed about four weeks. Tom Monkhouse was another visitor, and the Beaumonts were guests for a few days on their way to Keswick. Dorothy and the Wilberforces dined with them at Miss Barker's in Borrowdale, and the next day, escorted by a shepherd, she and Miss Barker climbed to the top of Scafell. Never before had she beheld 'so sublime a mountain prospect'.

In February 1819, when Wordsworth learned what a huge library his friend Wrangham possessed, he answered with an emphasis akin to contrasuggestibility that he had not spent five shillings on *new* books in five years, and had not read a fifth of the books in his relatively modest collection. Soon afterwards, deeming perhaps that interest in his poetry was on the increase, he committed 'Peter Bell' to his publisher, after adding two stanzas suggested by 'Haydon's noble picture of Christ's Entry into Jerusalem'. J. H. Reynolds' 'antenatal Peter' skit excited wider interest in the poem than it would otherwise have received, and in two weeks another impression was required. Wordsworth sent a copy to Lamb, who did not dare to tell him his views, except that he ought to have added 'The Waggoner'. This hint probably tipped the scale, for 'a most abominably abusive critique' of 'Peter Bell' had so incensed the ladies of Rydal Mount that they urged him to publish 'The Waggoner' and 'give them another bone to pick'. Lamb was delighted to find that it was dedicated to him.

The mockery and abuse of 'Peter Bell' did little to stem the tide of approval which was flowing for Wordsworth, yet there was nothing in contemporary criticism to equal twentieth-century eulogies of its brilliance in narration and psychology. The most lasting animus it generated was political. Leigh Hunt sent his review of the 'didactic little horror' to Shelley, who promptly wrote the long lampoon which, fortunately for Wordsworth, was not published until 1839. In her accompanying note, Mrs Shelley stated that nobody admired Wordsworth's poetry more than her husband had done. It must have been his earlier poetry, for nobody relished his 'damnation' more than Shelley, turning thoughts of one of his Thanksgiving odes into praise of the Devil for making Carnage and Slaughter and Peterloo massacres serve his purpose, and attributing the 'double damnation' of his incurable dullness to the gentility which followed his acceptance of a sinecure from Lord MacMurderchouse of the Devil's party.

Wordsworth's 1818 poems include a pleasing fantasy of the mighty fallen and the humble exalted in 'The Pilgrim's Dream', and interesting images in the moralizing of 'Inscriptions supposed to be found in and near a Hermit's Cell'. As winter approached he revised two sonnets, and wrote nineteen others, for his Duddon sequence; three more, notably on Malham Cove and Gordale, were prompted by Yorkshire scenes which William Westall's sketches had recalled. 'William has done nothing lately except a few sonnets, but these are exquisitely beautiful', Dorothy wrote the following summer, as if she were half deploring his failure to resume *The Recluse*. Besides more Duddon sonnets, these may have included 'I watch, and long have watched', a poem which could have reminded her of 'Strange fits of passion': the sudden drop of a star below the parapet of Loughrigg Fell is a reminder of death, a feeling awakened in the poet 'not once only, but a hundred times' from the same spot, at Rydal Mount, as he watched such occurrences. Another possibility is 'I heard (alas! 'twas only in a dream)', a sonnet based on the fusion of two ideas in Plato's *Phaedo*, that man is too weak and slothful to rise above earth's hollows to heights nearer heaven, and that the swan is the bird of Apollo because, foreseeing the joys of heaven, it sings and rejoices more than ever as it approaches death. 'The Haunted Tree' lacks the intensity of 'Yew-trees'; it betrays a failing of the imagination and a partiality for classical fancies. The thought inspired by the song of birds in 'September, 1819', that the poet in the autumn of life may still be strong, makes Wordsworth glance critically at contemporary poets, and wonder if the purer and nobler poetry of classical times can be revived.

The River Duddon was published in April 1820, with 'Vaudracour and Julia' and other poems, and 'A Topographical Description of the Country of the Lakes'. It was a stream Wordsworth remembered from his schooldays, when he became familiar with its upper reaches; from student vacations when he stayed at Broughton;[3] most of all, from sight-seeing with Mary as they returned from Bootle in 1811. The fourteenth sonnet was the first to be composed, and this together with the twenty-sixth was revised when the majority were written in November 1818. The dedicatory stanzas to Christopher Wordsworth are not the least interesting part of this publication. William commemorates the visit of carollers on Christmas Eve 1819, and wishes his brother could have been present, and seen a revival on other faces of the radiance which had been theirs on such occasions in childhood. He sees a sure defence of 'wholesome laws' in ancient manners; early memories are endeared by them, as they are by 'emerald fields' and streams 'more pure and bright Than fabled Cytherea's zone Glittering before the Thunderer's sight'. He hopes that Christopher, by the Thames at Lambeth, will find time to recall 'humbler streams, and greener bowers', and profit from 'those kindly rays That through the clouds do sometimes steal, And all the far-off past reveal'.

Although arranged to give impressions evoked by the river from source to sea, the sonnets as a whole have little coherence or continuity. They begin with the 'child of the clouds' or 'nursling of the mountain' that turns into 'a glistering snake' as it thrids 'with sinuous lapse' the rushes, or glides through dwarf willows and by ferny brake, until it meets cottages, trees, and flowers. Wordsworth wonders whether the first inhabitants of the area were 'nursed in hideous usages, and rites accursed'. He thinks of Sunkenkirk, the Druid circle above the lower valley, to which he had ridden with schoolfriends from Hawkshead; the eagle is a reminder of the Roman soldiers who camped on Hardknott above the upper valley; and the Danish raven recalls other invaders. Wordsworth indulges in pretty fancies, collectively and individually (vii, xii, xxii), having reason, it seems, to describe fancy as 'too industrious' an elf (probably an unconscious recollection from Keats's 'Ode to a Nightingale', which had appeared in July 1819). He makes too much of the silly unsooth of folklore (xi); he is distractingly reminded of a Red Indian tradition in Humboldt's *Travels* (xvi); and the more Miltonic and classically-minded poet sees the beauty of Elysium in the 'liquid lapse serene' of a river 'countenanced like a soft cerulean sky' amid the flowery plain of Donnerdale, before it has to change its temper and 'Dance, like a Bacchanal, from rock to rock, Tossing her frantic thyrsus wide and high' (xx). The recollection of happy times with friends and relatives before the death of his cousin Mary of Whitehaven, who had married John Smith of Broughton, produces an impressive image of triumphant Memory, breaking from her 'cloudy stall of Time' with 'glistening tresses bound, yet light and free As golden locks of birch, that rise and fall' (xxi). He wishes his wife Mary could be transported to him, for without her nothing pleases to the full (xxv). Some sonnets are made memorable by particular images: of bleak winds roaring through 'the stiff lance-like shoots of pollard ash' with a swell of sound 'loud as the gusts that lash The matted forest on Ontario's shore' (xiii), or the 'choral multitude' of streams pouring down, 'Pure as the morning, fretful, boisterous, keen, Green as the salt-sea billows, white and green', from the 'sullen reservoirs' which he viewed with 'flying inquest' in his boyhood (xxvi). 'Seathwaite Chapel' (xviii) ends in a tribute to the Revd Robert Walker, whom he had already honoured in *The Excursion*, and on whom he wrote a long historical note for this edition: 'A pastor such as Chaucer's verse portrays; Such as the heaven-taught skill of Herbert drew; And tender Goldsmith crowned with deathless praise!' 'The Kirk of Ulpha' (xxxi) is a poem of unusually satisfying imagery and unity. Then follow three sonnets which bring the series to its grand conclusion. The river widens majestically as it meets the sea; it is comparable to the Thames estuary, though its vessels are more humble and peaceful. The poet hopes he will advance with the same spirit towards his life's end, 'Prepared, in peace of heart, in calm of mind And soul, to mingle with Eternity', and concludes with 'Afterthought', one of the finest philosophical poems of all time, in purest English undefiled. Here we have wisdom which is universal and imperishable, transcending creed and system:

Enough, if something from our hands have power
To live, and act, and serve the future hour;

And if, as toward the silent tomb we go,
Through love, through hope, and faith's transcendent dower,
We feel that we are greater than we know.

The capitalization of 'Still glides the Stream, and shall for ever
glide; The Form remains, the Function never dies' helps to express
the spiritual meaning. Some idea of this will be found in a passage
with less imaginative overtones, at the end of 'Brook, whose society
the poet seeks', a sonnet (not later than March 1804) where Wordsworth states that, if he had to choose a 'type' or emblem of a
stream, it would not follow the human style of the Greeks:

It seems the Eternal Soul is clothed in thee
With purer robes than those of flesh and blood,
And hath bestowed on thee a better good;
Unwearied joy, and life without its cares.

All four publications from the 'Thanksgiving Ode', etc. of 1816
to *The River Duddon*, etc. of 1820 were bound in one volume and
made available in 1820 as the third volume of Wordsworth's *Miscellaneous Poems*. The same year a pocket edition of all this poetry
appeared in four volumes, followed by the second edition of *The
Excursion*. Wordsworth had at last been recognised. With the successful conclusion of his second political campaign for the return
of the Lowthers in May, the time had come for a respite. His eyes
had troubled him for months, but he was free. All the children
were now being educated away from home, John at Sedbergh,
Dora at Ambleside, and Willy in London, at the school of the
former curate and schoolmaster of Grasmere, Mr Johnson, whose
enthusiasm for the new teaching method had come to the notice of
Andrew Bell, its initiator, and earned his promotional transfer.
The Wordsworths planned a holiday tour in Europe. Dorothy was
already in London, checking the proofs for the new four-volume
edition of *Miscellaneous Poems*.

Recollections of William and Mary's stay with Robert Jones at
Souldern, and at Oxford, on their way to London, are recorded in
'A Parsonage in Oxfordshire' and the two sonnets 'Oxford, May
30, 1820'. In the latter Wordsworth describes how he felt as if he
were a young student again, and wishes Mary could be equally
exhilarated. The song of birds at Richmond Hill, with another
recollection of Collins' 'Ode on the Death of Thomson' (as in a
poem of 1789) is the subject of 'Fame tells of groves'.

In London, where the sculptor Chantrey completed a bust of William, the Wordsworths stayed with Christopher at Lambeth. They attended Tom Monkhouse's wedding on 8 July, and he, his young wife, and her sister joined the party which set off for Europe three days later. From Calais they proceeded to Bruges (regretting they could not stay much longer to study its 'magnificent architecture'), Brussels, and Cologne. They visited many places as they made their way along the Rhine to Switzerland, where they spent most of August. At Lucerne Mrs Monkhouse, who was not equal to climbing in the Alps, left with her sister and their maidservant to join the remainder of the party at Geneva after visiting friends at Berne. Joined by Crabb Robinson, the more intrepid travellers made their way over the St Gotthard Pass to Lake Como and Milan. Here Dorothy lingered with the statues on the cathedral roof while the others ascended the 'giddy, central spire'. Their return route (much improved in the Gondo gorge) taking them the way William had come with Jones thirty years earlier, they crossed the Simplon, visited Chamonix for views of Mont Blanc, and reached France via Geneva.

After being captivated by the splendours of historic Fontainebleau, William found nothing more interesting in Paris than the Jardin des Plantes. He was moved almost to tears by 'this apparently boundless exhibition of the wonders of the creation', but disappointed to find that the Temple, where Louis XVI and his family had been immured, and the 'memorable spot' where the Jacobin Club had held its meetings, had disappeared. Meeting Miss Williams, whose poems he admired in his youth, he accomplished what he failed to do on his first visit. Four weeks were spent in Paris, principally to meet Annette Vallon. Caroline, whose openness in addressing Wordsworth as 'father' seemed indelicate to Robinson, had married Jean Baptiste Baudouin in 1816; they had two little girls, and Annette lived with them in the Rue Charlot. In order to see them as much as possible, the Wordsworths took lodgings in the same street. William had been making up Caroline's dowry in annual instalments of £30, which were continued until 1835, when they were handsomely completed with a further £400.

At the end of October the Wordsworths, whose companions had returned to England, stayed with their old friend Miss Barker at Boulogne; rough seas delayed their departure. Two weeks were spent in London, where they met the Lambs, Samuel Rogers, and

Coleridge. At Cambridge William and Mary stayed with Christopher, now Master of Trinity College, before proceeding to the Beaumonts' at Coleorton. In the meantime Dorothy was at Playford Hall, the home of the Clarksons near Ipswich, and Willy spent most of his holiday with her. His parents reached home just before Christmas, after an absence of seven months.

Dorothy's journal provides the best descriptive account of the tour. Wordsworth's record is to be found in *Memorials of a Tour on the Continent*, most of the poems in this collection being written for insertion in the journals kept by Mary and Dorothy, which had the effect of suggesting subjects and even expression at times. Perhaps it would have been better had he waited for creative memory to inspire him. Whether he composed these poems *seriatim* is unknown, but their level declines rather quickly, and few can be admired as a whole. He can write a fine sonnet on the ugliness of Calais fishwomen, two on the architecture and 'cloistral silence' of Bruges, and another on scenery by the Meuse which he preferred to that of the Rhine. He has an interesting sonnet on the field of Waterloo, and another contrasting the relics of Charlemagne with the enchantments of romance. 'In the Cathedral of Cologne' fascinates by the use of musical metaphor to express the powers it would need to complete a work of such magnificence. The best of the subsequent Rhineland poems is the hymn which Wordsworth imagined sung by the Heidelberg boatmen. A graceful tribute to Aloys Reding as the opponent of Napoleon introduces the poems on Switzerland, most of which are disappointing, as may be seen by comparing 'Engelberg, the Hill of Angels', one of his most striking subjects, with the account of the kind of scene which suggested angels singing while the monks built the abbey below, as it is presented in Wordsworth's letter to Lord Lonsdale (19.viii.20).

Among succeeding poems there are two, 'Fort Fuentes' and 'Stanzas composed in the Simplon Pass', which are rendered almost unreadable by the tum-tee-tee verse in which they are cast. The 'golden lot' prophesied for the Italian itinerant is not without a tinge of poetry, but Dorothy's account is far more alive and interesting. 'The Last Supper, by Leonardo da Vinci' is wrought with feeling but suffers from inadequacies. A sonnet on the column intended by Bonaparte for a 'triumphal edifice' in Milan savours more of rhetoric than of imaginative force. Wordsworth's confident claim that 'The Eclipse of the Sun, 1820' combines 'beauty,

majesty and novelty, nature and art, earth and heaven' with 'a
degree of lyrical spirit and movement' rarely attained in English
odes may be true, but it is not an outstanding composition except
perhaps in the highly wrought passage on the 'aerial host' of figures
decorating the roof of Milan Cathedral. More memorable and
glowing, in 'The Three Cottage Girls', is the association of the
Helvetian maid with Wordsworth's Highland girl, the 'bright
spirit' whom his imagination had endowed with immortality.

The tribute to an American in 'Elegiac Verses' was made at
Robinson's request; he had introduced the young man to the
Wordsworth party, and they had spent some time together very
happily before parting on the Rigi summit; three days later he was
drowned while attempting to cross Lake Zürich. As imaginative
description, 'Echo, upon the Gemmi' is remarkable, even in its
moralizing conclusion; its evocation of Cynthia and the stars has
an astonishing Grecian vitality. 'Processions' has some admirable
verses on ancient rites; its main interest is in the thoughts raised by
the propinquity of glaciers and religious processions, on links
between Christianity, pagan worship, and the mythical interpretation of nature. 'Desultory Stanzas', added on the advice of
Robinson, who hoped Wordsworth had not forgotten 'those
patriotic and pious bridges at Lucerne' and 'the equally affecting
Senate house not made of hands' at Sarnen, has that appearance
of professional improvization which characterizes too much of
Wordsworth's later verse; it is the Alps which inspire him most, but
the greatness he attains is never long sustained.

'The Italian Itinerant' suggested the ode 'To Enterprise', a
finely executed work which is imbued with the living spirit for adventure and exploration by land, sea, and air. Wordsworth thinks
of enterprise for evil, sending hosts and armies to 'their destined
punishment', with a final glance at the dissolution of Napoleon's
army in Russia, their suffering and madness forgotten as they are
wrapped in a winding-sheet of spotless snow. His wish for resolution in those who, like himself, are no longer young, reaches its
final expression in a stern image, 'fixed resolves by Reason
justified' cleaving to their object 'like sleet Whitening a pine tree's
northern side, When fields are naked far and wide'. Finally he
prays for enterprise in his favourite island, the redoubt of freedom;
without it, hope could hardly survive.

Before most of these poems were composed, however, Wordsworth became strenuously engaged in another enterprise. At

Coleorton he spent much time with George Beaumont choosing the site for a parish church, and their conversation may have been the deciding factor in giving a new subject priority. Catholic Emancipation was in the air, and Wordsworth's apprehensions sprang from the conviction that the Church of England had been a stabilizing factor among the people, and that any threat to it was a threat to national progress. He lost no time; much research needed to be done, and many sonnets were ready by March, including one at least on King's College Chapel. By the summer a large proportion of *Ecclesiastical Sketches* must have been written, for a recurrence of eye-trouble held up the work for months, and this sonnet sequence and *Memorials of a Tour on the Continent*, on which Wordsworth was working in January 1822, were with the printers in February. The sonnets follow a chronological order, in three parts, the 1822 series numbering 102; by 1845 there were 132. Wordsworth rightly claimed that they are the more impressive from continuous reading, the pictures often being 'so closely connected as to have jointly the effect of passages of a poem' in stanzas; he realized none the less their 'obvious disadvantage' for readers unfamiliar with the relevant history.

As with liberty, he thinks of the course of Church history as a stream; its English origin may be uncertain, but he can gaze upon 'the growing rill'. He regards the luxury and refinements of the Romans in Britain as a lure from 'hardy virtue' and as 'instruments of deadliest servitude'. Three notable sonnets (xiv—xvi) are based on Bede, the last even more on Fuller, its subject being Paulinus's image of life when, before Edwin of Northumberland, he compared it to a sparrow flitting from cold to cold through his warm banqueting-hall. Three fine sonnets on eremitical life (xxi—iii) end in praise of the venerable Bede; two (xxvi—vii) pay tribute to Alfred and his descendants. Part I ends significantly with Papal domination.

A bright gleam of the river reflects Edward the Confessor's virtues in one of the best of the sonnets (vii) preceding the period of monastic corruption. Subjects which lift Wordsworth include monks and scholars, the dissolution of the monasteries, idealization of the evicted nun (xxii), saints, the translation of the Bible, Edward VI (chiefly in praise of Chaucer, the 'great precursor, genuine morning star'), the martyrdom of Protestants (xxxiv—v), and the plight of the English reformers in exile. A sonnet from *Memorials* is brought in (xliii) to illustrate the troubles of the

Church during the period of zealotry which ensued. The sonnet on Laud, although redeemed by the simile 'Like a poor bird entangled in a snare Whose heart still flutters, though his wings forbear To stir in useless struggle', suggests, when compared with the general introductory I.F. note and his own vindicatory comment, that Wordsworth did not always allow himself time to do justice to the subjects of *Ecclesiastical Sonnets*, as the series was entitled from 1837.

The patriotic fears which initiated these poems are well expressed at the opening of Part III in a sonnet introduced by one of the loveliest in the series, on a dream in which a vision of Dora came and went, exciting Wordsworth's apprehension. His note on its composition, on the road from Grasmere to Rydal, and how, unlike some sonnets which cost him labour, it had never been changed, illuminates his 1798 statement in question form, 'Think you . . . That nothing of itself will come, But we must still be seeking?' He is at ease with Jeremy Taylor, the Cambridge Platonists, and Milton (iv), even more with Walton's *Lives* (in one of his greatest and most delightful sonnets), and he emphasizes how much lovers of civil liberty such as Algernon Sidney and Lord William Russell owed to the Church, insisting that, 'if spiritual things Be lost, through apathy, or scorn, or fear', civil liberties will be short-lived: 'What came from heaven to heaven by nature clings, And, if dissevered thence, its course is short.' The link between God and man is the spiritual imagination on which Wordsworth enlarged in *The Prelude*. After his historical survey has reached Sacheverel, with scorn for 'High' and 'Low' − 'as if a Church, though sprung from heaven, must owe To opposites and fierce extremes her life' − Wordsworth, adapting a sonnet from *Memorials*, suddenly ends his voyage down the stream of time.

At this point, in 1842, he inserted three sonnets on Christianity in America. Originally he began his rather miscellaneous conclusion with sonnets on the influence of rural churches and parsonages, and on the 'stupendous mysteries' of the liturgy throughout the year, with recollections of catechizing and of the Westmorland rush-bearing processional custom which would have delighted Laud and Hooker. (Between these he subsequently added sonnets on various special services.) Three sonnets are devoted to a church to be erected (that proposed by Beaumont), and more to great cathedrals and King's College Chapel, before the sequence closes with the prospect of a stream of 'living waters' flowing on to the eternal City.

Here in this final medley we have some of Wordsworth's best poetry. 'Ejaculation' is a *Gloria* which shows how, even if not identical at all points, his religion of nature had become inseparably fused with Christianity. The motif of change from 'Old Abbeys' to 'New Churches' is introduced in 'Mutability', a poem which rises above criticism, so subtly musical is it, and so enriched in the concluding octet with visual images, the second perfected with a line remembered from the unpublished 'Fragment of a "Gothic" Tale' and originating in Gilpin: the outward forms of Truth

> drop like the tower sublime
> Of yesterday, which royally did wear
> Its crown of weeds, but could not even sustain
> Some casual shout that broke the silent air,
> Or the unimaginable touch of Time.

Such ineffable music concludes 'Inside of King's College Chapel, Cambridge', better known but not greatly superior to the second on the subject. It is the poetry of thought, not of sensuousness; nevertheless, one must ask whether the intricacies of fan-vaulting could be more exquisitely suggested, or whether the intimations of the last line could have been more melodiously conveyed. There are some kinds of poetry in which Wordsworth remains unexcelled.

More Trachoma, Poetry, and Travel (1822–31)

In February 1822 Wordsworth had the misfortune to read a mischievous article at his expense in one of the copies of *The London Magazine* he had obtained principally to read some of Lamb's essays. Hazlitt's 'On Consistency of Opinion' included an anecdote which he had heard from Charles Lloyd and dressed up as an illustration of the poet's 'impertinence' and 'ostentatious servility'. It describes how, about 1802, a romantic acquaintance who was 'smit with the love of simplicity and equality' (Wordsworth) used to call on a gentleman (Lloyd) in the evening, and snuff out one of the two candles on the table because he thought it 'a shame to indulge in such extravagance' when many a cottager had not even a rush-light. In 1816 this hater of luxury asked his extravagant friend to dine with him and a lord (Lowther), and lend him his man-servant to wait at table. Just before they were about to sit for dinner, the friend heard him (Wordsworth) instruct the servant to have six candles on the table. It was left to Mary Wordsworth, in an indignant letter to Tom Monkhouse, to deny the 'cant' about the rush-light, and to explain that William had once snuffed out a candle at Brathay because the light hurt his eyes, that Lloyd's servant attended the dinner to watch and restrain his master, after his return from a Birmingham asylum, and that Lord Lowther had brought his own servant to wait at table. To add that Wordsworth had asked Lloyd's servant to bring two candles in addition to the two already in place rather spoils a story which exemplifies the creative malice of a writer envenomed by personal pique and political hatred.

1822 brought unforeseen anxieties. During the previous year Edward Quillinan and his wife had come to live by the Rothay river (at the house which was later called 'The Stepping Stones');

their second daughter, who was born soon afterwards, was named after the stream. Quillinan, son of an Irish wine-merchant in Portugal, was now retired on half-pay after serving with the dragoons in the Peninsular War; he wrote poetry, and had an engaging personality. In the spring the family moved to Ivy Cottage, where Mrs Quillinan recovered from the mental breakdown which followed Rotha's birth but was most severely burned; she was nursed by Dorothy Wordsworth, but died while her husband was in London. In the summer Willy came home very ill from Charterhouse, the school to which he had recently been transferred; his life was despaired of, but he was well in three weeks, and remained at Rydal the next six years or more, a good-natured, spoilt boy, who (like John) had not proved to be very academically gifted. There were many visitors; Christopher and his three sons stayed at Ivy Cottage, and Robert Jones spent three weeks with the Wordsworths. Dora had left school; when she and Sara Hutchinson departed in September for a holiday at Stockton-on-Tees, Dorothy, who needed a change, left with Joanna Hutchinson for Scotland, intending to return in two weeks but staying away seven, mainly because Joanna needed warm-bath treatment in Edinburgh for lumbago. Willy was very ill again when they returned, but he recovered before Christmas.

Wordsworth had suffered much anxiety on his account. His responsibilities as Distributor of Stamps for an area which had increased, not very lucratively, by the addition of Maryport, Cockermouth, and Workington, were far from light; and trachoma afflicted him for months on end, especially in the spring and summer. During this period he may have written only one poem, 'To the Lady Fleming', on the foundation of the new church at Rydal. Studiously penned, it contains a striking image on the disbeliever who, 'shipwreck'd, kindles on the coast, False fires, that others may be lost'; a later modification, on time's 'pathetic sanctity', anticipates the gentle admonitory sound of the clock across the lake when the churchyard 'Is ruffled o'er with cells of death; Where happy generations lie . . . tutored for eternity'.

Wordsworth and Mary left Rydal in February 1823, and stayed three weeks at Coleorton on their way to London, where they were Tom Monkhouse's guests, and hosts at dinner to Coleridge, Rogers, Moore, the Lambs, and Crabb Robinson; according to Monkhouse, Coleridge was most eloquent and Lamb most witty (without being unsteady). Then, after five weeks at Lee Priory in Kent, home of Quillinan's brother-in-law, they made a tour in the Netherlands. After a visit to Bolton Abbey and two weeks at Harrogate, where William drank the waters, they returned home in July. John Wordsworth, who had spent an extra year at Sedbergh and been advised not to enter St John's, Cambridge, because he was weak in mathematics, began a course of study in October at New College, Oxford, admission to which had been facilitated by John Keble.

Wordsworth began translating the *Aeneid* in the autumn as an experiment; he continued it as a pastime, not intending to go beyond the fourth book. In setting out to improve on Dryden's translation, he wished above all to convey the '*genuine* ornaments' and tenderness of Virgil. He broke off in the middle of the third book to visit London with Dorothy, after a month at Coleorton. They met many friends, including Coleridge, who told him that his translation had been a waste of time. At Cambridge their plans were changed; Dora, who had been staying with a friend in London, was homesick, and travelled back with her father. She accompanied her parents to North Wales at the end of August, Robert Jones joining them with a servant and conveyance for much of their tour. They left him at Devil's Bridge, and spent the next three weeks at Hindwell, where Tom Monkhouse had come for rest and fresh air; he was in 'a very alarming state of health' (and died in February 1825).

The most remarkable poems of 1824 are addressed to Mary. They include 'Let other bards of angels sing', 'How rich that forehead's calm expanse!', possibly 'What heavenly smiles!', and 'O dearer far than light and life are dear', a moving lyric expressing a troubled spirit. When she and Wordsworth left Tom Monkhouse, they feared it was for the last time. William lacked the assurance that friends 'by death disjoined' would meet again, and turned to seek comfort from Mary's faith. The poem almost achieves greatness; it is robbed of it in the very last line, where the poet tries to express the faith he does not possess. If 'Look at the fate of summer flowers' (with its allusion to Francis Quarles's 'Our life is but a winter's day' and its reference to Spenser's 'An Hymne in Honour of Beautie') was written with Dora in mind, the contrast with 'Let other bards of angels sing' has a heightened interest. 'A Flower Garden' originated from Coleorton, with suggestions from the garden of Lady Caroline Price (wife of the landscape gardener, Sir Uvedale Price) at Foxley, Herefordshire, which Wordsworth visited the previous September. Wales produced three sonnets, the most memorable lines being on a spot of time conjured up by the torrent at Devil's Bridge, where the poet was reminded of the Rhine at Viamala, as he saw it with Jones in 1790:[4]

> There I seem to stand,
> As in life's morn; permitted to behold,
> From the dread chasm, woods climbing above woods,
> In pomp that fades not; everlasting snows;
> And skies that ne'er relinquish their repose.

The 'very pretty small poems' mentioned by Dorothy (13.xii.24) include a sonnet on Mary Monkhouse written specially to please her father Tom ('Unquiet childhood here by special grace Forgets her nature'), another addressed to Rotha Quillinan ('Rotha, my spiritual child'), and probably 'Such age how beautiful', on Lady Fitzgerald, after a description by Lady Beaumont. All three are transfused by delicacy of thought. Almost wholly admirable is 'Elegiac Stanzas' on Mrs Fermor, Sir George Beaumont's sister-in-law (whom Wordsworth had visited at Worcester after leaving Wales, and who had bequeathed him £100 in appreciation of his work). The poem revives views expressed by the Pedlar on excessive grief; its imagery shows a poet's tender sympathies, and its close suggests that the philosophy of *The Excursion* is not empty:

> Thou takest not away, O Death!
> Thou strikest − absence perisheth,
> Indifference is no more;
> The future brightens on our sight;
> For on the past has fallen a light
> That tempts us to adore.

The most bard-like notes of Wordsworth in 1824 are found in lines 'Written in a Blank Leaf of Macpherson's Ossian'; and this is strange, for in his 'Essay, Supplementary to the Preface' (1815) he had written:

All hail, Macpherson! hail to thee, Sire of Ossian! The phantom was begotten by the snug embrace of an impudent Highlander upon a cloud of tradition − it travelled southward, where it was greeted with acclamation, and the thin consistence took its course through Europe, upon the breath of popular applause.

Wordsworth seems to have regretted this high-spirited, parodic derogation, after being moved by Ossianic passages. His lines begin with appealing poetic imagery, which conveys the thought that authentic genius, communicated in snatches, is a reward in itself, and that its appreciation is not diminished by lack of perfection throughout. Reflections follow on genius in the course of time: the complete loss of ancient poets, the thousands who have died young, and those who have not fulfilled their promise. Here Wordsworth was thinking of Hartley Coleridge, now Willy's teacher at Ambleside. He had been described by Dorothy as 'the oddest looking creature you ever saw', not taller than De Quincey, 'with a beard as black as a raven', and 'exactly like a Portuguese Jew'. His discipline was poor, but he was still steady and regular. Dorothy's apprehensions are clear; Wordsworth's had been alerted in 1823, when he wrote 'Memory', a short poem of remarkable grace and originality which concludes with the yearning for a life on which one can look back conscience-clear, 'With heart as calm as lakes that sleep, In frosty moonlight glistening'.

Wordsworth's impressive 'Address to Kilchurn Castle' may belong to this period, the scene being revived by a passage in Dorothy's *Recollections*. He had 'thrown off' the first three lines on first seeing the ruin in 1803, and it is doubtful whether he could have written better had he completed the poem when his impressions were fresh. Two features are especially striking. Wordsworth still believes in 'the God of Nature': there are Powers that 'touch each other to the quick in modes Which the gross world no sense hath to perceive, No soul to dream of', and Ben Cruachan submits all that this God has conferred on him, and 'all that he holds in common with the stars', to 'the memorial majesty of Time' which is impersonated in the castle's 'calm decay'. All nature seems to pay homage to this 'shade of departed power'; and Wordsworth, imaginatively awakened by past and present, activity and stillness, in Time's memorial (as in the 'woods decaying, never to be decayed' of the Gondo gorge), sees the thought in a natural image so appropriate that they become one:

> Yon foaming flood seems motionless as ice;
> Its dizzy turbulence eludes the eye,
> Frozen by distance; so, majestic pile,
> To the perception of this age, appear

Thy fierce beginnings, softened and subdued
And quieted in character . . .

Much of Wordsworth's time in 1825 was devoted to Willy's
education (in the hope that he would gain a place at Oxford) and
to the entertainment of visitors, including Edward Quillinan and
the Foreign Secretary George Canning. He attended festivities at
Storrs Hall, and a regatta on Windermere, chiefly in honour of
Canning and Sir Walter Scott. Scott and his son-in-law Lockhart,
who were staying at Elleray with John Wilson, breakfasted at
Rydal Mount before visiting Southey at Keswick with Wordsworth. Lockhart's smile haunted Dora 'like an evil thing'; she
could not forgive him for his remarks on her father in *Blackwood's
Magazine*. Wordsworth then spent more than a month at Coleorton with Mary and Sara, returning via Manchester, where they
stayed a few days with Miss Jewsbury, a young writer who had
become friendly with Dora during a seaside holiday with the
Wordsworths near Grange in July. When he heard that Lady
Fleming wanted Rydal Mount for her aunt, Wordsworth bought
the slope below and had plans prepared for building a house near
the new church; these measures proving to be unnecessary, the
land was given to Dora, and subsequently called 'Dora's Field'.

The little poetry that was written during the year contains verses
of quality on birds. Keen critical selectivity, lyrical expression,
harmony of idea and image, make 'To a Skylark' ('Ethereal
minstrel! pilgrim of the sky!') characteristic of much that is best in
Wordsworth. Closer unification of the subject with the creative
idea central to his belief ('Type of the wise who soar but never
roam; True to the kindred points of heaven and home!') arose from
the transfer of the middle stanza ('To the last point of vision, and
beyond') to 'A Morning Exercise'. This poem, though dated 1828
when published, probably belongs to 1825, as the I.F. note
indicates; its subject is the contrast between the skylark and other
birds whose echoed notes are associated with melancholy. 'The
Contrast', on Mrs Luff's parrot and a wren, would have been
better confined to the parrot, its description being vivid, arch, and
distinctive. (Now a widow, Mrs Luff, after spending much of her
time and money on improvement to the house and surroundings,
lived at Fox Ghyll, which the De Quinceys had occupied, by the
Rothay river.)

Two poems on May (the first tinged with 'poetic diction')

developed largely in 1826 from a stanza ('How delicate the leafy veil') which perpetuates the sight of a small church gleaming through a screen of half-opened leaves in the vale of Newlands. 'The Pillar of Trajan' was written when Wordsworth noticed that it was the subject for the Newdigate Prize at Oxford; as John did not respond to the hint that he should compete, his father showed him 'what might, without difficulty, be done on such a subject'. More artistic in a lighter vein of pleasing fancy and originality is 'On Seeing a Needlecase in the Form of a Harp', written in 1827 on the handiwork of Southey's daughter Edith.

Among the new poems in Wordsworth's published collection of 1827 are several sonnets of which the composition dates are conjectural. They include 'To S. H.', on the happiness created by domestic spinning (unheeded by those who promote factories), with its soothing murmur, 'Soft as the dorhawk's to the distant ear, When twilight shades bedim the mountain's head'; 'Decay of Piety', recalling attendance for worship, whatever the weather, of those who seemed even then 'like fleecy clouds That, struggling through the western sky, have won Their pensive light from a departed sun'; and, in confirmation of Cowper (*The Task*, ii.285–304), '*There is a pleasure in poetic pains*', on the delight given by composition from which all 'hindrance and obscurity' are removed, leaving thought clear and

> Fresh as the star that crowns the brow of morn;
> Bright, speckless, as a softly-moulded tear
> The moment it has left the virgin's eye,
> Or rain-drop lingering on the pointed thorn.

To this group belong 'Scorn not the sonnet', composed almost extempore during a walk on the western side of Rydal Water, and 'To —', in recollection of the time when, after hearing Dorothy read three of Milton's sonnets in 1801, Wordsworth 'took fire' and wrote three the same afternoon. He delights in the 'perfect shape' of expression:

> Happy the thought best likened to a stone
> Of the sea-beach, when, polished with nice care
> Veins it discovers exquisite and rare,
> Which for the loss of that moist gleam atone
> That tempted first to gather it.

Writing to Alexander Dyce (c.22.iv.33), he observed, on 'that pervading sense of intense unity' wherein resides 'the excellence of the sonnet', that, instead of regarding this form as a piece of architecture, he had been 'much in the habit of preferring the image of an orbicular body, − a sphere − or a dew-drop'.

Wordsworth's political *angst* continued in the early part of 1826, generated less by the menace of Catholic Emancipation than by Brougham's third bid to free Westmorland from Lowther domination. Towards the end of the year he made efforts to secure a more enterprising publisher than Longman. He seems to have had little time or proclivity for any major poetic enterprise. 'He has lately written some very good sonnets. I wish I could add that the "Recluse" was brought from his hiding-place,' Dorothy wrote in December. Southey's *History of the Peninsular War* continued to give him interest and pleasure. He could not agree with the author's views that, but for Wellington, Napoleon would have remained master of Europe; he was convinced that Providence would not have allowed the overthrow of tyranny to depend on any particular individual, that (as Lord Wellesley observed) Bonaparte was the kind of man who creates great reverses for himself, and that 'it is of the nature of tyranny to work to its own destruction'.

Sir George Beaumont died in 1827, leaving Wordsworth an annuity of £100; when Lady Beaumont died in 1829, William, Dorothy, and Mary had lost two of their greatest friends. Among their visitors in the summer of 1827 were Christopher's three sons, all distinguished scholars, John and Christopher at Trinity, Cambridge, and Charles at Christ Church, Oxford; with other students and a tutor, they found rooms at Bowness, and combined outings with study. (Two years later Charles had the distinction of organizing the first boat race between Oxford and Cambridge, and of rowing in the event.) During the winter William and Mary, after three weeks at Coleorton, spent a long period at Brinsop Court, Tom Hutchinson's new home near Hereford, where Dora had been taken for the sake of her health.

John was ordained at Cambridge in March. After Lord Lonsdale's inability to provide a curacy, he accepted one which had been reserved for him at Whitwick near Coleorton. Contrary to Sara Hutchinson's expectation that he would be 'quite *lost* among the stocking weavers', he was happy there. Dorothy managed his house from November to the following June, when, after little more than a year in Leicestershire, he moved to Cumberland. He had accepted Lord Lonsdale's offer of the Moresby living near Whitehaven before the end of 1828.

After leaving John at Whitwick in April 1828, Wordsworth had stayed at Cambridge, and then in London, where he hoped to find a position for Willy, whose wish to enter the army (his own youthful ambition) he opposed. Mary and Dora joined him, and they lived at Quillinan's home in Bryanston Street, meeting most of their friends, including Sir Walter Scott. A visit to Lamb in retirement with his sister at Enfield produced the heartfelt 'Farewell Lines' in which the peace of their 'lonely union' is likened to that of a pair of herons on an islet after a storm. Suddenly it was agreed that Wordsworth, Dora, and Coleridge would take a holiday abroad, while Mary stayed at Whitwick.

The tourists set off on 22 June and returned on 6 August, after travelling through Belgium (where they spent four hours on the field of Waterloo) to Cologne, up the Rhine to Bingen, and down to Nijmegen, thence to Arnhem, Amsterdam, Rotterdam, and Antwerp, much of the journey by boat. Wordsworth looked more like a mountain farmer than a 'lake poet', wrote the novelist Thomas Colley Grattan, who accompanied them part of the way from Brussels. 'Tall, wiry, harsh in features, coarse in figure, inelegant in looks', he was 'roughly dressed' in a long brown *surtout*, striped duck trousers, fustian gaiters, and thick shoes. 'There was a total absence of affectation, or egotism; not the least effort at display, or assumption of superiority over any of those who were quite prepared to concede it to him.' The tour produced only two poems, 'Incident at Bruges' and 'A Jewish Family'. Coleridge enjoyed it greatly, and Dora's health benefited. After two weeks at Whitwick, she returned home with her parents.

At the beginning of 1828 Wordsworth took an unprecedented step, agreeing to supply, for one hundred guineas, twelve pages of verse for *The Keepsake*, an annual of some distinction. He did this mainly in order to give John financial assistance, but also in gratitude to the editor, who had brought him considerable relief by recommending blue-stone as a salve for trachoma. His five contributions consisted of two sonnets, 'A Gravestone upon the Floor of the Cloisters of Worcester Cathedral' and 'A Tradition of Okker Hill in Darley Dale', 'The Gleaner' (rather laboured), 'The Triad', and 'The Wishing-gate'. The thoughts of the last were evoked by the old gate on the Ambleside road above the lake at Grasmere,

Wordsworth defending the 'superstitions of the *heart*', and assuming that 'the local Genius' or spirit of nature will kindle only worthy desires. The poem ends with the possibility that the wise man who is above superstition may pause by the gate and wish for insight to allay misgiving when 'the crimson day in quietness withdraws',

> Or when the church-clock's knell profound
> To Time's first step across the bound
>   Of midnight makes reply;
> Time pressing on with starry crest,
> To filial sleep upon the breast
>   Of dread eternity.

(A later poem, 'The Wishing-gate Destroyed', though regretting the loss of an object prompting beneficial sentiments, enjoins that firm resolve be followed by action, 'And life be one perpetual growth Of heaven-ward enterprise'.) 'The Triad' is more ambitious; it presents impressions of Edith Southey, Dora Wordsworth, and Sara Coleridge. Wordsworth thought much of it was 'as elegant and spirited' as anything he had written; there is, however, so much inventive prologizing and excursive heightening that reality is diminished, coming most to life with the natural gaiety of Dora, which makes her conscience light as air,

> Leaving this daughter of the mountains free
> As if she knew that Oberon king of faery
> Had crossed her purpose with some quaint vagary,
> And heard his viewless bands
> Over their mirthful triumph clapping hands.

Wordsworth turned to the composition of narrative poetry in 1828. 'The Somnambulist', a fanciful Gothic tale with a startling conclusion, was suggested by a true story he heard when he visited Lyulph's Tower by Ullswater with Beaumont and Samuel Rogers in 1826. More successful is 'The Egyptian Maid', an Arthurian romance delightfully conceived after hearing a nephew describe the appearance and movement of a vessel, and say that her name was 'The Water-Lily'. There must be many who would never expect Wordsworth to excel in this kind of story; it is a nonpareil. Had it been written by Keats or Tennyson, or by Wordsworth before 1806, much would have been heard in praise of it. Wordsworth's sureness

of touch fails hardly in a syllable. Curiously, since he did not think
it well suited to narrative, the verse is one of its attractive features;
its varied measure consorts admirably with a subject which is
dignified without high seriousness, a style which is precise and
economical, and a story which pleases by continuity of movement,
surprising turns, and novelty from first to last. 'The Russian
Fugitive' is based on Peter Henry Bruce's *Memoirs*; the verse is
rather monotonous, and the story moves slowly, yet it has the
appeal of a romantic novel. Its author rightly deemed it 'a pleasing
subject for an opera or musical drama'.

News of Dorothy's illness with influenza in April 1829 alarmed
William. 'Were she to depart the phasis of my moon would be
robbed of light to a degree that I have not courage to think of', he
wrote. Mary went to take charge at Whitwick, and Willy, who had
been staying there, was 'the tenderest nurse possible'. Arrangements had been made for him to be taught German and French at
Bremen, but his tutor was not able to fetch him from London until
early June. As there was no parsonage at Moresby, Mary and Dora
travelled to Whitehaven in August, to ensure that John was 'comfortably established'. Wordsworth accompanied them, hoping to
sail thence to Ireland. After a delay and a change of route, he
crossed with Jane Marshall's husband and their son to Holyhead
and Dublin, where he was the guest of William Rowan Hamilton,
a young professor of astronomy at Trinity College who had already
visited Rydal Mount. It was a strenuous sight-seeing tour all the
way, lasting about six weeks, and best summed up by Wordsworth:

> We went by Holyhead to Dublin, where we remained 3 days, we
> then explored the Wicklow Mountains, and traced the courses
> of the Slaney, the Suir and Blackwater, where most interesting,
> visiting Wexford, Waterford and afterwards Cork, and so on to
> Killarney, which is worthy of its high reputation — We took
> pains with the County of Kerry, far the most beautiful in
> Ireland, saw the best parts of the Shannon, turned aside to
> Sligo, and by Enniskillen and the bank of the Erne etc etc etc
> and through Londonderry, and Coleraine we went to the Giants
> Causeway and along the coast, concluding by Belfast, and
> embarking at Donaghadee for Portpatrick.

They sailed in Bantry Bay, climbed Carrantuohill (the highest
mountain in Ireland), spent two days with the Edgeworths at

Edgeworthstown, and passed through Goldsmith's Auburn. Wordsworth enjoyed seeing new places, but he was disappointed with Irish scenery as a whole. The tour gave him mixed feelings; he was appalled by widespread evidence of poverty, and alarmed at the spread of 'Romanism' and 'Catholic bigotry'.

Among the poems assigned to 1829 'Gold and Silver Fishes in a Vase' is notable for its scintillating verse; the sequel 'Liberty' leads gracefully from thought on freedom-loving creatures to the freedom of the poet, with recollections of Horace and Cowley, and a conclusion addressed to the donor of the bowl, Miss Jewsbury, who was to die of cholera while with her missionary husband in India. After his wife's complaint that the original sequel was 'unwieldy and ill-proportioned', Wordsworth detached the portion entitled 'Humanity', which remains an unshapely fragment, the freedom theme being most obvious in an onslaught on the cupidity of those who worship 'the Wealth of Nations' and exploit factory-workers. As a comment on this and life in general, the finest poetical passage, though dressed in dazzling vestments rather than being the incarnation of thought, is true to the essence of Wordsworth's religion from 1797 onwards:

> Glorious is the blending
> Of right affections climbing or descending
> Along a scale of light and life, with cares
> Alternate; carrying holy thought and prayers
> Up to the sovereign seat of the Most High;
> Descending to the worm in charity;
> Like those good angels whom a dream of night
> Gave, in the field of Luz, to Jacob's sight
> All, while *he* slept, treading the pendent stairs
> Earthward or heavenward, radiant messengers,
> That, with a perfect will in one accord
> Of strict obedience, serve the Almighty Lord.

'This lawn, a carpet all alive' repays careful reading; the subject would have commended itself to few poets, yet it is profoundly true to Wordsworth, and the result is fascinatingly poetical. The I.F. note, though communicated long afterwards, seems to have been influenced by the discussion Wordsworth held with Hamilton in Dublin on the passage in *The Excursion* (iv.941–94) where scientists are accused of destroying grandeur through unremitting analysis. Wordsworth makes amends by stating that 'such processes being to a certain extent within the reach of a limited intellect, we are apt to ascribe to them that insensibility of which they are in truth the effect and not the cause'. Beauty, he affirms, 'is not made less but more apparent as a whole by more accurate insight into its constituent properties and powers. A *savant* who is not also a poet in soul and a religionist in heart is a feeble and unhappy creature.'

The ode 'On the Power of Sound' is the product of much wasted effort. Starting with lines first intended for 'The Triad', Wordsworth completed a first version in December 1828, but this was modified and considerably extended after his return from Ireland. It is a cumulative poem rather than a subject with a theme; the succession of images palls for want of a developing idea, and the design lacks inevitability, compensation being attempted in a climactic ending of universals, first with representatives of all sounds in praise of the Creator, and finally with a trumpet-like voice announcing the world's end.

Dorothy, after being ill again in the summer at Halifax, remained so invalided that she could no longer take lengthy or strenuous walks. Wordsworth had suffered from trachoma for long periods, and often Dora acted as his amanuensis. In January 1830 they were walking near Town End, Grasmere, when she spotted a bird's nest half filled with snow, an observation which soon led to the composition of the sonnet 'Why art thou silent!', the dramatic situation of which is developed from the image. William walked '*regularly* more than ever', and was 'still the crack skater on Rydal Lake', Dorothy wrote. In February he reported that Hartley Coleridge was 'wandering about like a vagabond, sleeping in barns, without the dignity of gipsy-life, and picking up a meal' wherever he could in and around Ambleside. The Wordsworths paid expenses he had incurred, and arranged for him to be boarded at Town End, hoping that he would maintain himself by writing. Periodically, however, his roving habits got the better of him, and almost inevitably he would be found drunk and ill on the road.

John stayed at Rydal Mount in March, and Wordsworth, having business at Ulverston, decided to accompany him on the first part of his journey to Whitehaven. They rode up the Duddon valley, John departing over Birker Moor, his father continuing to the Duddon source and Wrynose Pass, and returning home in raptures.

He realized that *The Recluse* would soon be beyond him, but did not let it weigh heavily on his conscience. He was more interested that spring in supervising the construction of a terrace near the top of 'Dora's Field'. At the end of July he could not remember having written any poetry that year. Soon afterwards, if their I.F. notes are reliable, he must have composed 'Presentiments', a rather impressive poem, and 'The Armenian Lady's Love'. The latter has a less satisfactory stanza; though adopted from 'The Spanish Lady's Love' (in Percy's *Reliques*) for its suitability to dialogue, it impedes the narrative, which is as unexciting as it is remarkable, being derived from *The Broad Stone of Honour* by Kenelm Digby, whom Wordsworth was to meet at Cambridge in November. Summer visitors included Mrs Hemans (whom her host admired despite her affectations), Professor Hamilton, and Christopher, Master of Trinity. The great event of the year was John's marriage in October to Isabella Curwen of Workington Hall and Belle Isle, Windermere. 'All Workington was abroad making a lane for the carriages to drive through − some on house-tops − all the windows crowded − The people shouted Hurra! Curwen for ever!' While Mary prepared John's new home, William stayed with Lord and Lady Lonsdale and other nobility at Whitehaven.

Shortly afterwards, hoping that Dora's health would benefit, they set off with her to Cambridge, leaving Sara and Dorothy in charge at home. Dora needed her pony, and the servant James took it to Lancaster, whence it was ridden by Wordsworth. On the way to Manchester he saw nothing which pleased him as much as 'a sweet little Gainsborough cottage girl' wheeling a tiny barrow of manure which she had collected from the road. He gave her a penny for her industry; she replied 'Thank you, sir' in 'the prettiest manner imaginable', and he forgot to ask her if she could read. At Tideswell he had no time to enter the church. It was the fifth of November, and the firing of guns and squibs in the evening gloom at Ashford was so alarming that he dismounted and led his horse to Bakewell. The next morning he visited Chatsworth; on the road to Derby he composed a sonnet to that 'splendid domain' during a drenching storm which was so violent that his horse chose to encounter it slantwise. A rather Quixotic figure on his pony Pegasus, he composed 'Elegiac Musings' in memory of Beaumont while riding thirty-seven miles in an even worse storm, after leaving Coleorton, where he stayed a week with Mary and Dora. About five weeks were spent at Cambridge. At the end of the term he was the guest of James Spedding, one of the Trinity 'Apostles', son of his school friend, and a close associate of Tennyson and Edward FitzGerald. (Tennyson and Arthur Hallam had left for Somersby the previous day.) He chatted freely with Spedding and five other students until nearly two in the morning. They tried to lure him into philosophical discussion, but he preferred to talk on revolutions, which he did with fervour and alarmist conviction.[5]

He had intended to return home after a few days in London, but Christopher persuaded him to prolong his holiday and join him at his Buxted rectory in Sussex. On 23 December they dined at Lambeth Palace with the Archbishop of Canterbury and his wife, Lady Beaumont's parents. Dora's pony was taken to Buxted, where the party stayed until the spring. Wordsworth dined five times with Lord Liverpool and twice with a prince. He sometimes stayed in London with Quillinan, visiting the Bishop (Dr C. J. Blomfield, whom he had met before he became Bishop of Chester), sitting for his bust, and being cordially received at a Brixton school by Joseph Hine, the first editor of a selection of his poetry for schools. Quillinan described the visit. After wine and cake, they were ushered into the schoolroom; 'Composed upon Westminster Bridge' was written down line by line, and recited; the meaning of 'The river glideth at his own sweet will' was discussed; Wordsworth then explained and, after remonstrating with the persistent head, consented to read the poem. He never read better, Quillinan thought. There was 'a thunder of applause' from the boys; Wordsworth thereupon requested a half-holiday, the granting of which evoked 'thunders on thunders'.

When the early part of 'The Primrose of the Rock' was written is uncertain. The whole poem is dated 1831, but its 'after-lay' suggests a resumption after a considerable interval. In the first four stanzas, which constitute an independent poem, the poet thinks of the 'Glow-worm Rock' on which he and Dorothy and Coleridge had noticed the primrose growing in 1802; he alludes to the Napoleonic war which had been fought and won in the long interval. Each part expresses a traditional point of view, the first being intellectually rooted in the 'chain of Being' theory, the second being spiritual and other-worldly, its emphasis on redemption after death ('eternal summer' after the winter of life).

Willy returned from Germany in March, and he was left in Sussex to ride Dora's pony back to Rydal. The other three travelled by coach toward the end of April, but Mary was so afflicted with lumbago that, when they reached Nottingham, Wordsworth, knowing nobody there, turned for help to fellow-authors, William and Mary Howitt, and was pleased to accept their hospitality, leaving Mary and Dora with them for twelve days. Sudden anxiety about his responsibilities as Stamp-Distributor, aggravated by certainty that Reform would be accelerated by the oncoming elections, hastened his journey home. Whatever his fears, the summer was 'brilliant' with unprecedented 'gaiety in regattas, balls, dejeuners, picnics by the lake side, on the islands, and on the mountain tops − fireworks by night − dancing on the green sward by day'. In the room where Wordsworth wrote this (9.ix.31) 'forty beaus and belles, besides matrons, ancient spinsters, and greybeards' had attended a dance three days previously, and 'tomorrow in this same room we are to muster for a venison feast'.

During that summer John Stuart Mill, who owed his spiritual renewal to Wordsworth's poetry, met the poet at Rydal, and was struck by 'the extensive range of his thoughts and the largeness and expansiveness of his feelings'. Wordsworth talked 'on no subject more instructively than on states of society and forms of government'. His 'comprehensiveness and philosophic spirit', his ability to see both sides of every question, were impressive. On subjects peculiarly his, he was 'probably the first person who ever combined with such eminent success in the practice of the art, such high powers of generalisation and habits of meditation on its principles'. Mill thought he was 'the best talker' he had ever heard; his whole demeanour was marked by benignity and kindliness, with 'a perfect simplicity of character . . . delightful in any one, but most of all in a person of first-rate intellect'.

After being delayed almost three weeks by an unusually sharp attack of trachoma, Wordsworth set out, driven by Dora, on a Scottish tour, primarily to see Sir Walter Scott before he left Abbotsford to winter at Naples for his health. 'Ther's a man wi' a veil, and a lass drivin',' exclaimed an urchin, as they entered Carlisle (five weeks before Willy began work there as sub-Distributor to his father). Dora was twenty-seven, a young woman of independent judgment, whose fun and awareness of the incongruous in no way lessened her deep attachment to her father; he doted on her, worried about her health, and loved her blithe spirit. He knew that Scott had been stricken with paralysis, but found him more 'sadly changed' than he expected. Yet Scott not only enjoyed entertaining his visitors; he had great pleasure in accompanying them to Newark Tower above the Yarrow, the setting for the narration of *The Lay of the Last Minstrel*, the poem which had brought him immediate fame. 'Yarrow Revisited' is coloured by Wordsworth's hopes and fears. It stresses two powers: that of localized romance (in which Yarrow was rich) to 'Sustain the heart in feeling Life as she is — our changeful life, With friends and kindred dealing', and that of the imagination to give life to the world around us. Wordsworth hopes that classical fancy will combine with Scott's to preserve his heart from sinking in Italy. When the party was returning, he noticed a rich but sad light, purple rather than golden, over Eildon. Shortly afterwards he wrote the noble sonnet 'On the Departure of Sir Walter Scott from Abbotsford, for Naples'. Deep feeling finds expression in heightened language: 'Blessings and prayers in nobler retinue Than sceptred king or laurelled conqueror knows, Follow this wondrous potentate.' The thought of his genius revives the idea of a kinship between the spirit of nature and of man: 'spirits of Power' assembled over 'Eildon's triple height' complain at the departure of 'kindred Power', while Tweed saddens his voice repeatedly. One of the most moving moments in the Wordsworths' farewell came when Sir Walter returned Dora's album, in which he had written some verse, and said, 'I should not have done anything of this kind but for your father's sake: they are probably the last verses I shall ever write.'

An extensive tour followed, Wordsworth delighting to show Dora many of the beauty spots he had seen. The weather was generally favourable, though it ruled out visits to Glencoe and Staffa; they had 'most beautiful appearances of floating vapours, rainbows and fragments of rainbows, weather-gales, and sunbeams innumerable'. Wordsworth had never viewed Scotland 'under a more poetic aspect'. He composed several poems en route, one of the best in Roslin Chapel, where he was detained for hours in a storm. Less admirable is his sonnet on the Trossachs; unlike several sonnets written on this tour, it has a pleasing unity of idea, but it is rather commonplace and only superficially attractive, its expression marred by the poeticizing vagueness of 'Nature's old felicities' and the expletory circumlocution of 'the pensive warbler of the ruddy breast'; it is tainted with fabrication, though honoured by Walter Bagehot when he selected it and 'Composed upon Westminster Bridge' as 'luminous examples' of the pure style in poetry. 'Suggested at Tyndrum in a Storm' opens arrestingly ('Enough of garlands, of the Arcadian crook, And all that Greece and Italy have sung Of swains reposing myrtle groves among!') and leaves the poet aspiring to be on cloud-sequestered heights with the mountaineer, and one of 'Nature's privy council', witnessing 'To what dread Powers He delegates his part On earth, who works in the heaven of heavens, alone'. 'Bothwell Castle', recalling the landscape, praises the power of memory to present 'vivid dreams, that are not fugitive'. A longer poem on the Highland brooch ends happily with the thought that one may be found by dint of 'Blind Chance, a volunteer ally, That oft befriends Antiquity, And clears Oblivion from reproach'. 'Roman Antiquities' (at Penrith), one of the poems added in conclusion, to bring these itinerary pieces nearer home, ends with lines which have the stamp of a master-poet. Sceptical about the overconfident theories to which relics give rise, and of their relevance to undiscoverable truth, Wordsworth asks, 'Heaven out of view, our wishes what are they?', and answers: 'Mere fibulae, without a robe to clasp; Obsolete lamps, whose light no time recalls; Urns without ashes, tearless lachrymals!' His 'Apology for the Foregoing Poems' endorses Dora's view that the tour and the writing of verse had helped to take her father out of the dreaded world of political Reform.

To the Sunless Land
(1831–50)

At the end of 1831 and in the early months of 1832, Wordsworth revised *The Prelude*. It was a rewarding pastime during a troubled period. He had little respite from trachoma; Dorothy's illness worsened; and fears of Reform grew until the passing of the Reform Bill in June, when he was certain that the flood-gates had been opened to a torrent which threatened to sweep all before it.

Friendship with Dr Thomas Arnold, headmaster of Rugby School, brought relief, though Arnold was politically progressive. In the summer of 1832 they climbed Helvellyn, Wordsworth thinking sadly of his ascent with Scott and others, several of whom were dead or sinking. (Ten days earlier Sir Walter had been brought home in a coma from Naples; he died in September.) Wordsworth helped to negotiate the purchase of the Fox How estate, where the house which became the Arnold holiday home was built.

While with John at Moresby in June, he had been visited by Walter Savage Landor, with whom he spent a day in Wastdale. Lord Lonsdale had presented John a richer living at Brigham near Cockermouth, and Wordsworth looked forward in 1833 to the time when his grand-daughter would enjoy picking flowers and gathering pebbles by the river which furnished the same delights for him sixty years earlier. He and John accompanied Crabb Robinson to Scotland in the summer, chiefly to see Staffa and Iona. They sailed from Whitehaven, its atmosphere darkened with smoke from the Lonsdale mines, first to the Isle of Man, then to Greenock and Oban, returning via the Burns country after only two weeks' absence. Robinson, who had stayed at Inverary to see more of Scotland when the weather improved, left Rydal Mount in September with 'enhanced admiration of the great man' who was 'so ill appreciated'.

In February Wordsworth told Quillinan that a year had elapsed since he wrote 'any poetry but a few lines'. The previous spring he had written 'Devotional Incitements', a poem which invites comparison with 'Lines Writen in Early Spring' and 'To my Sister'. The presentation of the subject differs more than its interpretation. Instead of revealing the 'universal birth' of love which nature seemed to breathe thirty-four years previously, it emphasizes the religious awareness inspired by nature. Wordsworth proclaims no holy plan, but transfers his worship to nature, which is endowed with the spirit of rejoicing; it is no longer a medium, but an agent of praise. Christianity meant much to him in his later years, but he was no strict conformer. 'Devotional Incitements' recognises the impermanence of Churches and their peculiar creeds: 'the sanctities combined By art to unsensualize the mind Decay and languish'; 'solemn rites and awful forms Founder amid fanatic storms'. The *jubilate* of nature, on the other hand, never dies:

> Yet evermore, through years renewed
> In undisturbed vicissitude
> Of seasons balancing their flight
> On the swift wings of day and night,
> Kind Nature keeps a heavenly door
> Wide open for the scattered poor.
> Where flower-breathed incense to the skies
> Is wafted in mute harmonies;
> And ground fresh-cloven by the plough
> Is fragrant with a humbler vow;
> Where birds and brooks from leafy dells
> Chime forth unwearied canticles,
> And vapours magnify and spread
> The glory of the sun's bright head —

Nature is a perpetual reminder that we live 'not by bread alone' or 'what a hand of flesh can give', and 'That every day should leave some part Free for a sabbath of the heart'. Few religious poems from the seventeenth century onwards show sustained flights of comparable lyricism or an apter choice of words.

'Thoughts on the Seasons' (December 1832) is a pleasingly wrought poem on life from youth to age. 'Calm is the fragrant air', an evening voluntary by Grasmere, closes with a moralizing note, but manifests above all the poet of eyes and ears. Further evening

voluntaries were written at Moresby in the spring of 1833, 'The sun
is couched', after a storm at sea, which made Wordsworth wish
that the gratitude of mariners for deliverance were audible as in
the past, and hope that their silent thoughts would be heard in
heaven. The past elicits the most poetic touches: 'those vesper lays
Sung to the Virgin while accordant oars Urge the slow bark along
Calabrian shores' and 'those hymns that soothe with graver sound
The gulfy coast of Norway iron-bound; And, from the wide and
open Baltic, rise With punctual care, Lutherian harmonies'.
'Composed by the Sea-shore' directs the imaginative reader to the
longings of sailors for home. 'On a High Part of the Coast of
Cumberland' recalls 'It is a beauteous evening, calm and free', but
is less evocative, Wordsworth being less interested in the 'mighty
Being' than in his own spiritual grace; the 'earth-voice of the
mighty sea' whispers a gentle note which prompts the prayer that,
during the brief course of life reserved for him, he will gladly
accept the most softly voiced admonitions of the 'Power supreme'.

'To — upon the Birth of her First-born Child, March, 1833'
(addressed to John's wife) opens memorably through association of
an image from Lucretius with the Cumbrian coast:

> Like a shipwreck'd sailor tost
> By rough waves on a perilous coast,
> Lies the babe, in helplessness
> And in tenderest nakedness,
> Flung by labouring Nature forth
> Upon the mercies of the earth.

Similarly, but more incidentally, the snowstorm through which the
poet rode from Moresby when he composed 'The Warning' (a
sequel) is reflected in one of its images (1.21). Here the main interest
lies in the way the verse becomes an outlet for obsessional alarm at
the passing of the Reform Bill. Wordsworth sees 'lost people, trained
to theoretic feud', even more the bewildered working class, capable
of being excited by politicians into mob action or the illusion that
boundless suffrage will lead to universal justice and plenty. He
returns briefly to the subject in 'If this great world of joy and pain':

> Woe to the purblind crew who fill
>   The heart with each day's care;
> Nor gain, from past or future, skill
>   To bear, and to forbear!

His Scottish tour produced a crop of poems, chiefly sonnets, most of which read too much like compositional exercises. The Derwent at Brigham raised thoughts on the parsonage being built for John ('Pastor and patriot'), and at Workington (in one of the better poems), on the landing of Mary Queen of Scots. Cocker-mouth Castle recalled boyhood daring in dungeon darkness. Passing St Bees Head in a steamboat reminded Wordsworth of his visit in March to the principal of the theological college, and of the excellent work done by a pre-Reformation order, at St Bees. He wishes that the spirit of the past could be revived in the new institution, but wonders whether it will withstand the overconfident, calculating, contemporary spirit. It required fortitude and trust in God for St Bega to cross the Irish Sea and found the monastery named after her. Such humility and wisdom are not engendered when matter and spirit are regarded by Prowess as 'one machine', typified in the steamboat which monotonously pursues its 'straight-lined progress' as if 'locked in certainty'. The same scorn, not for science but for the overconfidence it breeds, enters the three sonnets (xii–iv) which follow, ending in splendid affirmation:

> The universe is infinitely wide;
> And conquering Reason, if self-glorified,
> Can nowhere move uncrossed by some new wall
> Or gulf of mystery, which thou alone,
> Imaginative Faith! canst overleap,
> In progress toward the fount of Love . . .

Three of the Isle of Man sonnets have links with Wordsworth's family, one alluding to the rescue of a drowning man by Willy (probably in 1828), another to the retirement to the island of Mary's sailor brother Henry, who wrote the third (xix). 'In the Frith of Clyde, Ailsa Crag' contains thoughts on the cheerfulness of labourers which are not wholly consistent with Wordsworth's earlier views: though poor, they are rich without the culture of books 'Or aught that watchful love to Nature owes For her mute Powers'. Two of the Staffa sonnets link the cave with Fingal; another finds it a 'school For the presumptuous thoughts that would assign Mechanic laws to agency divine; And, measuring heaven by earth, would overrule Infinite Power'. '"There!" said a stripling' recalls how 'the repose of earth, sky, sea, and air, was vivified' when Wordsworth learned that he was gazing at Burns's farm and the field of 'To a Mountain Daisy'. The greatest of the sonnets suggested on the homeward journey is 'Monument of Mrs. Howard', a poem which breathes a tender spirit and conveys the nobility of Nollekens' art. In 'Steamboats, Viaducts, and Railways' Wordsworth rises above old poetic prejudices against technological advance, after being impressed by the magnificence of a viaduct over the Eden valley. In 'Lowther' he goes to the other extreme, seeing in the Castle an emblem of England's glory, rooted in religion and the preservation of political rights won by war. Alarm at the swelling of 'the democratic torrent' makes him exaggerate 'the strength of backward-looking thoughts' and end his 1833 travel series in anticlimax.

Four evening voluntaries belong to 1834. 'By the Side of Rydal Mere' and 'The leaves that rustled on this oak-crowned hill' (composed near Grasmere) contain addresses respectively to the nightingale and the owl, but it is their opening imagery which is remembered, especially the dreamlike reflections of Grasmere which hold a spell recalling scenes from Wordsworth's boyhood in *The Prelude*. 'Soft as a cloud is one blue ridge' illustrates the poet's fanciful skill in moralizing a scene (from Rydal Mount). 'Not in the lucid intervals of life' begins as a variant of 'The world is too much with us', but takes its bias mainly from Byron, Wordsworth being convinced that we belong to nature in 'rational and manly sympathy' only by 'grace divine', without which there can be no respite from care, or help for the 'distempered intellect'. The Westmorland cottage of 'The Redbreast' seems to be fictional, but the invalid inmate is Dorothy, for whose pleasure the poem, based as much upon her observation as the poet's, was written. The blank verse of 'Lines' ('Beguiled into forgetfulness of care') moves with ease and clarity, its subject (a portrait of Quillinan's elder daughter Jemima) leading to the story told by the painter Wilkie when the poem was under way, to the effect that it is the picture with its permanence which is the substance, and we, the transitory spectators, who are the shadows. The most pleasing of the 1834 poems, and the most harmonious, is the sonnet 'Most sweet it is with unuplifted eyes'.

Coleridge's death at Highgate was followed by that of Lamb in December. The following spring William and Mary spent five weeks in London, where he revised 'Postscript, 1835' for publication in

Yarrow Revisited and other Poems, and made unavailing efforts to secure a better post for Willy. At Cambridge he saw his portrait (painted at Rydal Mount by Pickersgill for St John's College in the summer of 1832) and met his old school friend Greenwood, Fellow of Trinity. When they reached home, they were alarmed at the state of Dora's health. By June influenza had turned the house into a hospital, as Mary described it. Dorothy was thought to be near death's door, but it was Sara Hutchinson who died, after being delirious with rheumatic fever. With her 'blessed face' perpetually before him the night after her death, Wordsworth composed the last seven lines of 'Upon seeing a coloured Drawing of a Bird of Paradise in an Album' (the colourful 'divinity' of which subject he attempted with no mean success, here and in 'Suggested by a Picture of the Bird of Paradise'):

> How happy at all seasons, could like aim
> Uphold our spirits urged to kindred flight
> On wings that fear no glance of God's pure sight,
> No tempest from his breath, their promised rest
> Seeking with indefatigable quest
> Above a world that deems itself most wise
> When most enslaved by gross realities!

Much later, when he was reading one of Sara's favourite passages (the latter part of his sonnet 'Methought I saw the footsteps of a throne'), the 'heavenly' expression of her countenance returned, and he honoured her memory in a sequel (taking its title from the date of composition, November 1836) which concluded:

> Oh! if within me hope should e'er decline,
> The lamp of faith, lost friend! too faintly burn;
> Then may that heaven-revealing smile of thine,
> The bright assurance, visibly return:
> And let my spirit in that power divine
> Rejoice, as, through that power, it ceased to mourn.

He wrote little poetry in 1835. Two poems entitled 'To the Moon', the first composed by the seaside, the second at Rydal, have little to commend them, unlike 'Airey-Force Valley', where a light pendent ash 'in seeming silence makes A soft eye-music of slow-weaving boughs'. 'Written after the Death of Charles Lamb' was composed in response to Mary Lamb's request for an epitaph. For this three lines ('Still, at the centre of his being, lodged A soul by resignation sanctified: O, he was good, if e'er a good man lived!') were abstracted from the first part, which was modelled after Chiabrera. An addition allowed Wordsworth to allude to the protective role which tragic circumstances had compelled Charles to assume towards his sister; the image of them as 'a double tree with two collateral stems sprung from one root' reminds one of the natural ties between William and Dorothy, and of the mental disorder which became evident in the latter soon after this poem was completed. It was the death of 'the Ettrick Shepherd' James Hogg that released Wordsworth's poetic feeling; curiously, for he had no high regard for him as a person. He was reminded of his first visit to the Yarrow with him, and of his last with Scott. From Scott his mind turned to other fellow-authors dead – Coleridge, Lamb, Crabbe, and Mrs Hemans. Half an hour after reading the news of Hogg's death, he asked a niece to write down his 'Extempore Effusion'. Very little of it was changed; and it shows how, moved by an appropriate subject, Wordsworth was still capable of matching his best verse. The poem begins with apparent naturalness, but nothing can disguise the art of the whole, its subtle linking and rounding off, and its effective use of light and shade. Nowhere is it more expressive than in the lines on Coleridge's genius; such generous recognition suggests that all grievances had been forgotten.

A visit to Italy had long been in Wordsworth's mind. In January 1834 he believed one would be of inestimable value as a means of laying in 'a store of images, poetical and others, against the blindness' he predicted for himself. Not until March 1837, after preparing another edition of his collected poems and receiving an advance from his new publisher Edward Moxon, was he able to undertake this project. Crabb Robinson agreed to travel with him, and Moxon accompanied them as far as Paris, where Wordsworth met the Baudouins and did much sight-seeing. The weather was wintry, with heavy snow in the north of France, and hail, snow, and rain as they approached Italy along the Riviera. From Genoa they travelled via Lucca, Pisa, and Siena to Rome, where they lodged in the Piazza d'Espagna. They became acquainted with the painter Severn, and talked with him of Keats. After four weeks of sight-seeing, they turned north via Assisi and Perugia to Florence, with excursions to 'the three great Tuscan sanctuaries' of Laverna, Camaldoli, and Vallombrosa. After visiting Milan and Venice, they journeyed through Alpine country to Salzburg, Munich, Heidelberg, Brussels, and Calais. At Salzburg Wordsworth was smitten with contrition for being harsh to his 'inestimable fellow-labourer' Mary while making corrections for the last edition of his poems. He spent several weeks in the south of England, mainly for the health of Dora, who had been staying with Edith Southey, now married in Sussex.

Restrictions on the Italian tour, and the poems written to commemorate it, are explained in Wordsworth's note:

> The tour of which the following poems are very inadequate remembrances was shortened by report, too well founded, of the prevalence of cholera at Naples. To make some amends for what was reluctantly left unseen in the south of Italy, we visited the Tuscan sanctuaries among the Apennines, and the principal Italian lakes among the Alps. Neither of those lakes, nor of Venice, is there any notice in these poems, chiefly because I have touched upon them elsewhere.

In the introduction to these 'memorials' ('Musings near Aqua-pendente', written in 1841) Wordsworth imagines he is high up near the town named after the snow-white torrent which seems to hang in the distance. The blank verse tends to be cumbrous, but it flows more freely in two passages: first, when the broom beside him, in his resurrection of the Italian scene, reminds him transitionally of Lakeland mountains, the ascent of Helvellyn with Scott, and the latter's painful visit to the Janiculum; secondly, where he describes the coast near Savona, and seems imbued with the 'pure poetic spirit' of Chiabrera, who spent much of his life there. Thoughts on the early Christians, St Paul in particular, give rise to despondency as the poet thinks of his own generation − 'a chilled age, most pitiably shut out From that which *is* and actuates', blinkered by abstractions and lifeless facts, devoted to science and expediency, and neglectful of wisdom or 'godlike insight'.

In Rome Wordsworth was moved most by the interior of St Peter's; the glory of the city came, he thought, from endless 'combinations of old and new caught in ever varying connection with the surrounding country' as seen from its hills or neighbouring eminences. Significantly he placed 'The Pine of Monte Mario at Rome' at the head of his sonnets on Rome. He had caught sight of

it from the Pincian hill soon after his arrival. Spared by the intervention of Sir George Beaumont, it meant more to Wordsworth, as
a living emblem of the artist's attachment to natural beauty, than
'the whole majesty of Rome'. He was less interested in buildings
than in permanent issues. Two of the poems in this group indicate
a live interest in the cause of Italian freedom. Others bear on
imaginative knowledge: if ancient monuments disappoint the eye,
they emphasize the need for a true comprehension of the past. The
scepticism of Niebuhr and other modern historians of Rome's
'morning splendors' cannot destroy Wordsworth's conviction that
faith is needed to achieve great ends; 'for exciting youth's heroic
flame, Assent is power, belief the soul of fact'.

'The Cuckoo at Laverna' (a poem which convinced William
Hale White that the common distinction between sacred and pro-
fane, or religion and nature, meant nothing to Wordsworth) is the
only Italian memorial he attempted on the tour. It shows an
intuitional understanding of St Francis which was far ahead of
contemporary views; he wished to write a poem on his life and
character, but was unable to find a book on the subject while 'the
heat was upon' him. 'At Vallombrosa', though it recalls Milton, is
disappointing, Wordsworth's wrong choice of metre making it
hardly readable. Whatever pleasing images Italy supplied, it did
little to waken his poetic inspiration. The later poems in the series
are a patchwork, including two translations of Michelangelo
sonnets, protests against the torpid acceptance of foreign rule
(emblemed in the dreary sight of Lago Morto), and, to conclude,
'The Pillar of Trajan' (1825–6).

The caution advocated in 'At Bologna, in Remembrance of the
late Insurrections, 1837' (three sonnets transferred to a late collection on liberty and order) reflects the fears which political
sectarianism roused in Wordsworth at home and abroad. He
reasons from nature: the most sudden sunrise in the tropics 'yields
a temperate ray', and each human generation in 'the Being' of a
great country is like another succession of leaves to a tree, which
should not be injured by rash zealots. When 'passions hold the
scales', nations struggling for freedom are 'doomed to flounder on,
like wounded whales Tossed on the bosom of a stormy sea'.

For many years before his visit to Italy, Wordsworth had lacked
a defined objective in poetry, but subjects had arisen (more often
than is usually recognised) which had kindled his full artistic
response. Thereafter he was rarely able to rise above the contrived

and mediocre. How forced his verse could be is exemplified by the ending of 'To the Planet Venus' (January 1838). Anything that stirred him, it appears, seemed suitable for a sonnet. 'Protest against the Ballot' and 'Said Secrecy to Cowardice and Fraud' convey a suspicion which must seem incredibly benighted: only the powers of darkness could support the bill for secret voting, and St George's vigilance is invoked, 'for, if the State comply, From such Pandorian gift may come a pest Worse than the dragon'. Two sonnets, 'A Plea for Authors, May 1838' and 'A Poet to his Grand-child' testify to Wordsworth's laudable and long-sustained endeavours to amend the law cancelling copyright on all published work after its author's death. With John now seeking pupils, after the Curwens' loss of their coalmines through sea-flooding (4.i.38), he had good reason to think of his children's prospects, and an additional motive for publishing *The Prelude* posthumously.

The University of Durham bestowed the degree of Doctor of Civil Laws on him in the summer of 1838, an honour repeated by Oxford the following year. He derived much pleasure from working at the final revision of *The Prelude* in the spring of 1839. In December he read the manuscript of 'Thoughts', which expresses a wise tolerance and humility, like his other poems on Burns; when he came to the end, feeling on the brink of the vast ocean on which he 'must sail so soon', he added:

> But why to him confine the prayer,
> When kindred thoughts and yearnings bear
> On the frail heart the purest share
>   With all that live?
> The best of what we do and are,
>   Just God, forgive!

Isabella Fenwick had become Dora's devoted friend in recent years, and she was very dear to Mary and William. His letters to her suggest a new animation in his life; sometimes they have a warmth and glow rarely found in his contemporary poetry, even in the I.F. sonnets. She had accompanied him to her home county Northumberland and to Carlisle, before they travelled by train to Durham for his degree ceremony. In 1841 she took a house in Ambleside, and in the winter of 1842–3 she stayed at Rydal Mount and recorded, with Edward Quillinan's assistance, Wordsworth's comments on his poems. The dates he assigned to composition are frequently misleading, and he is guilty of long digressions, yet many of his recollections and perceptions are of rare biographical or critical value. Miss Fenwick was one of six who accompanied Wordsworth on a seven-day tour to Keswick, Buttermere, Ennerdale, Wastdale, Eskdale, the Duddon valley, Furness Abbey, and Coniston in the summer of 1840.

Wordsworth's confession in the I.F. note to *The River Duddon* on how his wife made him lose his temper completely is quite endearing. How much he loved her is reflected in 'To a Painter' and 'On the same subject', two of the best of his later poems; possibly also in 'What heavenly smiles!' and 'Yes! thou art fair', which were first published in 1845. The latter includes a statement of Wordsworth's philosophy of nature which suggests that, apart from his admission of free will, there had been little change in his ideas of Necessity over the years:

> Be pleased that nature made thee fit
>   To feed my heart's devotion,
> By laws to which all forms submit
>   In sky, air, earth, and ocean.

Soon after his Lakeland tour, he was delighted to escort Queen Adelaide and her party from the lower to the higher waterfall near Rydal Mount. Two months later, as he was climbing Helvellyn, he composed a sonnet on Haydon's picture of Wellington at Waterloo, an etching of which he had received from the artist. Dora, who performed the rare feat of riding to the summit, and Edward Quillinan accompanied him. Their proposed engagement more than two years earlier had shocked Wordsworth, partly because he did not wish to lose Dora, more because he knew that Quillinan, who lived most of the time with relatives, could not afford the kind of home and attention that she, with her delicate constitution, needed. Miss Fenwick persuaded him to accept the engagement in 1839, and two years later the marriage took place from her home at Bath. John officiated and Willy was the best man, but Wordsworth was so overcome that, like Dorothy at the time of his wedding, he could not bear to attend the service. Before the married couple left for their honeymoon at Rydal Mount, they travelled with him and Mary, and Miss Fenwick, to the haunts around Alfoxden and Nether Stowey which William had not seen for more than forty years. The Wordsworths took Isabella to Exeter and

Plymouth (where they had a delightful afternoon at Mount Edg-cumbe) before returning along the coast, and via Salisbury (with a visit to Old Sarum) and Winchester to London. After several days at Coleorton, Wordsworth assumed he had completed his 'farewell visits for life'.

Meanwhile, though John's financial prospects had improved with the grant of a living at Plumbland, those of Willy at Carlisle had not changed for the better. In 1842, however, when Peel became Prime Minister, Wordsworth persuaded him to transfer to his son the Distributorship of Stamps for Westmorland and Cumberland. Anxious now for his parents, who had sacrificed half their income, Willy was not relieved until, a few weeks later, his father was granted a Civil List pension of £300 a year for life. When Southey died in 1843 the Poet Laureateship was offered to Wordsworth, who declined it on the score that he was too old for the responsibilities it imposed; he changed his mind when Peel assured him that the position was merely honorary.

Wordsworth's last poems are notable for their diversity rather than their number. Conservationists may take delight in 'Poor Robin' (the Ragged Robin), a subject which made the author wonder what would happen after his death to Rydal Mount and all its walls and steps with their beautiful mosses, ferns, and wild flowers. A present from Miss Fenwick on his seventieth birthday, soon after the composition of this poem, suggested the night-thoughts of 'The Cuckoo-Clock', in which the poet recalls the 'wandering voice' of 'To the Cuckoo' and the flowers and sunshine of childhood. The subject becomes imaginatively restricted through recourse to common ecclesiastical imagery, the solaces that come to sufferers at night being borne by angels from 'founts above the starry sky'.

Poems chiefly of Early and Later Years, published in 1842, included *The Borderers* and 'Guilt and Sorrow', the final version of 'Salisbury Plain'. For this volume Wordsworth wrote 'Prelude', in which he defines his higher aims as a poet: to bring, as he wrote in the prospectus for *The Recluse*, blessed consolations in distress, through devotion to love, beauty, nature, and human sympathies. With reference to the agitations of contemporary Britain, he adds the hope that his verse will promote gratitude for benefits that survive through faith in progress.

'Wansfell! this household has a favoured lot', the most com-pletely satisfying of Wordsworth's later sonnets, was written with the Arnolds in mind, after the sudden death of Dr Arnold in 1842 and the removal of his family to Fox How.[6] Thinking also of his own death and the glory which the hill above Ambleside had lavished on his life, the poet generalizes in conclusion:

> Bountiful son of earth! when we are gone
> From every object dear to mortal sight,
> As soon we shall be, may these words attest
> How oft, to elevate our spirits, shone
> Thy visionary majesties of light,
> How in thy pensive glooms our hearts found rest.

'Grace Darling', written early in 1843, has a vivid account of the rescue which won the heroine fame. Her good deeds are 'a theme for angels', but the final *laudate* carrying her name to 'celestial choirs' is pitched too high. Most young people would have been more interested in her story, than in the two stories Wordsworth wrote for children. 'The Norman Boy' and its sequel (published in 1842) belong to an era of pious credulity, in complete contrast to 'The Westmoreland Girl' of 1845, which is based on rare contemporary fact, though only the first part could have been intended for Wordsworth's grandchildren. The I.F. note on the former, protesting that 'children will derive most benefit from books which are not unworthy the perusal of persons of any age', suggests that he may have judged the subject of 'The Westmoreland Girl' more suitable for the young.

One bright day in July 1844, near Loughrigg Tarn, Wordsworth and some learned friends were admiring the splendour of the Langdale Pikes when, looking down, he saw a smooth stone which displayed, it seemed, 'a dark star-shaped fossil of most distinct outline'. On closer inspection this proved to be the shadow of a daisy 'projected with extraordinary precision by the intense light of an almost vertical sun'. The thoughts to which this 'minute but beautiful phenomenon' gave rise may be gauged from 'So fair, so sweet, withal so sensitive', the early stanzas of which are exquisitely phrased. The poet sees beauty created by light on the small scale and the large, but dismisses the idea that, in the words of 'Intimations', 'The moon doth with delight Look round her when the heavens are bare' as a fancy, knowing that (to use Coleridge's words) the inexhaustible treasure of the loveliness and the wonders of the world before us depends on the mind and heart of the observer; we need to 'converse with nature in pure sympathy'. The pleasure which Wordsworth derived from 'God's works' was not impaired, but he regretted that the spirituality of his nature did not expand as he approached the grave (19.ix.44).

It has already been seen that his attitude to railways was progressive. He enjoyed travelling on them, but consistently objected to the spoliation of natural beauty. His opposition in 1844 to the proposed railway to Windermere arose less from this reason than from the threatened invasion of the Lake District by hordes of people, ill prepared to respect its character and amenities. Not only did he campaign locally; he wrote to Gladstone and *The Morning Post*, which published his letters and the two sonnets 'On the Projected Kendal and Windermere Railway' and 'Proud were ye, mountains'. The menace struck more grievously when he discovered that the Workington-Cockermouth line was scheduled to pass between John's vicarage and the river, cutting off the garden about ten yards from the house.

When this news reached his father, John was in Rome with his wife Isabella; she had settled abroad for health reasons. In 1845 he took his children out to her, and at Christmas heard that his youngest boy had died and two of his children were seriously ill. Wordsworth thought his lost grandson 'one of the noblest creatures both in mind and body' he had ever known, and wrote the consolatory sonnet 'Why should we weep or mourn . . .?' Anxieties increased: he knew that Christopher, who had retired from Trinity in 1841, was dangerously ill at Buxted (where he died within two weeks); he was worried about Dora's health, and saddened at the rapid decline of Richard's son John, who had caught consumption abroad and was now at Ambleside to be near his guardian uncle and aunt. In these distressful circumstances 'Where lies the truth?' was written, a poem which invites comparison with Hardy's 'The Darkling Thrush' and underlines the strength of Wordsworth's faith.

His 'natural piety' had not been starved. It was a special pleasure for him to visit places dear to him from boyhood. On 20 May he informed Henry Crabb Robinson that James had driven Mary, Miss Quillinan, and himself 'down Windermere side, and home by Hawkshead and the beautiful vale, my old school-day haunts, which I make a point of seeing every year'. He noted the changes: 'In my time we had more than a 100 boys playing and roaming about the vale; now not one was to be seen, the school being utterly deserted.'

Dora's prospects had not improved with the years. Her husband's resources had been further straitened through having to assist in reparations for a fraudulent transaction committed by the family of Sir Egerton Brydges, his first father-in-law. He had no settled home or occupation, apart from translating the Portuguese poet Camoens; and Dora needed the gifts she received from her family and friends. In 1845 she accompanied her husband to Portugal; her health improved there, and she kept a descriptive journal (which Moxon published in 1847). On their return in 1846 they settled at Loughrigg Holme, a cottage formerly occupied by John Carter, Wordsworth's clerk, between the Stepping Stones and Fox Ghyll. Her consumption was aggravated by a cold she caught at Christmas, when she was at Carlisle helping Willy to prepare a home for the reception of his bride. So ill was she in the spring of 1847 that her parents hastened back from London, and had her removed to Rydal Mount. Her cheerfulness to the end alleviated sorrow, but it was long before Wordsworth recovered after her death in July; ministering to Dorothy was a relief.

Dora's illness had made it impossible for the Poet Laureate to write the choral ode which Prince Albert had requested for his installation as Chancellor of the University of Cambridge in July; it was planned and composed almost wholly by Quillinan, and Wordsworth did little more than revise it. After this, as far as is known, he attempted no more poetry. His previous verse includes 'Forth from a jutting ridge' (1845), which was added to 'Poems on the Naming of Places' in the hope that it would preserve 'in blended memory' Mary and Sara's love of natural beauty. 'Illustrated Books and Newspapers' is challenging: Wordsworth regards the pictorial page as a retrogressive medium, and deplores a trend that would make literature subservient to a dumb art, in accordance with the prevailing taste of 'this once-intellectual land'. Two other poems of 1846, 'I know an aged man' and 'Sonnet to an Octogenarian', are related, the second seemingly a comment on the former, which illustrates how 'love for living thing can find a place' in the heart of one who has no human friend, a subject which would have appealed to Wordsworth nearly fifty years earlier when he was preparing *Lyrical Ballads*.

'How beautiful the Queen of Night' is probably a late poem. Its changing image seems to typify the characteristic attitude of Wordsworth to life, and his ability through temperament and philosophy to retain a 'cheerful faith'; it recalls one of his late lyrics, 'A Night Thought', in which the sky-scene (on his way home from Mrs Luff's) provides an illuminating parallel to reflections on 'ingrates who wear a smileless face The whole year through'. But Wordsworth's 'patient cheer' was dimmed in 1846; the clear sky into which the moon is expected to emerge (in 'Who but is pleased to watch the moon on high') proves to be 'in truth the stedfast face Of a cloud flat and dense, through which must move (By transit not unlike man's frequent doom) The wanderer lost in more determined gloom'. In May of that year Wordsworth wrote to Isabella Fenwick:

> My dear wife keeps herself quite well by marvellous activity of mind and body. I wish I could do the same − but many things do not touch her which depress me, public affairs in particular. . . . My pleasures are among birds and flowers, and of these enjoyments, thank God, I retain enough; but my interests in literature and books in general seem to be dying away unreasonably fast − nor do I look or much care for a revival in them. . . . Mason the poet used to say latterly that he read no poetry but his own. I could not speak in this strain, for I read my own less than any other − and often think that my life has been in a great measure wasted.

Wordsworth did not remain under a cloud during his last years. He was pleased to admit visitors to his grounds, and to receive many indoors. He visited and succoured the poor and needy, was generous to tramps on the road, and was popular with children, for whom he would cut ash-sticks from hedges. To celebrate his seventy-fourth birthday, over three hundred young people, and 'nearly half as many adults', were entertained at Rydal Mount, Miss Fenwick making a generous provision to ensure that this was a very special occasion for all. Wordsworth was in his element, and wished such meetings could be held more commonly, to create greater friendship and unity between members of all classes. He treated his servants as members of his family, working with them outdoors whenever he pleased. He had never lived in a world of Arcadian illusion about rustics, though Harriet Martineau, a newcomer to Ambleside, was convinced that his ideas of 'rural innocence' bore little relation to the truth. He had kept in touch with old acquaintances but, with interests extending, and often taking him, much further afield, he knew less and less about the local peasantry, except from hearsay; and the gossip collected by H. D. Rawnsley after his death shows that they knew little about him.

Mary wisely persuaded him to visit his sons at Carlisle and Brigham in the spring of 1848. He liked Willy's wife, was happy with John and his children, and with the walks he and John took in the country of his boyhood near Cockermouth. His nephew Christopher had been authorized to prepare his memoirs, and it was a great comfort to have him and his wife at Rydal Mount towards the end of the year, and to give him all the information and help he could.

When Hartley Coleridge died in January 1849, Wordsworth, who had befriended him whenever possible, insisted that he should be buried near his own family graves at Grasmere. He and Mary made their last long excursion together to see Tom Hutchinson, who was seriously ill near Great Malvern, after falling from his horse. Robinson visited them, and noted that Wordsworth was able to walk twice over the Malvern Hills, but had lost his 'strength' of mind. At Rydal he still enjoyed walking, usually with Mary. It was after outings, first to Grasmere, then to a cottage at White Moss Common, that he developed pleurisy in March 1850. It wore off, but Wordsworth's energy had been sapped. Mary's hope of his recovery revived when she read to him on the evening of his eightieth birthday; the next morning it had gone. Two weeks later, she tried to comfort him by saying, 'William, you are going to Dora'. He did not seem to hear, but the next morning, when his niece entered his room, he asked, 'Is that Dora?' It was the day of his death, 23 April, and the anniversary of Shakespeare's.

On hearing that William was dying, Dorothy summoned up resolution and was very considerate for Mary. After his funeral she relapsed into the querulous demanding self to which, afflicted in mind and body, she had been reduced in her later years. She lived until January 1855. Mary sent Wordsworth's autobiographical poem to Moxon for publication, entitling it 'The Prelude'. It appeared in July 1850, the proofs being read by Quillinan, who died a year later. Mary lived until 1859, enjoying 'an old age serene and bright, And lovely as a Lapland night'.

Part IV: Supplementary

Tradition and Innovation

Wordsworth's tendency to idealize a rural, pre-industrial past is illustrated in the I.F. note to his late poem 'Love Lies Bleeding'. He believed that 'trade, commerce, and manufactures, physical science, and mechanic arts' had made his countrymen 'infinitely less sensible to movements of imagination and fancy' than their forefathers had been 'in their simple state of society'. Something of the spirit which quickened the imagination of the Greeks (as described in *The Excursion*, iv) must have swayed the 'fancy-stricken youth or heart-sick maid' who named the flower 'Love Lies Bleeding'. One cannot expect a revival of imagination and fancy, Wordsworth argues, as the influence of towns continues to spread:

> Refinement, for the most part false, increases the desire to accumulate wealth; and while theories of political economy are boastfully pleading for the practice, inhumanity pervades all our dealings in buying and selling. This selfishness wars against disinterested imagination in all directions, and, evils coming round in a circle, barbarism spreads in every quarter of our island. Oh for the reign of justice, and then the humblest man among us would have more power and dignity in and about him than the highest have now.

Wordsworth's sympathies were with the poor to the end; he remained a democrat. There is every justification for his claim in a letter to James Losh (4.12.21):

> If I were addressing those who have dealt so liberally with the words Renegado, Apostate etc, I should retort the charge upon them, and say, *you* have been deluded by places and persons, while I have stuck to principles — I abandoned France, and her rulers, when they abandoned the struggle for liberty, gave themselves up to tyranny, and endeavoured to enslave the world.

Wordsworth had lived near enough to the French Revolution and its aftermath to see an unenlightened people led by demagogues into violence and horrible crime, and a movement for freedom turn into imperialistic aggression and despotism. Rather than risk the loss of rights and liberty which had been achieved through centuries of struggle and conflict, he believed in the slower but more assured evolutionary route of enlightened progress. In 'Blest statesman he, whose mind's unselfish will' he declares that wisdom does not exist apart from high principles, and finds his ideal in one who is 'prompt to move, but firm to wait', knowing that, for a country which is 'strong by her charters, free because imbound', sweeping change (the emphasis here shows a significant departure from *The Faerie Queene*, V.ii.36) is perilous, and chance unsound. 'I have witnessed one revolution in a foreign country, and I have not courage to think of facing another in my own', he wrote to his brother Christopher in 1832. How much the people were to the fore in Wordsworth's mind when he thought of freedom is instanced in the sonnet 'Emperors and kings . . .' which he wrote after Napoleon's overthrow. He contrasts impious thanksgiving in celebration of triumphant wrong with rejoicing in freedom won, and urges reinstated dynasts to avoid oppression, and be just and grateful to the peoples who fought for their restoration.

Wordsworth's readiness to accept changes in the best interests of the country is clear from his sonnets on railways. Caroline Fox records his view (6.x.44) 'that railroads and all the mechanical achievements of this day are doing wonders for the next generation'; he then added, in an access of patriotic fervour which is not typical of his later years, 'indeed, it is the appropriate work of this age and this country, and it is doing it gloriously'. The 'Sonnets upon the Punishment of Death' express an evolutionary rather than a reactionary spirit; they present a case for the retention of capital punishment for certain crimes, after its abolition in 1837 for numerous minor offences. Such arguments have no novelty for our crime-ridden age, but they are based on the hope that the need for the death penalty will wither away as social rights prevail and 'Religion deepens her preventive care'. As Wordsworth expected, there was an outcry from 'weak-minded humanitarians', notably from a sonneteer who fired 'a battery of nineteen fourteen-pounders' and was satisfied that he had blown his adversary to atoms.

The I.F. note to 'The Force of Prayer' laments the passing of cottage industry, and its usurpation by the evils of 'mechanic power' in factories. As political economy offered no remedy, Wordsworth insisted that 'we must look to something deeper, purer, and higher'. In *The Excursion* (ix) his hopes are based over-optimistically on education. 'Humanity' (1829) voices a fearless protest against the 'cupidity from heartless schools' which urges on mechanic power, reduces workers to slaves, and prizes least 'the power . . . which thinks and feels'.

In 'Postscript, 1835' Wordsworth condemns 'combinations of masters' formed 'to keep down, unjustly, the price of labour', and recommends joint-stock companies so that workers can invest, not only for their own profit, but to create respect for the investments of others, and reduce the temptation to join 'unjust combinations'. In his support for the Poor Law Amendment Act, he declares that all who are unemployed or unable to procure adequate wages 'are entitled to maintenance by law', and that, if the State can con-script in time of war, it has a corresponding duty to support its citizens whenever they cannot support themselves. The 1834 Act assumed too readily that unemployment could be avoided, and ignored the fact that those who are abandoned lose respect and virtue, and that habituation to misery hardens the heart of the community (a view quite contrary to that of 'The Old Cumberland Beggar'). The sonnet 'Feel for the wrongs to universal ken Daily exposed' was intended for those who considered that evils could be removed by 'measures ungoverned by moral and religious prin-ciples'; it reveals Wordsworth's unfailing humanitarianism:

> feel for all, as brother men!
> Rest not in hope want's icy chain to thaw
> By casual boons and formal charities;
> Learn to be just, just through impartial law;
> Far as ye may, erect and equalise;
> And, what ye cannot reach by statute, draw
> Each from his fountain of self-sacrifice!

The education of his children, family deaths, and relief at national deliverance, combined with triumph (as it seemed) of principle against might at the end of the Napoleonic war, strengthened the attachment that had been steadily growing between Wordsworth and the Church of England. The study of its history (as revealed in *Ecclesiastical Sonnets*) made him appreciate all the more how much civilization in England owed to it. For this reason he eyed with alarm the growth of Nonconformity and the pressures for Catholic Emancipation. Sectarianism bred division and discord, and 'such a preponderancy' had been given by the Reform Bill to interests in opposition that the Church seemed doomed to fall. Such fears caused Wordsworth to dream that the flood he had seen at Cambridge threatened the foundations of King's College Chapel, a gathering crowd assisting in the assault until the buttresses were removed and the roof and walls fell, crushing the people (14.v.34). Eighteen years earlier he had been incensed to find that the son of Mr Carus Wilson (original of the Calvinist Brocklehurst in *Jane Eyre*) had been ordained by the Bishop of Gloucester; Wordsworth described him as a 'rank Methodist' (a term of opprobrium for offending Nonconformists, whatever their denomination) who 'preached the other day in Kendal, in a chapel which under the management of a person I will not name has long been a scandal to the Establishment'.

Wordsworth feared Catholicism more than Protestant dissent. Catholics might be a majority in Ireland in 1808, but he told his more tolerant friend Wrangham that he was not prepared to see 'the Catholic religion' its Established Church. He was opposed to concessions in 1821, first, because he was certain that the Catholics were intent on Irish independence; next, because they insisted on papal infallibility; finally, because concessions would 'set all other Dissenters in motion' and weaken the Church of England, which was 'not only a fundamental part of our Constitution, but one of the greatest upholders and propagators of civilization in our own country, and, lastly, the most effectual and main support of religious toleration'. He believed that free discussion was the only safeguard of liberty, and never ceased to stress the surrender of private judgment which Catholicism imposed. In 1825 he held that Protestant supremacy should be maintained in Ireland, by force of arms if necessary; he was convinced that its Catholic Church throve on the poverty and ignorance of its peasantry. Writing to Blomfield, Bishop of London, when the passing of the Catholic Emancipation Act was imminent, he described the Catholic Church as idolatrous, persecuting, 'evasive and unbindable'; and asked how the Church of England could be preserved against infidels, Dissenters, and Catholics. Her 'most pressing enemy' was the Church of Rome. During his visit to Ireland, after the passing of the Bill in 1829, he was dismayed to find how widespread was its power. His views were never substantially modified, as his letter to Gladstone in March 1844 indicates:

> As to Romanism, having lived much in countries where it is dominant, and being not unacquainted with much of its history, my horror of it . . . is great indeed . . . we must never lose sight of its manifold attractions for the two extremes of our artificial society, the opulent and luxurious, never trained to vigorous thinking, and . . . the extreme poor, who are greatly in danger of falling under the influence of its doctrines, pressed upon them by a priesthood so constituted.

The Tractarian or Oxford movement for the revival of Catholic observances and ritual within the Anglican Church did appeal to Wordsworth, but, as one who believed that poetry is 'the impassioned expression which is in the countenance of all Science', he could never have supported its reactionary doctrine. In a note to 'Musings near Aquapendente' he refers to his friend Frederick Faber, one of its leaders, and remarks, 'Much of the work they are undertaking was grievously wanted, and God grant that their endeavours may continue to prosper. . . .' Newman stated that Wordsworth, Coleridge, and Scott, 'with essential differences one from another and perhaps from any Church system', had all shown religious thought 'deeper and truer than satisfied the last century'.

Wordsworth did not wish the Church of England to change radically. He favoured a judicious redistribution of its wealth, but his 'Postscript, 1835' shows that he believed in its hierarchical system, recognised that its standards and good influence owed much to ministers who belonged to the gentry, and argued that, as long as this obtained, it was in the interest of the country as a whole that stipends should be scaled to encourage their admission. Such views explain the social status of the Pastor in *The Excursion*. Stipendiary equality would tend to diminish incentive. He defended the system whereby curates assisted incumbents with pluralities. It gave them opportunities to study, and to be transferred if mistakes made transfer advisable. Their enthusiasm often rekindled the zeal of incumbents, but they had much to learn about people and society (including 'the constitution of civil government') before taking charge of parishes. Wordsworth opposed voluntary churches, and argued that all should be made to support the Church of England, since it existed for everyone's benefit. New communities created a need for new churches, and it behoved thriving manufacturers and wealthy landlords to provide them. His 'Jacobinism' is exposed when he suggests that those whose vast estates had been 'lavished upon their ancestors by royal favouritism or purchased at insignificant prices after church-spoliation' could thus make a return for which their tenantry and dependents would 'learn to bless their names'.

It is doubtful whether any poet, even Milton, devoted so much of his thought to his country as Wordsworth did from 1793 to 1850; first in bitter disagreement with national policy, then in strenuous support against Napoleonic aggression, finally in the long, anxious post-war era of disturbance and reform. When he told an American visitor that he had given his mind twelve hours to 'the conditions and prospects of society' for every one to poetry, he seems to have been thinking mostly of this period, during which his patriotic fears appear more pronounced than at any time during the war; they were obsessively prolonged. The contrast between his post-war trepidation and his confidence in popular judgment during the Napoleonic struggle is more remarkable than any change in the evolution of his poetry. He had faith in the people as long as they were wisely governed. Even during the war the allegiance of Whigs and Radicals was uncertain, and it was for this reason that Wordsworth became convinced that the future of the country was safer under Tory leadership, though his support was never uncritical. In 'November, 1806', when England was left without an ally, after the overthrow of Prussia, he wrote:

> We shall exult, if they who rule the land
> Be men who hold its many blessings dear,
> Wise, upright, valiant; not a servile band,
> Who are to judge of danger which they fear,
> And honour which they do not understand.

He protested against lack of statesmanship in the Convention of Cintra. After the war, especially in industrial cities and areas, agitators and political demagogues were responsible for Ludditism, mob violence, and what seemed to Wordsworth a frightening recrudescence of 'Jacobinism' which could lead to anarchy.

The fact that Wordsworth numbered aristocrats among his friends has often been turned against him by political adversaries from Hazlitt onwards. He was never a sycophant; before accepting the Distributorship of Stamps from Lord Lonsdale, he made it plain that he could not sacrifice any of his principles. Sir George Beaumont warned his guests Haydon and Wilkie in 1809 against Wordsworth's 'democratic' views, and it is worth remembering that Macaulay judged *The Prelude* in 1850 'to the last degree Jacobinical, indeed Socialist'. He was quite sure that it had been published posthumously for this reason; yet in no respect is it inconsistent with what Wordsworth was known to stand for during his life. If he spent far too much time and energy supporting the Lowther faction at elections, it was not from a sense of gratitude; it was because he thought they represented beneficial forces that were indispensable for national progress in the post-war years.

Events had made Wordsworth an 'alarmist' by April 1817, when he felt that the suspension of the Habeas Corpus Act was 'a measure approved by all the well disposed'. His confidence was undermined by the conviction that the 'moral cement' of social cohesion had been dissolved by 'a quickened self-interest'. Expedience was preferred to principle, but 'if our present constitution in church and state is to last, it must rest as heretofore upon a moral basis; and they who govern the country must be something superior to mere financiers and political economists'. Wordsworth believed the Reform Bill of 1832 was unsound in principle, agreeing that it encouraged extremists to work on the grievances of unenlightened workers for the promotion of 'extensive, sudden, and experimental innovation . . . diametrically opposed to the principle of progressiveness'. For this reason he injudiciously described it as 'a greater political crime than any recorded in history' (24.ii.32); a year later he concluded that 'an unbridled democracy is the worst of all tyrannies'. Not surprisingly, Henry Crabb Robinson labelled him a *despairing* alarmist in June 1833. By November 1834 he was resigned to the worst; it was, he told Robinson, simply a question of time.

Hindsight makes it tempting to ridicule such fears, but it would be truer to historical perspectives to claim that any Englishman who felt deeply for his country had ample cause for apprehension. Wordsworth wanted reform; most of all he wished to ensure that it was not imperilled by inflammatory speeches and passions but proceeded through orderly and enlightened measures for the common good. Matthew Arnold and George Eliot felt similarly in their turn, as *Culture and Anarchy*, *Felix Holt*, and 'Address to

Working Men, by Felix Holt' disclose. Drawing from an exception-
ally wide range of political experience, Wordsworth matured into
a Burkeian democrat, as he admitted (6.x.32):

> A spirit of rash innovation is every where at war with our old in-
> stitutions, and the habits and sentiments that have thus far sup-
> ported them; and the ardor of those who are bent on change is
> exactly according to the measure of their ignorance. − Where
> men will not, or through want of knowledge, are unable to, look
> back they cannot be expected to look forward; and therefore,
> caring for the present only, they care for *that* merely as it affects
> their own importance. Hence a blind selfishness is at the bottom
> of all that is going forward − a remark which in other words was
> made by Mr Burke long ago. . . .

Wordsworth realized the danger of placing too much political
representation in the hands of large landed proprietors (as in the
pre-Reform era); nevertheless he supported an electoral system
based on property, in the assurance that ownership instilled a
sense of responsibility and concern for improvements in areas of
future benefit to the nation. Seeing progress endangered by dazzling 'political nostrums', he felt that an uneducated people could
be exploited, as the French had been, even to despotism. He
remained a fervent believer in liberty, insisting on the necessity for
a vigorous Opposition in Parliament, and even more for the freedom of the press. He knew that its abuses needed curbing, but
there was 'scarcely any abuse' he would not endure rather than
'sacrifice, or even endanger' this freedom; it was 'the *only* safeguard of liberty' (4.xii.21).

His fears for 'the tottering realm' (as expressed in 'The Warning',
after the Reform Bill had been passed), particularly from politically
exploited mobs with blood-stained hands, may seem wildly
exaggerated, but Wordsworth, who was well informed, denies this
in his I.F. note, and is content to leave the verdict to history. Earlier,
when the passing of the Bill was imminent, his inescapable pre-
possession had determined the conclusion of 'Upon the Late
General Fast' (March 1832, after a serious cholera epidemic):

> Oh that with aspirations more intense,
> Chastised by self-abasement more profound,
> This people, once so happy, so renowned

For liberty, would seek from God defence
Against far heavier ill, the pestilence
Of revolution, impiously unbound!

Three other sonnets show his disgust with writers who defended the excesses of the French Revolution ('Portentous change when history can appear As the cool advocate of foul device') and his hope that 'long-favoured England' would not be misled by 'monstrous theories of alien growth' lest it suffer from 'alien frenzy' and bloodshed. The poet's anxieties passed with the years. When Thomas Cooper, the Chartist, called at Rydal Mount in 1846, not long after his release from prison, he was astonished to find that Wordsworth fully concurred with the aims of the Charter. 'I have always said the people were right in what they asked; but you went the wrong way to get it.' Force must never be used, he counselled, but he was confident that the people would have the franchise as knowledge advanced. Cooper left with 'a more intense feeling of having been in the presence of a good and great intelligence' than he had ever known.

Wordsworth's public advocacy of State education for all went back to *The Excursion*, yet more than sixty years were to pass before it was fully operative at an elementary level. In the full sense of the word, including the humanitarian, the imaginative, the moral, and the spiritual, education had been one of his preoccupations from 1797. 'Every great poet is a teacher; I wish either to be considered as a teacher, or as nothing,' he wrote in 1808. It would be absurd to expect from Wordsworth expert advice on method or curricula, but his remarks on educational aims are perennially valid. By 1829, it is worth noting, he had some reservations on free education; he doubted whether the child could be grateful to a public institution as much as to parents who 'spare from their scanty provision a mite' for his benefit. He had become concerned too about the emulation encouraged by Dr Bell's 'Madras System', which he once admired. More radical than most of his countrymen, he knew that little progress was possible without educational reform, in schools and universities, for the middle and upper classes.

In a letter (?1808) to a friend Wordsworth reflects the views he expressed in *The Prelude* (v) on the 'model' schoolboy for whose 'unnatural growth' the teacher is responsible. He condemns the rote-learning which was characteristic of most teaching, and stresses the importance of awakening the imagination through tales, biography, history, and natural life. In 1829, after deploring the separation, through infant schools, of juveniles from their mothers, and the inability of parents to attend to their children, he distinguishes between 'education' and 'tuition'. He satirizes cramming, is certain that bookish attainments are of no avail when divorced from moral influence, especially of the home, and decries the mummery of teaching natural history from pictures. 'A moment's notice of a red-breast pecking by a winter's hearth is worth it all.' Such strictures have been repeated in the twentieth century with reference to our whole educational system:

> Its centre of gravity lies in the intellect, and its chief tool is the printed book. . . . What is wanted is an appreciation of the infinite variety of vivid values achieved by an organism in its proper environment. When you understand all about the sun and all about the atmosphere and all about the rotation of the earth, you may still miss the radiance of the sunset. . . . We want concrete fact with a high light thrown on what is relevant to its preciousness.[1]

The strength of a country, Wordsworth declared (28.iii.11), lies not in its military power but in its people, 'the augmentation of their virtue and happiness', and their progress in knowledge, science, and civilization. England needed 'a new course of education, a higher tone of moral feeling, more of the grandeur of the imaginative faculties, and less of the petty processes of the unfeeling and purblind understanding, that would manage the concerns of nations in the same calculating spirit with which it would set about building a house'. He could not comprehend how a curriculum could be complete without religious education. Opening a new school at Bowness in 1836, he regretted that religious teaching was 'too often given with reference, less to the affections, to the imagination, and to the practical duties, than to subtle distinctions in points of doctrine, and to facts in scripture history, of which a knowledge may be brought out by a catachetical process'. Too much attention was given to arithmetic and mathematics to the neglect of natural and civil history. Education 'comprehends all those processes and influences, come from whence they may, that conduce to the best developement of the bodily powers, and of the moral, intellectual, and spiritual faculties which the position

of the individual admits of'. Parental co-operation with teachers
and ministers was indispensable, for parents 'become infinitely the
most important tutors of their children, without appearing, or
positively meaning to be so'. Wordsworth did not underestimate
the effect, for good or ill, of influences outside schools and homes.
In 'Musings near Aquapendente', with the calculations of political
economists in mind, he hopes for wiser governing:

> Zealous co-operation of all means
> Given or acquired, to raise us from the mire,
> And liberate our hearts from low pursuits.
> By gross utilities enslaved we need
> More of the ennobling impulse from the past,
> If to the future aught of good must come
> Sounder and therefore holier than the ends
> Which, in the giddiness of self-applause,
> We covet as supreme.

Wordsworth had the good of his country at heart. Much had
changed in the affairs of the outer world since he declared his
democratic principles to his friend Mathews in 1794, but his
political views had remained radically the same. He did not believe
then in violence and 'inflammatory addresses to the passions of
men'; a writer, like himself, who had 'the welfare of mankind at
heart', should 'let slip no opportunity of explaining and enforcing
those general principles of the social order which are applicable to
all times and to all places . . . they include an entire preservative
from despotism, they will guide the hand of reform, and if a
revolution must afflict us, they alone can mitigate its horrors and
establish freedom with tranquillity.' In 1843 he declared that he
was a democrat who believed that the people should govern themselves as far as they were capable. When, as he tells us in 'At
Florence', he dared to sit reverently on the stone reputed to be
Dante's favourite seat, it was with thoughts of his own dedication,
not to poetry but to patriotism. The better his endeavours during
war and peace are known, the greater the justification that will be
found symbolized in that singular act.

Poetic Theory and Practice

Wordsworth's critical writings are more substantial than their number suggests. They consist of the preface to *Lyrical Ballads* in the three forms of 1798 (brief), 1800, and 1802 (substantially enlarged); and two essays which were added to the 1815 edition of his poems. Arguments in the former provoked hostility which damaged Wordsworth's poetic reputation for a long period. It was written, he maintained, 'solely to gratify' Coleridge.

They must have thought their publication more innovative than it really was; but for the prefaces of 1800 and 1802 *Lyrical Ballads* would have excited much less controversy, and perhaps little at all. Only in a few poems was the style patently experimental and, as Wordsworth did not continue writing in this manner, they could hardly be elevated into a literary *casus belli*. The emphasis on 'poetic diction' and its 'gaudiness and inane phraseology' from 1798 onwards, as a contrast first of all to the poetic use of 'the language of conversation in the middle and lower classes of society', then of 'a selection of the real language of men in a state of vivid sensation', finally of 'a selection of the language really spoken by men', gives a false impression of eighteenth-century poetry, and especially (from the title-page epigraph which was added in 1800) of Pope. Wordsworth's contentiousness carries him too far when he argues (paradoxically, in conjunction with the definition of the poet which immediately precedes his statement) that the poet's language 'must often, in liveliness and truth, fall short of that which is uttered by men in real life'. This claim suggests that he was thinking primarily of one type of poetry in *Lyrical Ballads*, the dramatically lyrical, whether direct as in 'The Complaint of a Forsaken Indian Woman', or introduced by the poet as in 'The Last of the Flock', or entirely mediated by an imaginary narrator as in 'The Thorn'. Examples can be easily adduced (from, for example, *King Lear* or the vernacular of *The Mayor of Casterbridge* and *The Woodlanders*) of the high efficacy of simple language in conveying the most heartfelt emotions, but it remains at least equally true that most people cannot find words to express their deepest feelings adequately, and that the language of great poets is not restricted to the simpler forms of expression in communicating moments of great emotional appeal. Often such emotions are conveyed in elevated language, as in Macbeth's 'No, this my hand will rather The multitudinous seas incarnadine' or in Wordsworth's 'The Affliction of Margaret':

> Perhaps some dungeon hears thee groan,
> Maimed, mangled by inhuman men;
> Or thou upon a desert thrown
> Inheritest the lion's den;
> Or hast been summoned to the deep,
> Thou, thou and all thy mates, to keep
> An incommunicable sleep.

The poet is 'a man speaking to men', but in his poetic role he is more. Wordsworth knew that in copying the language of life, vivid and moving though it often is, effects may be weakened. The question is how far the poet may go without selection or without 'composing accurately in the spirit of such selection'. In his experimental poems Wordsworth realized the risk he took with such expressions as 'Sad case it was, as you may think', admitting that 'Goody Blake and Harry Gill' was one of the 'rudest' poems in the collection. Elsewhere he seeks a safeguard in referring to the language of living poetry as 'closely resembling that of real life'. His main purpose is to validate a poetic medium which is real and permanent, as opposed to the meretricious and fashionable;[2] a language which, capable of communicating throughout the ages, is consonant with its subject, which is 'truth, not individual and local, but general, and operative; not standing upon external testimony, but carried into the heart by passion'. Through its language therefore, poetry is 'philosophical' in the Aristotelian sense, being based on a judgment of what gives perennial appeal. The tenor of the general argument which Wordsworth eventually assembled is sound, but it is unfortunate that he did not take pains at all points to ensure its explicitness and consistency.

The permanent value of his stress on simpler, non-literary language as the medium of poetry which will evoke a full response to human situations may be felt in such poems as 'Michael', where he achieves, at a more sustained level than elsewhere perhaps, 'an art, a music, and a strain of words' that is 'life' or 'its acknowledged voice'. Sir Walter Scott must have sympathized with his aims. After telling his son-in-law Lockhart that he was 'too apt to measure things' by literary standards, he said:

> God help us! What a poor world this would be if that were the true doctrine! I have read books enough, and observed and conversed with enough of eminent and splendidly cultivated minds, too, in my time; but, I assure you, I have heard higher sentiments from the lips of poor *uneducated* men and women, when exerting the spirit of severe yet gentle heroism under difficulties and afflictions, or speaking their simple thoughts as to circumstances in the lot of friends and neighbours, than I ever yet met with out of the pages of the Bible.[3]

Wordsworth's use of the word 'language' is neither precise nor consistent. If he referred to no more than vocabulary when making the elliptical affirmation that 'there neither is, nor can be, any *essential* difference between the language of prose and [the language of] metrical composition', few would wish to contest the argument as a statement of a general, rather than absolute, principle, in contradistinction to Thomas Gray's claim that 'the language of the age is never the language of poetry', and that English poetry, unlike French, 'has a language peculiar to itself'. Gray is thinking of words and phrases. Most poets, he continues, have enriched our language with new or 'foreign' idioms and derivatives, Shakespeare and Milton particularly, none being more licentious than Pope and Dryden, 'who perpetually borrow expressions from the former'. Adherence to either 'poetic diction' or to 'the language of men' can lead to inadequacies of expression. When Mary Hutchinson objected to 'sickness had by him' in 'Resolution and Independence', Wordsworth defended its truth to speech, then changed it (only slightly for the better) to 'sickness felt by him'. Occasionally he went to the other extreme in circumlocutory evasion of common words. Until 1832 'the beverage drawn from China's fragrant herb' did duty for 'tea' (Ex.ix.530–1); 'itinerant vehicle' remained injudiciously unaltered in *The Prelude*, probably for metrical reasons. This factor, coupled with the need for alternative expression, explains the anticlimactic 'indigenous produce' of 'The power of armies is an invisible thing'. Technical words present a special problem, but nothing can justify the periphrasis for 'the barometer' (in 'The Italian Itinerant ') of 'the well-wrought scale, Whose sentient tube instructs to time A purpose for a fickle clime'. These are extremes; Wordsworth's usual practice is indicated when he states that 'One of the first duties of a writer is to ask himself whether his thought, feeling, or image cannot be expressed by existing words or phrases' (23.xii.29).

His remarks in the 1800 preface on the lines in Gray's sonnet which he could not distinguish from prose might suggest that his primary consideration was vocabulary, for the first and third are examples of poetic inversion, and 'lonely anguish' in the second is an obvious poeticism; furthermore, he calls attention to 'fruitless' for 'fruitlessly' as exceptional to his case. However, when he speaks of rhyme as another distinguishing feature, he implies larger considerations; and this conclusion is borne out when he refers to 'language, though naturally arranged, and according to the strict rules of metre', and states that 'not only the language of a large portion of every good poem, even of the most elevated character, must necessarily, except with reference to the metre, in no respect differ from that of good prose, but likewise that some of the most interesting parts of the best poems will be found to be strictly the language of prose when prose is well written'. This last passage claims no more than the admissibility to poetry of language which in every way (order being significant) is like prose. What Wordsworth appears to have done is to posit this principle as a general rule; and yet he nowhere observes that poetry precludes language arranged in accordance with principles which are inadmissible in prose. In reacting against the artificialities of 'poetic diction' and its adjuncts, he may have intended no more than a new emphasis and freedom, not a prescription.

Coleridge was surprised that Wordsworth, whose style seemed to him more individual than that of any poet after Shakespeare and Milton, attached so much importance to the *lingua communis* of prose and poetry which was to be found in Chaucer, Spenser, and seventeenth-century poets such as Herbert. How far his reasoning diverted him from a fundamental truth may be gauged by the degree to which lyricism in Donne, Browning, and Hardy, is enhanced through an unhesitating adoption of conversational idiom and tone. He seems to have forgotten that Wordsworth is interested in the language of poetry only as a medium. Every poet worthy of the name has his idiosyncratic style whether, apart from rhyme and metre, his language differs from prose or not. Wordsworth knew that in reacting against 'poetic diction' he would be accused of '*nimia simplicitas*', but was confident that such criticism would diminish 'the more an intimacy with our best writers' was cultivated. Matthew Arnold drew a valid distinction between this kind of 'natural simplicity' and the *simplesse* or 'artificial simplicity' to which Tennyson sometimes declined. No informed reader can assume that a natural style came readily to Wordsworth in his best poetry, and was not the product of both critical ruthlessness and creative strength. The perfect naturalness of a line such as 'And all the air is filled with pleasant noise of waters' reflects a higher kind of art than all the patent artfulness of Tennyson's 'The league-long roller thundering on the reef'. With exceptions here and there the language of 'Michael' follows, or closely approximates, the order of prose; it is most simple at the most moving points of the story; the artistry is expressed throughout in the superb control of rhythms which vary according to the subject.

Wordsworth's addiction to personification, which he selects in the preface as an eminent feature of mechanical or conventional eighteenth-century poetry, is manifest in the bedizened verse of *An Evening Walk* and *Descriptive Sketches*. It was Burns more than any other poet who, with his manly conversational tone and his lyricism, brought home to him the genuine power of a poetic style close to speech. His convictions were reinforced by ballads, after he attained his basic style by strenuous endeavour in *The Borderers* and 'The Ruined Cottage'. He was influenced too by the conversational manner of Coleridge in some of his best poems. In 1798 he wrote poetry as diverse as 'The Last of the Flock' and 'Tintern Abbey'. Among the poets who contributed to his development, Milton is probably the most important, though his stylistic groundwork has a greater affinity with plainer writers such as Daniel. Whatever the influences, Wordsworth had to forge his style, and he practised it to such effect that it came too readily at times. Among the many poems which he wrote during the long period of decline, when he had no great cause to inspire him, 'poetic diction' – a heightened language where a simpler would suffice – recurs, sometimes with pleasing indulgence, sometimes in contrived verse. Gerard Manley Hopkins rightly attributes a

Parnassian quality (a poetic style devoid of inspiration) to much of the later verse, which varies from high to low, from chance inspiration to heavy prosaic manipulation.

Long before Keats abandoned it in *Hyperion*, on the grounds that 'English ought to be kept up', Wordsworth had recognised the artificiality of classically constructed blank verse in Milton. More than any other poet, he succeeded in bringing blank verse constructively close to the language of speech and prose without diminishing its poetic power. Deep human appeal in 'Michael', moving reflections in 'Tintern Abbey', and numerous evocations of scenes instinct with feeling in *The Prelude* are communicated through this medium. The second book of the last work (ll.419–51) attains a stirring, climactic grandeur in a passage constructed according to the syntax of periodic prose. Wordsworth generally follows a prose order; the danger, especially in the greater freedom which blank verse gives over rhymed stanzaic forms, is that without continual vigilance one may write too freely, as Wordsworth does in *The Prelude*, and more copiously in *The Excursion*. Departures from the norm may be dictated by metrical convenience, as in 'Me, rather, it employed' (Pr.vii.598), a kind of Miltonic inversion which Keats came to regard as the product of 'an artful, or rather, artist's humour' (22.ix.19). They may arise from higher aims, such as rhythmic enrichment or an intensification of imaginative effect. The latter is illustrated in lines of Miltonic order and diction in 'Yew-trees', where each trunk is described as 'a growth Of intertwisted fibres serpentine Up-coiling, and inveterately convolved'. The rejection of prose order for rhythmic effect is to be found in some of the best passages of *The Prelude*. 'Magnificent the morning rose' when Wordsworth felt that he was a dedicated spirit. He recalls the hooting of the owls by Windermere, 'concourse wild of jocund din'; the peak that upreared its head 'as if with voluntary power instinct', and seemed to stride over Ullswater after him; and skating on Esthwaite with his school friends 'in games confederate'. An interesting conversion of Miltonic order occurs in *The Prelude*. Originally the foppish London preacher had calculatingly produced a smile of 'rapt irradiation exquisite'. The insertion of a comma in the later version (vii.561) changes this into clipped conversational English, with an emphatic concluding comment:

> There have I seen a comely bachelor,
> Fresh from a toilette of two hours, ascend

His rostrum, with seraphic glance look up,
And, in a tone elaborately low
Beginning, lead his voice through many a maze
A minuet course; and, winding up his mouth,
From time to time, into an orifice
Most delicate, a lurking eyelet, small,
And only not invisible, again
Open it out, diffusing thence a smile
Of rapt irradiation, exquisite.

If the language of true poetry resembles that of life, it acquires 'dissimilitude' partly from selection (which eliminates 'vulgarity and meanness') but principally from metre. Wordsworth rather exaggerates the importance of the latter, since poetry depends far more on the satisfaction of those rhythmical expectations which subject and presentation arouse. He implies that metre creates a degree of excitement, but stresses its value in 'tempering and restraining' the reader's feelings when they would otherwise be over-excited. This theory may have more significance for the writer than for the reader, for lack of artistic control tends to reduce the intensity of sympathetic response. How important metre is may be seen negatively and positively in Wordsworth's poetry: first, in the unfortunate choice of jaunty metres in such poems as 'The Reverie of Poor Susan', 'Star-Gazers' (where it would be more appropriate to listeners enjoying hurdy-gurdy music), and 'At Vallombrosa'; secondly, in the life and gaiety which it quickens in 'The Idiot Boy'. A note on 'The Thorn' illustrates Wordsworth's attention to the technicalities of poetic communication; it was necessary, he says, that the poem should move slowly, to be natural, yet he hoped that 'by the aid of metre, to those who should at all enter into the spirit of the poem, it would appear to move quickly'. To this he adds a comment on the value of repetition, not only in rousing emotional responses, but more particularly in expressing the verbal limitations of his 'talkative' narrator. Coleridge's inability to 'enter into the spirit of the poem' is indicated in *Biographia Literaria* (xvii) by his unacknowledged repetition of Southey's hostile criticism of 1789: 'it is not possible to imitate truly a dull and garrulous discourser, without repeating the effects of dullness and garrulity.' The comment is seriously weakened by the introduction of 'truly'.

Wordsworth's passage on 'emotion recollected in tranquillity' recalls T. S. Eliot's account of the poet's role at the time of composition. Eliot's assumption that the poet acts like a catalyst, and that successful composition demands 'a continual extinction of personality' is deliberately anti-romantic and reactionary; his own poetry is proof enough that personality is implicit in a writer's expression and thought, however much he eliminates his egotistic self. Wordsworth's definition of poetry as 'the spontaneous overflow of powerful feelings' may astonish, until one remembers how strongly he was roused in mind and body during composition. Poetry begins, he says, with emotion recollected in tranquillity (often, the evidence shows, with impressions contemplated there and then); contemplation leads to loss of tranquillity until an emotion kindred to the first is generated, and composition begins. The question of kinship between these two emotions leaves room for debate. What seems certain from a comparison of 'I wandered lonely as a cloud' or 'Resolution and Independence' with the original experience is that the process of contemplation and the consequent complex of emotion are artistic in the main, and that Wordsworth's views and Eliot's are not as far apart as may first appear. Wordsworth points out that the pains of poetic parturition are balanced by pleasures, and his sonnet '*There is a pleasure in poetic pains*' gives definition to both.

One brief observation on his 'ballads' is highly significant. He is less interested in story and exciting events than in the flux and reflux of thought and feeling. He wishes to make incidents and situations interesting by following 'the primary laws of our nature', particularly 'the manner in which we associate ideas in a state of excitement'. In an age that thirsted after 'outrageous stimulation' in literature, his poems differed from popular poetry (including translations of Bürger) in this respect, 'that the feeling therein developed gives importance to the action and situation', and not vice versa. As the 'Action is transitory' speech of *The Borderers* suggests, he had already made the mind of man, the inner world of sensation, his 'haunt' and the 'main region' of his song. In subject as well as in style, he wished to keep his readers 'in the company of flesh and blood'.

Nowhere is Wordsworth's poetic vision more laudable and challenging than in his declaration of 1802 that 'Poetry is the breath and finer spirit of all knowledge; it is the impassioned expression which is in the countenance of all Science'. Specialization in education has hindered this development. There are no subjects, potentially, which are outside the poet's province; 'he will follow wheresoever he can find an atmosphere of sensation in which to move his wings'; 'the remotest discoveries' of science will be 'as proper objects of the poet's art as any upon which it can be employed, if the time should ever come when these things shall be familiar to us, and the relations under which they are contemplated' by scientists 'shall be manifestly and palpably material to us as enjoying and suffering beings'. Here we see Wordsworth's yearning for an enlargement in the area of knowledge and wonder. His 'atmosphere of sensation' implies thoughts 'steeped in feeling', as does Keats's 'O for a life of sensation rather than of thoughts'; but he knows that life's mystery, and poetry therefore, extend beyond the finite reach of science, which is 'a succedaneum, and a prop to our infirmity' (Pr.ii.212−15), 'a precious visitant', 'a support, Not treacherous, to the mind's *excursive* power' (Ex.iv. 1251−63).

Wordsworth's linguistic and psychological objects in *Lyrical Ballads* are part of his aim to present 'incidents and situations from common life' in such an imaginative way that 'ordinary things' appear 'in an unusual aspect'. The subject of 'The Thorn' may not be ordinary, but the poem affords striking examples of the unusual manner in which ordinary things can be presented; the same is true of 'Lucy Gray', as Wordsworth points out in the I.F. note, where he contrasts his 'spiritualizing' of the subject with Crabbe's matter-of-fact style. The arguments in favour of choosing 'low and rustic life' may or may not be answerable; they show in what direction Wordsworth's sympathies, like Hardy's, lay. When he discusses the language of country people, and stresses the advantage it derives from lack of 'social vanity', he gives a hint of class prejudice. His criticism of 'sickly' and 'fickle' tastes in the wider reading public was valid, no doubt, but his aggressiveness suggests a strong social bias which would lose him the sympathy of many readers when he became the target of Jeffrey's invective.

The 1815 preface was occasioned principally by Wordsworth's new arrangement of his published poems in categories. The most important section relates to fancy and imagination, a distinction first attempted in the 1800 note to 'The Thorn', and illuminatingly treated in parts of *The Prelude*. After differentiating between the image-recall of memory and the creativity of the imagination, Wordsworth illustrates the conferring and abstracting properties of the latter. In 'Over his own sweet voice the stock-dove broods', the active word suggests the prolonged note of the bird's cooing and a quiet satisfaction 'like that which may be supposed inseparable from the continuous process of incubation'. The abstracting power of the imagination in 'Shall I call thee bird, Or but a wandering voice?' implies the mobility of the cuckoo, which is frequently heard at different points but never seen. Visual images in 'Resolution and Independence' exemplify how, by a process of combining and modifying which abstracts and confers, a state bordering on inanimation in the leech-gatherer is presented. Wordsworth refers to imagination as it deals with thoughts and sentiments, regulates the composition of characters, and determines the course of actions, citing the Scriptures and Milton as the 'grand storehouses' of religious and meditative imagination, commenting on its allegorical form in Spenser, and contenting himself with one example of its human and dramatic manifestations in Shakespeare. He supplies interesting illustrations of the aggregative or associative fancy, but does not go far enough in distinguishing it from imagination. Apart from the aggregative as opposed to the unifying (Coleridge's 'esemplastic') process, more needs to be said on the light and intellectual forms which fancy takes, in contrast with the wholeness of imaginative experience, where all one's conscious being (mind, spirit, feeling) is simultaneously engaged, with no dissociation of thought or awareness. (For this reason, imagination quickens and renews, its effect in counterbalancing distress probably explaining the cathartic effect of great tragedy.)

The 1815 'Essay, Supplementary to the Preface', provoked by Jeffrey's taunts and criticism from 1807 to his hostile reception of *The Excursion* (on which its author had set high hopes), could have done little to help Wordsworth's cause. His long attempts to explain why readers can easily be misguided, especially in the assessment of original works, seem rather a useless exercise; only a continual irritant could have made him write so unprofitably. After the dubious generalization that simplicity accompanies 'the wisdom of the heart and the grandeur of the imagination' in higher poetry, he admits that his observations on readers are ungracious, and professes to make them reluctantly. He then proceeds to show how great writers from Spenser onwards failed for long periods to gain the recognition they merited. Between *Paradise Lost* and Thomson's *Seasons*, he claims, English poetry does not contain 'a single new image of external nature' except 'the nocturnal Reverie of Lady Winchilsea' and 'a passage or two in the Windsor Forest of Pope'. Hence Thomson's success, despite his 'vicious' style; yet his imaginative genius was not perceived, and his *Castle of Indolence* remained neglected. Collins was hardly noticed, yet the spurious imagery of Macpherson's *Ossian* was highly acclaimed:

> From what I saw with my own eyes, I knew that the imagery was spurious. In nature every thing is distinct, yet nothing defined into absolute independent singleness. In Macpherson's work, it is exactly the reverse; every thing (that is not stolen) is in this manner defined, insulated, dislocated, deadened, − yet nothing distinct. It will always be so when words are substituted for things.

The unassuming poetry of Percy's *Reliques* redeemed English verse, and Wordsworth is happy to admit his obligations to it; it had been treated with contempt, while Bürger became 'the delight' of Germany.

From this Wordsworth takes comfort in the thought that his poems will endure despite their hostile reception. Every *original* author, he concludes, has to create 'the taste by which he is to be enjoyed', shaping his own road like Hannibal in the Alps. To change the taste of an age demands 'a co-operating *power* in the mind of the reader', and only a great poet can evoke it. This 'widening of the sphere of human sensibility' is the only infallible sign of genius in the fine arts. Wordsworth concludes by putting his trust in the people rather than in 'the public', whose judgments are governed by 'the factitious influence' of fashionable tastes. On this, in a letter stressing the imperative for a great poet to 'rectify men's feelings' and make them 'more sane, pure, and permanent, in short, more consonant to nature, that is, to eternal nature, and the great moving spirit of things', he had written (7.vi.02):

> But where are we to find the best measure of this? I answer, from within; by stripping our own hearts naked, and by looking out of our selves towards men who lead the simplest lives most according to nature; men who have never known false refinements, wayward and artificial desires, false criticisms, effeminate habits of thinking and feeling, or who, having known these things, have outgrown them. This latter class is the most to be

depended upon, but it is very small in number. People in our rank in life are perpetually falling into one sad mistake, namely, that of supposing that human nature and the persons they associate with are one and the same thing. Whom do we generally associate with? Gentlemen, persons of fortune, professional men, ladies, persons who can afford to buy or can easily procure books of half-a-guinea price, hot-pressed, and printed upon superfine paper. These persons are, it is true, a part of human nature, but we err lamentably if we suppose them to be fair representatives of the vast mass of human existence. And yet few ever consider books but with reference to their power of pleasing these persons and men of a higher rank . . .

On the subject of poetry Wordsworth's critical essays contain several fine and original observations which have become part of our heritage. Nevertheless, one cannot resist the thought that he would have enhanced his contemporary reputation more surely had he devoted himself more to poetry, and surrendered less of his time and thought to provocative argumentation in self-defence.

Dorothy's journals and Wordsworth's letters contain ample evidence of his concern for exact expression, as both poet and critic. His statement that language is not the dress, but the incarnation, of thought springs from the convincing authority of experience. Not surprisingly, though his best poems and passages bear witness to his high regard for art, he despised artificialities. Gray failed as a poet, he writes (15.iv.16), because he lacked animation:

> he had little of that fiery quality to begin with; and his pains were of the wrong sort. He wrote English verses, as he and other Eton school-boys wrote Latin; filching a phrase now from one author, and now from another. I do not profess to be a person of very various reading; nevertheless if I were to pluck out of Gray's tail all the feathers which, I know, belong to other birds he would be left very bare indeed. Do not let any body persuade you that any quantity of good verses can ever be produced by mere felicity . . .

On this subject he wrote the sonnet which begins:

> *A poet!* He hath put his heart to school,
> Nor dares to move unpropped upon the staff
> Which art hath lodged within his hand — must laugh
> By precept only, and shed tears by rule.

True poetry, he continues, depends on truth to one's self and truth to nature (or life and experience). He had been disgusted by the frequency with which the word 'artistical' (adopted with 'other impertinences from the Germans') was used for the artificial in poetry.

Wordsworth had not disdained to borrow plumes for the decoration of his early poetry. A quotation in one of the 1794 extensions to *An Evening Walk*, on children playing around churchyard graves, illustrates the manner in which he was to borrow from poets, especially Milton and Spenser, and from prose-writers: 'sensible warm motion' from *Measure for Measure* is not an ornament for outward show; it has been adopted because it expresses the poet's thought and feeling in a way which he finds unsurpassable. The inclusion of such quotations was welcomed by scholarly readers; it was traditional. Their incidental allusiveness is usually no more than a pleasurable association. Sometimes they have indispensable overtones of meaning, as in those allusions to Miltonic parallels in *The Prelude*, where they act as reminders of a Paradise Lost-Regained theme, and in '*A little onward lend thy guiding hand*', where Wordsworth thinks of the blindness that may befall him.

Beside the richly sensuous style of Keats, who believed that 'poetry should surprise by a fine excess' and that every 'rift' of the subject should be loaded with 'ore', Wordsworth is often spare or ascetic. It is a mistake, however, to think of a single style in Wordsworth or any great writer. Authors usually develop; Keats's poetry becomes quieter, less florid, and more English as he matures; Wordsworth has many voices (not just the two which are the delight of parody-lovers, or those more fairly enunciated by Hartley Coleridge in 1837: 'more a man of genius than talent, for whilst the fit of inspiration lasts he is every inch a poet; when he tries to write without it he is very dragging'). George McLean Harper misleads by oversimplification:

Take from Wordsworth's poetry all its lines of Virgilian elegance, of Tennysonian grace, of Miltonic majesty, and you will still have, in what is left, the true Wordsworth, the central, unmistakably personal qualities of which the rest is but a far circumference, dull and wan in some quarters, splendid enough in others, but not always bound to the midmost point by a true radiation.

Not many of Wordsworth's lines can be truly described as Tennysonian, and few would banish 'Laodamia' to a peripheral place, though it undoubtedly possesses the 'majestically plain and touching' qualities he found in Virgil. 'Majesty' is not quite the word one associates with those elevating qualities which make some of Wordsworth's blank verse (in *The Excursion* as well as in *The Prelude*) comparable to Milton's, but such poetry indisputably belongs to the central body of Wordsworth's poetry as he developed. That the best of it belongs to a few years around 1800, and that in any period it has a particular style, are commonly accepted fallacies. The 'true Wordsworth' is found as much in 'The Thorn' as in 'Tintern Abbey' (both written in 1798); in the concluding sonnet of *The River Duddon* as in 'The Solitary Reaper' or 'Intimations of Immortality' or 'The world is too much with us'. In language or tone, these poems show marked differences, just as do 'The Waggoner', 'The White Doe of Rylstone', and the conclusion of *The Prelude*. One can find poems on lighter subjects which belong to Wordsworth's later years and honour him more than many passages in *The Prelude*. Humanly interesting and exceptional in presentation as some of the poems in *Lyrical Ballads* are, they have a quirkishness which does not raise them to the unrivalled elegance of such late poems as 'Mutability' and 'Inside of King's College Chapel, Cambridge'; the Wordsworth of 1798 lacked those subtler skills which successful composition on such subjects required, nor had he the maturity which enabled him to write with the deep feeling of 'On the Departure of Sir Walter Scott from Abbotsford' (1831) and 'Extempore Effusion on the Death of James Hogg' (1835). It would not be difficult to illustrate a wider diversity in the best of Wordsworth's poetry; one might ask, for example, what poet has written a romance more delightful in subject and execution than 'The Egyptian Maid' (1828). There are too many prejudgments on 'the true Wordsworth' and his stylistic qualities.

To do justice to the varying characteristics of Wordsworth's best poetry would require a full-length study. His ability to rise above conscious art has already been glanced at. Though tricks of craftsmanship are more likely to appear in his less inspired versification, one of his finest descriptions illustrates how the impression of stern, unrelenting pursuit is reinforced by alliterative ('st') persistence:

> When, from behind that craggy steep till then
> The horizon's bound, a huge peak, black and huge,

As if with voluntary power instinct
Upreared its head. I struck and struck again,
And growing still in stature the grim shape
Towered up between me and the stars, and still,
For so it seemed, with purpose of its own
And measured motion like a living thing,
Strode after me.

Like Milton, Wordsworth rejoices in the poetry of place-names, whether British, as in 'To Joanna' (where they are used to best effect) and 'Yew-trees' ('from Glaramara's inmost caves'), or classical, as in the sonnet on Sir Walter Scott's departure for Naples ('Be true, Ye winds of ocean, and the midland sea, Wafting your charge to soft Parthenope!').

Incidental imagery reveals a poet's interests, and Wordsworth's are predominantly in nature. He is as sensitive to nature as waters are to the sky. He wanders lonely as a cloud; the knight of 'Hart-leap Well' had ridden down from Wensley Moor with the slow motion of a summer cloud; and St Basil's life hung 'In bright remembrance, like a shining cloud O'er the vast regions of the western Church' ('The Tuft of Primroses'). Peter Bell's glance is as keen as the wind that cuts along the hawthorn-fence; the Highland girl's difficulty in speaking English reminds Wordsworth of tempest-loving birds beating up against the wind. Weakness suggests a breaking wave in 'A Poet's Epitaph'; the Presences of Nature make the whole visible round of the earth's surface 'With triumph and delight, with hope and fear, Work like a sea'. Speaking of the girl he met beside the churchyard yew, Matthew says that no fountain ever tripped so freely from its rocky cave, and that she seemed as happy as a wave that dances on the sea. Many of Wordsworth's similes, especially in his later poems, provide exquisite vignettes. The 'easy man' sits at his door and, 'like the pear That overhangs his head from the green wall, Feeds in the sunshine' ('The Old Cumberland Beggar'); the murmur of the spinning-wheel is 'Soft as the dorhawk's to a distant ear When twilight shades darken the mountain's head' ('To S.H.'). Against the 'huge fermenting mass of human-kind' in London, a subject that stirs interest and feeling is like a sunbeam in a valley against the black storm on the mountain top (Pr.vii.619–25); in the midst of domestic calamity, the Solitary's wife had remained 'Calm as a frozen lake when ruthless winds Blow fiercely, agitating earth and sky' (Ex.iii.650–1). 'To Enterprise' includes the hope that 'a veteran few' will cling to stern resolves 'by reason justified'

> like sleet
> Whitening a pine tree's northern side,
> When fields are naked far and wide,
> And withered leaves, from earth's cold breast
> Up-caught in whirlwinds, nowhere can find rest.

Wordsworth speaks of 'fair trains of imagery' which came to him when he mused 'on man, on nature, and on human life'. The association between life and nature was so close and persistent that either was apt to conjure up some form of the other. An example of this reciprocal process is afforded by the two sonnets 'Composed near Calais' and 'Why art thou silent!' The contrast revealed in the former between the spirit of France in 1790 and that of 1802 made Wordsworth 'pensive as a bird Whose vernal coverts winter hath laid bare'. Years later the sight of a bird's nest filled with snow in a leafless hedge suggested the human situation which is imaginatively dramatized in the second poem. With Wordsworth 'The clouds that gather round the setting sun' take 'a sober colouring from an eye That hath kept watch o'er man's mortality'; imagination and sympathy are such that 'the meanest flower that blows' can evoke 'Thoughts that do often lie too deep for tears'. The daisy, that 'unassuming commonplace of nature', renews in him 'the homely sympathy that heeds the common life'; it has a greater 'concord with humanity' than any other flower, and plays an apostolical role, in teaching, by its cheerfulness in suffering all things, how man can find hope in adversity. Phases of the small celandine make Wordsworth think of man in his youth and decay, and wish that the surplus energy and cheerfulness of early manhood could be reserved for old age. In 'Yarrow Revisited' thoughts of time and change, of fear and hope (especially for Sir Walter Scott) are intermingled with the scene:

> And if, as Yarrow, through the woods
>   And down the meadow ranging,
> Did meet us with unaltered face,
>   Though we were changed and changing;
> If, *then*, some natural shadows spread
>   Our inward prospect over,
> The soul's deep valley was not slow
>   Its brightness to recover.

How far the moon came by association almost to symbolize hope
for Wordsworth has been discussed with reference to 'A Night
Thought' and 'How beautiful the Queen of Night'. Confirmation
may be found in 'To the Moon (Rydal)':

> May sage and simple, catching with one eye
> The moral intimations of the sky,
> Learn from thy course, where'er their own be taken,
> 'To look on tempests, and be never shaken';
> To keep with faithful step the appointed way
> Eclipsing or eclipsed, by night or day,
> And from example of thy monthly range
> Gently to brook decline and fatal change;
> Meek, patient, stedfast, and with loftier scope,
> Than thy revival yields, for gladsome hope!

Wordsworth's disposition towards classical imagery in his later
poems, notably in 'The Brownie's Cell' and 'Love Lies Bleeding',
reflects the revival of his interest in classical literature. The
sympathy he shows for pagan anthropomorphism (Ex.iv) contrasts
with the distaste for such fancies which he expressed earlier, as a
believer in the 'Eternal Spirit' of nature, in 'Brook! whose society
the poet seeks'. The angelic imagery to which his later approach to
orthodoxy made him readily incline is less convincing than the
reverence for ecclesiatical tradition which appears in '*A little
onward lend thy guiding hand*', where the interior of woods and
forests (nature's temples) is sought:

> In the still summer noon, while beams of light,
> Reposing here, and in the aisles beyond
> Traceably gliding through the dusk, recall
> To mind the living presences of nuns;
> A gentle, pensive, white-robed sisterhood,
> Whose saintly radiance mitigates the gloom
> Of those terrestrial fabrics, where they serve,
> To Christ, the Sun of righteousness, espoused.

Wordsworth has some lengthy similes, one, introduced in epic
style (Pr.05.viii.711), of thirty-one lines; but these are rare. More
impressive and redolent of thought are his simple metaphors: the
sleep that is among the lonely hills, and the fields of sleep; the

weight of many a weary day, of all this unintelligible world, of chance-desires, or of custom 'Heavy as frost and deep almost as life'. The old, mannered personifications are reduced to animating verbs which present pictures to the imaginative: flowers *laugh* in the observance of duty; the sky *rejoices* in the morning's birth; Skiddaw is *glad* with the cry of the hounds; and (onomatopoeically) a leaping fish sends through the tarn a lonely *cheer*. How richly imbued is 'The harvest of a quiet eye That broods and sleeps on his own heart' (the poet's thoughts steeped in feeling) in 'A Poet's Epitaph' may be seen from the parallel between Milton's image of the heavenly Muse which 'dove-like' sat 'brooding on the vast abyss' before Creation and Wordsworth's image (on the creative power of the imagination) of the mind that feeds upon infinity as it 'broods over the dark abyss' in the scene from the top of Snowdon near the end of *The Prelude*. This association is confirmed at the beginning (Pr.i.139–41), when he states that the poet's mind is 'best pleased While she as duteous as the mother dove Sits brooding'.

Wordsworth's greatest poetic qualities are too various to be found in close conjunction. He writes for the thoughtful, imaginative reader. As he matured, his eye 'made quiet' by deeper powers, he rarely indulged in natural description for its own sake. In *The Prelude*, where (in A. N. Whitehead's words) 'the concrete facts of our apprehension' are expressed 'to the height of genius', it is subordinate to other ends. The effect, in context, of 'Ships, towers, domes, theatres, and temples' is quite contrary to what the bare catalogue presentation might at first suggest, the repeated emphasis helping to convey clear-cut details in an imaginative scene. When they are not forced, philosophical subjects and thoughts come to Wordsworth more lyrically and imaginatively than to any other English poet: in 'She was a phantom of delight'; in the 'exultations, agonies, And love, and man's unconquerable mind' of 'To Toussaint l'Ouverture'; above all, in 'Ode to Duty' and 'Mutability'. He combines sense with deep feeling and an ear for the ineffable music of words. He can write with conversational grace and dignity, or in grander strains. The distinctness which is characteristic of much of his verse reflects clarity of vision, intellectual discrimination of a high poetic order, and unusual attention to diction. His emphasis on 'the logical faculty' in poetic composition (24.ix.27) suggests that his view of the poetic process was not radically different from T. S. Eliot's:

The logical faculty has infinitely more to do with poetry than the young and the inexperienced, whether writer or critic, ever dreams of. Indeed, as the materials upon which that faculty is exercised in poetry are so subtle, so plastic, so complex, the application of it requires an adroitness which can proceed from nothing but practice, a discernment which emotion is so far from bestowing that at first it is ever in the way of it.

Wordsworth's range of tone and style (which are one) corresponds with his range of subject, from 'joy in widest commonalty spread' (birds and flowers, for example) and 'random thoughts', through grief and tragedy to man's higher moral and spiritual resources (individual and national), to the most exalted form of imagination, 'that which is conversant with, or turns upon infinity (21.i.24).

Critical Reactions

Hostility to Wordsworth began with the publication of his poems in 1807, principally from Francis Jeffrey in *The Edinburgh Review*. Jeffrey's onslaught on the 'new school of poetry' (the Lake poets, who had little in common) was long sustained. He conceded that the popularity of *Lyrical Ballads* testified to their merit, but stressed their 'childishness, conceit, and affectation', and claimed that the new volumes confirmed the justice of his previous censure. He hoped that the public would pronounce against the present publication, and gave reasons for accelerating such a verdict. The diction lacked elegance, dignity, and melody; and the subjects (including a leech-gatherer) were ridiculous. He found lines of philosophic weight in 'Ode to Duty' 'utterly without meaning', 'Intimations of Immortality' beyond all doubt 'the most illegible and unintelligible' poem in the collection, and 'Alice Fell' trash, an insult to public taste.

Such blind, insensitive, and inhuman criticism is inevitably self-defeating. Jeffrey was a relic of the age of reason, and much of his Wordsworth appraisal remains a monument to unintelligent arrogance. It voices the prejudices of one who made it his business to stamp out innovation, especially anything that savoured dangerously of sympathy with the 'poor and vulgar'. He had some respect for the sonnets, but trusted condescendingly that Wordsworth would be cured of his follies, and that his 'open violation of the established laws of poetry' would be a warning to others. The frequency of this last form of conservative opposition in contemporary and subsequent criticism makes it clear that Wordsworth's arguments on the extent to which the language of poetry should coincide with prose and rustic speech contributed largely to the hostility of critics for a long period.

Jeffrey resumed the attack the following year, when he contrasted Crabbe with Wordsworth and the 'misguided fraternity' who laboured to 'bring back our poetry to the fantastical oddity, and puling childishness of Withers, Quarles, or Marvel' (*sic*). Unlike Crabbe's rustics, those of the new school expressed 'fantastical' feelings or 'wide and wilful aberrations from ordinary nature'. After making fun of 'The Thorn', he returned to Crabbe.

He is remembered for his opening remark on *The Excursion*, 'This will never do'; and few would wish to take issue with it. His criticism of this work is not all abuse; he admits that it contains some moving stories, and lines and images like gems in 'the rubbish that has been heaped around them'. He thinks it absurd that an old Scottish pedlar should be wise, and dismisses the bulk of the poem as 'a tissue of moral and devotional ravings, in which innumerable changes are rung upon a few very simple and familiar ideas'. He wishes that the tendency to extravagance and puerility to which self-indulgent genius is betrayed had been repressed. There were sympathetic reviews of *The Excursion*, one in *The British Critic*, another by the poet James Montgomery in *The Eclectic Review*; but Jeffrey pursued his onslaught with his attack on *The White Doe of Rylstone*, which combined, he said, 'all the faults, without any of the beauties' of the school of poetry to which it belonged, and revealed the poet in 'a state of low and maudlin imbecility'. By this time, when Leigh Hunt had got over the worst of his personal pique and political prejudice, and had the good sense to rate Wordsworth as our greatest poet 'since the days of Spenser and Milton', Jeffrey was beginning to defeat his ends by ridiculous excess. Instead of taking advantage of opportunities to be discreetly critical, he continued an abusive rearguard action against *The River Duddon*, *Memorials of a Tour on the Continent*, and *Ecclesiastical Sketches*. The chief characteristic of these volumes was their 'emphatic inanity', the author disguising his barren and feeble thought under 'a sententious and assuming manner and a style beyond example verbose and obscure'. In 'Southey and Porson' (*Imaginary Conversations*, 1824) Landor has two comments on Wordsworth which deserve to be remembered: one, that 'clear writers, like clear fountains, do not seem as deep as they are'; the other (with reference to Jeffrey) exhorting us to 'recollect that God in the creation left his noblest creature at the mercy of a serpent'.

Though Hazlitt's vindictiveness against Wordsworth led him to make the most of Jeffrey's more common aspersions, his review of

The Excursion in *The Examiner* was relatively liberal. He appreciates the imaginative presentation of the natural scenes, but decries the 'intense intellectual egotism' which 'swallows up everything', and sees the pedlar, the solitary, and the pastor as 'three persons in one poet', whose mind magnifies 'the littleness of his subject'. He goes out of his way to disagree with Wordsworth's attitude towards country people, and condemns their manners and morals. Hazlitt's accumulating venom was secreted in a footnote to a review prompted by a revival of *Comus* in 1815. Motivated by political prejudice and personal spite, he jibes at the fortitude ascribed to George III in Wordsworth's humanitarian sonnet 'November, 1813', draws attention to the omission of 'The Female Vagrant' from the 1815 edition of his poems, and refers to it as a story which 'very beautifully and affectingly describes the miseries brought on the lower classes by war, in bearing which the said "royal fortitude" is so nobly exercised'.

Wordsworth's indifference seems to have had two effects on Hazlitt: it hardened his assurance of the poet's egocentricity, and it gave an uncontrollable bias to his own criticism. In his 1818 lectures on the English poets, it reaches an almost *saeva indignatio* when he attacks Wordsworth's 'Letter to a Friend of Burns', sneers at his 'wisdom and purity', and concludes with impudent misrepresentation that 'no common link of sympathy' existed between Wordsworth and Burns. He does not finish with his quarry until he has flung it aside with these words:

> His taste is as exclusive and repugnant as his genius. It is because so few things give him pleasure, that he gives pleasure to so few people. It is not every one who can perceive the sublimity of a daisy, or the pathos to be extracted from a withered thorn!

In the last of the lectures, 'On the Living Poets', he attempts some reparation, praising poems in both volumes of *Lyrical Ballads* for their fine, deep vein of thought and feeling. Wordsworth is 'the most original poet now living'. After such praise, the reader must be wary. Hazlitt alludes to his own favourable review of *The Excursion* ('I did what little I could to help to launch it . . .') and, after quoting 'Hart-leap Well' at full length, begins to show his teeth. His criticism of 'the Lake school of poetry' turns into a travesty of Wordsworth's aims in *Lyrical Ballads*, and ends with an enlargement of a view he had blended with his initial praise.

Wordsworth is 'his own subject'; 'he sees nothing but himself and the universe'. 'He hates all science and all art; he hates chemistry, he hates conchology; he hates Voltaire; he hates Sir Isaac Newton . . . he hates all poetry but his own.' It is astonishing that Hazlitt had the insolence to mix so much deliberate untruth with a little truth and much more misrepresentation. In *The Spirit of the Age* he reveals his imposture to a remarkable degree by reversing many of these assertions. He gives Wordsworth high praise, but flattens it by reference to 'the hebetude of his intellect', the meanness or triviality of his subjects, his commonplaceness as a man, and the self-conceit which made him resentful of censure; the fact that the tide had turned in his favour might save him from becoming 'the God of his own idolatry'. Such criticism pursues a private vendetta, and tries unsuccessfully to conceal it by making concessions to prevailing judgments.

Young and impressionable, Keats was much influenced by Hazlitt and his lectures when he asked, with Wordsworth in mind, 'are we to be bullied into a certain philosophy engendered in the whims of an egotist?' The distinction he drew between 'negative capability' (28.xii.17) and 'the Wordsworthian, or egotistical sublime' (27.x.18) is a useful one, however unjust to Wordsworth. A wiser, more balanced appraisal is to be found in Keats's comparison of Wordsworth and Milton (3.v.18). He poses the question 'whether Wordsworth has in truth epic passion, and martyrs himself to the human heart, the main region of his song', then admits that he cannot judge until he has more experience, 'for axioms in philosophy are not axioms till they are proved upon our pulses'. He recognises Wordsworth's genius in exploring those dark passages which must be followed to assess 'the balance of good and evil' in life, and concludes that he had thought more deeply than Milton on the heart and nature of man.

Keats, it would seem, was more capable of looking deeply into Wordsworth's poetry than Coleridge proved to be. If Wordsworth had expected his quondam friend to come to his rescue, he must have been disappointed with *Biographia Literaria* in 1817. Coleridge had given his work much thought; it contains brilliant writing, and its past impressions of Wordsworth often warm into a poetic glow. It is, none the less, the product of an intellectual with wasting assets, dependent mainly on prejudgments, and incapable of sustained intensive criticism. A rambling compilation, it bears eloquent and tedious testimony to undisciplined genius. Nobody can read it without being aware of the writer's complete self-assurance. It contains many admirable expressions on the nature of poetry and the imagination. Not least praiseworthy is the attack on unprincipled reviews, *The Edinburgh Review* in particular, with Jeffrey obviously as his chief target. It could have been more vigorous and open, but it is good to find Coleridge illustrating the idiocy of Jeffrey's judgments, and even coming to the defence of the pedlar as a wise commentator on life in *The Excursion*.

If he had taken half as much trouble to write about Wordsworth's poetical merits as he did on the wrongness of his theories and the defects of his poetry, Wordsworth might have fared better. The controversy he had provoked on the related questions of diction and prose style in poetry had already done him enough harm. With unfortunate lack of tact, Coleridge chose to settle that issue with complete thoroughness. On this question, it should suffice to say, as T. S. Eliot saw, that Wordsworth's meaning was so essentially right that little more needed to be said, and it is a pity that Wordsworth did not clarify his meaning before Coleridge got to work on the subject. Wordsworth must have been exasperated by his irrelevance, his occasional misinterpretation (for example, when he discusses whether the order of words in a poem could be that followed by a rustic), and a summing-up (at the end of xviii) to which no fair-minded reader of the prefaces to *Lyrical Ballads* could ever arrive.

Philosophical chapters lead eventually to the distinction between fancy and imagination. On this Coleridge adds nothing essentially new to what Wordsworth had already written in his essays and, more importantly, in *The Prelude*, including the lines on the child (ii.255–60) which imply that the imagination is a factor in the eternal act of creation. Wordsworth was surely right in insisting that the aggregative and associative power belongs 'as well to the imagination as to the fancy'; the two faculties work differently.

Nobody has written more finely in general terms on certain aspects of Wordsworth's poetry than Coleridge at various points in *Biographia*, but he has blind spots, and there are times when theory deadens his sensibilities. He believes that 'Alice Fell' and 'The Sailor's Mother', for example, would be better in prose, and he is baffled by the author's intention in 'The Idiot Boy' and 'The Thorn'. His comments on the defects and beauties of Wordsworth's poetry are based, unlike those of *The Edinburgh Review*, on critical principles. He repeatedly insists that the defects are small compared with the beauties, but he gives the former greater attention: Wordsworth's unevenness of style is such that he sinks 'too often and too abruptly' into what would be better in prose; he is too matter-of-fact (Coleridge could have chosen better examples than the passage from *The Excursion* to confirm an argument uncertainly shored up by Aristotelian and Horatian principles); he has an undue predilection for the dramatic in some poems (on this dubious proposition Coleridge says little); he is guilty of prolixity, repetition, and eddyings of thought; and lastly, his thoughts and images are sometimes too great for his subject.

Here the quotations from 'I wandered lonely as a cloud' seem quite inoffensive; Coleridge's comment on the child as the 'best philosopher' loses much of its force at a later stage when, in defence of 'Intimations of Immortality', he says that 'the ode was intended for such readers only as had been accustomed . . . to venture at times into the twilight realms of consciousness, and to feel a deep interest in modes of inmost being, to which they know that the attributes of time and space are inapplicable and alien'. His comment on 'thou eye . . . deaf and silent' reflects a spirit markedly different from Ruskin's on the subject of 'blind mouths' in 'Lycidas';[4] and the alleged 'faulty and equivocal syntax of the passage' illustrates the petty criticism to which Coleridge is partial.

The Wordsworthian excellences which he categorizes include an austere purity of language and perfect appropriateness of words to meaning; a correspondent weight and sanity of thoughts and sentiments, which are drawn from the poet's own meditative observation, and which 'are *fresh* and have the dew upon them'; sinewy strength and originality of single lines and paragraphs; meditative pathos (here Coleridge's *idée fixe* does Wordsworth the injustice of restricting attention to him as the *spectator ab extra*, rather than the fellow-sufferer); last and pre-eminently, the gift of imagination in the highest and strictest sense of the word. Coleridge was 'fully convinced' that his criticism 'must conduce, in no mean degree,' to Wordsworth's reputation. It undoubtedly did, but there was a degree of meanness about it. Coleridge had to depend too much on accumulated ideas, and it is notable that he still considered Wordsworth capable of producing 'the FIRST GENUINE PHILOSOPHIC POEM'.

Coleridge's self-assurance assumed various forms, until in the end he seems to have dwelt in an inner world of conviction, remote from the realities of much in Wordsworth's poetry. His self-congratulatory comments on the characteristics of mountain people (8.viii.20) form the premise to an acerbic attack on Words-worth's 'nature-worship' which ill becomes one who had fervently apostrophized 'the one Life within us and abroad' and responded enthusiastically to *The Prelude*, that 'linkéd lay of truth, Of truth profound a sweet continuous lay':

> I will not conceal from *you*, that this inferred dependency of the human soul on accidents of birth-place and abode, together with the vague misty, rather than mystic, confusion of God with the world & the accompanying Nature-worship, of which the asserted dependence forms a part, is the trait in Wordsworth's poetical works that I most dislike, as unhealthful, & denounce as contagious . . .

The remarks that follow show what a decline had taken place in Coleridge's spirit. Magnanimously generous in his creative prime (which coincides with his devotion to 'William, my head and my heart', and Dorothy, 'eager of soul, my most affectionate sister'), he now indulges in shallow witticism and snide suggestion:

> while the odd occasional introduction of the popular, almost the vulgar, religion in his later publications (the popping in, as Hartley says, of the old man with a beard) suggests the painful suspicion of wordly prudence (at best a justification of *masking* truth (which in fact is a falsehood substituted for a truth with-held) on plea of expediency) carried into religion. At least, it conjures up to *my* fancy a sort of *Janus*-head of Spinoza and Dr Watts, or 'I and my brother, the dean'.

In this can be seen Coleridge's displeasure that Wordsworth, instead of being dogmatic, had attempted persuasion by 'dram-atic' means in *The Excursion*. How far the hardening of prepossessions affected Coleridge's criticism of Wordsworth is evident from statements recorded in *Table Talk* (21.vii.32, 16.ii.33). He was confident that 'a great philosophical poet ought always to teach the reader himself as from himself', and had no admiration for argumentation in poetry or 'the practice of ventriloquizing through another's mouth'. This prejudice had already influenced his remarks on Wordsworth's dramatic poems, any success in which he had been reluctant to admit from the first. In *Table Talk* he seems to have become utterly oblivious of them, as well as of such narratives as 'Michael' and that of Ellen in *The Excursion*. Wordsworth and Goethe shared the 'peculiarity of utter non-sympathy with the subjects of their poetry'; they both had 'feeling *for*, but never *with*, their characters'. This categorical assertion is the *ne plus ultra* of the fatal misjudgment which led Coleridge rapturously to encourage concentration on *The Recluse*. Wordsworth would have done better to ignore his friend's advice, and keep his poetry more close to the world of men and women.

More than half a century passed without producing criticism of striking or lasting value on Wordsworth. *The Prelude*, posthumously published in 1850, created interest rather than excitement; it seemed antiquated, as if it belonged to the end of the previous century and could add nothing to the stature of a familiar author. In the 1870s deeper, more disinterested studies of Wordsworth began to appear, in attempts to assess the quality of his work as a whole. The first of these is that of Pater, whose disciplined economy affords a refreshing contrast to the divagations of Coleridge. Pater revised his essay after the publication of 'Home at Grasmere' in 1888. He had been hampered, it seems, by Wordsworth's arrangement of his poems: 'the mixture in his work, as it actually stands, is so perplexed, that one fears to miss the least promising composition even, lest some precious morsel should be lying hidden within.' His task of extricating 'the figure of the more powerful and original poet, hidden away, in part, under those weaker elements in Wordsworth's poetry', produced an essay which is remarkable in range, perspicacity, and depth. He does not see everything in true proportion; swayed undoubtedly by the fragment of *The Recluse*, 'Home at Grasmere', he exaggerates the placidity of Wordsworth's life; similarly he is too restrictive in describing him as the poet of nature 'in its modesty'. (In turning aside from mountain grandeurs, and holding that Wordsworth's genius, with its 'power to open out the soul of apparently little or familiar things, would have found its true test had he become the poet of Surrey', Pater is not as wide of the mark as may appear to readers who associate Surrey with suburbia, for its hills and valleys were not widely different from the Somerset country where Wordsworth enjoyed the spring of his true poetic inspiration.) Finally,

Pater, caught up in Arnold's 'machinery' of ends and means, sees Wordsworth through his own aesthetic spectacles, claiming that his life-aim was contemplation 'in the spirit of art', with no desire 'to teach lessons' or 'stimulate us to noble ends'.

Even so, his sympathetic discernment enables him to see Wordsworth's aims and achievement more surely than any previous critic had done. He draws attention to his importance in the 'pantheistic' movement, the moral and spiritual life he found in natural objects, and the value he attached to 'the almost elementary expression of elementary feelings'. When he states that human life for him was, at first, 'only an additional, accidental grace on an expressive landscape', he has in mind Wordsworth's youthful development as it is traced in *The Prelude*. He does justice to his portrayal of rural life, and finds a resemblance to it in the works of George Sand. Perhaps he exaggerates the passion of Wordsworth's new pastoral world; it is invested with 'a sort of biblical depth and solemnity', and he sees its influence in 'our best modern fiction' (George Eliot's, most probably). He is aware of those subtle relations between Wordsworth's mind and external scenes which have fascinated modern critics, and gives due importance to his higher imaginative moods and their faultless expression, the words being 'thought and feeling; not eloquent, or musical words merely, but that sort of creative language which carries the reality of what it depicts, directly, to the consciousness'.

Wordsworth distrusted ratiocination, and never schematized his beliefs. They were subject to uncertainties and change. How far his faith in the one Life was modified, and how closely it merged with Christianity, is impossible to gauge. It was not in the number of his beliefs that Wordsworth was exceptional, but in their quality, and in the intensity with which they were held, whether religious or political. They were simple and never intellectualized. Leslie Stephen's attempt in 'Wordsworth's Ethics' to show that they 'fall spontaneously into a scientific system' may create a misleading impression. More truth and wisdom will be found in Pater's observation that Wordsworth uses 'bold speculative ideas' with 'a very fine apprehension of the limits within which alone philosophical imaginings have any place in true poetry; and using them only for poetical purposes, is not too careful even to make them consistent with each other'. This is particularly true with reference to the Platonic assumptions or 'seemings' which Wordsworth adopted in 'Intimations'. Reasoned passages, in which he tries to justify certain views, are to be found in *The Excursion* (the most important belonging to an early period), but these have no necessary link with the rest of Wordsworth's poetry. In fact, Stephen's essay does not reflect a system of axiomatic and co-ordinated views; rather, a collection of Wordsworth's beliefs and attitudes to which the author has given some semblance of integration. As John Morley wrote in 1888, 'It is best to be entirely sceptical as to the existence of system and ordered philosophy in Wordsworth.' The poet's religion was based on intimations of ultimates which came, not from philosophizing but from intuitional communion with the natural world.

Wordsworth's views on immortality, for example, are neither consistent nor certain. He presents physical and spiritual aspects in 'A slumber did my spirit seal' and 'Lines' on the expected death of Fox. If his faith 'looks through death', what are the implications of 'the sunless land' in 'Extempore Effusion upon the Death of James Hogg' and 'the approach of all-involving night' in 'Ejaculation', the penultimate poem in *Ecclesiastical Sonnets*? 'The Primrose of the Rock' (ll.42−7) is much more confident, but Wordsworth's faith could not withstand the shock of Tom Monkhouse's death. In 'O dearer far than light and life are dear' he admits his apprehension that 'friends, by death disjoined, may meet no more', and turns to Mary for spiritual comfort. He approached death, it seems, not with assurance but hope, as may be seen in his 'Conclusion' to *The River Duddon* ('Prepared, in peace of heart, in calm of mind And soul, to mingle with eternity') and in 'Thoughts on the Seasons' ('So may our autumn blend With hoary winter, and life touch, Through heaven-born hope, her end!').

The main interest of Stephen's essay derives from its influence, particularly on the calculations of Matthew Arnold, who reached the conclusion that, if Wordsworth was to occupy the high place he merited in public esteem, he needed 'to be relieved of the poetical baggage' which encumbered him. With considerable emphasis and justification he added his belief that Wordsworth's poems 'will never produce their due effect until they are freed from their present artificial arrangement, and grouped more naturally'. (How naturally, following Greek genres, Arnold arranged the selection which his essay introduced in 1879 is open to question.) After urging that 'poetry is at bottom a criticism of life', and that 'the greatness of a poet lies in his powerful and beautiful application of ideas to life, − to the question: How to live' (which is very much Wordsworth's subject), he adduces Stephen's findings as typical of 'the fervent Wordsworthian', and maintains that 'the disinterested lover of poetry' can have no place for Wordsworth's philosophy. He refers erroneously to the intimations of 'the famous Ode' as 'those corner-stones of the supposed philosophic system of Wordsworth', and quotes from *The Excursion* to prove how inimical to poetic truth philosophy can be. He does not show, as could easily be done, that some of Wordsworth's greatest poems are philosophical to a high degree. One does not have to be a systematic philosopher to write philosophical poetry, in which thought on life is inseparable from deep feeling, and imaginatively conveyed.[5]

Arnold's conclusions are oversimplified. He sees Wordsworth's poetry as part of a 'great movement of feeling', not of mind (he 'cared little for books, and disparaged Goethe'). His greatness is due to the extraordinary power with which he feels 'joy in widest commonalty spread'. His best poetry is inevitable; he has no style; it is as if nature takes the pen out of his hand, and writes for him with 'her own bare, sheer, penetrating power'. Except for the generalization that 'wherever we meet with the successful balance, in Wordsworth, of profound truth of subject with profound truth of execution, he is unique' (which is hardly surprising), the rest is adventitious. The same oversimplification characterizes reflections on Wordsworth in 'Memorial Verses': 'He laid us as we lay at birth On the cool flowery lap of earth; Smiles broke from us and we had ease.' He speaks of 'Wordsworth's healing power', a quality not to be discounted in a poet who, recognising that hope is a dominant characteristic of life, dared to proclaim it. In an 'iron time Of doubts, disputes, distractions, fears', Arnold took comfort from his predecessor's fortitude and patient cheer. He seems to have assumed that Wordsworth did not have to face greater stresses, and to have undervalued his manliness and philosophical insight, concluding that he had 'put by' the 'cloud of mortal destiny'. With sharper definition, in 'Obermann', he affirms that 'Wordsworth's eyes avert their ken from half of human fate'. It would be more true to say that Arnold's eyes averted their ken from half of the world reflected in Wordsworth's poetry.

Full-length scholarly works on Wordsworth began more than a century ago, but no new study of great importance for modern readers appeared before A. C. Bradley's essay. It is surprisingly wide-ranging, but notable for certain emphases which have exerted a strong critical influence. He cannot agree with Arnold that the reason for Wordsworth's greatness is simple, or that he ignores half of human fate:

> Unquestionably then he saw the cloud of destiny, and he did not avert his eyes from it. Nor did he pretend to understand its darkness. The world was to him in the end 'this unintelligible world', and the only 'adequate support for the calamities of mortal life' was faith. But he was profoundly impressed, through the experience of his own years of crisis, alike by the dangers of despondency, and by the superficiality of the views which it engenders.

Bradley's wise observation reflects a truth to life which is often ignored. He is more difficult to follow when he states that the main reason for doubting whether Wordsworth could have reached his highest level in love poetry is that 'he did not strongly feel — perhaps hardly felt at all — that the _passion_ of love is a way into the Infinite'. This limitation is probably true of some of the finest writers of love lyrics, whatever the link between spiritual love and the Infinite in the poetry of Dante or between physical love and the Infinite in the poetry and prose of D. H. Lawrence. Unlike Hazlitt, Bradley rightly insists on Wordsworth's sympathetic tolerance in questions of morality, but one wonders whether it extended as far as the anti-respectability of Browning's deliberately provocative 'antinomian' attitudes. Disagreeing with Pater's view that Wordsworth is the poet of nature in her modesty, Bradley emphasizes and illustrates the 'mystic', 'visionary', and 'sublime' aspects of the poetry in which Wordsworth excels.

It is not always an easy area in which to draw conclusions. Wordsworth undoubtedly believed that the 'impulses of deeper birth' which came to him in solitude were intimations of the universal Soul, but the question whether he was a mystic, or to what degree, seems unanswerable. Some of the experiences to which Bradley refers suggest the supervention of momentary trancelike states when 'bodily eyes were utterly forgotten'. Repeatedly, it seems, the external scene became 'a prospect in the mind' of Wordsworth. This explains those impressions, imagined or remembered, in his poetical account of his meeting with the leech-gatherer, and of his sudden interest in the more universal or symbolic implications of the label attached to the blind beggar who caught his attention as he wandered with the crowd in a London street, thinking that everyone he saw was an unknown, 'a mystery'. His mind turned round 'as with the might of waters', and he looked at the fixed face and sightless eyes 'as if admonished from another world'. No visionary experience is implied; it was 'as if . . .'. Similarly, after listening to the leech-gatherer, Wordsworth's mind turns inwards, towards his former thoughts; before they redefine themselves, the whole body of the man becomes like one met in a dream, or like one sent from some far region to give strength 'by apt admonishment'. The dream image is transitional in an imaginative process of heightening what might be called a 'heaven-sent' example. In the passage describing the scene encountered after crossing the Alps, the changing features (suggesting energy and continuity, or life and eternity) are like workings of one mind, or like signs of the great Apocalypse . . . In a succession of similitudes, the poet's imagination invests a recollected scene with 'types and symbols of Eternity'. He is reminded of the eternal act of creation; he does not recall a mystical experience.

It would be a mistake to ignore Aldous Huxley's essay 'Wordsworth in the Tropics', or assume that it is the last word on Wordsworth's religion. Its premises may seem incontrovertible. Any 'pantheistic' worshipper of nature is 'liable to have his religious convictions somewhat rudely disturbed' in the tropics, where nature is alien or hostile or terrifying. The traveller in an equatorial jungle experiences not a sense of solitude but 'the uneasy feeling that he is an alien in the midst of an innumerable throng of hostile beings'. 'Wordsworthian adoration of Nature' is possible, Huxley continues, only in a country where nature has been wholly or almost wholly enslaved by man, and only for 'those who are prepared to falsify their immediate intuitions of Nature'. 'Adoration', it should be observed, is used pejoratively, and does not represent the breadth and depth of Wordsworth's attitude to nature. Huxley's second conclusion cannot be substantiated; Wordsworth was not false to his intuitions (even if they were wrongly conceived), nor was he ignorant of nature. The schoolboy who helped to destroy ravens' eggs did not need to be told that nature was red in tooth and claw; horrors consequent on the operation of natural law in the Alps are faced unflinchingly in *Descriptive Sketches*; and their association with 'the God of peace and love' in 'Ode, 1815', theologically strange though it be, does not suggest that Wordsworth's faith was based on 'the cosy sublimities of the Lake District'.

The tragedy of the Greens in 1808 could no more be ignored than the loss of Wordsworth's brother John at sea. The cloud of destiny which the poet saw and pondered, without pretending (in Bradley's words) to understand its darkness, included nature's terrors and the calamities befalling man more generally. When Huxley wrote his essay, he was influenced by his friend D. H. Lawrence, but Lawrence would not have agreed with his major contention. He knew the terrors of the natural world, but believed to the end of his life in a universal spirit, and sought communion with it. 'One could say "God", but the word "God" is somehow tainted. But', he continued, 'there *is* a flame or a Life Everlasting wreathing through the cosmos for ever and giving us our renewal, once we can get in touch with it.'[6] Lawrence's faith is not radically different from Wordsworth's, and both were convinced that science does not hold the key to life.

If nature seems, as a result of scientific discovery, to be neutral or even hostile to man, the question is not relevant to the appreciation of Wordsworth's poetry. Whether nature does or does not kindle or restrain, nothing can destroy or weaken those imaginative experiences which he communicates to illustrate the ministry which Nature employed (as he believed, at the height of his power) in moulding his moral being. Nor, as has been hinted earlier, is Wordsworth's Nature wholly spiritless or inanimate today, since it is often inseparable from human life. Additionally, as in memories of his childhood guilt, and in 'Peter Bell', it represents an externalization of the internal reality; its workings are psychological.

Huxley presents his case cleverly but misleadingly. He identifies the 'something far more deeply interfused' with 'the god of Anglicanism', and argues that such a belief made 'the world seem delightfully cosy'. Then, the Lawrentian bias directing his course, he tells us that, to live well, one must live 'with the whole being – with the body and the instincts, as well as with the conscious mind'; the poet, as Blake remarked of Milton, should be 'of the devil's party without knowing it'. Wordsworth (Huxley continues) betrayed his nature, and deserted to the side of the angels. In consequence the poet was doomed; he became a philosopher, and interpreted nature 'in terms of a divine, anglican unity', living 'comfortably at home with a man-made and, therefore, thoroughly comprehensive system'. This change was 'symptomatic of his general apostasy'. Huxley took from literary tradition what suited his purpose, in particular the systematic philosophy and the apostasy. He was skating on thin ice, for he had clearly not made a study of Wordsworth. His *parti pris* interpretation of the poet's remark after gazing on the sculpture of Cupid and Psyche (as reported by Haydon) is of little moment; but what are we to think of a writer who pretends that Wordsworth's decline began with his religious love of nature, and who concludes that his poetry would have benefited had he 'learned once more to treat Nature naturally, as he treated it in his youth'? The only natural poetry of any consequence in Wordsworth's pre-religious period is *An Evening Walk* and *Descriptive Sketches*. Huxley's lack of chronological sense makes nonsense of his comments on Wordsworth's poetry; he was led astray principally by his identification of 'the one Life' with 'the god of Anglicanism'.

One cannot expect a revival of religion centred in the soul of nature such as that which made God real for William Hale White. Yet nature cannot be alien or neutral, since man is part of it. Wordsworth's nature is humanized to a higher degree than is commonly thought. The commingling of the human spirit with the universal is expressly the subject of 'Lines' on the expected death of Fox; it is implicit in the sonnets on Toussaint l'Ouverture and the departure of Scott for Naples. The assumption of a national spiritual legacy, of Powers working for good or ill, is probably as inherent in Wordsworth's fears for England as it was in the traditional link between freedom and mountainous regions. Such imponderables are of perennial interest. Those who think 'there is nothing left remarkable beneath the visiting moon' are less wise than Wordsworth, for the source of life and universal energy is a mystery, and any religion inadequately related to it is frail.

Conclusion

Though it recalls Hamlet, Pope's philosophical summing-up of man as the glory, jest, and riddle of the world is not ironical; it reflects the age of reason and considerably less optimistic expectations of the human race than those of Wordsworth inspired by 'reason in her highest mood'. Both poets thought the cosmos beyond scientific explanation, but Wordsworth's view of God as the soul of universal nature was no rationalization like his predecessor's. To him the 'something far more deeply interfused' was an elevating presence. Man's highest being was spiritual; it depended not merely on intellectual growth, but on the development of imagination, feeling, intuition, and love. Wordsworth's 'converse with the spiritual world' (the highest reach of the imagination) was the offspring of seventeenth-century Christian Platonism and eighteenth-century reason; and Pope's vast chain of Being remained central to it (Pr.viii.485–94):

> In the midst stood man,
> Outwardly, inwardly contemplated,
> As, of all visible natures, crown, though born
> Of dust, and kindred to the worm; a being,
> Both in perception and discernment, first
> In every capability of rapture,
> Through the divine effect of power and love;
> As, more than anything we know, instinct
> With godhead, and by reason and by will,
> Acknowledging dependency sublime.

At the end of *The Prelude* Wordsworth rests his hope of man's redemption on the twin development of the imagination and love or altruism; they are inseparable. 'By love subsists all lasting grandeur', and man's completion comes when he has risen 'to the

316

height of feeling intellect'. Finally, and more euphorically, he looks forward to man's redemption through the imagination, the human mind being potentially 'more divine' and 'a thousand times more beautiful' than the earth on which he dwells. It is for this reason, more than any other, that the main region of his prospective song was the mind of man.

Thinking of those memorable boyhood experiences he had already described, he claims (Pr.iii.173ff.) to have spoken of 'genius, power, creation, and divinity itself'; not of outward things, but of his heart and youthful mind. He regards with awe the 'might of souls' while yet (in terms of 'Intimations') 'the yoke of earth is new to them'; it is a subject meet for 'heroic argument' (an anticipation of his 'prospectus'), but on the whole it is beyond the reach of words. Everyone will have known such godlike hours, and felt what we inherit 'as natural beings in the strength of Nature'. 'The vision and the faculty divine', as the imagination is described in *The Excursion*, is the 'birthright of our being' (Pr.ii.271).

The question of retrospective attribution has already been raised. How much of 'the glory and the dream' investing recollections of childhood is due to transmutations effected in the mind during the course of time; how indissociable, in fact, are memory and imagination? It would be erroneous to assume that the boyhood experiences described by Wordsworth are recalled with fidelity, and not modified by associated thoughts and moods, consciously and subconsciously operative during the intervening years. His awareness of the creative process of memory is implied in his use of 'impregnations' (Pr.viii.632ff.). He refers to other, immediate, processes, the observer becoming spellbound by a scene, until it seems to become part of oneself, 'a dream, a prospect in the mind'; or the scene enters 'unawares' into the mind, to emerge clearly in recollection (Pr.ii.348–52, v.384–8). The 'fallings from us, vanishings' of a boy who often grasped a wall or tree to recall himself from 'an abyss of idealism' seem to require a psycho-physical rather than a mystical explanation; and the tendency in modern criticism to equate 'visionary' with 'mystical' with reference to too many of Wordsworth's boyhood memories is unfortunate. Especially is this true of the 'spots of time' passages which he transferred to a late section of *The Prelude*. Close study of the text shows that their visionary essence came not from intimations of immortality (of the infinite, to be more exact) in the initial experiences, but from the working of pleasurable or fearful emotions there and then, and in the course of time. The recollections are not endowed with extra-temporal or extra-sensory effects; they are 'islands in the unnavigable depth Of our departed time' (PR.641).

Misinterpretation of Wordsworth's comment on the 'spots of time' in which he found 'a renovating virtue' (Pr.xii.208ff.) has led to more serious errors. If he drinks from them 'as at a fountain' (he wrote this as early as 1799), it is not because they are the fountain-light of *all* his day, like those intimations of the invisible world and of 'God, who is our home'. The experiences he refers to are based on 'outward sense', and illustrate the effect of feeling in their imaginative re-creation:

> This efficacious spirit chiefly lurks
> Among those passages of life that give
> Profoundest knowledge to what point, and how,
> The mind is lord and master − outward sense
> The obedient servant of her will.

Wordsworth had found that his imagination was stimulated by imaginative scenes which came to mind from his own life; they were 'scattered everywhere' from his 'first childhood' onwards. He regrets that as he grows older these 'hiding-places of man's power' (of 'creation and divinity itself', as he states elsewhere) open only to close as he attempts to 'approach' them. Once he recalled them clearly; now he sees them by glimpses; he fears they will weaken with age. Neither here nor in 'Intimations of Immortality' is there any thought of poetic decline. Such, however, is a common reading, well illustrated in F. R. Leavis's *Revaluation*, where it is stated that the Wordsworth of 'Ode to Duty' had 'seen the hiding-places of his power close', and 'the exquisitely fine and sensitive organization of the poet no longer informed and controlled his pen'.

If we consider the subjects which inspired Wordsworth during the *annus mirabilis* of 1797−8, no connection between the 'visionary gleam' of his boyhood and his poetical power will be found. The master light of his seeing remained to be defined in the triumphant conclusion of *The Prelude*; it is inseparable from the 'mighty mind' and 'majestic intellect' which is imaged in the scene from the top of Snowdon. It is a power which derives its genius from the Deity, and feeds on infinity; it knows the grandeur which springs from spiritual and intellectual love. This 'amplitude of mind' comes with maturity. The 'factitiousness' in 'Intimations' of which Dr Leaves complains is inherent in the contrived explanation of the fading 'vision splendid'. Wordsworth's mature poetic strength is to be found in his affirmations relative to the 'years that bring the philosophic mind', and they carry an impressive weight of conviction.

It would be exceedingly difficult to diagnose when Wordsworth's poetic genius began to fail. One can point to various factors which help to explain his decline: growing family responsibilities and duties (such as the Stamp-Distributorship) which made it impossible to think long and deeply on poetical subjects, as he had been able to do; accompanying this, a facility in verse achieved after years of toil, which tended to dull critical perception; the recurring affliction of trachoma which made it difficult to read or write at length for much of the second half of his life; growing discouragement for a long period from the continued hostility of critics; and post-war political anxieties that were often obsessionally distracting. The major obstacle in the way of Wordsworth's progress, however, was *The Recluse*, and the greatest misfortune in his poetical career was his acceptance of Coleridge's advice to write a great philosophic poem. Had they not thought so highly of each other's genius, this would not have happened. As it was, Wordsworth wasted the greater part of his best years on a subject so vast and vague that he thought nothing could be foreign to it. Flattery and euphoria may have got the better of his judgment at first, and a sense of duty and fear of failure may have caused him to perservere; otherwise it is strange that one usually so independent in judgment allowed a task for which he had less and less appetite to preoccupy him for long periods with no prospect of conclusion. Had he gone his own way, the probability is that nothing of value in *The Prelude* and *The Excursion* would have been lost. He could have dealt more effectively with smaller units, and given more attention to human situations, instead of philosophizing at length. 'The Ruined Cottage', for example, would have been more satisfactory had it been completed outside a context which was intended to show the unnaturalness of immoderately protracted grief. Wordsworth (who has one passage at least which manifests ability to write imaginatively of great voyages) might have proved capable of writing well, if not at epic length, on some of the more epic subjects mentioned in his introduction to *The Prelude*.

The Recluse became his albatross; he regarded its completion as a duty, to Coleridge, to his family, and to mankind; its continual deferment sowed a sense of guilt and failure, thereby sapping his creative zest for long periods. Except in the ordinary sense of the word (one's attitude to life), he was not a philosopher; he tended to scorn the analytical mind. Coleridge's recommendation 'to deliver upon authority' and as a *spectator ab extra* 'a system of philosophy' which would show the way of redemption for mankind indicates a misjudgment of the poetic role. Its inimicality to poetry is further suggested in a letter on *The Excursion* (30.v.15), where Coleridge summarizes his plan as a discussion of the human faculties, an affirmation of 'a Fall in some sense, as a fact', and 'a grand didactic swell on the necessary identity of a true philosophy with true religion' as a substitute for the 'sandy sophisms of Locke, and the mechanic dogmatists'. How remote from poetry the subject could become may be guessed from some of the *Biographia* chapters.

For many years after concluding 'Intimations' Wordsworth showed that he was able to rise to subjects which appealed to him; yet the completion of this ode is commonly associated with the inception of his decline. His 'Ode to Duty' belongs to the same period, and Leavis hazards the guess that 'few to whom Wordsworth matters would grieve much if some very inferior bard were proved to have written it'. Such a boomerang statement makes one wonder how far and how deeply its author appreciated the best of Wordsworth's poetry. Only a very great poet could have written lyrically, imaginatively, and personally on such a mature subject, with the control and distinction which inform this poem. Leavis finds evidence of Wordsworth's decline in the patriotic sonnets which were under way in 1802. 'The worst of them', he says (referring to 'It is not to be thought of'), 'are lamentable clap-trap, and the best, even if they are distinguished declamation, are hardly distinguished poetry'. Some political animus against patriotic poetry may be suspected here. There is a single touch of jingoism in the sonnet which caused offence, but Wordsworth rarely slipped into it; he was thinking with some pride of England's record in the cause of liberty compared with that of other nations. His was not a popular patriotism; it was above war and conquest, and appealed to magnanimity. He was highly critical, knowing that genuine freedom and national greatness depend on moral and spiritual forces which are rarely exerted. On this subject he never wrote clap-trap; there are far more soul-animating strains in his patriotic sonnets than will be found in Milton's.

But for his preoccupation with *The Recluse*, the range of Wordsworth's poetry might have increased. It contains a greater variety than is usually assumed, or can be briefly indicated; in, for example, such different modes as 'The Thorn' and 'The Idiot Boy', 'Tintern Abbey' and 'Yew-trees', 'Michael' and 'The Afflic-tion of Margaret', 'A slumber did my spirit seal' and 'Extempore Effusion upon the Death of James Hogg', 'Elegiac Stanzas' (suggested by Peele Castle) and 'The Waggoner', 'Surprised by joy' and 'Mutability', 'Hart-leap Well' and 'Laodamia', 'Peter Bell' and 'The Egyptian Maid'. Entirely original, the last is a delightful romance, as astonishing in the fineness of its texture as is its con-tinued neglect. In addition to most, if not all, of the above poems, the best of Wordsworth would contain sonnets on many subjects, the form being one in which he excelled at least as often as Shakes-peare, and far more often than any other English poet. To these must be added an impressive selection of lyrics, containing some of Wordsworth's supremely finished work; *The White Doe of Rylstone*, a poem of disciplined execution on a subject deeper and more universally significant than all the romantic allure and trappings of verse romances by Byron and Scott; the whole of the two-part opening of *The Prelude* which was concluded in 1799, and several passages from the remainder of that work. Many would think the whole indispensable; despite its unevenness, it is Wordsworth's greatest achievement, and the earlier and later versions afford the best guide to his development and thought.

Part of Wordsworth's lasting appeal comes from his poetic per-sonality. Not one of our greatest poets has written so largely or more sincerely on his own experience and thoughts. This is an advantage despite the longueurs to which his philosophizing is prone (whether ventriloquized or adapted) in *The Excursion*. Most of those who knew Wordsworth recognised his readiness to listen and consider other people's views. *The Excursion* does not reveal a dogmatist but an author who realized that convictions were not to be changed lightly or reasoned away. Aware that his poetry had the traditional aim of instructing as well as of pleasing, he sought to present his views, 'not standing upon external testimony, but carried alive into the human heart by passion', through 'nature' or experience, whether personal or imaginary, individual or national. Rejecting Coleridge's advice, he therefore evaded lengthy dogmatizing in *The Excursion* for a more dramatic narrative. Nor could he publish *The Prelude* in his lifetime; it was 'a thing unprecedented in literary history that a man should talk so much about himself'. He wrote it from 'real humility' and not 'self-conceit', intending it as an introduction to the major work for which he was yet inadequate. Its background and self-exploration are invaluable. The personal note is strong elsewhere in his poetry, from childhood to manhood, in joy and in sorrow; even in the most tedious I.F. notes there are passages of delightful candour and significance which few would wish to miss.

Combined with his veneration for man as man, this sincerity places him (as it does Burns) far ahead of his generation. His later political apprehensions should be forgiven, for Wordsworth never wavered in the cause of enlightened advance to democracy; his distinction between the public and the people remained unshaken. It is reflected in his remarks (Pr.xiii.186ff.) on the successful books of his age:

> seeking their reward
> From judgments of the wealthy few, who see
> By artificial lights; how they debase
> The many for the pleasure of those few;
> Effeminately level down the truth
> To certain general notions . . .
> flattering self-conceit with words,
> That, while they most ambitiously set forth
> Extrinsic differences, the outward marks
> Whereby society has parted man
> From man, neglect the universal heart.

A study of Wordsworth reminds us of the perils of political movements and revolutionary zeal among the unenlightened. He knew better than most people of his age or ours that freedom is always liable to exploitation, until the major issues of life are realized and people act in the belief that 'we have all of us one human heart'.

Scepticism may help to sharpen our interest in the stranger aspects of Wordsworth's natural religion. Whatever the reason, solitude in nature such as he knew enables many of us to think more calmly and clearly about life, and we may therefore experience some of those common feelings which were basic to his faith. One question which arises in studying Wordsworth is whether the inspiring belief which he found in nature changed intrinsically as it lost its freshness. There is no evidence that it did, though he tended after 1802–4 to express it more frequently in terms of orthodox Christian belief. A remarkable passage in a letter to Sir George Beaumont (28.v.25) ends with reflection on the recent spring; never had he relished the beauties of the season more highly, and he thought what 'manifold reason' they had for gratitude to Providence:

> Theologians may puzzle their heads about dogmas as they will; the religion of gratitude cannot mislead us. Of that we are sure; and gratitude is the handmaid to hope, and hope the harbinger to faith. I look abroad upon Nature, I think of the best part of our species, I lean upon my friends, and I meditate upon the Scriptures, especially the Gospel of St John; and my creed rises up of itself with the ease of an exhalation, yet a fabric of adamant.

This affirmation ends as strongly as that of 'Tintern Abbey', but it is more reasoned and qualified. Its distinguishing feature is the Johannine gospel, with its emphasis on God as the spirit of love working for good. For Wordsworth this spirit worked through the whole of the creation, its most crucial link being with man as part of nature. Seen as 'a universal birth' in 1798, it is proclaimed in both *The Prelude* and *The Excursion* as man's highest possession: 'Life, I repeat, is energy of love Divine or human; exercised in pain, In strife, in tribulation' (Ex.v.1012–14). The spirit of nature helped to develop Wordsworth's boyhood and character and his mature imagination; it includes human aspirations, sympathies, and sense of right and wrong. The powers promoting the cause of Toussaint l'Ouverture exist in the air, earth, and skies as well as in the hearts and minds of men; as late as 1831, Wordsworth believed that 'spirits of Power' mourning the departure of stricken genius from Abbotsford for Naples were in league with 'the world's good wishes'. The new world he postulates for 'higher minds' through imaginative development comes from mutations which they, 'Willing to work and be wrought upon', both 'send abroad' and 'catch'. By nature's spirit they become Powers; the spiritual nature of their imagination maintains 'A balance, an ennobling inter-change Of action from without and from within' (Pr.xiii.367–78, xiv.86–113).

In the post-war years of growing political rancour and industrialism, there must have been times when Wordsworth felt he had pitched his hopes of mankind too high, when the mood of 'The world is too much with us' returned, with the discouraging certainty that most people saw little in nature and were more spiritually dead therefore than the pagan Greeks.

It is often thought that Wordsworth's stature as man and poet is diminished by his optimism: 'We live by admiration, hope, and love.' So strong was this conviction that hope became for him 'the paramount *duty* that Heaven lays' on 'man's suffering heart'. Some may see this as a facile escape from reality, and find more wisdom in Keats's 'Where but to think is to be full of sorrow' or in Hardy's Darwinian outlook; yet the course of man's progress bears continual witness to the strength of 'love, and man's unconquerable mind'. Darwinism may dispel some illusions about nature, but it does not establish the wisdom of pessimism. For, as Hardy states memorably, the whole of nature, from the leaf on the tree to the titled lady at the ball, lives instinctively with 'the determination to enjoy'. Wordsworth's hopeful philosophy is rooted in life; he had known suffering and, like Hardy, had wondered how it could be consonant with belief in Providence. He had asked whether the 'great Cause and Ruler of things' could have as much love as the human race, but his belief in Immanence made him think of the human soul as it is, 'by nature and gift of God', and admire the goodness, courage, and disinterested love he saw in people everywhere. There could have been nothing narrow or shallow in one who realized 'the dread strife Of poor humanity's afflicted will Struggling in vain with ruthless destiny'. Human perception is limited, and wisdom is on the side of the Wordsworth who opposed the confident utilitarian rationalism of his age, and who held that 'faith is the highest individual experience, because it conquers the pride of the understanding − man's greatest foe'.[7]

Whatever allowance can be made for Wordsworth's failure, in deference to Coleridge, to follow his own star for long periods during his prime, his achievement in later years is disappointing. He had become too passive as a poet, too ready to accept what subjects came to hand, a victim perhaps of his own philosophy of nature: 'Think you . . . That nothing of itself will come, But we must still be seeking?' The only poetic work for which he studied at length was *Ecclesiastical Sonnets*; he wished to write a poem on the life and character of St Francis but was unable to find the requisite books when 'the heat' was upon him. The rarity of this kind of impulse gives some support to Arnold's criticism that Wordsworth, like other poets of his period, 'did not know enough'. Arnold had an axe to grind, and it should not be assumed that Wordsworth was ignorant of the world because he lived in the Lake District; many notable people were impressed by his knowledge and his ability to discuss the pros and cons of a wide range of topics. For all that, few could disagree with Arnold's conclusion that Words-worth's poetry lacks completeness; the expectations roused by both volumes of *Lyrical Ballads*, especially in sympathetic pictures of human life, were not fulfilled. T. S. Eliot expressed his dissatisfaction more dismissively, and in his peculiar way: Wordsworth 'had no ghastly shadows at his back, no Eumenides to pursue him; or if he did, he gave no sign and took no notice; and he went droning on the still sad music of infirmity to the verge of the grave'. Eliot generalizes, as he is apt to do, from his own experience, and his impatience is uncritical. Whatever Wordsworth needed to produce a great poem, it was not the Eumenides; and it is clear that, until his very last years, poetry was latent in him but insufficiently awakened through dearth of the right subjects.

Had he pursued the true course of his genius more vigorously in his later years, he would have written more to illustrate the indomitable spirit of man, and those human qualities on which his hopes rested. It is to his credit that, although he did not carry out his programme nearly as far as could be wished, he made his key subject the mind of man, with its propensities for good and evil, and the imaginative awakening of spiritual love for the benefit of mankind. No one has posed the problem more courageously. His message and the humanitarianism of much that lives in his poetry, profoundly personal or narrative or dramatically lyrical, were not lost on the more scientifically minded George Eliot, who grappled with the human condition in her own humanistic way in novel after novel. The altruistic tradition that stems largely from Words-worth leads through George Eliot to Thomas Hardy. 'We go to Wordsworth's poetry for something more lasting than pleasure, and for something more human than beauty', Herbert Read wrote, after making the less obvious statement that 'his singular distinction is the centrality and traditional validity of his philosophical faith'.[8]

Few writers agree on Wordsworth's singular distinction. If it is not to be found where Matthew Arnold placed it, in 'the extraordinary power with which Wordsworth feels the joys offered to us in nature' and 'in the simple primary affections and duties', there may be more justification for linking it with the power of the poet's 'feeling intellect', as John Stuart Mill claimed implicity in his *Autobiography*:

> What made Wordsworth's poems a medicine for my state of mind was that they expressed, not mere outward beauty, but states of feeling, and of thought coloured by feeling, under the excitement of beauty. They seemed to be the very culture of the feelings, which I was in quest of.

Perhaps we tend to exaggerate the aspect of his poetry which appealed most to the poet himself: 'the spirituality with which I have endeavoured to invest the material universe, and the moral relations under which I have wished to exhibit its most ordinary appearances' (1.vii.45). John Morley in 1888 thought Wordsworth's 'distinguishing title to fame and gratitude' lay in 'the extraordinary strenuousness, sincerity, and insight with which he first idealises and glorifies the vast universe around us', making it 'an animate presence, intermingling with our works, pouring its companionable spirit about us, and "breathing grandeur upon the very humblest face of human life"'. Very rightly he balanced this assessment with another from Ruskin's *Modern Painters*: 'Wordsworth's distinctive work was a war with pomp and pretence, and a display of the majesty of simple feelings and humble hearts, together with high reflective truth in his analysis of the courses of policies and ways of men; without these, his love of nature would have been comparatively worthless.'

His interest in nature was subordinate to his interest in human welfare. She linked the human soul that through him ran to her fair works, only to make him think grievously on what man had made of man. His sympathies, strengthened by revolutionary idealism, and in line with 'the great moving spirit of things', were consistently humanitarian and democratic in principle. How significant his contribution to the great tradition of English literature has been may be judged from a comparison of Fielding's attitude towards rustics in *Tom Jones* (1749) and George Eliot's more than a century later in *Adam Bede*. Like Scott, Wordsworth had the highest regard for the virtues of ordinary country people and for the moving quality of their linguistic inheritance. George Eliot's reverence and realism owe much to both, but no writer influenced her basic development and outlook more than Wordsworth.

He is a poet of sense and sensibility to an unusual degree. Directed by reason and truth to human nature, his poetry combines thought, imagination, and feeling along a human scale which extends from great issues to little things of lasting appeal. If he is an adult, rather than popular, poet, it is because he chose not to make the moving accident his trade, but to write for thinking hearts. His imaginative sweep is through space and time. He sees the individual as a traveller between life and death, and Kilchurn Castle as a memorial to the majesty of Time. The individual is part of nature's universe; Time sees the generations pass. For them the 'pangs' and 'the dread strife of poor humanity's afflicted will' are ready. As in external nature, all is change but continuity. The evolution of civilization, through enlightened freedom and altruism, is by implication the ultimate aim to which Wordsworth's thought most persistently turns; it springs from a hope which never seeks to evade vicissitude and human weakness. Believing in the power of ideas, and convinced (like Seneca) 'how poor a thing is man' unless he can rise above himself (Ex.iv.330–1), he appeals to the best in mankind. Life becomes worthy if we can achieve something that will 'serve the future hour', and if 'Through love, through hope, and faith's transcendent dower, We feel that we are greater than we know'. Wordsworth's greatness is well-reflected in what he wrote on Sir Joshua Reynolds (20.vii.04): 'It is such an animating sight to see a man of genius, regardless of temporary gains whether of money or praise, fixing his attention solely upon what is intrinsically interesting and permanent, and finding his happiness in an entire devotion of himself to such pursuits as shall most ennoble human nature.'

Wordsworth rescued poetry from artificiality and pretentiousness. More than any other poet, he made blank verse a living medium, whether in language of moving simplicity or in grander styles. His artistry is to be found most in shorter forms, the sonnet and lyrics particularly, as well as in passages which engaged his whole interest. Works of great length were beyond his management: *The Prelude* combines the intensive, the diffuse, the prosaic, and the highly imaginative; *The Excursion* sprawls as a whole, and is connected rather than integrated. Yet few poets have been as successful in the technical changes they have attempted. In this respect Wordsworth's influence on English poetry has been considerable, especially on diction and approximations to speech order and rhythms. The ideal which he repeatedly accomplished over a long period is envisaged in the closing lines of a fragment (PR.lvi, footnote) which belongs to the 1798–1800 period:

> In that considerate and laborious work
> That patience which, admitting no neglect,
> By slow creation, doth impart to speech
> Outline and substance even, till it has given
> A function kindred to organic power,
> The vital spirit of a perfect form.

The extent of Wordsworth's greatness will not be felt until he is better known. A necessary step in this direction is the removal of his poems from the shackling divisions in which he placed them, and where many have remained hidden from all but a relatively small number of scholars. Setting aside *The Prelude* and *The Excursion* for separate volumes, and a collection of larger items from *An Evening Walk*, *Descriptive Sketches*, and *The Borderers* onwards, the remainder of the poems would benefit considerably from being arranged as far as possible in chronological order. The same principle applies to anthologies. If full justice were done to Wordsworth, he would require a selection of greater length than would any other English poet.

Notes

1. Wordsworth was on his way to his 'father's house' (PR.23,*app.crit.*), probably in the summer of 1781, when his elder brother was ill at Hawkshead. On 1 July Mr Cookson's servant paid the Hawkshead accounts, and William probably accompanied him late in the afternoon on his return journey to Penrith, before being taken to Cockermouth. See Mary Wedd, 'Wordsworth's Stolen Boat', *The Wordsworth Circle*, XI.4, Autumn 1980.
2. T. W. Thompson (ed. R. Woof), *Wordsworth's Hawkshead*, London, 1970, pp. 211–15.
3. Compare Pr.i.425–63, where the cottage lights and village clock of Hawkshead are mingled with precipices, cliffs, and crags on the western side of Windermere. Skating took place also on the Tarns, north-west of Hawkshead.
4. Like that of the passage quoted earlier from 'Beauty and Moonlight', this imagery was appropriate by Coleridge at a time of financial stress for inclusion (undoubtedly with Wordsworth's permission) in 'Lewti' when it was published in *The Morning Post*, 13 April 1798.
5. In his 'fourteenth summer', PR.582–3.
6. Richard spent one night with them. He was now articled to his solicitor cousin, uncle Richard's son, at Branthwaite, between Whitehaven and Cockermouth.
7. B. R. Schneider, *Wordsworth's Cambridge Education*, Cambridge, 1957, pp. 166, 171.
8. See Dorothy's *Journal of a Tour on the Continent*, 9.ix.20.
9. F. M. Todd, *Politics and the Poet, A Study of Wordsworth*, London, 1957, pp. 221–5.
10. Mary Moorman, *William Wordsworth, The Early Years*, Oxford, 1957, p. 115n.
11. See H. D. Rawnsley, *A Coach-Drive at the Lakes*, Keswick, 1902, pp. 9–10.
12. W. J. B. Owen and J. W. Smyser (eds), *The Prose Works of William Wordsworth*, vol. I, p. 103.
13. This convenient abbreviation has the disadvantage of not indicating the subject of the poem. The actual title *begins*: 'Lines composed a few miles above Tintern Abbey'.
14. After being huntsman to the squires of Alfoxden, Christopher Tricky lived on the common near the entrance to the park. The facts were as narrated,

and his expression when the hounds were out, 'I dearly love their voices', is echoed in the poem. Though these words support Wordsworth's view that the poet's language often falls short of that uttered by men in real life, his argument would be sounder if it were qualified.

15. Wordsworth sometimes named his fictional characters after people he had heard of, for example, Vaudracour, after a lieutenant (de Vaudrecourt) in Beaupuy's regiment; Martha Ray was named after the mother of Basil Montagu senior. A singer and mistress of the fourth Earl of Sandwich, she was fatally shot by her disappointed suitor in 1779.

16. *Biographia Literaria*, XVII.

17. See the illustration to the article by Mary Jacobus in Jonathan Wordsworth (ed.), *Bicentenary Wordsworth Studies*, Ithaca and London, 1970, opp. p. 238.

18. How Wordsworth had anticipated the opening, and the thought at one point, of 'Tintern Abbey', may be seen in a brief fragment, PW5.340.

19. The phrase is used by Wordsworth in 'To the Moon (Rydal)', 1835, but with a moralizing, not a spiritual, significance.

20. Douglas Bush, *Science and English Poetry*, New York, 1950, p. 83.

PART II: 1798–1814

1. Wordsworth had used the name in 'Anecdote for Fathers'.

2. Berta Laurence, *Coleridge and Wordsworth in Somerset*, Newton Abbot, 1970, p. 169; and Mary Moorman, *William Wordsworth, The Early Years*, Oxford, 1957, p. 429.

3. Sara Hutchinson had no doubt about this; she substituted 'Mary' for 'Emma' in her copy (William Heath, *Wordsworth and Coleridge*, Oxford, 1970, p. 113).

4. The name is used anachronistically for lack of better reference.

5. This visit resulted in a remarkably sustained simile, Pr.05.viii.711–41.

6. William Heath, *Wordsworth and Coleridge*, pp. 129–31.

7. Compare, for example, Sir Thomas Browne, *Christian Morals*, III.xxix: 'The created world is but a small *parenthesis* in Eternity, and a short interposition for a time between such a state of duration as was before it and may be after it.'

8. For this version see E. L. Griggs (ed.), *Collected Letters of Samuel Taylor Coleridge*, vol. II, Oxford, 1956, no. 438; or *Essays and Studies by Members of the English Association*, Oxford, 1937, pp. 7–25.

9. See the paragraph on Wordsworth's 'Reply to Mathetes' in Chapter 6.

10. The case for this, and for considering the preamble as an account of that journey, is argued by J. A. Finch in Jonathan Wordsworth (ed.), *Bicentenary Wordsworth Studies*, Ithaca and London, 1970, pp. 1–13.

11. *Far Away and Long Ago*, XVII.

12. Jane Worthington Smyser showed that the idea of the dream, not its imagery, came from Descartes (PMLA, March 1956); see PR.539–40.

13. Suggested by ll. 125–8 of James Thomson's 'To the Memory of Sir Isaac Newton'.

14. When Lord Lowther (shortly to become Earl of Lonsdale) heard that

Wordsworth had been outbid, he authorized Wilkinson to purchase Broad How for £1000, on condition that Wordsworth paid no more than the £800 he had offered. Had he known, Wordsworth would not have agreed to this, for he had no definite plan to live there. The property remained in his hands until 1834.

15. Christopher had married Priscilla Lloyd, daughter of a Birmingham Quaker banker, in October 1804. Her brother Charles, after being coached by Coleridge at Nether Stowey in 1797, was treated for epilepsy by Dr Erasmus Darwin at Lichfield. Subsequently he quarrelled with Coleridge, and settled at Old Brathay near Ambleside.
16. Wordsworth quotes at length from his poem 'All Saints' Church, Derby' (1805) in the first of his essays on epitaphs.
17. *Table Talk*, 21 July 1832.
18. See Mary Moorman, *William Wordsworth, The Later Years*, Oxford, 1965, p. 182n.

PART III: 1814–1850

1. A disease known as 'Egyptian ophthalmia' from being carried to England by troops withdrawn from Egypt at the beginning of the century.
2. F. M. Todd, *Politics and the Poet, A Study of Wordsworth*, London, 1957, pp. 226–8.
3. In a note to l. 171 of *An Evening Walk* (1793), Wordsworth states, for the benefit of the 'curious traveller', that 'up the Duddon . . . may be found some of the most romantic scenery' in the Lake District.
4. Cf. *Descriptive Sketches*, ll. 162–3.
5. A. M. Terhune and A. B. Terhune (eds), *The Letters of Edward FitzGerald*, Princeton, 1980, vol. I, p. 60; and Robert B. Martin, *Tennyson: The Unquiet Heart*, Oxford, 1980, p. 126. 1830 had been a year of revolutionary outbreaks in Europe, one leading to Belgian independence.
6. Mrs Humphry Ward, *A Writer's Recollections*, London, 1919, p. 76.

PART IV: SUPPLEMENTARY

1. A. N. Whitehead, *Science and the Modern World*, Cambridge, 1932, p. 248.
2. Compare the lines (Pr.05.vi.600–6) which allude to the account of an Italian scene in *Descriptive Sketches*, and to Wordsworth's later style:

> While yet a youth, undisciplin'd in verse,
> Through fond ambition of my heart, I told
> Your praises; nor can I approach you now
> Ungreeted by a more melodious song,
> Where tones of learned art and nature mix'd
> May frame enduring language.

3. J. G. Lockhart, *Memoirs of the Life of Scott*, Edinburgh, 1837–8, vol. VI, pp. 60–1.

4. In J. Ruskin, *Sesame and Lilies*, London, Lecture I, 22.

5. Cf. Herbert Read, *The True Voice of Feeling*, London, 1953, p. 210: 'But Wordsworth was a philosophical poet, and not a poetical philosopher. This implies that his faith was based on intuitions rather than on processes of reasoning.'

6. From 'The Real Thing' in *Phoenix*, London, 1936, p. 202.

7. Horace N. Pym (ed.), *Memories of Old Friends, being Extracts from the Journals and Letters of Caroline Fox*, London, 1883, p. 199.

8. *The True Voice of Feeling*, p. 211.

Appendixes

i WORDSWORTH'S 'GUIDE TO THE LAKES'

The principal part of this work, first published anonymously with the inferior illustrations of the Revd Joseph Wilkinson, did not gain much attention until it was issued ten years later in *The River Duddon* (1820). In 1822 it was published separately, with additions; again, in a revised and enlarged form, in 1823. The final text appeared in 1835.

Interest in Lakeland 'picturesque' had grown through the medium of such writers as Dr John Brown, Thomas Gray, W. Hutchinson, Thomas West, William Gilpin, and James Clarke. Whether enthusiasts or guide-book writers, all except Brown were, unlike Wordsworth, visitors unfamiliar with the more subtly intimate scenic effects the region offered. Though he indulged in romantically sensational description, only Gray had looked at scenes with a poet's eye.

Wordsworth's principal aim was 'to furnish a guide or companion for the minds of persons of taste, and feeling for landscape' who wish to explore the Lake District 'with that degree of attention to which its beauty might fairly lay claim'. Yet, for practical reasons, he begins with a transferred chapter on approaches, views on the way, and more detailed advice for the area as a whole. The informed reader will find in the latter numerous hints on the poet's favourite walks and views.

The main work falls into three sections:
1. To give a general view of the whole region, Wordsworth imagines an aerial station midway between Great Gable and Scafell, whence eight valleys are seen radiating like the spokes of a wheel: Langdale and Windermere, Coniston, Duddon, Eskdale, Wastdale, Ennerdale, Buttermere and Crummock Water, and Borrowdale. The remainder (nearly half the circle) can be seen

from the top of Helvellyn: Wythburn and St John's Vale, Ullswater, Haweswater, and Grasmere with Rydal and Ambleside.

The author does not know where a greater variety of light and shade can be found in conjunction with sublime or beautiful landscape features. Describing the changes effected throughout the seasons of the year, he shows that (despite a commonly accepted view) he has a discriminating eye for colour. A characteristic poetic touch combines with geological interest in the remark that the decomposition of iron in the rocks leads in many steep places to 'an intermixture of colours, like the compound hues of a dove's neck'. In turn he deals with features of mountains, valleys, and lakes. The smallness of the latter, in close conjunction with mountains, is conducive to greater beauty, from the sublimity which is 'the result of Nature's first great dealings with the superficies of the earth' to the 'multiplicity of symmetrical parts uniting in a consistent whole' which has been wrought by her later operations. Observations follow on wild life, lake islands, tarns, streams, woods, ground plants, and climatic conditions during the year, the latter in terms which often recall descriptive scenes in Wordsworth's poetry.

2. This section turns from natural characteristics to changes in the country wrought by man. A historical survey leads to the subject of social equality among shepherds and agriculturists, followed by discussion of their homes in dales and mountain regions, where they are built of local stone and slate, and soon appear as if they are a natural part of the scene; their need for the pack-horse routes and bridges which abound; and features of their places of worship. At lower levels, in open country, there are halls and mansions, many built defensively against the Scots, in addition to middle-class homes with decorative gardens.

3. Changes during the last sixty years began when writers made the lakes celebrated. Visitors came from all parts of England, many to settle and introduce the visual discord of ostentatious homes and ornamental gardening. The craving for views made their artificiality all the more obtrusive to the eye. Wordsworth's advice is to work 'in the spirit of Nature, with an invisible hand of art'. Otherwise, unlike Kilchurn Castle, the puny efforts of elegance in modern edifices appear contemptible against the sublimities of nature. In gentler country, the same objection is not felt. Closely agreeing with Gilpin in *Observations on the River Wye*, he observes that white houses can be 'delightful and animating' in isolation,

but that, in close proximity, they disturb the repose of the land-scape, particularly at twilight. The principle of harmony with natural background should be applied to grounds and planta-tions. Shrubberies with exotic colours can be an eyesore, but Wordsworth objects even more to patches and plantations of larch, which is more suitable to barren and exposed expanses, where 'interposition of rocks would . . . break the dreary uniformity of which we have been complaining'. The growth of factories and decline of wool-spinning at home, leading to the impoverishment of *estatesmen* or farmers, and the sale of their property, increases the need for better taste among new pro-prietors.

A miscellany follows, first on the best times for visiting, with emphasis on colour in the autumn, and on bird song and lambing in the spring. A comparison with the scenery of Switzerland, of rather disproportionate length, suggests that beauty lies in small proportions, and concludes with two remarkable lake reflections, on Ullswater and Grasmere. Wordsworth then gives accounts of excursions to the top of Scafell Pike and along 'the banks of Ulls-water', each taken from Dorothy's (the first from her letter to Mr Johnson of October 1818, describing the climb she made with Miss Barker, the second from her journal of 7–13.xi.05), and each accompanied by one of Wordsworth's poems.

ii OBSERVATIONS AND EXPERIENCES WHICH DOROTHY RECORDED AND WHICH BECAME THE SUBJECT OF WORDSWORTH'S POETRY

Date of record	Poem	Date of composition
25.i.98	A Night-piece	25.i.98
18.iii.98	'A whirl-blast from behind the hill'	18.iii.98
10.vi(for 27.v).1800	Beggars	13–14.iii.02
3.x(for 26.ix).1800	Resolution and Independence	v–vi.02
16.ii.02	Alice Fell	12–13.iii.02
14.iii.02	To a Butterfly	14.iii.02

Date of record	Poem	Date of composition
15.iv.02	'I wandered lonely as a cloud'	1804 (I.F.note)
16.iv.02	Written in March	16.iv.02
24.iv.02	The Primrose of the Rock	1831 (I.F.note)
28.iv.02	Foresight	28.iv.02
31.vii.02*	Composed upon Westminster Bridge	

* *Dorothy's inclusive notes were entered under 27.vii.02. The I.F. note confirms that the sonnet was composed on 31 July; Wordsworth's date suggests that it was revised in London on 3 September 1802.*

Composed by the Sea-side,
near Calais, August, 1802
See Dorothy's inclusive entry under 27.vii.02.

4.x.02*	'Dark and more dark the shades of evening fell'	4.x.02

* *Dorothy's inclusive notes were entered under 24.ix.02.*

*   *   *

From the Scottish tour of 1803, Dorothy's recollections of which were written from September 1803 to May 1805, and subsequently revised:

27.viii and 12.ix	Rob Roy's Grave	1805 or 1806
28.viii	To a Highland Girl	1803, 'not long after our return'
31.viii	Address to Kilchurn Castle	31.viii.03 (ll. 1–3). finished 'long after'
8.ix	Sonnet, In the Pass of Killicranky	x.03
11.ix	Stepping Westward	3.vi.05
20.ix	The Matron of Jedborough and her Husband	between 1803 and 1805

*   *   *

From the Journal *of the 1820 tour on the Continent, written from November 1825 onwards, and copied in 1828. Unlike Dorothy's* Highland Recollections, *it was based on copious notes which she made on the tour. All the poems which follow were published in 1822:*

7.viii	Memorial near the Outlet of the Lake of Thun (to Aloys Reding)
9.viii	Scene on the Lake of Brientz
10.viii	On approaching the Staub-bach, Lauterbrunnen
14.viii	Engelberg, the Hill of Angels
19.viii	Our Lady of the Snow
20.viii	The Town of Schwytz
1.ix	The Eclipse of the Sun
6.ix	The Italian Itinerant
12.ix	Echo, upon the Gemmi
16.ix	Processions

---

iii TWO TOPOGRAPHICAL QUESTIONS

1. The 'stolen' boat (Pr.i.357ff.): Three alternatives have been proposed (PR.517 and Part I, note 1 above). The distinguishing feature of the peak which seemed to pursue Wordsworth is its likeness to a huge cliff (1805). From any point he was likely to reach (he was probably only eleven) towards the middle of the Patterdale end of Ullswater, this can apply only to St Sunday Crag. It is not likely that any boat was accessible on the Blowick side (Blowick is private, and some distance from the roadway, which was only a rough track). If one looks across the lake from this neighbourhood, however, it is evident that Wordsworth's description cannot apply to Black Crag above Stybarrow, and that the former was probably not visible to the rower. In line between St Sunday Crag and Blowick is a wooded height (1020 feet, known locally as Keldas), with a craggy face, between Grisedale and Glenridding. Wordsworth's shortest

and easiest route to the lake would take him along a road which made its way over rocks below this steep; the boat could have been secured in a recess among them, at the edge of the lake. As he rowed out, St Sunday Crag would appear above the craggy wooded height below which the boat had been tethered. See plate 4 *above*.

2. The 'meeting-point of two highways' (Pr.xii.287ff.): There is no crag which ascends steeply immediately above such a point in the area; nor is this implied in the text. The horses brought from Cockermouth in winter, when daylight was short, and ice and mists could create hazard for unridden horses, would come by the shortest and most reliable route; the Wrynose track seems out of question on all counts. The main road ran via Keswick and Grasmere Vale, from which the shortest way to Hawkshead was over Skelwith Bridge. Jefferys' 1770 map of Westmorland shows that from this point the most direct alternative routes (one via Skelwith Fold) meet at Outgate Inn, one mile north of Hawkshead. (This does not exclude the possibility of an approach over Brathay Bridge.) Wordsworth's look-out post would not be miles from Hawkshead; it would command a view of either road for quite a distance; it would be within hailing-distance of each, enabling him to descend and ride back to Ann Tyson's. There are craggy points fulfilling these requirements not far north of Outgate, the furthest possible (perhaps too remote) being High Crag.

---

iv SELECT BIBLIOGRAPHY

Works

Poetry: *The Poetical Works of William Wordsworth* in five volumes, with textual and critical notes by Ernest de Selincourt and Helen Darbishire, Oxford, 1940–9; *The Prelude* (containing the 1805 and 1850 texts), ed. Ernest de Selincourt, 2nd edition revised by Helen Darbishire, Oxford, 1959.

The Cornell Wordsworth, Ithaca, N.Y. and Hassocks, Sussex: The Salisbury Plain Poems (1975), *The Prelude* 1798–1799 (1977), *Home at Grasmere* (1977), *The Ruined Cottage* and *The Pedlar* (1979).

Prose: in three volumes, ed. W. J. B. Owen and J. W. Smyser,
Oxford, 1974.

Letters

The Letters of William and Dorothy Wordsworth, 2nd edition,
Oxford, 1967 (and later volumes).

Biography

Mary Moorman, *William Wordsworth: The Early Years*, Oxford,
1957; *The Later Years*, Oxford, 1965.

Critical Studies

W. Raleigh, *Wordsworth*, London, 1903.
G. W. Meyer, *Wordsworth's Formative Years*, Ann Arbor and
London, 1943. Valuable in the main, though outdated at some
points.
J. C. Smith, *A Study of Wordsworth*, Edinburgh, 1944.
Helen Darbishire, *The Poet Wordsworth*, Oxford, 1950.
Enid Welford, *Salisbury Plain, A Study in the Development of
Wordsworth's Mind and Art*, Oxford, 1966.
S. M. Parrish, *The Art of the Lyrical Ballads*, Cambridge, Mass.,
1973. Developed within an excellent survey of the critical rela-
tions between Wordsworth and Coleridge.

Critical Essays and Selections

Walter Pater, 'Wordsworth' (1874); recast for *Appreciations*
(1889).
A. C. Bradley, 'Wordsworth' in *Oxford Lectures on Poetry*,
London, 1909.
Aldous Huxley, 'Wordsworth in the Tropics' in *Do What You
Will*, London, 1929.
Basil Willey, *The Seventeenth Century Background* (XII) and
The Eighteenth Century Background (XI,XII), London, 1934
and 1940.

A. W. Thomson (ed.), *Wordsworth's Mind and Art*, Edinburgh, 1969.

Jonathan Wordsworth (ed.), *Bicentenary Wordsworth Studies*, Ithaca and London, 1970.

W. J. Harvey and R. Gravil (eds), *The Prelude*, London, 1972.

A. R. Jones and W. Tydeman (eds), *Lyrical Ballads*, London, 1977.

More Specialized Studies

W. H. White, *An Examination of the Charge of Apostasy against Wordsworth*, London, 1898.

Elsie Smith, *An Estimate of Wordsworth*, Oxford, 1932. Contemporary views and reviews from 1793 to 1822.

Edith C. Batho, *The Later Wordsworth*, Cambridge, 1933.

B. R. Schneider, *Wordsworth's Cambridge Education*, Cambridge, 1957.

F. M. Todd, *Politics and the Poet, A Study of Wordsworth*, London, 1957.

H. Lindenberger, *On Wordsworth's 'Prelude'*, Princeton, 1963.

Melvyn Rader, *Wordsworth, A Philosophical Approach*, Oxford, 1967.

Jonathan Wordsworth, *The Music of Humanity*, London, 1969. On 'The Ruined Cottage' and 'The Pedlar'.

M. H. Abrams, *Natural Supernaturalism: Tradition and Revolution in Romantic Literature*, New York and London, 1971. Wordsworth is the principal subject, with parallels from English and German literature and philosophy to denote 'the spirit of the age' after the failure of the French Revolution.

Mary Jacobus, *Tradition and Experiment in Wordsworth's Lyrical Ballads*, Oxford, 1976.

Index

Abercrombie, Lascelles 85
Addison, Joseph 25–6,44,90,
  ('The Vision of Mirzah')132, 171
Adelaide, Queen 262
Alfoxden House 68ff.,107,262,
  329–30
Allan Bank 144,177,180,185,186,
  187
Ambleside 17,109,124,135,180,
  189,190,238,261,264,265,267
Anderson, Dr 122,211
Arnold, Matthew 105,124,126,
  163,164,277,286,309,310–12,325,
  325–6
Arnold, Thomas 252,264

Bagehot, Walter 250
Barker, Miss 191,223,228,335
Bartram, William 101,143
Beattie, James 14,16,18,38,43,
  44,46
Beaumont, Sir George and Lady
  135–6,142,144,156,164,166,169,
  171,172,185,188,212,214,215,223,
  229,231,232,237,241,243,247,248,
  260,277,323
Beaupuy, Michel 34–5,47,49,59,
  74,76,86,148,164
Belgium 29–30,228,259; and
  Holland 235–6,242
Bell, Andrew 189,227,279
Bield Crag 203
Blake, William 21,79,91,150,168,
  204–5,314
Blois 33–5,49
Blomfield, C. J. 248,274
Bolton Abbey 172–6 passim, 236

Bonawe 10,131–2
Bowles, William 27–8
Bowness 13,221–2,241,280
Bradley, A. C. 311–13,314
Branthwaite 26,53,329
Brigham 252,255,268
Bristol 50,53,54,72,99,172
Broad How 161,330–1
Brontë, Charlotte 167,(Jane Eyre)
  274
Brougham, Henry 222,223,241
Brougham Castle 24,169–70
Broughton 13,26,41,225,226
Browning, Robert 85,222,285,
  312
Bürger, Gottfried 65,73,('The
  Lass of Fair Wone'),76,80,99–100,
  101,114,115,289,292
Burke, Edmund 28,30,49,59,158,
  278
Burns, Robert 20,100,101,125,
  131,134,143,162–3,217,218,252,
  255–6,261,286
Buxted 248,265

Calais 128,129,228,229,259
Calgarth Hall 18,57
Calgarth Park 48
Calvert, Raisley 51,53,191
Calvert, William 50,51
Cambridge 10,14,18,20ff.,73,
  137,151,154,157,185,229,236,
  247–8,257,266; King's College
  Chapel 231,232,233,274
Carlisle 131,249,261,266,268
Carlyle, Thomas 50–1
Carter, John 190,266

Chamonix   28,46,47,228
Chantrey, Francis   228
Chatsworth   247
Chatterton, Thomas   14,16,124–5
Chaucer   25,122,226,231,285
Chiabrera, Gabriello   183,187,
    258,259
Christian, Edward   14,63
Christian, Fletcher   8,63
Clarke, James   38,45–6
Clarkson, Thomas and Catherine
    121,122,128,142,160,170,185,198,
    229
Cockermouth   6–9,51,108,172,
    235,268,338
Coleorton   169,171,185,188,229,
    230–1,235,236,239,241,247,263
Coleridge, Hartley   138,169,172,
    180,188,214,238,246,268,294,307
Coleridge, S. T.   28,54,65,68–73
    passim,   78,86,90,91,99,100,
    107–8,110,112–13,114,117,121,
    123,125,131,136–7,138,142,144,
    155,169,176,177,180,181,185,186,
    189,221,228–9,235,236,242,248,
    256,258,282,286,339;   *The
    Friend*   67,92,180,183;
    'Ode: to Dejection'   140,154,
    168;   and *The Recluse*   71,
    107,145–6,156,168,169,183,
    192–3,319–20;   criticism of
    Wordsworth   37,46–7,76–7,
    117,124,157,173,174–5,236,285,
    288,304–8
Coleridge, Sara   172,243
Collins, William   14,16,18,27,38,
    44,73,227,292
Colthouse   11,16,20,21,23,24
Como, Lake   29,46,228
Coniston   10,188,262;
    Coniston Water   10,18,107
Cookson, Christopher (uncle Kit)
    20,26,51,107,108
Cookson, Rev. William   20–1,31,
    35,36,50,128,185
Cooper, Thomas   279
Cottle, Joseph   54,71,72,99,106,
    107
Cowper, William   18,30,38,44,240

Coxe, William   28,44
Crabbe, George   25,258,290,302

Daniel, Samuel   122,286
Darwin, Erasmus   74,331
Darwinism   81,95,123,201,
    313–14,324
Day, Thomas   149
De Quincey, Thomas   172,177,
    180,181,212,222,238,239
Descartes   330
Devil's Bridge   236,237
Dovedale   23,(Derbyshire)105
Dryden, John   44,236
Duddon (river and valley)   11,188,
    225–7,246,262,331,333
Durham (University)   261
Dyer, John   18,44

Edridge, Henry   166
Edwards, John   171
Einsiedeln   29,46
Eliot, George   61,77,91–2,95,137,
    194,198,277–8,325,326
Eliot, T. S.   38,288–9,299–300,
    305,325
Ennerdale   108,118,172,262,333
Esthwaite   9,11,13,14,107,157

Fenwick, Isabella   261–3,267
Fergusson, Robert   125
Fisher, Molly   109,202
Fleming, John   14,18,21
Forncett   20–1,25,26,30,37,50
Fox, Charles James   110,119,129,
    158,166,167
French Revolution, the   26,28,33,
    36,47,48,59,63–4,86,107,145,181,
    193,199,271–2,279
Furness Abbey   13,262

Germany   58,71,99ff.
Gillies, R. P.   211
Gilpin, William   23,38,47,50,61,
    99,334–5
Godwin, William   53,57,59,60,62,
    66,74,110,166,186;   *Caleb
    Williams*   63,65;   *Political
    Justice*   49,53,59,64

Goethe 308,311
Goldsmith, Oliver 38,226,245
Gondo gorge, the 28–9,44,228, 238
Goodrich Castle 50,72,80
Gordale Scar 112,172,224
Gosse, Edmund 85
Grande Chartreuse, the 28,46, 179
Grasmere 7,51,52,108–10,128, 130–1,135,179,186,187,201,246, 253,268; the lake 114,117, 144,172,256,335; the Vale of 13,15,94–5,108,114,117,144,146, 334
Gray, Thomas 14,18,23,25,28,38, 43,44,47,103,143,284,285,293,333
Green, Sally 177,185
Greenwood, Robert 13,21,257
Gustavus IV (of Sweden) 170,182

Hacket 186,188,201
Halifax 9,50,51,103–4,172, 246
Hamilton, W. R. 244,245,247
Hardy, Thomas 67,77,89,118, 144,196,201,202–3,265,285,290, 324,325
Harrington, James 36,49,130
Hartley, David 60,69,192
Hawkshead 3,8,9–11,17,18,69, 102,103,107–8,115,195,202,265, 338
Haydon, Benjamin 214,215,221, 262,277,315
Hazlitt, William 71,72,85,136, 194,214,218,221,234,276–7, 302–4,312
Helvellyn 160,252,259,262,333–4
Hemans, Mrs 247,258
Herbert, George 226,285
Hindwell 185,189,212,236
Hofer 182
Hogg, James 211,212,258
Hopkins, G. M. 286–7
Hudson, W. H. 148
Hunt, Leigh 214,224,302
Hutchinson, George 108,112
Hutchinson, Henry 65,180,255

Hutchinson, Joanna 112,113,131, 134,235
Hutchinson, Mary 8,15,24,52,65, 100,106,110,112,113,117,121,122, 127,284; *see* Wordsworth, Mary
Hutchinson, Sara 108,112,117, 121,125,127,130,144,161,169,178, 180,183,185,188,195,211,212, 221,235,239,('To S.H.')240,257, 266,330
Hutchinson, Thomas 26,106,112, 144,185,241,268
Huxley, Aldous 313–15

Ireland 244–5,274
Isle of Man 252,255
Isle of Wight 50
Isola, Agostino 25–6
Italy 29,228,258–60

Jeffrey, Francis 70–1,106,190, 195,206,215,217–18,290,291, 301–2,305
Jewsbury, Maria 239,245
Jones, Robert 28–30,42–3,50,51, 112,129,227,235,236,237

Keats, John 15,38,105,123,170, 187,200–1,221–2,225–6,258,287, 290,294,304,324
Keble, John 214,236
Kendal 23,51,108,169,172,195, 202,274
Keswick 51,56,108,109,110,112, 127,135–6,160,165,262
Klopstock, Friedrich 99

Lamb, Charles and Mary 68,69, 95,128,144,165,166,169,185,186, 213,220,221,223–4,228,234,235, 242,256,257–8
Landor, Walter Savage 211,213, 252,302
Langhorne, John 25,41,44
Lawrence, D. H. 81,139,312,314
Leavis, F. R. 318,319,320–1
Lloyd, Charles 166,234
Locke, John 39,60,192,320

Lockhart, J. G.   239,284
London   8,27,30−1,36,53,70,99,
    127−8,130,146,149,150−1,166,
    172,177−8,185,214−15,228−9,235,
    248,256−7,263,312−13
Lonsdale, Lord (Sir James Lowther)
    6,20,36,59,127
Lonsdale, Lord (cousin and successor)
    165,189,190,214,222,229,242,247,
    277,330−1
Lucerne   29,228,230
Luff, Mr and Mrs   161,173,199,
    239,267

Macaulay, Thomas   277
Malham   112,172,224
Martineau, Harriet   267
Marvell, Andrew   130,302
Mary Queen of Scots   130,221,255
Masefield, John   89
Mathews, William   31,52−3,281
Michelangelo   26,164,167,260
Mill, J. S.   249,326
Millom   6,12
Milton   9,15,18,25,36,38,39,41,
    44,47,49,55,83,128,130,146,
    150−1,179,182,211,215,218,226,
    232,260,276,286,287,291,294−5,
    299,304,321
Monkhouse, Thomas   221,223,
    228,235,236,237
Montagu, Basil   53,54,65,70,121,
    128,166,185,186,189,191,330;
    his son Basil   53,54,59,80,
    190−1
Moorman, Mary   85,329,330,331
Moresby   7,242,244,253−4
Morley, John   310,326
The Morning Post   110,114,121,
    135,140,265,329
Moxon, Edward   258,266

Napoleon (Bonaparte)   58−9,128,
    129,162,170,180−3,214,229,230,
    241,272
Nelson, Lord   161,164,165
Nether Stowey   65,66,68,70,262
Newbiggin Hall   3−6,51,107−8
Newton, Sir Isaac   15,21,27,90,157

Nollekens, Joseph   256
Nottingham   171,249

Orléans   32,33,35,36,49
Ossian   30,135,211−12,237−8,292
Oxford   99,214,227,236,240,261

Paine, Thomas   49
Palafox   182
Paris   33,35,36,228,258
Park House   144
Pater, Walter   308−9,312
Patterdale   3,160,161,337
Penrith   3,6−7,8−9,12,15,18,20,
    24,52,53,121,157,183,190,251
Percy's *Reliques*   75,99,173,247,
    292
Pickersgill, Henry   257
Plato   138,224
Pollard, Jane   20,(Mrs Marshall)
    112,172,173,244
Poole, Thomas   66−7,68,70,80,
    110,115,119
Pope, Alexander   14,41−2,91,
    282,291−2,316

Quarles, Francis   236,302
Quillinan, Edward   234−5,239,
    242,248,253,256,261,262,266,268

Racedown (Lodge)   53,54,65,68,
    74,106,145
Rampside   53,164
Read, Herbert   325,332
Reding, Aloys   229,337
Reform Bill, the (1832)   251,254,
    274,277,278
Reynolds, J. H.   84−5,223
Richardson, Samuel   30
Robinson, Henry Crabb   158,178,
    185,189,218,221,228,230,235,252,
    258,268,277
Robinson, Mary   108,('the maid of
    Buttermere')131,155
Rogers, Samuel   27,44,166,228,
    235,243
Rousseau, Jean-Jacques   29,44,49,
    54,59,60
Ruskin, John   306,326

Rydal 108,232,235,268;
Rydal Mount 178,189−90,212,
214,216,220,221,224,239,252,256,
261,263,266,267; Rydal Water
51,108,109,167,190,240,256

St Bees 255
St Francis 260
Salisbury Plain 50
Scafell 223,333,335
Scotland (Wordsworth's visits to)
121,131−4,211,249−51,252
Scott, (Sir) Walter 114,134,135,
160−1,162,168−9,170,172,(editor
of the 'Border Minstrelsy')173,
173−4,239,242,250,252,258,259,
284,297,321,326
Selincourt, Ernest de 85,156,338
Shakespeare 9,25,30,(*Romeo and
Juliet*)34,38,61,291,(*Measure for
Measure*)294
Shelley, P. B. 85,103,163,178,
216,222,224
Sidney, Algernon 36,49,130,232
Simplon Pass, the 28,228,229
Skiddaw 6,45,46,136,299
Snowdon 31,46,145,152,299
Sobieski, John 217
Sockbridge 3
Sockburn-on-Tees 26,65,100,
106,108
Southey, Edith 240,243,259
Southey, Robert 54,112,136,144,
166,189,239,241,263,288
Spenser, Edmund 9,25,26,34,38,
55,122,142,146,176,215,236,291,
294; *The Faerie Queene*
55,173,272
Spedding, John 51; his son
James 247−8
Spinoza 68−9,307
Staffa 250,255
Stephen, Leslie 310,311
Switzerland 28−9,44−7,130,170,
181,228−30,335
Sympson, Rev. Joseph 110,179,
202,204

Taylor, William 14−15,22,53,102

Tell, William 29,212
Tennyson, Alfred (Lord) 126,
248,286,294−5
Thelwall, John 68,99
Thomson, James 14,18,38,44,45,
91,122−3,199−200,291−2,330
Thompson, T. W. 102,329
Threlkeld 108,169
Tyson, Ann 10−13,16,20,22,23,
26,119,131−2,202

Ullswater 3,108,112,122,143,145,
147,243,334,335,337
Uri, Lake 29,46,212

Vallon, Annette 33−4,35−6,43,
49−50,51,63,65,76,100,101,122,
127,128,199,214,228; her
daughter Caroline 36,127,128,
129,214,228,258
Vaughan, Henry 136,137,138−9
Virgil 27,213−14,219,236,294−5

Walker, Rev. Robert 202,226
Wastdale 108,172,252,262,333
Waterloo 216,229,242,262
Watson, Richard (Bishop of
Llandaff) 48−9
White, William Hale 260,315,
340
Whitehaven 3,6,7,14,24,26,53,
172,190,214,244,246,247,252
Whitehead, A. N. 280
(quotation),299
Whitwick 241−2,244
Wilberforce, William 215,223
Wilkie, David 166,256,277
Wilkinson, Thomas 161,183
Williams, Helen Maria 14,17,34,
221,228
Wilson, John 78,92,186,198,218,
239
Winchilsea, Lady 25,37,39,
291−2
Windermere, Lake 10,11,13,23,
24,51,107,190,239,247,265
Windsor 35,128,185
Windy Brow 51,53
Worcester 237,242

Wordsworths, the:

Ann (mother, née Cookson)   3,6, 8,9

Catherine (daughter)   180,185–9 *passim*,   212

Christopher (brother)   6,11,20,37, 128,166,189,202,221,225,228,229, 235,241(sons),247,265

Dorothy (sister)   6–9 *passim*, 18,20,24,25,26,28,29,30,35,37,42, 49–50,53–4,59,65,82,99,100,103, 104–5,106,113,114,118,122, 127–9,130–4,142,144,172,177, 185–6,188,190,191,212,220,223, 224,227–9,235,238,240,241–2, 244,246,248,256,258,266,268,307, 335;   journals   70,110–12,124, 130,141,173,198–9,293,335–7; *Recollections of a Tour in Scotland*   113,162,211,238,336

Dorothy (daughter: Dora)   142, 145,146,187,188,218,220,227,232, 235,236,239,242,243–50 *passim*, 257,261,262,265,266,268

John (father)   3–9 *passim*, 12–13

John (brother)   6,10–11,13,20,27, 107–8,110–12,114,121,128,144, 164;   in Wordsworth's poetry 117,118,160,163–4

John (cousin)   27,53

John (nephew)   265

John (son)   130–1,134,142,223, 227,236,240,241–2,244,246,247, 252,254,261,262,263,265,268

Mary (wife: *see* Hutchinson, Mary) 130–1,134,142,143,144,172,178, 180,186,189,211,214,221,225,226, 227,229,234,236,239,242,244,247, 248–9,259,261–8 *passim*

Richard (grandfather)   3

Richard (uncle)   3,7,27,30,51,53

Richard (brother)   6–10 *passim*, 13,20,27,36,50,127,221,265

Thomas (son)   166,187,189

William (son)   185,189,190,227, 229,235,238,239,242,244,248, 249,262,263,266,268

WORDSWORTH, WILLIAM

his writings (*for individual works, see pp. 347–51*): Gothic features   16, 18,55,143–4;   natural imagery 15,16–17,40–1,134,187,203–4, 296–7;   style   282–8,293–7, 298–300,309

and the imagination   82,94, 150–3,168,290–1,316–18

literary interests (non-English): classical   15,25,124,179,200, 204,212,213–14,219,220,224,230, 254;   Italian   25–6,34,38, 54,130,164,167,217

and Nature (the one life)   52,69, 81,83,87,90–1,158–9,307,313–14, 323;   its link with human life 18–19,52,81,83,94–5,118–19,140, 148–9,297,314,315

and pastoral poetry   110,117–20, 163,249–50,309

politics: democratic principles 271ff.,276ff.,279,281,292–3,322; national independence and freedom   129–30,181–3,260,278

views: books   9,60,81,93,150; capital punishment   272; childhood   51–2,80,84,138–9, 154,317;   the Church of England 158,231,232,273ff.   education and schools   149,204–5,279–81; immortality   139,310; industry   204–5,245,271,273, 324;   railways   256,265,272; science   81,200,245–6,255,259, 289–90,314;   the sonnet 240–1;   war   55,216–17

Workington   235,247,255

Wrangham, Francis   53,59,112, 128,176,189,223,274

Wrynose Pass   11,246,338

Wye valley, the   50,72,82

Yewdale   11,188

Yordas   112,(simile of thirty-one lines)298

Young, Edward   30,40,83

Zürich, Lake   29,230

WORDSWORTH'S POEMS AND PROSE WRITINGS

Advance — come forth from thy Tyrolean ground 183   The Affliction of
Margaret 121,283   Ailsa Crag, In the Frith of Clyde, 255   Airey-Force
Valley 257   Alas! what boots the long laborious quest 182   Alice
Fell 122,301,305,335   Anacreon 15   And is it among rude untutored
dales 183   Andrew Jones 89,101   Anecdote for Fathers 80
Animal Tranquillity and Decay 73   Anticipation 135   Apology for the
Foregoing Poems (*Yarrow Revisited, and other Poems*) 251   The Armenian
Lady's Love 247   Artegal and Elidure 169,215

A Ballad 16,89   Ballot, Protest against the 261   Beauty and Moonlight 15,16−17,56,329   Beggars 122,124,335   Beggars, Sequel to 220
Bishop of Llandaff, A Letter to the 48−9   Bird of Paradise, Upon seeing a
coloured Drawing of a 257   Bird of Paradise, Suggested by a Picture of the
257   Blest statesman he, whose mind's unselfish will 272   The Blind
Highland Boy 169   Bologna, At (in Remembrance of the late Insurrections) 260   *The Borderers* 8,54,58,59,60−4,68,70,87,263,286,
289   Bothwell Castle 251   Brave Schill! by death delivered 182
Brientz, Scene on the Lake of 337   Brook, whose society the poet seeks
227   The Brothers 108,117−18,119,215   Brougham Castle, Song at the
Feast of 169−70   The Brownie's Cell 211−12   Bruges, Incident
at 242   Burns, At the Grave of 163   (Burns) Thoughts, Suggested . . .
near the poet's residence 163,261   Burns, A Letter to a Friend of Robert
217−18,303   Burns, To the Sons of 163   Butterfly, To a 122,335

Calais, August 1802 129   Calais, Composed near 297   Calais, Composed by the Sea-side, near 336   Calm is the fragrant air 253   Celandine, The Small 103,142   Characteristics of a Child three years old 187,
199   Chatsworth! thy stately mansion 247   The Childless Father 115
Cintra, Composed while . . . engaged in writing a Tract . . . 183   *Cintra,
Concerning the Convention of* 180−2   Clarkson, To Thomas
170   Clouds, To the 178   Cockermouth Castle, Address to the Spirit
of 7,255   Collins, Remembrance of 73   Cologne, In the Cathedral
of 229   A Complaint 169   The Complaint of a Forsaken Indian
Woman 75−6,282   The Convict 65,73,113   The Contrast
239   Cora Linn, Composed at 211   Cuckoo, To the 122,139,263
The Cuckoo at Laverna 260   The Cuckoo-Clock 263   Cumberland,
On a High Part of the Coast of 254

Daisy, To the ('With little here to do or see' and 'Bright flower! Whose home is
everywhere') 123   Daisy, To the ('Sweet flower! belike to have one day')
163   The Danish Boy 102   Dark and more dark the shades of evening
fell 130,336   Dear native regions 18−19   Decay of Piety 240
Descriptive Sketches 30,31,35,36−7,42−7,286,313,315   Desultory Stanzas
230   Devotional Incitements 253   Dion 220−1   Dirge 16,17
Distressful Gift 163   Dover, Composed in the Valley near 129   Dover,
September 1802. Near 129   Duty, Ode to 136−8,167,301

Ecclesiastical Sonnets 8,158,231−3,273−4,302,310,324   The Eclipse of the

Sun 229–30   Effusion . . . near Dunkeld 211–12   The Egyptian Maid
243–4,295,321   Elegiac Musings (on Sir George Beaumont) 247   Elegiac
Stanzas (on Mrs Fermor) 237   Elegiac Stanzas (Peele Castle) 163–4
Elegiac Verses 230   Ellen Irwin 114–15   The Emigrant Mother 122,
124   Emperors and kings . . . 272   Engelberg, the Hill of Angels 229,
337   Enterprise, To 230   Epistle (to Sir George Beaumont) 187–8
Epitaphs, essays upon 183–5,202   Essay, Supplementary to the Preface
237,291–3   Esthwaite, The Vale of 17–18,37,39,80   Evening of Extraordinary Splendour, Composed upon an 138–9,159,218,220   *An Evening
Walk* 17,24,26,36–42,44,51,286,294,315   *The Excursion* 27,71,137,
150,153–4,168,180,186,188,190,191–208,211,215,221,237,273,275,291,295,
302,307,321–2   Expostulation and Reply 72,81   Extempore
Effusion on the Death of James Hogg 258,295,310

A Fact, and an Imagination 218   Fame tells of groves 227   A Farewell 127   Farewell Lines 242   The Farmer of Tilsbury Vale 115
Feel for the wrongs . . . 273   The Female Vagrant 54,73,303   Fidelity
160–1,203   Fleming, To the Lady 235   Florence, At 281   A Flower
Garden 236   Fly, some kind spirit, fly to Grasmere-dale 134   The Force
of Prayer 172,273   Foresight 336   Fort Fuentes 229   Friend, To a
('Pastor and patriot') 255

Gemmi, Echo upon the 230,337   General Fast, Upon the Late 278–9
General Thanksgiving Ode 85,216,217,227   Gipsies 171–2   The
Gleaner 242   Glen Almain 135   The Glow-worm 106,122   Gold
and Silver Fishes in a Vase 245   Goody Blake and Harry Gill 72,73–4,283
'Gothic' Tale, Fragment of a 61,233   Grace Darling 264   Grasmere,
Composed by the Side of 172   The Green Linnet 123   *Guide to the
Lakes* 183,333–5   Guilt and Sorrow 58–9,263

Happy Warrior, Character of the 137–8,164,167   Hart-leap Well 108,
115–17,138,198   The Haunted Tree 224–5   Haydon, To B. R.
215–16   Here pause: the poet claims at least this praise 187   Highland
Girl, To a 131,134–5   The Highland Broach (*sic*) 251   Home at
Grasmere 93,94–5,110,116–17,120,146,167,308   The Horn of Egremont
Castle 169   How beautiful the Queen of Night 266–7   How rich that
forehead's calm expanse 236   Humanity 245,273

I heard (alas! 'twas only in a dream) 224   I know an aged man 266
I love upon a stormy night 89   I wandered lonely as a cloud 143,289,
336   I watch, and long have watched 224   The Idiot Boy 77–80,
288   The Idle Shepherd-Boys 115,141   If this great world of joy and pain
254   Illustrated Books and Newspapers 266   Incipient Madness 196
Inscriptions . . . Hermit's Cell 224   Intimations of Immortality 52,80,92,
122,129,136,138–41,145,151,154,301,306,309,311,318,319   It is a
beauteous evening, calm and free 129,139,254   It is not to be thought of
135,320   The Italian Itinerant 229,230,285,337

A Jewish Family 242

Kent, To the Men of 135   Kilchurn Castle, Address to 176,238–9,336
Killicranky, Sonnet, in the Pass of 336   The King of Sweden 170
King's College Chapel, Cambridge, Inside of 233,295   Kirkstone, The Pass
of 220   The Kitten and the Falling Leaves 164

Lamb, Written after the death of Charles 257–8   Laodamia 213–14
The Last of the Flock 72,74,282   The Last Supper, by Leonardo da Vinci
229   Lauterbrunnen, On approaching the Staub-bach 337   The leaves
that rustled on this oak-crowned hill 256   Let other bards of angels sing
236   Liberty 245   *A little onward lend thy guiding hand* 218,294,
298   Lines ('Beguiled into forgetfulness of care') 256   Lines (on the
expected 'dissolution of Mr. Fox') 167,310,315   Lines written . . . in a Boat
at Evening 73   Lines written in early Spring 81,253   The Longest
Day 220   Look at the fate of summer flowers 236   Look now on that
adventurer 183   Louisa 121–2   Love Lies Bleeding 271
Lowther 256   'Lucy' poems 100,104–6,('Three years she grew')147
Lucy Gray 103–4,290   Lycoris, Ode to 219–20   *Lyrical Ballads* 27,
49,64,65,71–83,99,295;   second volume 89,112–13;   prefaces 112,
282–90, 305

The Mad Mother 75   March, Written in 122,123,336   Mary Queen of
Scots 255   Mary Queen of Scots, Lament of 221   Maternal Grief 199
Mathetes, Reply to 92–3,138,183   The Matron of Jedborough and her
Husband 135   'Matthew' poems 14,102–3   May, To 239–40   May
Morning, Ode, Composed on 239–40   *Memorials of a Tour on the Continent* 83,229–30,231,302   Memory 238   Methought I saw the footsteps of a throne 257   Michael 74,110,113,117,118–20,283–4,286,287
Monument of Mrs. Howard 256   Moon, To the 257   Moon (Rydal), To
the 257,298   A Morning Exercise 239   Most sweet it is with unuplifted
eyes 256   Musings near Aquapendente 259,275,281   Mutability 233,
295,299   My heart leaps up 122,140–1

Naming of Places, Poems on the 113–14,266,('To Joanna')296   A Needle-
case, On seeing . . . in the form of a Harp 240   A Night-piece 70,335
A Night Thought 267   The Norman Boy 264   Not in the lucid intervals
of life 95,256   November, 1806 170,276   November, 1813 214,303
November, 1836 257   November 1 215   Nuns fret not 130
Nutting 87,103,147,219

O dearer far than light and life are dear 236   O nightingale! thou surely
art 171   The Oak and the Broom 114   Octogenarian, Sonnet to
an 266   Ode, 1814 216   Ode, 1815 216–17   Okker Hill, A
Tradition of 242   The Old Cumberland Beggar 49,66,71,73,86,
273   Ossian, Written in a Blank Leaf of MacPherson's 237–8   Our Lady
of the Snow 337   Oxford, May 30, 1820 227

Painter, To a 262   A Parsonage in Oxfordshire 227   Personal Talk
170,173   A Pet-Lamb 115   Peter Bell 50,71,84–90,101,116,122,
223–4   The Pilgrim's Dream 224   The Pillar of Trajan 240,260

The Pine of Monte Mario at Rome   259—60   A Plea for Authors   261   A *poet!* He hath put his heart to school   293—4   A Poet to his Grandchild   261 A Poet's Epitaph   101,184,299   Postscript, 1835   256—7,273,275   The power of armies is an invisible thing   285   Power of Music   166—7   Power of Sound, On the   246   Praised be the art   187   Preface to the Edition of 1815   290—1   Prelude   263   *The Prelude*   18,21,78,82,84,91,103, 105,106—7,119,137,140,143,145—60,167,179,192,232,261,268,279,287,290, 295,308,309,316—17,318,321,322   Poor Robin   263   Portentous change when history can appear   279   Presentiments   92,154,247   The Primrose of the Rock   91,248,310,336   Processions   230,337   Projected Kendal and Windermere Railway, On the   265   Proud were ye, mountains 265   Punishment of Death, Sonnets upon the   272

The Recluse   71,101,103,107,117,146,150,156,167,168,178,192,208,247,308, 319,320;   its prospectus   93—4,151,168,192,263,317   The Redbreast 256   The Redbreast and the Butterfly   123   Repentance, A Pastoral Ballad   110   Resolution and Independence   114,122,124—6,178,284,2 89, 291,313,335   The Reverie of Poor Susan   115,288   *The River Duddon* 224,225—7,262,295,302,310   Rob Roy's Grave   162,222,336   Roman Antiquities   251   Roslin Chapel, Composed in . . . during a storm   250 Rotha, my spiritual child   237   The Ruined Cottage   42,54,55,56,65,66, 68,71,81,94,117,122,193—4,195—8,206 —7,286,319   The Russian Fugitive 244   Ruth   101—2   Rydal Mere, By the side of   256

Said Secrecy to Cowardice and Fraud   261   The Sailor's Mother   122,124, -305   Saint Bees' Heads, Stanzas suggested in a Steamboat off   255   Salisbury Plain   50,51,55—6,71   Salisbury Plain, Adventures on   54,56—9,61, 63   Scorn not the sonnet   240   Scott, On the departure of Sir Walter . . . from Abbotsford, for Naples   250,295,296,315,323   Schwytz, The Town of   337   Sea-shore, Composed by the   254   Seasons, Thoughts on the 253,310   September, 1815   215   September, 1819   225   September 1, 1802   129   Septimi Gades   52   The Seven Sisters   114   S. H., To 240   Simon Lee, the Old Huntsman   72,74—5   Simplon Pass, Stanzas composed in the   229   Sister, To my   81,253   Skylark, To a ('Ethereal minstrel')   239   Sleep, To   170   So fair, so sweet, withal so sensitive 264—5   Soft as a cloud is one blue ridge   256   The Solitary Reaper   104, 161—2   A Somersetshire Tragedy   66—7   The Somnambulist   243 Spade of a Friend, To the   161   The Sparrow's Nest   7,122   Star-Gazers 166—7,288   Steamboats, Viaducts and Railways   256   Stepping Westward   162,336   Stray Pleasures   166—7   Such age how beautiful   237 The sun is couched   254   Surprised by joy   212   Switzerland, Thought of a Briton on the Subjugation of   170

The Tables Turned   72,81,200   There is a little unpretending rill   51 *There is a pleasure in poetic pains*   240,289   Those words were uttered as in pensive mood   130   This lawn, a carpet all alive   245—6   The Thorn 16,72,76—8,282,288,290,295   The Three Cottage Girls   230   The Three Graves   65,72,74,76   Thomson's 'Castle of Indolence', Stanzas written in 122—3   Tintern Abbey, Lines composed a few miles above   69,72,81—3,101,

287,330   'Tis said, that some have died for love   115   To — ('Happy the feeling')   240   To —, on her first Ascent . . . of Helvellyn   218   To — upon the Birth of her First-born Child   254   Toussaint l'Ouverture, To 129,299,315,323   The Triad   242,243,246   The Trosachs (*sic*)   250 The Tuft of Primroses   178—9,180,200   The Two Thieves   115 Tyndrum in a Storm, Suggested at   250—1

Up with me! Up with me into the clouds!   123   Unquiet childhood here by special grace   237

Vallombrosa, At   260,288   Vaudracour and Julia   34,225   Venetian Republic, On the Extinction of the   129   Venus, To the Planet   261 Vernal Ode   218—19

The Waggoner   154,164—6,169,223,321   Wansfell! this household has a favoured lot   263—4   The Warning   254,278   The Waterfall and the Eglantine   114   Waterloo, After visiting the Field of   216   We are Seven 50,52,80   Weak is the will of man   215   Westminster Bridge, Composed upon   128—9,248,336   The Westmoreland Girl   264   What if our numbers   135   What heavenly smiles!   236,262   When I have borne in memory   135   Where lies the truth?   265   A whirl-blast from behind the hill   70,335   *The White Doe of Rylstone*   169,172—6,177,178,214,302, 321   The Wild Duck's Nest   220   The Wishing-gate   242—3   The Wishing-gate Destroyed   243   Who but is pleased to watch the moon on high 267   Who weeps for strangers?   178   Why art thou silent!   246,297 Why should we weep or mourn?   265   Worcester Cathedral, A Gravestone . . . the Cloisters of   242   The world is too much with us   93,142,200,256, 324

Yarrow Revisited   95,250,297   Yarrow Unvisited   135   Yarrow Visited 212   Yes, it was the mountain-echo   167   Yes, thou art fair   262 Yew-tree, Lines left upon a Seat in a   66,71,73,92   Yew-trees   143—4,224, 296   Young Lady, To a   121—2